\<creative html design.2\>

FTP
FORMES
FORMS
BUTTONS

SERVER
SIDE

lynda weinman
william weinman

design: ali karp

Creative HTML Design.2
By Lynda Weinman and William E. Weinman

International Standard Book Number: 0-7357-0972-6
Printed in the United States of America

First Printing: April 2001
05 04 03 02 01   7 6 5 4 3 2 1

Interpretation of the printing code: The rightmost double-digit number is the year of the book's printing; the rightmost single-digit number is the number of the book's printing. For example, the printing code 01-1 shows that the first printing of the book occurred in 2001.

Trademarks

Warning and Disclaimer

▶ credits

Publisher
David Dwyer

Associate Publisher
Al Valvano

Executive Editor
Steve Weiss

Product Marketing Manager
Kathy Malmloff

Managing Editor
Sarah Kearns

Development Editor
Jennifer Eberhardt

Technical Editors
Rich Evers
Derek Pell

Cover Designer
Bruce Heavin
stink.com

Book Designer & Prepress
Ali Karp | alink newmedia
alink@earthlink.net

Ducks In A Row, Illustrator
Joan Farber

Indexer
Cheryl Lenser

About the Authors

Lynda Weinman is a writer, designer, animator, teacher, and mom. She lives in southern California with her daughter, her daughter's numerous pets, her husband Bruce (who painted the wonderful book cover to this and Lynda's other books), and her dad. She writes for a lot of magazines, lectures at a lot of schools and conferences, and writes a lot of books. Oh yeah, in her alleged free time she updates her web site: http://www.lynda.com.

William E. Weinman is a musician, electronics engineer, programmer, writer, father, son, husband, and notorious abuser of commas. Bill was born under the sunny skies of Hollywood, California, sometime during the Eisenhower administration, to the cheers and cries of Carolyn and Donald Weinman while the Brooklyn Bums finished out their final year at Ebbet's Field by losing yet another World Series to the Bronx Bombers before moving west to grow up in the same town as your humble co-author. (The Dodgers are 21-1 for games in which Bill Weinman has been in attendance.) Bill now lives in Dallas, Texas (The Dodgers haven't won a single game since he left the southland), with his wife, artist Lee Harrington, stepdaughter Megan, and cats Max, Brooke, and Jeeter. His son, David, lives in Hawaii (the surfing is not very good in Dallas). If all the intervening electrons are doing their job, you can find Bill's web site at http://bw.org (wouldn't it be neat if you could click on a book?).

Dedication

This book is dedicated to our grandmother, Lillian Weinman (who would have been 102 years old at this book's publication). Always a strong example of strength and courage, thanks for reinforcing our positive self-image. We wish you were here to read the fruits of your labor with us. —**Lynda and Bill**

Lynda and Bill before they wrote *Creative HTML Design.2*.

Our grandmother Lillian with our Dad (1935).

After they wrote *Creative HTML Design.2* (shown with Dad). You be the judge.

Book designer Ali and her partner, Adam, actually use Lynda's books for reference all the time at their full-service, multimedia design studio—[alink newmedia].

Lynda's Acknowledgments

Special thanks to my **daughter Jamie**, who asked once if she could have "Jamie-dot-com," only to change her mind: "Mom, I'm not calm. I should be Jamie-dot.excited."

Extremely special thanks to my wonderful **husband Bruce**, who is the most supportive person I've ever known and helps me more than I can convey.

More special thanks to our **book designer Ali Karp**, [alink newmedia | alink@earthlink.net], who cares so passionately about bringing content and design together to communicate effectively. Her talents, as usual, were indespensible in this project.

Even more special thanks to **Jan Kabili**, **Training Director** in Adobe products at lynda.com, who helped develop many of the Photoshop exercises.

Last but not least, major thanks to our favorite awesome **development editor Jennifer Eberhardt**, who went beyond the call of duty time and again to help make this book (and my other books) as good as we all wanted.

Bill's Acknowledgments

First and foremost, thanks to **my wife**, **partner**, and **best friend**, **Lee Harrington**, without whom it would have been impossible to get any of this done.

Special thanks to my **sister Lynda**, for her excellent teaching skills.

To my **son David** and my **stepdaughter Megan** for their constant reminder of what is and is not actually important.

Thanks to **David Rogelberg** and his staff at **Studio B** for their constant support.

Thanks to **David Dwyer**, **Jennifer Eberhardt**, **Ali Karp**, and all the other people who worked long and hard on this book.

And finally, I'd like to thank the Academy... Oh, sorry, wrong speech.

A Special Thank You To:

Our **Readers**

All the **Readers** and **Fans** of the original printing of *Creative HTML Design*, who through your support and encouragement, have helped give this book a second life.

Forté (http://www.forte.com/), for the Agent Newsreader.

Adobe (http://www.adobe.com), for Photoshop, Illustrator, and so much else!

Macromedia (http://www.macromedia.com), for Director, Flash, Dreamweaver, and FreeHand.

WebMonster Networks (http://www.webmonster.net), for giving us a place to pass files back and forth and for hosting the site for this book (http://www.htmlbook.com/).

Joan Farber, Ducks In A Row (http://www.ducks.htmlbook.com/), for being the guinea pig and letting us use their web site project for this book.

A Message from New Riders

As the reader of this book, you are our most important critic and commentator. We value your opinion and want to know what we're doing right, what we could do better, in what areas you'd like to see us publish, and any other words of wisdom you're willing to pass our way.

As the Executive Editor for the Graphics team at New Riders, I welcome your comments. You can fax, email, or write me directly to let me know what you did or didn't like about this book—as well as what we can do to make our books better. When you write, please be sure to include this book's title, ISBN, and author, as well as your name and phone or fax number. I will carefully review your comments and share them with the authors and editors who worked on the book.

Please note that I cannot help you with technical problems related to the topic of this book, and that due to the high volume of mail I receive, I might not be able to reply to every message. If you run into a technical problem, it's best to contact our Customer Support department, as listed later in this section. Thanks.

Email: steve.weiss@newriders.com

Mail: Steve Weiss, Executive Editor
Professional Graphics & Design Publishing
New Riders Publishing
201 West 103rd Street
Indianapolis, IN 46290 USA

Visit Our Web Site: www.newriders.com
On our Web site, you'll find information about our other books, the authors we partner with, book updates and file downloads, promotions, discussion boards for online interaction with other users and with technology experts, and a calendar of trade shows and other professional events with which we'll be involved. We hope to see you around.

Email Us from Our Web Site

Go to www.newriders.com and click on the Contact link if you

• Have comments or questions about this book.

• Want to report errors that you have found in this book.

• Have a book proposal or are interested in writing for New Riders.

• Would like us to send you one of our author kits.

• Are an expert in a computer topic or technology and are interested in being a reviewer or technical editor.

• Want to find a distributor for our titles in your area.

• Are an educator/instructor who wants to preview New Riders books for classroom use. In the body/comments area, include your name, school, department, address, phone number, office days/hours, text currently in use, and enrollment in your department, along with your request for either desk/examination copies or additional information.

Call Us or Fax Us

You can reach us toll-free at: (800) 571-5840 + 9+ 3567 (ask for New Riders). If outside the U.S., please call 1-317-581-3500 and ask for New Riders. If you prefer, you can fax us at 1-317-581-4663, Attention: New Riders.

▶ **note**

Technical Support and Customer Support for this Book

Although we encourage entry-level users to get as much as they can out of our books, keep in mind that our books are written assuming a non-beginner level of user-knowledge of the technology. This assumption is reflected in the brevity and shorthand nature of some of the tutorials.

New Riders will continually work to create clearly written, thoroughly tested and reviewed technology books of the highest educational caliber and creative design. We value our customers more than anything—that's why we're in this business—but we cannot guarantee to each of the thousands of you who buy and use our books that we will be able to work individually with you through tutorials or content with which you may have questions. We urge readers who need help in working through exercises or other material in our books—and who need this assistance immediately—to use as many of the resources that our technology and technical communities can provide, especially the many online user groups and list servers available.

- If you have a physical problem with one of our books or accompanying CD-ROMs, please contact our Customer Support department.

- If you have questions about the content of the book—needing clarification about something as it is written or note of a possible error— please contact our Customer Support department.

- If you have comments of a general nature about this or other books by New Riders, please contact the Executive Editor.

To contact our Customer Support department, call 1-317-581-3833, from 10:00 a.m. to 3:00 p.m. U.S. EST (CST from April through October of each year—unlike the majority of the United States, Indiana doesn't change to Daylight Savings Time each April). You can also access our tech support Web site at http://www.mcp.com.

▶ table of contents

●   **Introduction**   **xix**

1   Start   **1**
Types of Internet Providers   2
ISP or IPP?   3
Does Your Provider Have Enough Bandwidth?   4
Do They Have Enough Overhead?   4
Other Services   5
HTML Software   7
HTML Versus Design   8
Text-Based Editors   9
Dedicated HTML Editors   10
WYSIWYG HTML Editors   11

2   First Page   **13**
How Does the Web Work?   14
Hyperlinks—Web-Like Relationships   15
Creating Your First Page   16
Understanding What You Just Did   18
Carriage Returns in HTML   19
HTML Capitalization   19
File Naming Conventions   20
Spaces in Tags and Attributes   21
Uploading the Page   22
    Windows FTP Instructions   22
    Mac FTP Instructions   24
Link Me Up   26
Linking with Images   27
Adding Color to the Page   28
Add Some Color!   29
Using a Background Pattern   30
Adding a Background Tile   31

3 Speedy Graphics — **33**

How to Read the True File Size	34
How GIF Compression Works	37
Making Small GIFs	38
Reducing Colors in GIFs Using Photoshop 6.0	38
Anti-Aliasing Versus Aliasing	44
Aliasing Type in Photoshop 6.0	46
To Dither or Not to Dither?	50
GIF Compression Tables	51
Dither Settings in Photoshop 6.0	52
Making Small JPEG Files	54
JPEG Compression in Photoshop 6.0	55
JPEG or GIF?	60
PNG	61
PNG Gamma Correction	61
PNG Alpha-Channel Transparency	62
PNG Compression Options in Photoshop 6.0	63

4 Web Color — **65**

Designers Versus Everyone Else	66
What Does the Browser-Safe Palette Look Like?	67
RGB Color	69
Hexadecimal RGB	70
Hexadecimal Colors in HTML	71
Hexadecimal Resources	73
Web Hex Converters	73
Hex Calculators	73
When to Use Browser-Safe Colors?	74
HTML-Based Color Choices	75
How to Load a Browser-Safe Palette into Photoshop 6.0	76
Previsualizing Colors in Photoshop 6.0	78

Experimenting with Hex Color Choices   82
Color Pickers   86
Illustration-Based Artwork   87
How to Check and Fix Dithering of an Image   88
How to Ensure Your Artwork Stays Browser Safe   93
Photographic-Based Artwork   94
Adding Color to a Web Page with HTML   96
Using Color Names Instead of Hex   96
Coloring Individual Lines of Text   98
Coloring Links   99
Adding Color to Tables   100
HTML Tags that Support Color   101

5   Clickable   103

Identifying Hot Images   104
Creating Linked Images and Text   105
Turning Off Image Borders   106
Importance of ALT Text   107
The Importance of WIDTH and HEIGHT   108
Resizing Using WIDTH and HEIGHT Info   109
Aesthetics of Interlaced Graphics   110
Linked Graphics Options   111
What Are Imagemaps?   112
Client-Side or Server-Side Imagemap?   113
Create a Client-Side Imagemap in ImageReady 3.0   114
Understanding the Client-Side Imagemap Code   118
Creating Server-Side Imagemaps   120
The Importance of ALT Text   121

6   Tiles   125

Tiling Backgrounds   126
Determining Tiled Pattern Sizes   127
Full-Screen Body Backgrounds   128
File Formats for Patterned Background Tiles   130

Seams or No Seams?   130
  Seams   131
  No Seams, the Photoshop / ImageReady Way   131
A Seamless Tile in ImageReady 3.0   132
Special Effects Tiles   145
Aesthetics of Backgrounds   146
How to Color Tiles in Photoshop and ImageReady   148
  Anit-Aliased Example in Photoshop 6.0   148
  Anti-Aliased Example in ImageReady 3.0   153
  Aliased Example in Photoshop 6.0   157

7   Bullets & Rules   161

Horizontal Rules   162
Horizontal Rules, the HTML Way   162
Fancier Horizontal Rule Tags   163
Horizontal Rules the Do-It-Yourself Way   164
Vertical Rules   164
Clip Art Rules, Too   165
Bullets   165
Creating HTML Bulleted Lists   166
Creating Ordered and Definition Lists   167
Alphabetical and Roman Ordered Lists   168
Button Clip Art   169
Creating Custom-Made Bullets   170
Changing Bullet Size in Photoshop 6.0   171
Linked Bullets   173

8   Transparency   175

Transparency Tricks   176
Creating Background Color the Hex Way   178
Background Color Using Solid Patterns   180
Creating Background Color in ImageReady 3.0   181
Transparent GIFs   185
When to Use Transparent Artwork   186

Making Clean Transparent GIF Artwork 187

Glows, Soft Edges, and Drop
    Shadows with GIF Transparency 188

GIF Transparency Compositing 188

HTML for Transparent GIFs 190

Transparent GIF Software 190

Creating a Transparent GIF in ImageReady 3.0 191

Creating a Transparent GIF in Photoshop 6.0 195

PNG Transparency 199

9   Alignment   201

Text Alignment Tags 202

Using P to Align Text 203

Using DIV to Align Blocks of Text 205

CENTER 206

Graphic Alignment Tags 207

IMG ALIGN Attribute 208

Floating Graphics 209

Insert a Line Break with BR 210

Image Gutters 212

The Single-Pixel GIF Trick—Part I 213

HTML Tables 214

Table Basics 214

Coloring and Spacing in Tables 217

Space Between Table Cells 218

Tables for Spacing 220

Spacing Text with Tables 221

Tables with Odd Numbers of Cells 223

Tables for Graphics 225

Slicing an Image in Photoshop 6.0 226

Piecing the Artwork Back Together 229

The Single-Pixel GIF Trick—Part II 231

Table Tricks and Tips 231

Bulleted List 232

Center an Object on the Page 232

Vertical Rules 233

10 Typography   235

Limited Choices	236
HTML Type Versus Graphical Type	237
HTML-Based Typography	238
HTML Font Choices	240
Font Face Attribute	240
Which Fonts?	241
Web Type Blues	242
Verdana and Georgia	243
Embedding Options	245
TrueDoc	245
TrueType Embedding and OpenType	245
Aliasing Versus Anti-Aliasing	246
Graphics-Based Typography	248
The HTML to Place Your Text Graphics	248
Leading Techniques	249
Indent Techniques	252
Digital Font Foundries	253
Interesting Typography-Based URLs	253

11 Planning   255

Looking Ahead	256
Organizing Your Site	256
Mind Maps	257
Ducks In A Row Goals	259
Art Direction	260
Metaphors	262
Flowcharting	263

12 Organization   265

Simplicity Versus Chaos	266
What's in a Name?	266
The Parts of a URL	267
Absolute and Relative URLs	268

Paths in Relative URLs   269
Relative URL Examples   270
Relative URLs as Links   272
Directory Structure   274
Repeating Elements   275
Server-Side Includes   276
How SSI Works   278

13 Style Sheets   283

Cascading Style Sheets   284
How CSS Style Sheets Work   285
Adding a Style Sheet   286
The Anatomy of a CSS Style Sheet   288
Type and Measurements   290
Text-Related Properties   292
Selectors   293
The SPAN Tag   294
Absolute Positioning   295
Layering Text and Images   297

14 Navigation   305

Frames   306
How Frames Work   307
(...Frames (...Within Frames))   309
Adjusting the Size of Frames   310
Borderless Frames   311
Navigating Frames   312
Scrollbars in Frames   314
Margins in Frames   315
Aesthetics of Frames   316
Size Considerations   318
Size Considerations Navbars/Frames   320
Making Thumbnails and Small Graphics   324
Fragments   325
    A URL with a Fragment   326

15 Rollovers 329

Creating Rollover Graphics	330
From Lynda's Perspective	330
From Bill's Perspective	330
ImageReady 3.0 Rollover Techniques	331
JavaScript for Rollovers	336
Pointing Rollover	337
Make Your Own Pointing Rollover	343
Slideshow Rollover	344
Make Your Own Slideshow Rollover	349
Highlighting Rollover	351
Highlighting Rollover File Naming Convention	352
Make Your Own Highlighting Rollover	357
Extra Rollover Example	358

16 Forms 361

The FORM Element	362
Widgets	362
The Feedback Form	364
Using Tables with Forms	366
The IMAGE Type	369
How Can I Use the Data?	370
Using mailform.cgi	371

17 Animation & Sound 373

Animation Process	374
Ducks In A Row Animation Case Study	375
Creating Artwork For an Animation in Photoshop 6.0	377
Animating Artwork in ImageReady 3.0	380
LOWSRC Animation Trick	388
Client Pull for Slideshows	389
The Aesthetics of Animation	390
Web Animation Technology Overview	391

Animated GIFs   391
Animated GIFs in Detail   393
Sound on the Web   395
Shockwave Case Study   395
Sound Aesthetics   397
Getting Sound Files into Your Computer   397
To Stream or Not to Stream?   399
Making Small Audio Files   400
Audio File Formats   401
Tips for Making Web-Based Sound Files   403
HTML for Downloading Sound Files   404
Other Sound Options   405

18 Get Listed   407

Using Search Engines and Directories   408
Search Engines   409
Directories   410
List Your Site with Search Engines   410
META Tag for Search Engines   411
Ad Banners: From Heaven or Hell?   412
Click Here   413

19 Good HTML   415

Why Write Good HTML?   416
HTML Terminology   417
What You See AIN'T What You Get   418
Cleaning Up After a WYSIWYG Editor   419
Common HTML Gotchas   421
What's in a Quote?   421
Hanging Quotes   422
Straddling Containers   422
Line Endings   423
Entities vs. Numbers vs. Embedded Characters   425

20 HTML 4.01 Reference   427

Introduction   429
    What Version of HTML Is This?   429
    Are They Tags or Elements?   430
    The Concept of Content   431
    General Content Models   432
    Reference Layout   433
    Global Attribute Groups   435
    Core Attributes   435
    Internationalization Attributes 436
    Event-Related Attributes   437
Categorized Reference   438
Alphabetized Reference   463
Supplemental Reference   486

Glossary   491

Index   499

▶ contents @ a glance

●	Introduction		12	Organization	265
1	Start	1	13	Style Sheets	283
2	First Page	13	14	Navigation	305
3	Speedy Graphics	33	15	Rollovers	329
4	Web Color	65	16	Forms	361
5	Clickable	103	17	Animation & Sound	373
6	Tiles	125	18	Get Listed	407
7	Bullets & Rules	161	19	Good HTML	415
8	Transparency	175	20	HTML 4 Reference	427
9	Alignment	201	●	Glossary	491
10	Typography	235	●	Index	499
11	Planning	255			

Dad's Foreword

a reputable source

When they were children, my son Bill and his sister Lynda already demonstrated clear signs of the exceptional talents they later revealed. Lynda, even in third grade, demanded every available color of Crayola the company offered, and later in her teens, purchased sets of Magic Markers with exotic and unusual shades.

Bill, on the other hand, quickly outshone his poor father whose successful construction of a HeathKit High Fidelity amplifier, tuner, and speakers gave himself such pride of accomplishment. Bill proceeded to build better and more powerful units from scratch, using parts he purchased at Henry's Radio.

All of us have been involved with computers from an early date. Bill owned an Altair, the first Personal Computer, built from a kit and described and featured in the July, 1975 issue of *Popular Electronics*. Lynda learned to hack on an Apple II Plus, and eventually bought the first available Macintosh in 1984. Bill became a DOS wizard, and I bought a Commodore 64 myself.

I was thrilled and proud of the opportunity to write a foreword to their book, and I read the chapters one by one as they emerged from the printer. As a casual computer user, not very deeply involved in the programming or technical side of it, I found this book amazingly clear and instructive.

I have "surfed" the web since being introduced to it about three years ago. But the details of just how and through what magic process I could find myself visiting the Louvre or researching the works of Shakespeare were a complete mystery to me. Now, they are not that big a mystery.

My hope is that you will enjoy reading this book as much as I did.

Introduction

Lynda: Can HTML Be Creative?

One of the coolest things to happen to me in 1993 was my discovery of the web. One of the uncoolest things was the simultaneous discovery that I had to learn HTML in order to create web content. I was the product of the GUI generation (raised and bred on the Graphical User Interface), and in no way associated myself with programming languages or command line interfaces.

I'd always heard programming was a creative act, though as a visual-type person, I was highly suspicious of people who claimed this. I knew I kept wanting to do things with HTML that it wouldn't easily let me do, and the process of working with it felt far from "creative."

And yet, look at the web today, a mere few years later, and you'll find a creative playing field in full force. My brother and I hope to get you to the point where that's how it feels, and where HTML is a willing vehicle to help you communicate what you want to say effectively and creatively.

The web has an amazing way of bringing together divergent technologies, people, and practices. My brother and I qualify as part of this weird phenomenon. We barely knew

each other as we were growing up. I mean, he was a boy! Another species...but that's another story! He was the *build-MITS-kit, teach-your-self-assembly-language* and *hack-your-way-through-music-and-programming* type. I was the I *have-my-Mac-hear-me-roar-try-to-outdo-this* type. We both viewed each other in the nose-up position, and rarely discussed computers when we spoke.

So the web caught us off guard. Each of us at opposite ends of computer careers (myself a digital designer/animator, and he a programmer) the web let us face each other squarely eye-to-eye to say, "Hey, I want to learn what you do! You're not so uncool after all!" I wrote some design books, he wrote some programming books, and we finally said, "Let's do one together!" And here it is.

When I wrote my first book in 1995 (*Designing Web Graphics*), I could barely get publishers to understand that graphic designers would ever want to publish on the web. It was not considered at that point to be a design medium. Things have changed—look around the web today, and you'll find stellar examples of beautiful visual design. (You'll also see some not-so-stellar examples, but more about that later.)

To be honest, there hasn't been an HTML book until now that I could wholeheartedly recommend. I like some of the visual quickstart guides, and the teach yourself guides, but they always raised more questions for me than they answered. It seemed to me that a different kind of HTML book was needed—one that walked the reader through the web site creation process—which contained lessons and source files handy to try out. Even though there are a glut of HTML books in the bookstores, I saw a glaring need for a different type of HTML book that offered a more holistic approach to teaching the subject matter. I've never met anyone more knowledgeable about HTML than my brother, so when he agreed to partner with me on this book, I was thrilled.

Mitchell Waite (Waite Group Press and Waite Online) once pegged me perfectly. He said, "Oh, I get what you do! You write books for yourself!" He couldn't have been more correct. I write books in a way in which I would want things explained to me. There's a certain amount of required organization, a certain amount of required detail and background information, and a whole lot of concrete, "Oh, so THAT's how you do it!" To be concise, I'm the practical type, not the theoretical type.

My brother and I are both well-worn travelers in this weird HTML/Web landscape, and hope to share our hard-earned lessons with you. We hope you get down, get dirty, and get creative with this HTML/Web stuff. We've learned a lot of tricks and techniques that will help you get past the tools and into the creative process.

▶ creative html design.2

Lynda's Goals for This Book

My area of expertise is graphics, and my brother's is programming. To date, my books have included tips, techniques, and exercises to learn how to create web graphics. I look at the HTML books on the market and don't think they include enough information about graphics, but also see the necessity to focus on HTML as the main subject when first starting in web publishing. It's my hope with *Creative HTML Design.2* that we've bridged the two worlds—graphics and programming—and created a single resource that can get people started on the right track.

My brother and I really enjoy sharing knowledge with each other. This has been a fantastic opportunity for us to blend our knowledge, get it down on paper, and put it in one place. We both write conversationally, and in some respects, this book invites you to witness our lively and educated conversation about web design and web programming.

Artists care about how things look, that colors match, and that artwork aligns exactly the way we planned. The web is a disconcerting medium because it's been designed to be customizable by the end user and the browsers, creating a situation where the results of your design efforts can easily look different than you planned. This book will help artists and programmers control what they can and accept and identify what they can't.

Bill: Can Programming Be Creative?

Conventional wisdom says that programming is technical, and graphics is creative. That's the sort of thinking that got us into this mess. If more programmers (and project managers) understood that programming is first a creative act (not unlike painting or music), we would have more innovative software and less "me too" bloatware screaming at us to believe that, contrary to appearance, it's actually innovative.

It's worth repeating: Programming is first a creative act.

Technology is "The knowledge and means used to produce the material necessities of a society" (Webster's, 1981). Programming is much more than that—it's a tool of expression, a set of skills with which you can create the reality of a vision. It is an art that will not be recognized as such until our children are grown because our contemporaries don't understand it. That makes it a technology in their eyes.

I've spent most of my life in the creative application of new technologies. I'm a fundamentally creative person, who just happens to love playing with new technology. I started out life as a musician, playing guitar, keyboards, and drums in rock-and-roll bands. On the side, I built custom synthesizers and designed sound reinforcement systems. I never drew that much of a distinction between all of those activities because I see them all as creative pursuits.

When the web came along, I saw a new way to explore the creative application of emerging technology. With transistors getting smaller and faster, processor speed being measured in hundreds of MEGAFLOPS (**M**illions of **F**loating **P**oint **O**perations **P**er **S**econd), memory prices falling and high-end graphics display hardware following suit, the web couldn't have happened at a better time. Now we can start really having fun!

In bringing together the visual arts with the programmatic arts, the web has also brought me together with my long-lost sister. Lynda didn't mention the part where she spent 18 years in the Himalayas spinning yak wool with the Swami Bawgdhagda Dhogdhoo. But upon her return, with the web exploding like Krakatau on a bad hair day, it became necessary for her to finally look up her propeller-head brother. Isn't life strange?

Us programmers are so terribly misunderstood.

▶ creative html design.2

Bill's Goals for This Book

Computers are obstinate about precision. Miss a period here or a semi colon there, and you'll get pistachios instead of caviar every time. That's why it's important to know how a language works before you try to write something in it.

Before we wrote this book, I had not yet seen a thorough and accurate book on HTML and its associated disciplines. There were some good books on graphics, but their HTML was weak; there were some technically accurate books on HTML, but they weren't really complete, or they just didn't teach the subject well. So when Lynda and I realized that we each wanted to write the same book, we both got really excited about combining our disparate skills and perspectives to create a uniquely useful book about HTML and how to build a web site.

Building a web site is more than just HTML. If you want to learn how to use tables to stitch irregular parts of a graphic together, you need to also learn how to make the graphic; or, if you want to learn how to use JavaScript to make rollover controls, it's good to also know how to make rollover graphics that invite the user to engage them.

My sister Lynda is the undisputed master of on-line graphics, and she has added generous tips, tricks, and insights where necessary to help you accomplish your ultimate goal: a web site that says what you want it to say—with compelling graphics and flawless HTML.

Lynda and Bill rode together long before they wrote together.

In the process of writing this book, I have learned what a wonderful teacher my sister is. She has a knack for teaching like Mozart had a knack for a catchy tune (I don't hear too many people whistling Mahler on their way to work). Combined with my propensity for bits and bytes, I hope we have created a book that will inspire you as much as it educates you.

In short, I want to see some more innovation. Make something new, and send me the URL.

How This Book Works

This book is designed to work on a number of levels. It can be read in linear order, or it can be surfed, much the way you would gather information on the web. Everyone learns differently— some people learn from theoretical books, others from manuals, others from step-by-step exercises, and some from simply diving in head first and doing. We have tackled this book from all these angles. We wanted to do more than a how-to book, more than an exercise book, and more than a theory book. Our goal was not simply to present information, but to also explain why it was necessary, how you would do it, and where could you find resources related to it.

Creative HTML Design.2 walks you through building a real working web site, specially created for the lesson plans in this book. In the process, you will have a chance to read about all the phases of site design. This book includes a complete HTML 4.0 reference with details on all current HTML elements.

What's New About Creative HTML Design.2?

A lot has changed since we first wrote this book in 1998, so our goal with this second edition was to update its content with new information about WYSIWYG (**W**hat **Y**ou **S**ee **I**s **W**hat **Y**ou **G**et) editors, new graphics applications, and new HTML and graphic techniques.

As HTML and graphic editors are writing HTML automatically, many might wonder why a book on HTML is needed at all. I (Lynda) tend to adopt these sorts of WYSIWYG tools much more readily because I am not a programmer like my brother, and they are fast and convenient to use. We've decided that there are likely two distinct camps of people who will read this book: those like me and those like him!

This book is useful to those people who plan to use HTML and web graphic editors because it will give you the knowledge of what those tools are doing behind-the-scenes. If you plan to do this work professionally or interact with other professionals, that knowledge will at minimum make you feel more confident, and at maximum will help you troubleshoot a problem down the road.

More than learning to write HTML yourself, our goal was to show how to integrate graphics editing with HTML editing and share tips and techniques that will make your work easier and sites more creative. Trial versions of Adobe's Photoshop and ImageReady are included on the CD-ROM, so you can follow along and learn to make all kinds of web-specific artwork while you're writing code.

System Requirements

To do most of the exercises in this book, you will need a computer with a Windows or Macintosh operating system capable of viewing and creating both graphics and text. Because the graphic exercises are conducted in either Adobe ImageReady or Photoshop, the RAM requirements for those programs are at least 64MB. You will sometimes want to have a browser, an imaging application, and a text editor open at the same time. This may cause you to want more RAM than 64MB, especially if you are using a Macintosh computer. That's because the Macintosh operating system doesn't manage RAM as flexibly as Windows.

While it's possible to write HTML on any operating system, Adobe ImageReady and Photoshop is only written for newer Macintosh and Windows operating systems (Win 95, Win 98, OS 7.1 and above).

For those of you using Linux (or virtually any X-Windows system), it is possible to do the exercises using The Gimp (http://www.gimp.org/). While The Gimp is conceptually similar to Photoshop there are some differences in its capabilities and user interface, so the Photoshop exercises will not work step-for-step.

Bill has tried The Gimp he sees it as a tremendous step forward for people who want to step outside the box of commercial software while retaining the power and flexibility of today's high-end applications. The Gimp combines the features of Photoshop with the power of an open-source development model to provide a user-driven graphics program that out-performs the commercial competition in speed and reliability. bill has seen the future and it looks very promising.

▶ **tip**

Web Site Information and Email Contacts

The *Creative HTML Design*.2 web site (http://www.htmlbook.com) is there to help you by providing updates to the book and tips and pointers that will be kept current as new technology emerges.

The Ducks In A Row web site (http://ducks.htmlbook.com) is a live implementation of the examples and exercises in this book. In fact, this book represents the actual process that we went through in building this site.

Lynda and Bill both live active email lives. Lynda's email address is lyndachd@lynda.com; and Bill's is chd@bw.org. Please feel free to contact us with questions, comments, complaints, and even kudos. We love kudos.

We hope you enjoy reading this book as much as we've enjoyed writing it. We both learned a ton from each other, and it's our hope that you will benefit from the results.

Our Lesson Approach

Once you're up to speed on web publishing, you will design your site in the following stages:

- Concept

- Planning

- Collecting Assets (artwork, text, etc.)

- Producing Graphics and Layouts

- Writing Code, HTML Editing, Scripting, etc.

- Publishing to a Server

We did not choose to teach you how to create your web site in this order because we agreed that it would not be the best order to learn from. How can you develop a concept if you don't understand the limitations of the medium? How can you plan a site if you've never built one before? How can you collect assets if you don't understand what you need? How can you produce graphics and layouts if you've never authored for the web? How can you publish something you don't know how to make yet?

For this reason, we organized the materials in a logical manner for learning web publishing with HTML and graphics. If you find that there's something you already know, feel free to skip ahead to the next section or chapter. If you're curious about something that hasn't been discussed, turn to the Index to locate it and flip ahead.

You will find all the related files to each exercise in its respective chapter folder on the <chd.2> CD-ROM.

About the Ducks In A Row Site

The Ducks In A Row web site (http:// www.ducks.htmlbook.com) was designed for the educational purpose of this book. The rubber stamp company is real and is owned by Mainway, Inc. The Ducks In A Row artwork on the <chd.2> CD-ROM was created by Joan Farber, and can be used for the exercises in this book only. You may post this artwork to the web in the context of following our exercises, but you may not freely distribute this art or resell the artwork in any form or manner. **Hint:** If you like Joan's artwork, she is an independent illustrator and will be happy to consider any projects you, might want to hire her for. Joan Farber's artists representative for national/ international advertising campaigns and private commissioned fine art is:

Vicki Prentice Associates Inc.

630 5th Avenue (20th floor)
Rockefeller Center, NY NY 100111
212.332.3460 / fax: 212.332.3401

Creative HTML Design.2 walks you through creating the Ducks In A Row web site. The CD-ROM includes all the art and programming files needed for the book's step-by-step exercises. In the process, you'll learn about seamless tiles, rollover buttons, navigation bars, frames, tables, cascading style sheets, fragments, animation, sound, transparency, web typography, site organization, and more. The lessons in the book start simple, and advance to more complex assignments. In the end, you will create a real working web site, and will be able to apply the process to your own site design projects.

Ducks In A Row

http://www.ducks.htmlbook.com

▶ contents @ a glance

• Introduction xix

1 **Start** 1
web publishing
internet providers
presence providers
html editors

2 **First Page** 13
how the web works
creating your first page
viewing it locally
uploading to a server

3 **Speedy Graphics** 33
fast graphics
reading true file size
making small gif files
making small jpeg files
reducing techniques

4 **Web Color** 65
browser-safe color
hexadecimal color
color for illustrations
color for photographs
html color tag

5 **Clickable** 103
linked images
alt text
width and height info
client-side imagemaps
server-side imagemap

6 **Tiles** 125
patterned-based images
seamless patterns
size of source patterns
file formats for patterns
html for tiled images

7 **Bullets & Rules** 161
html horizontal rules
custom rule artwork
html bullets
custom bullet artwork
clip art rules and bullets

8 **Transparency** 175
transparency tricks
matching backgrounds
clean transparency
transparency software

9 **Alignment** 201
text alignment tags
graphic alignment tags
html tables
coloring tables
spacing text within tables
complex tables

10 **Typography** 235
html typography
web fonts
font embedding
leading techniques

11 **Planning** 255
mind maps
determining goals
determining navigation
determining art direction
metaphors
flow charting

12 **Organization** 265
url anatomy
absolute urls
relative urls
server-side includes

Continues …

▶ contents @ a glance cont...

13   Style Sheets   283
redefining your tags
cascading style sheets
css for formatting

14   Navigation   305
frames
frames aesthetics
navbar aesthetics
thumbnails
fragment

15   Rollovers   329
rollover graphics
javascript rollovers
rollover exercises
dhtml

16   Forms   361
the form element
widgets
tables
cgi

17   Animation & Sound   373
animation process
animation production
aesthetics of animation
animation technologoies
sound technologies
sound production

18   Get Listed   407
using search engines
types of search engines
listing your site
using meta
ad banners

19   Good HTML   415
why write good html?
html terminology
what you see
what you get
common html gotch

HTML 4 Reference   427
introduction
categorized reference
alphabetized reference
supplemental reference

Glossary   491

Index   499

"In the beginning, there was this fish ..."
—The Firesign Theater

Start
tips and advice

contents

web publishing
internet providers
presence providers
html editors

If you have never created a web site before, you'll likely find yourself in the market for an Internet connection and a home for your web site. Our advice in this area is targeted to help you make informed choices based on the size and scope of your web site publishing needs.

Because this is an HTML book, as well as a design book, we know you're also interested in discovering which types of HTML editors and learning methods exist to get you up to speed fast. This chapter includes our opinions and recommendations about WYSIWYG (What You See Is What You Get) editors, HTML editors, and plain vanilla text editors.

Start

Types of Internet Providers

Selecting an Internet provider can be a frustrating experience. Most of the hype you hear is nothing more than the technological equivalent of the double-speak in George Orwell's *1984*, and what little accurate information is available is so technical that it might as well be double-speak. To head off disappointment, don't expect selecting an Internet provider to be easy, and don't expect to be satisfied with your initial choice.

First, it's important to understand the difference between an **Internet Service Provider** (ISP) and an **Internet Presence Provider** (IPP), which is also commonly called a **hosting company** or a **web hosting company**.

Your computer's modem connects to a phone line, which dials your ISP's "dialup" lines and connects to the Internet through their computers and routers.

Internet Service Provider (ISP): This is the company that you use to connect your computer to the Internet. An Internet connection enables you to look at web pages; get email; and send your artwork, media, and code to your own web site. This is the same whether you use a modem, DSL, T1, or cable modem.

Internet Presence Provider (IPP): This is a company that hosts your actual web site, and that is its sole purpose. If you use an IPP to host your web site, you still need an ISP so that you have some place to dial in to in order to send your files to the IPP, receive email, browse the web, and so on.

ISP or IPP?

If you're just starting with your first web page, you might decide for economic reasons to have your Internet Service Provider (ISP) also host your web site. ISPs typically have a less-expensive rate when providing connection services and web hosting services as a bundled deal. Although this makes sense for a first-time, casual web publisher, it may not make sense if you are creating a site on which you expect high traffic and visibility. This section evaluates the process of deciding between going with an all-purpose ISP or a dedicated IPP.

Most ISPs will gladly host your web site, but this usually is not the best choice. Often, an ISP will host your web site on the same machines that perform many other tasks, such as email, usenet news, and other services. More often than not, the web sites will connect to the Internet through the same connections that also carry other types of traffic. That's because the ISP's primary business is to host dial-up users, and hosting your web site is just another service they provide. This can result in poor performance for a high-traffic web site during peak traffic times because the lines connecting your site to the net are busy serving many dial-up customers. Choosing to house your web site with an ISP can result in a slower web site, which may not be reliably available to your users. If you have a high-traffic site, or if your web site is critical to your business, we recommend that you find a good Internet Presence Provider (IPP), in addition to your ISP.

A company that hosts web sites as its primary business is in a better position to do a good job than a company that hosts web sites as a side business. The dedicated hosting company typically runs banks of dedicated machines that do nothing but host web sites. This way your web sites get more bandwidth and overhead so that your visitors get a better response. By not sharing its resources with thousands and thousands of dial-up users, the likelihood of sluggish server response time is greatly reduced.

Although it's important that your ISP be local to your physical location (so that it's a local phone call to connect), there is no need to restrict yourself to local businesses for your web hosting. Instead, consider the following issues that actually affect your service.

Does Your Provider Have Enough Bandwidth?

Bandwidth is the measure of how much data a service can deliver in a given amount of time. It is one of the most important measurements of the quality of online service. If your ISP is short on bandwidth, you might not know because you are connected directly to their network with your modem. However, those who connect to your service will know because they connect through the Internet. There is no effective way of measuring the bandwidth of your provider. We recommend that you test your provider's speed by accessing their site from a connection that is not dialed right into their network. This will give you an objective evaluation of the speed of their service.

Keep in mind that many providers will quote a lot of figures and statistics about how much bandwidth they have. Most of these numbers are meaningless. It is very easy to describe a network that has huge amounts of bandwidth allocated, but there are no standardized measurements for the amount of available bandwidth, and that is what you would really need to know. So the only way to know is to test it.

Do They Have Enough Overhead?

Overhead is the measure of how much computing resources are allocated to your web site. Unless your site is large enough and busy enough to warrant a dedicated computer on a dedicated connection, you are probably sharing your computing resources with other web sites. That's not necessarily a bad thing. Problems occur when the computer you are sharing becomes overloaded.

Just like with bandwidth, there is probably no way to know from the provider's advertising materials if the provider has enough overhead. The only way to find out is to compare the response times of the other sites that are hosted on the same machine. Check some of those sites, preferably from some different locations and at various times of day. Get a feel for how responsive they are. Try to use sites that are about as busy as yours will be. Again, these are very subjective measurements, but they are really all you have to go on.

Other Services

You may also want to consider whether you will need other services from your provider. If any of the following are important to you, be sure to discuss them up front with your potential provider. Some of these items may be unfamiliar to you, but don't despair. They will all be explained later in this book.

- Do you need the ability to write and/or install your own CGI programs? (See Chapter 16, *"Forms,"* for more details about CGI.)

- Do you need access to SSI (Server-Side Includes)? (See Chapter 14, *"Navigation,"* for more details about SSI.)

- Does your provider have CGI scripts, such as email, guestbooks, and counters?

- If you need multiple email accounts, does your provider support that?

- Do you need access to mail-filtering scripts for your domain? These scripts give you control over your mail and allow for separate mailboxes, autoresponders, and mail-controlled web services such as list archives and databases.

- Do you need access to raw server logs to run your own statistics?

- How much space will they give you for the price you're being quoted? If you plan to put up movies, sound, or interactive content, you may need more than 10MB of storage. Is there an extra charge if you exceed your space allotment?

- Does the provider limit the traffic to your site? What are the charges if your traffic exceeds their limits?

▶ **tip**

ISP Comparison Study

The company C|Net runs an ongoing comparison of ISPs by area. You may want to look at this before deciding on an ISP. Note, however, that dedicated presence providers are not included in this survey.

http://www.cnet.com/Content/Reviews/Compare/ISP/area.html

▶ **note**

How the Authors Do It

We live in different states (Lynda's in California and Bill's in Texas), but we both house our web sites on dedicated servers at IPPs. Lynda uses an IPP in California, and Bill uses an IPP in Texas. We opted to use dedicated IPPs because we both have very busy sites. Compare our sites' speed to other web sites you visit as an example of how this choice has sped up our performance:

http://www.lynda.com

http://bw.org

HTML Software

HTML stands for HyperText Markup Language. It's the language with which web pages are written and designed, although most designers would cringe at the thought of calling HTML a layout language.

And that's precisely the point: HTML was not written to be a design language. It was written to be a display language, with the intent that it might display differently on different machines and operating systems. Ever notice how browser software enables you to change your fonts and their sizes, and whether images and links are turned on or off? HTML was supposed to be a transportable language that could be customized to the needs and taste of any end user.

Many of the chapters in this book teach you how to trick HTML into obedience, but the starting point is HTML. Whether we like it or not, HTML is the language of the web. Do you have to know HTML to design web pages? No, but it sure helps. Frankly, some of our all-time favorite sites were in fact designed by artists who never touched the code. They teamed up with HTML programmers and did what they knew best—design.

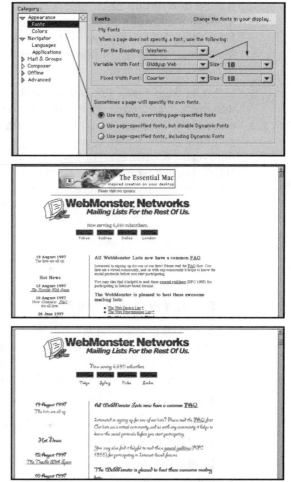

These three screens show the discrepancies between a page that was designed with certain settings and the results of the end user changing his or her browser preferences.

HTML Versus Design

A good description of designers is that we are control freaks. It is in our nature to want to control how our artwork looks; that's why we are good at what we do. Most of us, in fact, are passionate about making our artwork look just exactly to our liking. Web page design is definitely full of intense challenges, and you can decide to take them on or pass the buck to a programmer.

HTML is what made the web possible, but HTML has also become known as a designer's nightmare. There has never been a design medium that allowed its audience to change the content at whim. If you have ever created computer graphics before, you're used to having a sense of comfort that what you see as the final result is what everyone will see. When it's finished, it can never be changed. HTML plays havoc with a designer's quest for control. It is one of the strangest design mediums ever unleashed upon us, and that is because it was never intended to be a design medium in the first place.

▶ **note**

Should You Learn HTML?

It is great to know HTML, but it's not necessary in all cases. The advantage of knowing and understanding HTML is that you are in better control of knowing what is possible and what is not. You won't have to hear "No" from someone who might not care about your design as much as you do.

If you want to learn HTML, there are a few different camps to subscribe to:

Text-based editors: For those who want to learn HTML and understand what the tags do and mean.

Dedicated HTML editors: For those who want to use an HTML editor with automated tags.

WYSIWYG HTML editors: For those who don't want to know why anything works but want to get finished web pages anyway.

Text-Based Editors

This book teaches you to code in HTML inside a text editor, regardless of whether you plan to use one. Let's examine the options, pitfalls, and advantages of using different ways for creating HTML.

It's possible to learn HTML by using any off-the-shelf text editor. Try viewing the source of pages you like and learning from them as a starting point. It's perfectly acceptable to learn HTML this way. In fact, you'll find that most HTML pros used this learning method.

Different people have different learning methods, different aptitudes, different needs, and different goals. There is no right or wrong way to learn HTML. If you really want to understand what you're doing and why, writing code by hand works great as a starting point. It requires patience, persistence, and the acceptance that you'll make mistakes and won't get instant results. The payoff is that you'll understand what you're doing and will approach this medium with a greater degree of confidence.

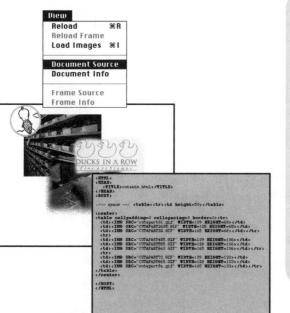

Most browsers allow you to "view the source" of HTML. Here's an example of viewing the source inside the Macintosh version of Netscape 4.0. Studying others' pages is a good way to pick up coding techniques.

▶ **note**

Online Tutorials for Learning HTML

Network Communication Design in Japan (an excellent visual online reference for learning HTML)
http://www.nchu.edu.tw/NCD/html/html_design.html

Microsoft's Design & Layout site
http://msdn.microsoft.com/workshop/design/

Brian Wilson's Index DOT HTML
http://home.webmonster.net/mirrors/bloo-html/

Dedicated HTML Editors

HTML editors are similar to dedicated word processors that have automated tags built in. Normally, these tags are accessible via menu commands or on handy toolbars. If you don't know a word of HTML, these types of editors certainly may baffle you. What good is an automated tag if you don't understand what tags do in the first place?

If you practice the methods of teaching yourself HTML in a standard text editor, you will eventually want and appreciate a text-based HTML editor. Some of them have spell-checkers, HTML checkers (to ensure that you've written correct HTML), and broken-link checkers, as well as search-and-replace functionality.

Most HTML editors are found on the web and can be downloaded for a free trial period. The best way to find HTML editors is on the web itself. Here are some good starting points:

Shareware
http://www.shareware.com

Yahoo
http://dir.yahoo.com/Computers_and_Internet/
Information_and_Documentation/Data_Formats/HTML/

If you are new to HTML, we suggest that you follow the exercises in this book using a text-editing tool, as opposed to an HTML editor. The lessons here enable you to graduate to an HTML editor and understand what you are doing, which will make working with an HTML editor much easier in the long run.

WYSIWYG HTML Editors

WYSIWYG (**W**hat **Y**ou **S**ee **I**s **W**hat **Y**ou **G**et) stands for a breed of HTML editors that profess to take the pain out of writing this stuff. At least that's the claim. WYSIWYG editors don't require you to know a word of HTML. In fact, many of them shield you from it so successfully that you might author pages and never understand or learn a single word of code.

In principle, there's nothing wrong with that! How many people write their own word processing software or PostScript commands? People who like and understand how to program really enjoy this stuff, and very few of the rest of us enjoy it much at all.

One problem is that HTML tags change frequently. New file formats, plug-ins, and browser features make this a changing landscape unparalleled by typical word processing or PostScript software. Web design and development is an emerging medium, and most of us are eager guinea pigs to propel it further!

The only way WYSIWYG editors could truly keep pace would be if they changed on a regular basis. This is not to suggest that they aren't useful at all. They can be wonderful. Anyone who has ever programmed frames or a complicated nested table will be in ecstasy letting a program do it for them without coding. WYSIWYG editors can be especially useful when you're in a hurry. They are fantastic time-savers that help you get your ideas out quickly without being bogged down by programming strange tags and adding slashes and opening and closing brackets everywhere.

The problem is that once you've been bitten by the web design bug, you'll want to try new things, such as newly introduced tags, plug-ins, or file formats, that the WYSIWYG editor won't support. And, if you've relied exclusively on the editor to compose pages, you won't have the necessary skills to understand how to extend its capabilities. WYSIWYG editors offer an easier programming environment, but they often limit what you can accomplish.

Another problem with WYSIWYG editors (at least the current crop of them) is that the HTML they churn out runs the risk of breaking when viewed on a new browser or a new version of a browser. WYSIWYG editors often throw in their own HTML tags that certain browsers don't recognize. This has been the case recently (as we write this). When the latest version of Netscape Navigator became available, a large number of sites lost their background colors because they had used a popular WYSIWYG editor that inserted an extra BODY tag. This bug didn't cause a problem with the previous version of Netscape, even though it's definitely incorrect HTML.

In the perfect world, the browser would also be the HTML editor. Every time the browser changed, the HTML editor would change, too. Well, without naming names, even the most popular browser's built-in editor doesn't fully support its own tags. These editors still have some growing up to do, and in the meantime, your site may be the victim of tags that don't work properly.

Chapter 19, *"Good HTML,"* discusses proper HTML versus WYSIWYG HTML. It will help you identify and clean up HTML that is created by outdated editors and should enable you to correct problems in your code that may haunt you down the ever-changing technology road.

▶ chapter one summary

Start

Being prepared for web publishing involves a lot of decision making in areas that might be new to you. Weigh your options carefully and make informed decisions. Often, there is no single correct way to go about doing this work. Diversity on the web is prevalent, and agreed-upon standards are rare. As much as we'd love to tell you otherwise, web publishing is a challenging—and changing—business!

*"If you can just get your mind together
then come on across to me
We'll watch the sunrise from the bottom of the sea
But first, are you experienced"*
—Jimi Hendrix, 1967

First Page
easy steps to follow

▶ **contents**

how the web works
creating your first page
viewing your page locally
uploading to a server

This chapter offers a number of short exercises that teach the fundamental principles of making web pages. We know you're anxious to get going, even though there might be a lot of holes in your knowledge of HTML and web design. In this chapter we encourage you to get your feet wet and leave more advanced concepts and techniques for later.

Throughout this book, we created a web site design for a rubber stamp company called Ducks in a Row. The `chap02` folder of the <chd2> CD-ROM includes all the image and text files you'll need to follow the exercises in this chapter. We'll quickly walk you through how to construct web pages, how to test them from your hard drive, and how to upload the files to your server. These exercises may raise a lot of unanswered questions for you because HTML and web design cannot be taught in a single chapter. Our goal is to start simple and build on this chapter as an introduction to the rest of the book. If you want to skip around, feel free to consult the Table of Contents, Index, Glossary, and the HTML Reference at any time.

2

First Page

How Does the Web Work?

Many people are confused by the distinction between the Internet and the World Wide Web. The web is a subset of the larger set called the Internet. For the purpose of this book, the web is defined as "anything on the Internet that you can access via a hyperlink." Many things that are available through a web interface are also available through more traditional Internet programs, such as FTP, Gopher, and WAIS.

Stated another way, the World Wide Web is a collection of documents on the Internet that are loosely knit through a concept called hypertext. Hypertext documents connect to each other by hyperlinks (or hotlinks) in a completely free-form manner. Any document can have links to any other document in the world. That's why it's called a web. There are no restrictions limiting any document from linking to any other.

▶ note

Definitions

Some of the terms used in this chapter may be unfamiliar to you, so here's a handy definition list. These terms are also listed in the Glossary at the back of this book.

Hypertext: Text that is linked to documents on the web

Hyperlink: Linked text, images, or media

Document: Any individual object (text, image, media) on the web

Element: An object in an HTML file

Object: Any distinct component, such as a tag, attribute, image, text file, etc.

Tag: An HTML directive, enclosed in "<" and ">" for example, <TAG>

Attribute: A modifier to an HTML tag, for example, <TAG ATTRIBUTE>

Container: An element that encloses other objects, for example,
<STRONG> </STRONG>

Hyperlinks—Web-Like Relationships

Each site on the web is made up of a collection of different pages. These pages are usually viewed with an application called a **web browser**. If you are interested in creating your own web site, you probably already have a browser, such as Netscape Navigator, Microsoft Internet Explorer, Mosaic, or any number of less common browsers. (Many sites on the web use specific features of specific browsers, so not all sites will work right on all browsers. We will do our best to note where this effect is significant within our lesson plan.)

The tangled web we weave.

When people want to see your web site, they connect to it with their browser. They might type in the URL (**U**niform **R**esource **L**ocator, a unique address assigned to each object on the web, such as http://www.blablabla.com/objectname) for your site, or, more likely, they will select it via a hyperlink from another page somewhere. The sequence of events from that point are helpful to understand as you create your web site:

- The browser connects with a server that contains your page.

- The browser sends a command to the server, asking for the page.

- The server sends the page, which is actually a file containing code in a language called HTML (**H**yper**T**ext **M**arkup **L**anguage).

- The browser reads the HTML and finds references to all the other objects on that page (for example, pictures, sounds, animation, and so on).

- One-by-one, the browser retrieves each of those other objects in the same way it got the page of HTML from the server.

- The browser assembles the page according to the instructions in the HTML and displays it for the viewer.

▶ e x e r c i s e

Creating Your First Page

This exercise requires that you use a text editor. It's best if you use NotePad (Windows) or SimpleText (Macintosh). A text editor is different from a word processor, and we strongly recommend that you avoid using a word processor to edit your HTML files. A word processor adds invisible formatting codes to your documents. Those invisible codes are very confusing to the browser that reads the HTML. For the exercises in this book, we also recommend that you avoid using a program that generates web pages for you, such as Microsoft FrontPage or Netscape Composer. The point of these exercises is that you learn HTML, and those programs tend to isolate you from the HTML. After you learn HTML, you will be able to use those programs much more effectively.

Any type of proprietary formatting, such as that of Microsoft Word, Microsoft FrontPage, Netscape Composer, or other word processing or HTML editing software, will cause the results of this exercise to break. Why is that? HTML is written in plain text, and that is the only way that the browser can interpret it properly to display web sites. HTML editors, such as FrontPage, Dreamweaver, GoLive, NetObjects, and Netscape Composer allow you to work in a WYSIWYG mode, and shield you from writing the code from scratch. If you write the code from scratch inside these visual editors, the code will not work. It would work only if you used these editors in "source" mode, which is the equivalent of writing the code in NotePad or SimpleText.

The bottom line is write this exercise in a plain text editor, and it will work. Write it in anything else, and it will not.

Step 1: Create a folder on your hard drive called ducks. Transfer the ylogo1.gif file from the chap02 folder of the <chd2> CD-ROM to your new folder. Open your text editor and type the following code exactly as it appears below:

```
<HTML>
<HEAD>
<TITLE>Ducks in a Row Homepage</TITLE>
</HEAD>
<BODY>
<H1>Welcome to Ducks in a Row
Online!</H1>
<P>Feel free to splash around . . .
<P><IMG SRC="ylogo1.gif">
</BODY>
</HTML>
```

Step 2: Inside the ducks folder you created, save the document as index.html or, if your system doesn't allow four-letter file name extensions, index.htm. Make sure you save it in text format and not a proprietary word processor format. See the note on the next page for background information about HTML naming conventions.

Step 3: Open your browser of choice (Netscape Navigator or Internet Explorer). Under **File**, choose **Open File** and locate the index.html document that you just created. This process is called "viewing a file locally," or from your local hard drive. Later in this chapter, we'll cover uploading this file to a web server so it can be "viewed globally" on the World Wide Web.

Here's what the results of the HTML would produce when displayed in Netscape Navigator.

Troubleshooting Note: If your file doesn't look like this, make sure you saved the document with the proper `.htm` or `.html` extension and that it was saved in **Text Only** mode, and not a proprietary word processing file format.

Understanding What You Just Did

In the HTML that you just wrote, notice the words that are placed within angle-brackets (for example, <HTML>). These are called *tags*. Tags are the instructions that tell the browser how you want certain parts of the page to be displayed.

Some HTML tags come in pairs. The second tag of the pair, called the end tag, has a slash (/) right after the left angle-bracket (for example, <TITLE> and </TITLE>). Tags that come in pairs are called containers because they enclose other objects. Everything between the begin tag and the end tag is said to be within the container.

Let's look at the code from the preceding exercise to break down what each element is doing:

```
1. <HTML>
2. <HEAD>
3. <TITLE>Ducks in a Row Homepage
   </TITLE></HEAD>
4. <BODY>
5. <H1>Welcome to Ducks in a Row
   Online! </H1
6. <P>Feel free to splash around . . .
   <P>
7. <IMG SRC=" ylogo1.gif">
   </BODY>
   </HTML>
```

1. The entire HTML document is within the HTML container. The document begins with <HTML> and ends with </HTML>.

2. The first element (every distinct object in an HTML document is called an element) within the HTML container is a HEAD container, and within that is a TITLE container. The HEAD element contains all the supplemental elements that don't belong in the body of the document, such as TITLE.

3. The text included inside the TITLE element will appear at the top of your browser window.

4. The BODY element contains all the content of the page, such as text, graphics, multimedia, and formatting specifications.

5. The line that says <H1> Welcome to Ducks in a Row Online!</H1> is called a heading. The typeface displayed on the browser will be different for headings. In most browsers, headings appear bigger and bolder than the normal type used in paragraphs of text. Notice the text Feel free to splash around... is outside of the H1 container. It appears in the default browser font for this reason. Generally, the header elements (H1–H6) will insert a line break before and after without requiring any additional code.

6. A paragraph is marked with a P tag. In most browsers, paragraphs are separated by empty lines. The P tag is a container, but it is different from some other containers in that it does not require an end tag (/P). You can leave out the end tag if the paragraph is followed by another paragraph. (In other words, you might want to use an explicit end tag </P> if what follows is not another paragraph.)

7. The line that says <IMG SRC=" ylogo1.gif"> shows an example of a tag and attribute combination. The tag is IMG, and the attribute is SRC=" ylogo1.gif". The IMG tag is used to place an image on the page. The SRC attribute tells the browser where to find the file to display as the image. IMG is not a container, so an end tag is not only unnecessary, it's not allowed. If you feel confused about which tags require end tags and which do not, never fear. The HTML reference at the end of this book clearly states which elements require end tags.

Carriage Returns in HTML

HTML can be very rigid in some areas and flexible in others. For the most part, HTML doesn't make any distinction between an end-of-line (what happens when you press the return key to make a new line on the computer) and a space (what happens when you press the spacebar). You could write the following code like this:

```
<HTML>
<HEAD>
<TITLE>Ducks in a Row Homepage</TITLE>
</HEAD>
<BODY>
<H1>Welcome to Ducks in a Row Online!
</H1>
<P>Feel free to splash around . . .
<P><IMG SRC=" ylogo1.gif">
</BODY>
</HTML>
```

or like this:

```
<HTML><HEAD>
<TITLE>Ducks in a Row Homepage</TITLE>
</HEAD>
<BODY>
<H1>Welcome to Ducks in a Row Online!
</H1>
<P>Feel free to splash around . . .
<P>
<IMG SRC=" ylogo1.gif">
</BODY>
</HTML>
```

We have placed line breaks in the book to help separate elements so they can be more clearly understood. It's a good rule of thumb to keep your lines within 80 characters wide because that is the lowest common denominator for text editors and computer screens. This means if someone needs to look at your code, they won't have to scroll sideways, and the text won't wrap. Use a fixed-space font in your editor, so you can easily tell when lines get too long.

HTML Capitalization

HTML tags are not case-sensitive. All the following versions of code will work the same:

```
<HTML>
<HEAD>
<TITLE>Ducks in a Row Homepage</TITLE>
</HEAD>
<BODY>
<H1>Welcome to Ducks in a Row Online!
</H1>
<P>Feel free to splash around . . .
<P><IMG SRC=" ylogo1.gif">
</BODY>
</HTML>
```

All caps: We have chosen this convention for the book in order to differentiate easily between code and content.

```
<html>
<head>
<title>Ducks in a Row Homepage</title>
</head>
<body>
<h1>Welcome to Ducks in a Row Online!
</h1>
<p>Feel free to splash around . . .
<p><img src=" ylogo1.gif">
</body>
</html>
```

All lowercase: This will also work just fine.

```
<HTML>
<head>
<title>Ducks in a Row Homepage</TITLE>
</HEAD>
<body>
<H1>Welcome to Ducks in a Row Online!
</H1>
<p>Feel free to splash around . . .
<P><IMG src=" ylogo1.gif">
</BODY>
</HTML>
```

Although a mixture of lowercase and uppercase code will also work, HTML tags are not case sensitive.

File Naming Conventions

The part of the file name after the period is called the file name **extension**. This part of the file name is often used to distinguish different uses for files. For example, in the file name index.html, .html is the extension. Files containing HTML must end in the .html extension (or .htm if your system doesn't allow extensions longer than three letters). In most cases, browsers will not recognize your files as HTML unless they have this extension.

It's a good idea to avoid capital letters and spaces in file names when you're working with objects for use on the web. Your web pages will likely be uploaded to a UNIX server someday, and UNIX systems distinguish between lowercase and uppercase letters in file names. For example, if you create a file called Index.html and someone tries to retrieve it as index.html, they get an error message instead of your web page. If your file is named index.html and your HTML code has different capitalization, such as Index.html, the file will not work either. The danger here is that some systems are case-sensitive and others are not. If you are not careful about case, it may still work on your system, but it won't work on someone else's.

Spaces within file names such as my index.html are problematic as well, and will likely cause errors. Instead of my index.html, name it my-index.html or my_index.html by using a dash or an underscore instead of a space.

If you're new to writing code, you might be shocked at how sensitive computers can be to otherwise-insignificant things like case and syntax. Trust us. A seemingly minor capitalization or spacing error will bring your web page functionality to an abrupt halt.

Spaces in Tags and Attributes

Spaces are never allowed between the initial "<" and the name of the tag. On the other hand, spaces are allowed before the closing ">" at the end of a tag.

For example, this is not legal: `< IMG SRC="ylogo1.gif">`

But this example would work: `<IMG SRC="ylogo1.gif" >`

According to the HTML specification, spaces are allowed around the equals sign (=) in HTML attributes. We have found, however, that some older browsers occasionally have problems with them.

In other words, while this is legal: `<IMG SRC = "ylogo1.gif">`

it's probably better to write it like this: `<IMG SRC="ylogo1.gif">`

▶ note

HTML Template

It's a good idea to keep a minimal document around that you can use as a template whenever you want to create a new web page.

Here's an example of a template you can use (we have provided a file named template.html in the chap02 folder of the <chd2> CD-ROM):

```
<HTML>
<HEAD>
<TITLE></TITLE>
</HEAD>
<BODY>
</BODY>
</HTML>
```

▶ e x e r c i s e

Uploading the Page

The last exercise taught you how to view the HTML document from your hard drive. This is called viewing the site locally. Next, it's time to learn how to post the page for the world to see by using an FTP program.

Windows FTP Instructions

If you're using Windows, you can use the **WS_FTP demo** program that we have included in the software/windows folder of the <chd2> CD-ROM. First, install the program by unzipping it into a temporary directory and running install.exe. Then, following these instructions, you will set up the connection with the information you got from your web site provider for your FTP connection.

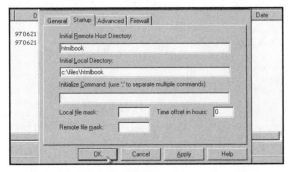

Step 2: Select the **Startup** tab to enter directory (folder) information. (You can skip this step if you want to select your directories manually.) Click the **OK** button.

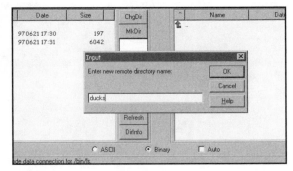

Step 3: Click the **MkDir** button on the Remote System side of the screen and enter the name ducks for the new directory.

You'll need to consult your Internet Service Provider for the session property settings. Do not fill in the settings as shown here; this needs to be filled in according to the instructions you receive from your ISP.

Step 1: Click on the **Connect** button to open the Session Properties dialog box.

Note: Select the **Save Pwd** check box only if you're sure no one else has access to your computer!

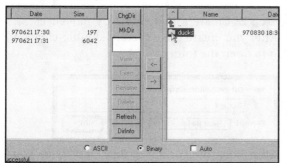

Step 4: Double-click on the new ducks directory to open it.

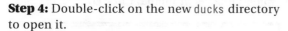

Step 5: To transfer your files, first select the appropriate transfer mode for the file. Always use ASCII mode for HTML files and Binary mode for images.

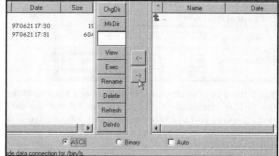

Step 6: Now you are ready to transfer your files. Select the file in the left window and click the right arrow button to upload the file to the server.

Mac FTP Instructions

For Mac users, download the program FETCH:
ftp://mac.archive.umich.edu/mac/util/comm/
fetch3.03.sit.

Open Connection...

Enter host name, user name, and password
(or choose from the shortcut menu):

Host: hendrix.htmlbook.com

User ID: lyndaw

Password: ••••

Directory:

Shortcuts: ▼   [Cancel]   [OK]

You'll need to consult your ISP to find out how to fill in the FETCH connection settings. Do not fill out the settings the way you see here because this information will be different for everyone reading this book. To get the exact settings for this dialog box, you must consult your Internet Service Provider.

Step 1: Launch **FETCH**. You will need to ask your ISP how to fill out the host and password information. When you're connected, choose Put File. You are prompted to locate the file. For this example, find the index.html document inside your ducks folder.

Directories
Change Directory...   ⌘D
Create New Directory...

✓ /home/lynda

Enter a name for the new directory:

ducks

[Cancel]   [OK]

Step 2: Create a new directory named ducks. After you create the directory, double-click on it to open the folder.

Save file on hendrix.htmlbook.com
bar.gif
Format: Raw Data ▼ [Cancel] [OK]

Step 3: Set the Format to **Raw Data** when you upload images or media. Click **OK**.

Save file on hendrix.htmlbook.com
company.html
Format: Text ▼ [Cancel] [OK]

Step 4: When you save the file, set the Format to **Text** when you upload HTML.

Note: Make sure you replicate your ducks folder exactly onto your web server. If you have your files inside a directory called ducks, for example, make sure you create a directory on the web server called ducks, too. This enables all your HTML links, images, and media to perform as they did on your hard drive. For more information on directory structure for HTML and the web, see Chapter 12, *"Organization."*

Now that you've uploaded the files, try viewing them from the web. We don't know what your exact URL will be because you have to get that information from your web administrator. Here's how the URL would look if it was on our server:

http://www.htmlbook.com/ducks/index.html

▶ note

Your Host and Directory

Occasionally, people write to us asking what to fill in for the host and directory information in the FTP exercise. We cannot answer that for you. The only people who can help you with that are the support people at your ISP or IPP.

It's a good idea to call your technical support people and get to know them anyway, as they can be valuable allies for the long-term as you build and maintain your web presence.

◗ exercise

Link Me Up

The most visible feature of the web is the ability to jump from one page to another just by clicking on an object with your mouse pointer. By using these "hyperlinks," it is possible to surf sites in the far corners of the earth, sometimes without even realizing that you've left one site and connected to another.

Here's an example of the Ducks in a Row home page with hyperlinks:

```
       <HTML>
       <HEAD>
       <TITLE>Ducks in a Row Homepage
       </TITLE>
       </HEAD>
       <BODY>
       <H1>Welcome to Ducks in a Row
       Online!</H1>
       <P>Rubber stamps or rubber duckies?
       Feel free to splash around to find
       out what we're about...
       <P><IMG SRC="ylogo1.gif">
       <P>Check out the
   1.  <A HREF="http://www.stampzone.com/">
       RUBBER STAMP ZONE
       </A> - an out-of-site
       rubber stamp page
       </BODY>
       </HTML>
```

1. This creates a link on your page that uses the text RUBBER STAMP ZONE to anchor the link. (The anchor text is usually rendered by the browser with an underline and/or in a different color text.) Clicking on this link displays the page at http://www.stampzone.com/.

Step 1: To create a link to another site, insert the A tag in your HTML document. It will look like this:

```
<P>Check out the
<A HREF="http://www.stampzone.com/">
RUBBER STAMP ZONE
</A> - an out-of-site rubber stamp page
```

Save this file as index.html inside the ducks folder you created in the first exercise. This will replace the preceding exercise file. You can open the file in your browser locally from your hard drive or upload it to your server to check the results.

You'll find an in-depth look at linked graphics in Chapter 5, *"Clickable."*

Here's how the linked RUBBER STAMP ZONE **text would appear inside the Netscape browser.**

Linking with Images

Your links don't have to be text. You can also use graphics for hyperlinks. Let's say you'd like to link the ylogo1.gif image to another page about the company Ducks in a Row. We've created a document called company.html, which is located in the chap02 folder of the <chd2> CD-ROM. Copy it to your hard drive's ducks folder.

Step 1: Put the IMG tag in place of the text for the link, and you will create a hyperlinked graphic.

```
<HTML>
<HEAD>
<TITLE>Ducks in a Row
Homepage</TITLE>
</HEAD>
<BODY>
<H1>Welcome to Ducks in a Row
Online!
</H1>
<P> Rubber stamps or rubber duckies?
Feel free to splash around to find
out what we're about...
1. <P><A HREF="company.html">
<IMG SRC="ylogo1.gif"></A>
<P>Check out the
<A HREF="http://
www.stampzone.com/">
RUBBER STAMPZONE
</A> - an out-of-site rubber stamp
page
</BODY>
</HTML>
```

1. By placing the <IMG SRC> element inside the anchor element (that is, between the <A> and the </A>), the graphic within the IMG tag will be linked to the specified URL (company.html).

   Now you have a graphic for the link. Be sure to copy the files ylogo1.gif and company.html to the ducks folder. You can open the file from a browser locally from your hard drive or upload it to your server to check the results.

Here's an example of the linked graphic. **If you click on the graphic, the document** company.html **should appear.**

Troubleshooting Tip: If your file doesn't appear as we've described, make sure you saved your files in ASCII text, that you used the .html (or .htm) extension, and that the files index.html, company.html, and ylogo1.gif are in your ducks folder.

Adding Color to the Page

HTML 4.01 allows you to make your pages more attractive by specifying particular colors for different elements on the page. You can change the background color, the color of the text, and the color of links from their default colors by using attributes to the BODY tag. The following BODY tag shows how:

```
<BODY TEXT="#FFFFCC" BGCOLOR="#669999" LINK="#CCCC66"
ALINK="#FFFF00" VLINK="#330033">
```

Colors in HTML are specified in hexadecimal (or, hex; base-16). Each color is represented as three pairs of hex digits, one pair each for the Red, Green, and Blue components, respectively. Hexadecimal digits range from 0 to F. In other words, if you were to count from 0 to 15 in hex (assuming you had 16 fingers), you would count like this:

```
0 1 2 3 4 5 6 7 8 9 A B C D E F
```

In the above BODY tag example, the background is a blue-green color. The Red part is 66 (or 102 decimal), the Green part is 99 (or 153 decimal), and the Blue part is also 99.

If you find all this talk about hex color confusing, don't fret yet. We have devoted an entire chapter to color (Chapter 4, *"Web Color"*), and it explains HTML color in detail.

> ▶ **note**
>
> ### Hash Marks
>
> When you specify hexadecimal values in HTML (for example, for colors in the BODY tag), the # symbol (called pound, hash, or that tic-tac-toe-looking thingy) is required, as are the quotation marks. Yes, we know it usually works fine without all that, but because it's required by the language, it's a good idea to just do it. That way, when the browser makers start enforcing the standard, your code will continue to work!

▶ e x e r c i s e

Add Some Color!

Step 1: To add color to the earlier example, type this HTML:

```
<HTML>
<HEAD>
<TITLE>Ducks in a Row
Homepage</TITLE>
</HEAD>
1. <BODY BGCOLOR="#669999"
TEXT="#FFFFCC" LINK="#CCCC66"
ALINK="#FFFF00" VLINK="#330033">
<H1>Welcome to Ducks in a Row
Online!</H1>
<P> Rubber stamps or rubber duckies?
Feel free to splash around to find
out what we're about...
<P><A HREF="company.html">
<IMG SRC="ylogo1.gif" BORDER="0"></A>
<P>Check out the
<A HREF="http://www.stampzone.com/">
RUBBER STAMP ZONE</A> - an out-of-
site rubber stamp page
</BODY>
</HTML>
```

1. BGCOLOR, TEXT, LINK, ALINK, and VLINK are attributes to the BODY tag. They control the following design elements:

BGCOLOR: Sets the background color of your page.

TEXT: Sets the color of text.

LINK: Sets the color of linked text, and the border around linked graphics that have not been visited yet.

ALINK: Stands for **Active Link**; it controls the color of the link while the mouse is pressed.

VLINK: Stands for **Visited Link**; the color that tells your users which of the sites they have visited and which may be new to them.

Step 2: Save this file as index.html to replace the preceding exercise file. You can open the file from a browser locally from your hard drive or upload it to your server to check the results.

Note: Chapter 4, *"Web Color,"* goes into detail about color issues and aesthetics on the web.

Here's what the page looks like in Netscape when we use the BODY tag. If this figure were printed in color, you would notice that some of the links are yellow, and some are blue. These colors are controlled by the LINK and VLINK attributes in the BODY tag. LINK is for links that have not yet been visited, and VLINK is for links that have already been visited by the user's browser.

Using a Background Pattern

You can also use a pattern for a background instead of just a flat color. This is done with the BACKGROUND attribute to the BODY tag. When you use a background image, it is displayed repeatedly as tiles until the entire display area is filled. This presents both challenges and opportunities for web designers. We'll teach you how to include a background pattern in the following exercise, and you can learn all the nuances and variations of this technique in Chapter 6, *"Tiles."*

With a background graphic, the BODY tag looks like this:

```
<BODY TEXT="#FFFFCC" BGCOLOR="#669999"
LINK="#CCCC66" ALINK="#FFFF00"
VLINK="#330033" BACKGROUND="tile.gif">
```

Notice that we didn't remove the BGCOLOR attribute. It still serves two purposes:

- Although certain browsers do not render background images, these browsers may still render the background color.

- In some browsers, the page starts to display before the background image is loaded. Leaving in a BGCOLOR ensures that the page displays with a background color that is close to the background image's dominant color, so there is less of a shock to the user when the image finally appears.

Adding a Background Tile

Copy the file tile.gif from the chap02 folder of the <chd2> CD-ROM into the ducks folder on your hard drive. Type in the following HTML (or change your existing index.html file):

```
<HTML>
<HEAD>
<TITLE>Ducks in a Row Homepage</TITLE>
</HEAD>
<BODY TEXT="#FFFFCC" BGCOLOR="#669999"
LINK="#CCCC66" ALINK="#FFFF00"
VLINK="#330033" BACKGROUND="tile.gif">
<H1>Welcome to Ducks in a Row
Online!</H1>
<P> Rubber stamps or rubber duckies?
Feel free to splash around to find out
what we're about...
<P><A HREF="company.html">
<IMG SRC="ylogo1.gif" BORDER="0"></A>
<P>Check out the <A
HREF="http://www.stampzone.com/">
RUBBER STAMP ZONE</A> - an out-of-site
rubber stamp page
</BODY>
</HTML>
```

Save this file as index.html to replace the preceding exercise file. You can open the file from a browser locally from your hard drive or upload it to your server to check the results.

Here's the page with the background image added.

Note: If this exercise didn't work, be sure that the file tile.gif is copied into the active ducks folder or directory. Chapter 6, *"Tiles,"* covers tile creation and aesthetic issues in much greater depth.

▶ chapter two summary

First Page

Now that you have a basic idea of what HTML is and how it works, take some time to experiment with the page. Change things around; add text and different graphics. This is the best way to learn any new language.

When you take the time to learn about the elements that were covered in this chapter, you will be anxious to learn about all the rest of the tags and features that HTML supports.

Subsequent chapters cover all the major groups of HTML tags and cover many of the areas we touched upon in this chapter in much greater depth.

3

"If I ever get out of here, I'm going to Katmandu."
—*Bob Seger*

Speedy Graphics
small, fast, and good

▶ **contents**

true file size
small gifs
small jpegs
reducing techniques

Authoring for the web is the first time most computer artists have to be concerned about file sizes. What this boils down to is that most people understandably don't know how to make small graphics, so most of the graphics on the web are too big. Large file sizes equal slow downloading speeds. A useful rule-of-thumb (albeit not 100% accurate) is that every kilobyte of data takes about a second to download for the average user. For example, using this measurement, a 30k file would take approximately a 1/2 minute to download. This is more true on slower connections (28.8 and lower) than on faster connections (ISDN and higher). However, as much as high bandwidth and faster connection options are hyped and touted in the industry, the majority of the web audience is still in the slow connection category.

You've surely explored the web and run into pages that take too long to load. Don't let your pages commit the same mistake! It doesn't matter if your site has stunning graphics; if they are too slow, very few people will stick around long enough to wait for them to load.

How to Read the True File Size

Web images are measured by *kilobytes*. For those who like number crunching, a kilobyte is 1,024 bytes; a *megabyte* is 1,048,576 bytes (1,024k); and a *gigabyte* is 1,073,741,824 bytes (1,024m). Graphics measuring in megabytes and gigabytes are obviously not acceptable for web delivery. Because of this, you'll often get the directive from a client to keep page sizes within a certain file size limit. Or you might have an internal goal of not exceeding 30k per page (another good rule-of-thumb). There's no set rule about how many kilobytes a single image should contain, but it's often necessary to understand how to read the file size of a document if you're trying to make it fall within a certain target range of acceptability.

| 584K/733K | ▶ |

How can you be sure of the number of kilobytes in an image? Most Photoshop users think the readout in the lower-left corner of a document informs them about the file size. Not true! These numbers relate to the amount of RAM Photoshop is using internally for the entire, uncompressed image.

rilly small			
Name	Size	Kind	Label
ps numbers	11K	Adobe Photoshop™...	—
radio.pict	132K	Adobe Photoshop™...	—
radiopict.dump	33K	Adobe Photoshop™...	—
radiopict.get info	44K	Adobe Photoshop™...	—

You also might look to your hard drive for the file size. Notice that the file size numbers are all nicely rounded figures: 11k, 132k, 33k, and 44k. Your computer rounds up the file size to the size of the next allocation unit it uses for allocating space on your hard drive. Have you ever had a file show two different file sizes on a hard drive and a floppy? That's because the computer allocates space in larger chunks on your hard disk.

mybook			
Name	Size	Type	Modified
Psp		File Folder	8/11/95 2:02 PM
_mssetup.exe	10KB	Application	3/23/92 12:00 AM
_mstest.exe	88KB	Application	3/23/92 12:00 AM
216.gif	14KB	Corel PHOTO-PAIN...	10/3/96 9:39 AM
acset.BMP	2,305KB	Bitmap Image	6/23/96 4:30 PM
acset.PCX	444KB	Corel PHOTO-PAIN...	6/23/96 5:01 PM
aolaln1.PCT	106KB	PCT File	10/15/95 7:53 AM

When using Windows, the file size shown in the folder directory is rounded to the nearest kilobyte. Again, this is the space allocated to the file, not the true size of the file!

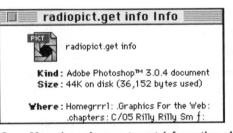

radiopict.get info Info

radiopict.get info

Kind: Adobe Photoshop™ 3.0.4 document
Size: 44K on disk (36,152 bytes used)

Where: Homegrrrl: .Graphics For the Web: .chapters: C/05 Rilly Rilly Sm f:

On a Mac, the only way to get information about the true byte size of a file is to do a Get Info command. First, highlight the file you want to check in the Finder; then go to the File menu and choose Get Info.

aolaln1.PCT Properties		
General		

aolaln1.PCT

Type: PCT File
Location: mybook
Size: 105KB (107,972 bytes)

To get the most accurate reading in Windows, click the file name using the right mouse button and select Properties from the pop-up menu. There you will find the true byte size.

▸ note

To Icon or Not to Icon?

On a Macintosh, Photoshop typically saves images with an icon. The icon is a small, visual representation of what the image looks like, which the file references. Photoshop icons take up a little extra room on your hard drive. This ultimately won't matter because when you send the files to your server, you'll transmit them as raw data, which will strip off the icon anyway. If your goal is to get a more accurate reading of the true file size, however, you should set your preferences in Photoshop to not save an icon automatically.

```
┌─────────────────── Preferences ───────────────────┐
│ ┌──────────────────────┐                           │
│ │ Saving Files      ▼ │              ┌──────────┐  │
│ └──────────────────────┘              │    OK    │  │
│   Image Previews: ┌─ Ask When Saving ▼┐ └──────────┘  │
│                   └────────────────────┘ ┌──────────┐│
│                     ☐ Icon               │  Cancel  ││
│                     ☐ Thumbnail          └──────────┘│
│                     ☐ Full Size          ┌──────────┐│
│                                          │   Prev   ││
│  Append File Extension: ┌─ Never    ▼ ┐  └──────────┘│
│                         └──────────────┘ ┌──────────┐│
│  ┌─ Options ────────────────────────────┐│   Next   ││
│  │ ☒ 2.5 Compatibility  ☐ Save Metric Color Tags └──┘│
│  └──────────────────────────────────────┘           │
└────────────────────────────────────────────────────┘
```

To set your preferences to not save the icon automatically, choose Edit:Preferences:Saving Files. In the Preferences dialog box, set the Image Previews to Ask When Saving.

▶ note

GIF Pronunciation

The definitive last word on the pronunciation of GIF from the author himself.

Sent: Wednesday, August 06, 1997 2:37 AM
To: Steve Wilhite
Subject: GIF pronunciation

Hope you don't mind that I've contacted you—I got your email address from Jack Paulus, who heard me speak about the GIF pronunciation controversy at SIGGRAPH. I'm the author of a series of books on web graphics, and am very curious if you would end the controversy for me and my readers. Is it a soft G as in "jiffy" or a hard g, as in "gift"? Inquiring minds want to know! Thanks.

From: Steve Wilhite
To: 'Lynda Weinman'
Subject: RE: GIF pronunciation
Date: Mon, 7 Aug 1997 17:04:55 –0400

a soft G as in "jiffy"

From: lynda@lynda.com
SMTP: lynda@lynda.com
Sent: Monday, August 11, 1997 11:53 PM
Subject: RE: GIF pronunciation

Thanks so much. Now, for another question—if you don't mind. Why a soft G, if the G in GIF stands for Graphics? I get asked this question often as well ;-)

From: Steve Wilhite
To: 'Lynda Weinman'
Subject: RE: GIF pronunciation
Date: Tue, 12 Aug 1997 09:44:05 –0400

That is the way I pronounced from day one and it stuck. No other reason.

How GIF Compression Works

The GIF file-compression algorithm offers impressive file size reduction, but the degree of file size savings has a lot to do with how you create your GIF images. Understanding how GIF's internal compression scheme (LZW—Lempel **Z**iv **W**elch) works is the first step in this process.

LZW compression looks for repeated patterns that it can represent with small tokens of data. When it encounters areas in an image that repeat or don't change, it can implement much higher compression. This process is similar to another type of compression called **R**un-**L**ength **E**ncoding (RLE—used in BMP, TIFF, and PCX formats), but LZW writes, stores, and retrieves its code a little differently. Because GIF images are stored in horizontal rows of pixels, the compression algorithm will find more uniform runs to compress when the image has repeating horizontal patterns.

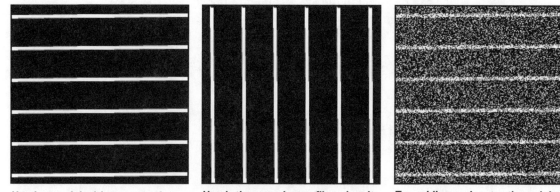

Here's an original image saved as a GIF that contains horizontal lines. It is 6.7k.

Here's the same image flipped on its side so that the lines are vertical. It's a whopping 42% bigger at 11.5k!

Try adding noise to the original. You'll be adding 88% to the file size. This one is 56k!

So what does the line test really teach?

- Artwork that has horizontal regularity compresses better than artwork that doesn't.

- Anything with Noise will more than quadruple a GIF image's file size.

- Large areas of flat color compress well, although complicated line work and dithering do not.

Making Small GIFs

The GIF file format works best on images that are composed of line art or flat color. In terms of making small GIF files, what can you do to ensure that you have large areas of flat color? Several factors can produce large GIF files. We will look at these culprits: too many colors, anti-aliasing, and dithering.

The two most valuable techniques for making small GIF files are to use the least amount of colors necessary and the least amount of dithering. The following exercises teach you how to do this. Compare the results of your efforts to our handy, full-color compression tables, ngif.html and dgif.html, which can be found in the chap03 folder of the <chd2> CD-ROM, inside the folder titled compression_tables.

▶ e x e r c i s e

Reducing Colors in GIFs Using Photoshop 6.0

Step 1: In Photoshop 6.0, open the image01.pct file from the chap03 folder on the <chd2> CD-ROM.

Step 2: Select **File:Save for Web** to open a new Photoshop 6.0 interface in which you can create and compare previews of optimization settings.

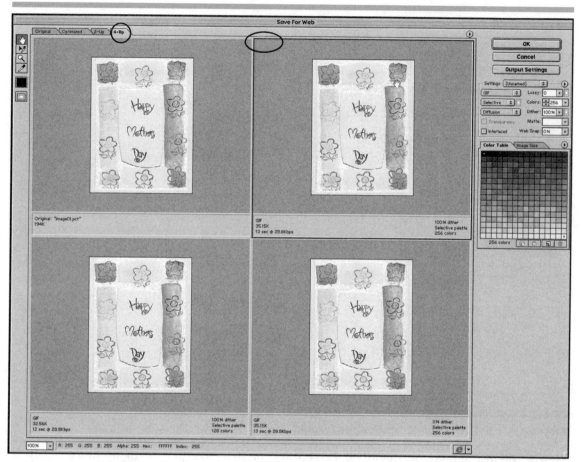

Step 3: Click the **4-Up** tab in the Save for Web window.

Step 4: Click the **preview pane** on the top right of the Save for Web window to select that pane.

Step 5: Choose **GIF** as the optimized file format.

Step 6: Choose either the **Adaptive**, **Perceptual**, or **Selective** palette to optimize a GIF in Photoshop. These palettes are based on colors in the original image and, therefore, will create an optimized image that looks most like the original.

Step 7: Choose **No Dither**. You'll experiment with dithering in the next exercise.

Step 8: Choose a **number of colors** from the drop-down **Colors** menu. Try starting with a low number of colors and increasing the number until the image quality is just acceptable. Notice the Color Table changes as you change the number of colors. The Color Table displays all of the colors from which the optimized image will be built.

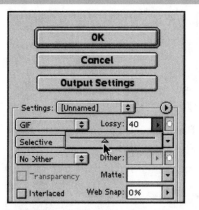

Step 9: To lower the file size even more, you can try adding some lossy compression by moving the **Lossy slider**. Keep your eye on the image quality as you add lossy compression. Lossy compression, which is a new feature for GIF optimization, used to be available only for JPEGs. Lossy means that the compression scheme reduces file size by discarding information, while Lossless means that it reduces file size without throwing away information.

Step 10: To get a closer look at the effects of the settings you chose, click the drop-down Zoom menu in the lower-left corner of the Save for Web window and choose **200%**. Be sure to return to the **100%** view to make your final choice of optimization settings, since 100% is the magnification viewers will see on the web.

Step 11: To view the effects of your settings on various parts of the image, select the **Hand** tool in the upper-left of the Save for Web window, and then click and drag the image in any preview pane.

Step 12: Click the **preview pane** on the bottom right of the Save for Web window and try some other settings for palette, number of colors, and lossy compression.

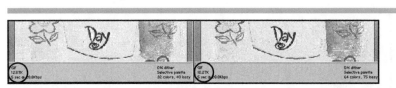

Step 13: Compare the estimated file sizes on the bottom left of each of the preview panes. Select the preview that offers the smallest file size at which image quality is acceptable.

Step 14: To view your choice in a web browser, click the **Show in Browser** icon at the bottom right of the Save for Web window and choose a browser from the drop-down menu.

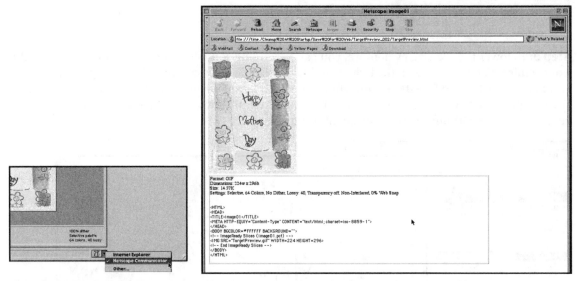

Step 15: When you have settled on the palette, number of colors, and amount of lossy compression, click **OK** in the Save for Web window.

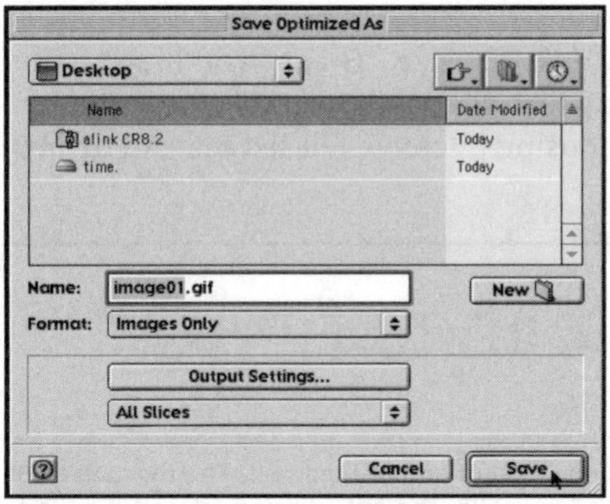

Step 16: In the Save Optimized As dialog box, make sure there is a **.GIF** extension at the end of the file name, saving the optimized image as image01.gif.

Step 17: Select **File:Close** to close the unchanged source file, image01.pct.

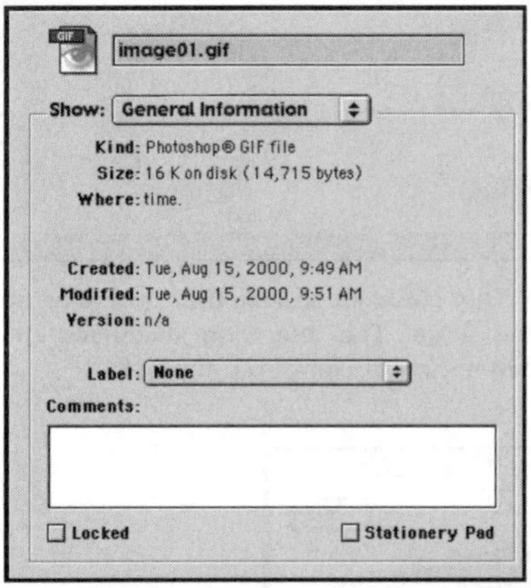

Step 18: Read the true file size of the resulting optimized GIF. Have you made it as small an image as you could have? Use the browser of your choice to open the file ngif.html in the compression_tables folder inside the chap03 folder of the <chd2> CD-ROM to see how the file size compares to the chart. If yours is the same or smaller, you've done well. If not, go back to Go and do not collect $200. I mean, go back and try your hand at optimization again.

Image01.pct is an excellent source file to practice reducing colors with. Because it is so colorful, it is easy to recognize the quality changes that take place with the addition and subtraction of colors. Using the techniques covered in this exercise, experiment with this file to see how small you can make it as a GIF and still retain the quality of the image.

Anti-Aliasing Versus Aliasing

We've established that the number of colors in an image affects file size. "Great," you may be saying to yourself. "But how do I really put this to practice when I'm creating artwork?" One technique that greatly reduces the number of colors in an image is choosing to create aliased instead of anti-aliased graphics.

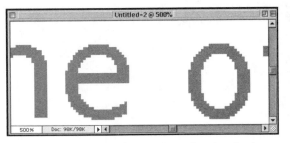

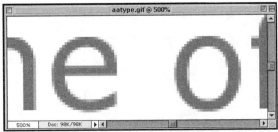

Here's an example of aliased text. The file totaled 3.8k when saved as a GIF.

Here's an example of anti-aliased text. The file totaled 5k when saved as a GIF. The anti-aliasing caused the file to be 24% larger.

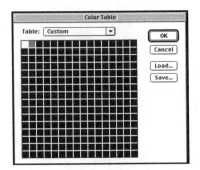

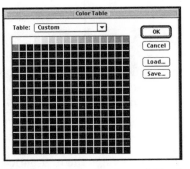

A close-up view: Aliasing does not disguise the jaggy nature of pixel-based artwork.

A close-up view: This close-up shows that anti-aliasing creates a blended edge. This blending disguises the square, pixel-based nature of computer artwork.

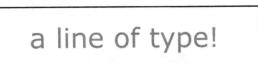

The aliased artwork used only 2 colors.

The anti-aliased artwork used 16 colors.

It's often assumed that artwork will always look better if it has anti-aliased edges. This is simply not true! Artists have never had to factor size of files into their design considerations. Having a file load 24% faster is nothing to balk at. In many cases, aliased artwork looks just as good as anti-aliased artwork, and choosing between the two approaches is something that web designers should consider when necessary.

This image is 571 x 499 pixels and takes up only 9k. Why? It has only two colors due to using aliased artwork.

Here's the aliased graphic in the context of a finished page. Not bad for a very low overhead effect.

In addition to considering whether to use aliased or anti-aliased graphics, you should also consider working with browser-safe colors when creating illustration-based artwork for the web. See Chapter 4, *"Web Color,"* for examples of how browser-safe colors can improve the quality of illustrations viewed in an 8-bit browser.

▶ e x e r c i s e

Aliasing Type in Photoshop 6.0

Try your hand at creating aliased type in Photoshop by following these steps:

Step 1: Select **File:New**.

Step 2: Choose **500** pixels by **200** pixels, and **72** pixels per inch, against a White background.

Step 3: Click the **Type** tool.

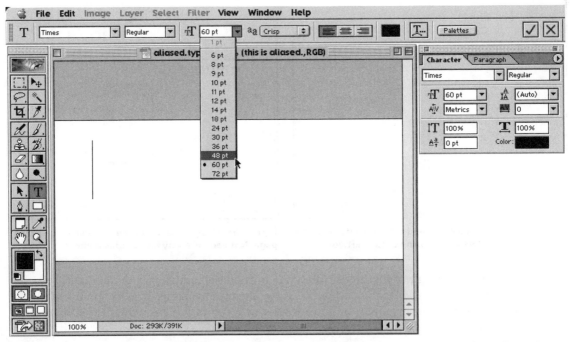

Step 4: In the Tool Information Title Bar located at the top of the screen, choose a large font size so you will be able to see changes take place.

Step 5: Click on the screen and type the sentence "this is aliased."

Step 6: In the Tool Information Title Bar at the top of your screen, choose **None** from the **Anti-Alias** (aa) drop-down menu. Using aliased type instead of anti-aliased type results in a smaller file size. **Note:** If you are working with anti-aliased text, Photoshop 6.0 has several to choose from— Crisp, Strong, and Smooth—each of which creates a different look.

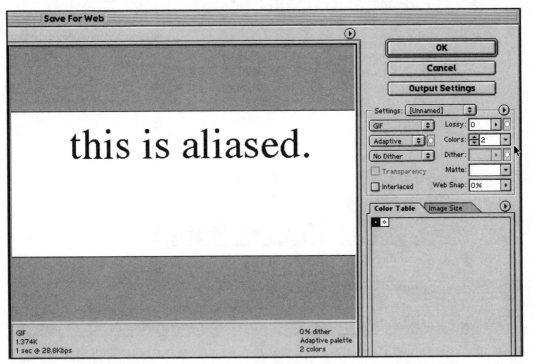

this is aliased.

This is what your text looks like when it is aliased. Notice the jaggy nature of the pixel-based artwork.

Step 7: Open the Save for Web window and make sure the optimized file format is set to **GIF**, the palette is set to **Adaptive**, and dithering is set to **No Dither**. The number of colors should be **2**.

Step 8: Click **OK** to save the aliased type file as a GIF. If you read the true file size of your aliased GIF, it will be smaller in comparison to choosing any of the anti-aliased options.

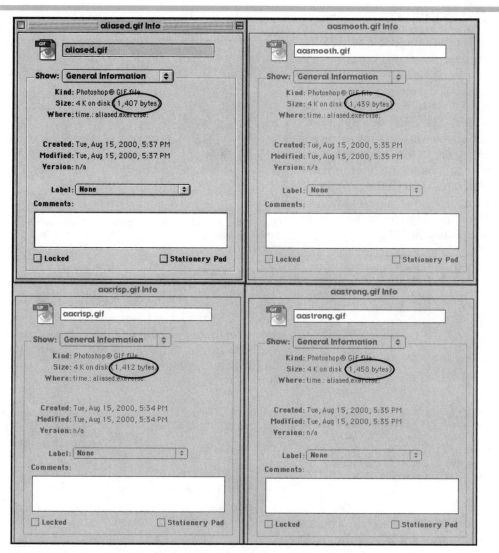

Step 9: Compare the file size of your aliased type GIF to the size of each of the following three anti-aliased type GIFs created in Photoshop 6.0: aacrisp.gif, aastrong.gif, and aasmooth.gif. You'll find these files in the chap03 folder of the <chd2> CD-ROM. Notice the byte size difference between the aliased GIF and the anti-aliased options.

To Dither or Not to Dither?

Dithering methods play a huge role in creating smaller GIFs. Any type of "visual noise," such as dithering or Photoshop noise filters, adds to the file size. Although you'll frequently try to eliminate dither to reduce file size, there will be times when you use dither in your optimized images. For example, you may want to save a photographic image as a GIF in order to include the photograph in an animated GIF or to make part of the photograph transparent. Dithering of one type or another must be employed to reduce a 24-bit color photograph to the 8-bit or lower bit-depth threshold of GIF.

This GIF saved with dithering is 28.2k.

This GIF without dithering is 21.5k.

In the example above, the GIF that did not use dithering is smaller. The problem is that it looks awful! Sometimes file size savings does not warrant loss of quality. When an image contains glows, feathered edges, or subtle gradations, you have to use dithering in order to smooth out the banding to maintain quality.

This 64-color GIF has been saved with Photoshop's 100% Diffusion dither method. The file size is 28.6k.

This 64-color GIF has been saved with Photoshop's Dither None method. The file size is 28.3k.

There's almost no difference in appearance between the two images above, regardless of whether a dithering method is used to convert to 8-bit color or Photoshop's Dither None method is chosen. Why? This image has a lot of solid areas of color to begin with. The file savings between 28.6k and 28.3k is not huge, but the non-dither method will still yield a smaller file size.

GIF Compression Tables

These two HTML documents show the file size savings that you can achieve by adjusting the color depth and choosing dithering methods. All images are GIFs optimized in Photoshop 6.0 with an Adaptive palette. The Dithered GIFs were optimized with 100% Diffusion dither.

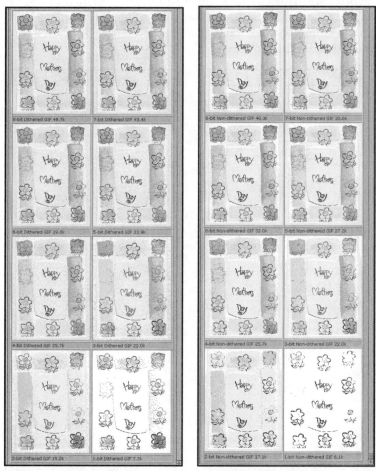

Dithered GIFs: This page can be viewed in color by opening the file dgif.html **inside the web browser of your choice. It's located in the** compression_tables **folder in the** chap03 **folder of the <chd2> CD-ROM.**

Non-Dithered GIFs: This page can be viewed in color by opening the file ngif.html **inside the web browser of your choice. It's located in the** compression_tables **folder in the** chap03 **folder of the <chd2> CD-ROM.**

Dither Settings in Photoshop 6.0

In Photoshop 6.0, you can determine the method and amount of dither while you are optimizing a GIF in the Save for Web window. Choose either No Dither or one of several dithering algorithms—Diffusion, Pattern, or Noise—which vary in appearance. Experiment with these dither methods and with the dither amount slider, taking into account the appearance of the image and its file size.

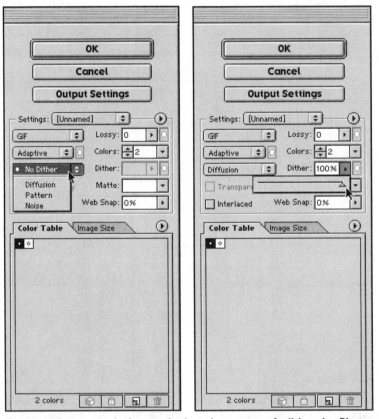

Settings that control the method and amount of dither in Photoshop 6.0 are located in the Save for Web window along with the other GIF optimization controls.

▶ **warning**

GIF Patent Controversy

There has been some measure of controversy in the past few years surrounding patent problems with the GIF file format. In short, Unisys, a very old and venerable computer company, owns a patent on the LZW compression scheme (U.S. Patent Number 4,558,302) used in the GIF file format. That seems to be the only fact that is not in dispute.

Over the past few years, Unisys has started charging license fees for programs that create GIF files, including programs that are free. This has led to the demise of free graphics programs that create GIF files. Additionally, starting in 1999, Unisys threatened to start charging web sites that display GIF files. This lead to the "*Burn All GIFs*" protest (http://www.burnallgifs.org/).

Unisys did eventually back down from their threat against the larger web sites, but they do still require license fees for all programs that create GIF images. As a result there is a large movement away from the use of the GIF format for images that require lossless compression. In fact, the U.S. government has started requiring that all graphics programs that it purchases support the newer, royalty-free, PNG format (covered later in this chapter).

Making Small JPEG Files

JPEGs are recommended for images that are photographic or use continuous-tone artwork. A key difference between GIF and JPEG is the fact that you can save JPEGs in a variety of compression levels. This means that more or less compression can be applied to an image, depending on which looks best.

The nuances of saving small GIFs are much more complex than the nuances of saving small JPEGs. Your primary decision is how much or how little JPEG compression to apply to the image. A fewer number of colors in a JPEG could potentially increase file size because JPEG compression was designed for complex, continuous-tone images.

The more compression you assign to an image the smaller it becomes, but the more it suffers in quality. A low-quality JPEG setting in Photoshop indicates a high amount of compression, and a higher quality setting indicates a low amount of compression.

You'll find that blurry, low-contrast photographs compress best as JPEGs. Therefore, to further reduce the file size of a JPEG, reduce the contrast in the source file. In Photoshop 6.0, use Adjustment Layers to reduce contrast of the original image outside of the Save for Web window. Another way to reduce the size of some JPEGs is to add blur to the optimized image. Photoshop 6.0's Save for Web window has a Blur slider for this purpose in the JPEG optimization controls.

JPEG Max Quality 67.6k   JPEG High Quality 30.5k

JPEG Med Quality 24.6k   JPEG Low Quality 21.7k

JPEG compression: You can see by this test that there's not a whole lot of difference between low-quality and high-quality compression in this example. Many people are reluctant to reduce their JPEGs to the lowest quality settings, but with most photographic images, low settings work well.

▶ e x e r c i s e

JPEG Compression in Photoshop 6.0

JPEGs are optimized for the web in Photoshop's Save for Web window. The process is similar to optimizing GIFs, except that there are fewer controls to set. Take advantage of the interactive previews in the Save for Web window to compare various JPEG compression settings, looking for the setting that results in the smallest file size with the best image quality.

Step 1: Open the image02.pct file from the chap03 folder of the <chd2> CD-ROM.

Step 2: Select **File:Save for Web**.

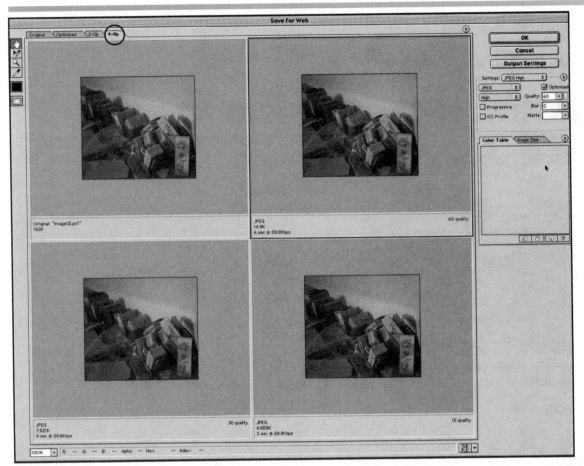

Step 3: Click the **4-Up tab**, where you can experiment with different quality settings. Choose **JPEG** from the drop-down format menu. Notice that there is no Color Table for a JPEG because JPEGs are 24-bit images and are not limited to a maximum of 256 colors as GIFs are.

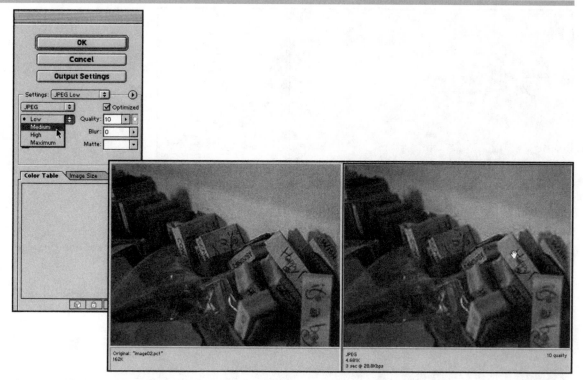

Step 4: Choose **Low**, **Medium**, **High**, or **Maximum** quality from the drop-down compression **Quality** menu. Alternatively, use the **Quality slider**, or type a number between 0 and 100 in the Quality field to set compression quality.

Step 5: As you vary quality, check each image preview for artifacts (areas of blocky color like those in the image above), which are the result of too much compression. You can zoom in to check for artifacts, but return to the 100% view to make your final optimization decisions.

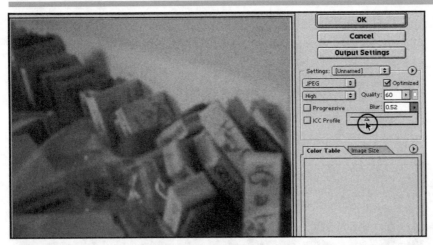

Step 6: Use the **Blur** slider to add a small amount of blur to the image to further reduce file size. Keep an eye on the image preview to make sure you don't make the image too blurry.

Step 7: Uncheck the **Progressive** check box. Read the Warning "Problems with Progressive JPEGs" for an explanation of why this is recommended.

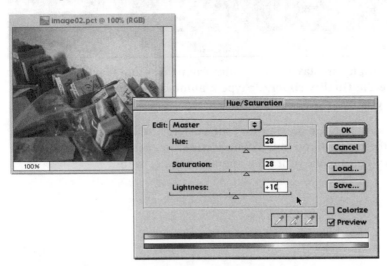

Step 8: When you finish setting the few JPEG controls in the Save for Web window, check the estimated file size in the selected preview pane. If it is still too high, consider exiting the Save for Web window and using Photoshop's Adjustment Layers to reduce contrast in the source image. One way to do this is to vary the Saturation, Lightness, and Colorize settings in the **Image:Adjust: Hue/Saturation** dialog box. Then return to the Save for Web window and reoptimize the image.

Save Optimized As

```
Desktop ▼                    ⬆  📖  🕐

  Name                          Date Modified  ▲
  📁 alink CR8.2                 Today
  💾 time.                       Today


Name:   image02.jpg              New 📁
Format: Images Only ▼

        Output Settings...
        All Slices ▼

?                    Cancel    Save
```

Step 9: When you are done, click **OK** to open the Save Optimized As window. Make sure the optimized file has a **.JPG** extension, and then click **Save** to save the optimized JPEG.

Step 10: Select **File:Save As** to save the source file if you made changes to it. Give the file a new name if you don't want to save over the original source file. If you have not made changes to the source file, close it without saving.

▶ **warning**

Problems with Progressive JPEGs

Progressive JPEGs render in stages, like interlaced GIFs. Many people like to use them because they give the illusion of loading faster than a standard JPEG. In reality they take just as long (if not longer), but your viewer has the advantage of seeing a low-resolution version of the image while she waits for it to fully download. The one serious drawback presents itself if you are targeting an audience that might be looking at your site with an older browser. Any browser before a 3.0 release does not recognize progressive JPEGs. In fact, they produce the dreaded broken image icon—meaning your audience has no chance of seeing the image at all.

JPEG or GIF?

The general rule is to use GIF for graphics that contain large areas of solid color or line art and JPEG for photographs or images that contain areas of continuous tone information (blurs, drop shadows, gradients, etc.). Although there are good reasons for saving photographs as GIF (animation, transparency, and interlacing), there are no good reasons for saving graphics that contain large areas of solid color or line art as JPEGs, unless the graphics are combined with photographs. With photographic content in general, don't be afraid to try low-quality settings; the file savings is usually substantial, and the quality penalties are not too steep.

Graphic GIF

Graphic JPEG

Photograph GIF

Photograph JPEG

Here is compelling evidence that proves that graphics compress better—and look better—if GIF compression is used. You can view the JPEG comparison by opening the file jpgcomp.html from the compression_tables folder in the chap03 directory of the <chd2> CD-ROM.

Here is compelling evidence that proves that photographs compress better—and look better—if JPEG compression is used. You can view the GIF comparison by opening the file dgifcomp.html from the compression_tables folder in the chap03 directory of the <chd2> CD-ROM.

PNG

PNG (**P**ortable **N**etwork **G**raphics, more fondly known as PNGs Not GIF) holds great promise as a new web file format. The W3C (**W**orld **W**ide **W**eb **C**onsortium at http://www.w3.org/pub/ WWW/Press/PNG-Pr.en.html) has made a formal endorsement of PNG, which strongly indicates that Netscape and MSIE will support it as an inline file format in the near future. As of this writing, Netscape Navigator 4.7 and later and Internet Explorer 5.0 and later (for Windows) recognize PNG files, but do not display full enhanced PNG transparency.

PNG uses a lossless compression method, meaning that no quality loss is incurred when it's applied to images. PNG is compressed by using any of a number of pre-compression filters and is then decompressed when viewed. This enables PNG to retain every original detail and pixel with no loss of quality.

Unlike GIF or JPEG, PNG can be stored at many different bit depths by using different storage methods. GIF, for example, can be stored only in 8-bit or lower bit depths. JPEGs must be stored in 24-bit, no lower. PNG can be stored in 8-bit, 24-bit, or 32-bit. This makes PNG one of the most flexible formats available for web images, and also somewhat more complicated to use. Expect a learning curve before you can use PNG files effectively for your web images.

PNG Gamma Correction

The PNG format also supports gamma correction for properly displaying images on different platforms without losing contrast or brightness in the translation. Differences in gamma between different platforms can make an image seem darker or lighter on a platform other than the one it was created on. The PNG format has the capacity to store a value that represents the gamma of the system on which the image was created. This value then can be used by the displaying system to correct for the image's gamma value, if known.

In order for all that to work, both the creating and displaying systems must know their own gamma, which is usually not the case in today's web world. This is a case of a great feature that, at the time this chapter was written, was unsupported.

> ▶ **tip**
>
> **PNG Resources**
>
> **PNG Home Site**
> http://www.libpng.org/pub/png/
>
> **PNG Specification at W3C**
> http://www.w3.org/TR/REC-png-multi.html
>
> **Greg Roelofs Article in Webreview.com**
> http://webreview.com/1999/08-13/ designers/08_13_99_2.5html

PNG Alpha-Channel Transparency

The PNG format has the capacity to store a variable transparency value known as alpha-channel transparency. This value allows your images to have up to 256 different levels of partial transparency (or translucency). For example, the image in the accompanying screen shot uses an alpha-channel to present a drop shadow that displays correctly against this irregular background.

This toucan image uses alpha-channel transparency.

One common misconception about PNG images is that you must use a 32-bit palette to use alpha-channel transparency. This is not true. The PNG format allows any entry in any palette to represent any channel—either Red, Green, Blue, or Alpha (these palettes are called RGBA instead of RGB).

In fact, the image of the toucan in the screen shot is only 12.5k in size because it uses an 8-bit RGBA palette, where some of the entries are used to represent the transparency mask instead of colors. We cover this subject in more detail in Chapter 8, *"Transparency."*

PNG Compression Options in Photoshop 6.0

Both Netscape and Microsoft have been promising PNG support for the past several versions, but so far neither has delivered the full spec. The reason is probably that it takes a lot of programming to properly support the format. It will be worth the wait if the support that comes includes gamma correction and alpha-channel transparency. (As of press-time, preview versions of Netscape Navigator 6.0 support the full PNG spec, including alpha-channel transparency. We expect all the major browsers to support PNG very soon now.)

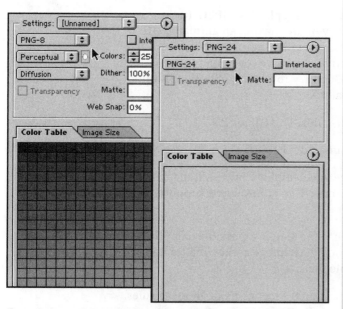

To optimize an image for the web in PNG format, select File:Save for Web and choose PNG-8 or PNG-24 from the drop-down file format menu. Select Interlaced to have a low-res version of the image display in a browser while the higher-res image is loading. Note: If there are transparent pixels in the image, you will have access to the Transparency box and will want to put a check mark in there to preserve transparency. If the Transparency box is not checked, transparent pixels will be filled with the color in the Matte field. See Chapter 8, *"Transparency,"* for more on the function of the Matte feature.

> ### ▶ warning
>
> #### Large 24-Bit PNG Files
>
> On low-resolution images for the web, the quality difference between JPEG and PNG is imperceptible. The fact that PNG uses lossless compression almost always results in much larger files than JPEG for 24-bit images. Our recommendation is that you always choose JPEG over PNG for photographic material. The only time PNG compression compares favorably in terms of file size is when it is used in 8-bit and lower bit depths. PNG has two advantages over JPEG and GIF: It can store gamma information to adjust automatically for the gamma (see Glossary) of its target platform, and it supports 8-bit transparency (otherwise known as alpha channels). You can find examples of PNG transparency in the "PNG Alpha-Channel Transparency" section of this chapter.

▸ chapter three summary

Speedy Graphics

You can create great-looking graphics that are also small and quick to download if you pay attention to what file formats you use and what options you select when saving them. In summary, remember the following:

- Try to keep your pages under 30 kilobytes total for all elements.

- Is the image a photograph? Use JPEG (unless you need transparency or are making an animated GIF. In those rare cases, optimize the photograph as a GIF using the Adaptive, Selective, or Perceptual palettes in Photoshop. Don't try to force a photograph into a web-safe GIF palette).

- Is the image flat-color? Use GIF or PNG.

- Is the image animated? Use GIF.

- Does the image need alpha-channel transparency? Use PNG (but only if your audience supports it in their browsers!).

- Make sure you use the smallest possible color palette in your GIF and PNG images; that makes for the smallest possible file size.

- You will find occasional exceptions to all these rules, but they are an excellent place to start.

In the next chapter, we look at the other side of the graphics equations, with a discussion of color use and the browser-safe color palette.

"Now I've discovered a new palette, a new canvas: light. My brushes are a keyboard and math."
—Lee Harrington

Web Color

safe specs

▶ **contents**

browser-safe color
hexadecimal color
color for illustrations
color for photographs
html color tags

In "real life," most people would consider choosing colors for artwork, text, and backgrounds a fun and creative act. In "web design life," choosing color is often more of a challenge, as you must field cross-platform color management differences.

Creating color artwork for the web is distinct from creating artwork for other color delivery mediums because you're publishing your work to people's screens instead of printed pages. The cross-platform realities of monitor differences can cause your artwork to render differently on different operating systems.

Computer screen-based color is composed of projected light and pixels instead of ink pigments, dot patterns, and screen percentages. In some ways, working with screen-based color can be more fun than working with printed inks. No waiting for color proofs or working with CMYK values, which are much less vibrant than RGB. No high-resolution files. No dot screens to deal with. Although presenting graphics via a computer screen is a lot easier than print in some ways, don't be fooled into thinking that what you see on your screen is what other people will see on theirs. Just like its print-based counterpart, computer screen-based color has its own set of gremlins.

Web Color

Designers Versus Everyone Else

A huge irony in web design is that most designers have much better computer systems than the audience they design for. A typical graphic designer's workstation generally consists of lots of RAM, a larger-than-average monitor, a fast processor, and a video card that supports thousands or millions of colors. The majority of your web audience doesn't use their computers for graphics. They probably use them for word processing, spreadsheets, or databases, where lots of color, RAM, screen real estate, and speed aren't critical.

The reality is that a part of your audience will see your web site through 256-colored (8-bit) glasses. If you create artwork using any of the millions of colors at your disposal, those visitors who have limited color systems will not be able to see your images the same way you can. Their systems will cause your artwork to look "dithered" (random dots of color) in an attempt to mix colors to simulate those they cannot display, or they will shift the colors you choose to the limited colors they can display.

So, what you see on your screen might not be what everyone you design for sees on their screens. It's important to understand what havoc 8-bit web browsers can wreak on your page design, so that you can build your images and color choices in a more indestructible manner.

Creating color images and screens for the web can be done without understanding the medium's limitations, but the results may not be what you are hoping for. In addition to teaching you the HTML behind web color, the focus of this chapter is to describe the web and computer color environment, and to clue you in on known pitfalls and solutions that offer maximum control over how your artwork is viewed.

As the web has matured as an authoring and delivery medium, the general public has become more and more computer literate, and computer systems have become more and more robust. Some of you may question whether the color limitations of 8-bit systems are relevant anymore. Our answer is: not always. Many of you can author web sites without using web-safe colors and your end users will not suffer for it. The web color palette will become a thing of the past as computer systems get cheaper, better, and more powerful. Meanwhile, should you learn this stuff? We think yes. The Web color palette has become an industry standard, and if nothing else, you will not have a well-rounded web design education if you do not understand its purpose or how to implement web pages with it.

What Does the Browser-Safe Palette Look Like?

The 216-color palette for the web has only 6 red values, 6 green values, and 6 blue values—each of which range in contrast. Sometimes this palette is referred to as the 6 x 6 x 6 palette, or the 6 x 6 x 6 cube. This system represents a predetermined palette that the browsers use—and that can't be changed—when the end user's computer system is set to 256-color mode. If you create artwork with colors outside of this system, the browsers will convert the colors you used to fit this palette, whether you want them to or not.

If you work with browser-safe colors, these are some important facts to understand:

- The RGB values found within the 216-color palette have some predictable similarities: The numbers are all formed from combinations of 0, 51, 102, 153, 204, and 255.

- The regularity of these numbers is even easier to see when viewed in the hexadecimal number system explained in this chapter: 00, 33, 66, 99, CC, and FF.

- These colors were picked for their mathematical properties— they are equally spaced in the available range of values—not for aesthetic reasons. Knowing the pattern of numeric values of the browser-safe colors is useful, because you can easily check your code or image documents to see whether they contain these values.

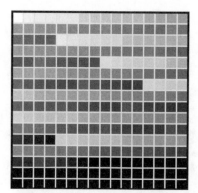

Notice how the browser-safe colors are organized by math? The organization is not useful when picking color combinations.

FFFFFF R: 255 G: 255 B: 255	FFFFCC R: 255 G: 255 B: 204	FFFF99 R: 255 G: 255 B: 153	FFFF66 R: 255 G: 255 B: 102
99FF66 R: 153 G: 255 B: 102	99FF33 R: 153 G: 255 B: 051	66FFCC R: 102 G: 255 B: 204	FFCCFF R: 255 G: 204 B: 255
FFCC66 R: 255 G: 204 B: 102	FFCC33 R: 255 G: 204 B: 051	CCCCFF R: 204 G: 204 B: 255	33FF66 R: 051 G: 255 B: 102
CCCC33 R: 204 G: 204 B: 051	99CCCC R: 153 G: 204 B: 204	FF99FF R: 255 G: 153 B: 255	99CC99 R: 153 G: 204 B: 153

You'll find nvalue.gif **(a portion of it is shown above) and** nhue.gif **in the** chap04 **folder of the <chd2> CD-ROM. These files are organized by color and lights and darks, and they are much more useful than the mathematical organization for aesthetic color picking.**

▶ **note**

Do Browser-Safe Colors Really Matter?

You may think that all this hubbub over browser-safe colors does not apply to you. If you think your site will be viewed only on computers that can display millions of colors (24-bit systems), you might be right. It's always important to investigate who your audience is before you design a site and create artwork that is appropriate for your viewers. There are some situations in which it is not unrealistic to assume that every visitor will be able to see 24-bit color. For example, you may have a site that appeals only to graphic designers, or a site that is on a company intranet.

Our recommendation is that if you are going to pick colors for backgrounds, type, text, links, and areas of solid color in illustrations and line art, that it's best to choose cross-platform compatible, browser-safe colors that everyone will see properly, regardless of his or her system. There may come a day when everyone has video cards that support more than 256 colors, but today many systems do not.

RGB Color

To create web page color schemes, you have to use hexadecimal (or for short, "hex") numbers in your HTML files. If you're scratching your head at this point, don't fret. Most people who aren't programmers have never had to understand hex. Fortunately, it's not hard. Just chalk it up to another web design skill you get to develop.

If you're used to picking RGB or CMYK color on the computer by using imaging software color pickers, chances are you have never had to pay much attention to the math used to represent the colors. Instead, you've probably based your choices on personal taste, such as, "I like this bluish-violet color."

The RGB color system uses a series of three numbers to represent color. The numbers represent the intensity of the Red, Green, and Blue color components that are projected from the computer screen in each pixel. With 24-bit color, each of these three numbers ranges from 0–255, which is 8 bits of storage in the computer. That's why the color system commonly used by designers is called 24-bit color (3 colors x 8 bits = 24 bits).

In most traditional imaging software, including Photoshop, the RGB values are represented in the decimal, or base-10, number system. So when you see 164,56,146, you get that nice bluish-violet color you like so much. Those three numbers represent the Red, Green, and Blue components of the color, respectively.

You've probably never noticed that the numbers are in decimal because we have all used the decimal system so much in our lives that we consider it "normal." We have ten fingers to count on, so it is perfectly natural for us to count in base-10. Unless you took advanced math or computer science in school (or were one of the blessed few who got "new math" in the '60s), you probably never even considered the possibility of another number system.

Hexadecimal RGB

The numeric values of RGB are represented in hexadecimal for
HTML. Hexadecimal is a base-16 number system. Just as the decimal system that you are already familiar with uses 10 different
digits (0, 1, 2, 3, 4, 5, 6, 7, 8, and 9), the hexadecimal system uses
16 different digits (0, 1, 2, 3, 4, 5, 6, 7, 8, 9, A, B, C, D, E, and F).
Letters are used for the digits over 9, rather than creating a whole
new set of symbols and pronunciations for everyone to learn.

Decimal Digits
0 | 1 | 2 | 3 | 4 | 5 | 6 | 7 | 8 | 9

Hexadecimal Digits
0 | 1 | 2 | 3 | 4 | 5 | 6 | 7 | 8 | 9 | A | B | C | D | E | F

The hexadecimal digits greater than 9 have the equivalent values
of the decimal numbers 10–15:

Hex	Decimal
0	0
1	1
2	2
3	3
4	4
5	5
6	6
7	7
8	8
9	9
A	10
B	11
C	12
D	13
E	14
F	15

Just as base-10 is natural for humans (who have five digits on
each limb), hexadecimal is natural for computers, which readily
work with multiples of two. The range of 0–F represents 16
possible different values, and 16 is as natural a value for a
computer as 10 is for a person.

Hexadecimal Colors in HTML

Colors are represented by three pairs of hexadecimal digits in HTML. Each pair of digits represents one of the RGB color components— Red first, then Green, and finally Blue. Just as the decimal representation of RGB colors uses a series of three values, so does the hexadecimal representation. But because the hexadecimal values are always two digits, there is no need for a comma to separate them.

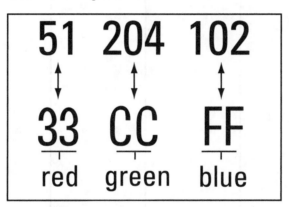

For example, the decimal color 51,204,102 would be 33CCFF in hex.

Here's a chart for converting RGB numbers (0–255) to hex. The browser-safe values are highlighted.

DEC	HEX	DEC	HEX	DEC	HEX	DEC	HEX	DEC	HEX	DEC	HEX
000	00	051	33	102	66	153	99	204	CC	255	FF
001	01	052	34	103	67	154	9A	205	CD		
002	02	053	35	104	68	155	9B	206	CE		
003	03	054	36	105	69	156	9C	207	CF		
004	04	055	37	106	6A	157	9D	208	D0		
005	05	056	38	107	6B	158	9E	209	D1		
006	06	057	39	108	6C	159	9F	210	D2		
007	07	058	3A	109	6D	160	A0	211	D3		
008	08	059	3B	110	6E	161	A1	212	D4		
009	09	060	3C	111	6F	162	A2	213	D5		
010	0A	061	3D	112	70	163	A3	214	D6		
011	0B	062	3E	113	71	164	A4	215	D7		
012	0C	063	3F	114	72	165	A5	216	D8		
013	0D	064	40	115	73	166	A6	217	D9		
014	0E	065	41	116	74	167	A7	218	DA		
015	0F	066	42	117	75	168	A8	219	DB		
016	10	067	43	118	76	169	A9	220	DC		
017	11	068	44	119	77	170	AA	221	DD		
018	12	069	45	120	78	171	AB	222	DE		
019	13	070	46	121	79	172	AC	223	DF		
020	14	071	47	122	7A	173	AD	224	E0		
021	15	072	48	123	7B	174	AE	225	E1		
022	16	073	49	124	7C	175	AF	226	E2		
023	17	074	4A	125	7D	176	B0	227	E3		
024	18	075	4B	126	7E	177	B1	228	E4		
025	19	076	4C	127	7F	178	B2	229	E5		
026	1A	077	4D	128	80	179	B3	230	E6		
027	1B	078	4E	129	81	180	B4	231	E7		
028	1C	079	4F	130	82	181	B5	232	E8		
029	1D	080	50	131	83	182	B6	233	E9		
030	1E	081	51	132	84	183	B7	234	EA		
031	1F	082	52	133	85	184	B8	235	EB		
032	20	083	53	134	86	185	B9	236	EC		
033	21	084	54	135	87	186	BA	237	ED		
034	22	085	55	136	88	187	BB	238	EE		
035	23	086	56	137	89	188	BC	239	EF		
036	24	087	57	138	8A	189	BD	240	F0		
037	25	088	58	139	8B	190	BE	241	F1		
038	26	089	59	140	8C	191	BF	242	F2		
039	27	090	5A	141	8D	192	C0	243	F3		
040	28	091	5B	142	8E	193	C1	244	F4		
041	29	092	5C	143	8F	194	C2	245	F5		
042	2A	093	5D	144	90	195	C3	246	F6		
043	2B	094	5E	145	91	196	C4	247	F7		
044	2C	095	5F	146	92	197	C5	248	F8		
045	2D	096	60	147	93	198	C6	249	F9		
046	2E	097	61	148	94	199	C7	250	FA		
047	2F	098	62	149	95	200	C8	251	FB		
048	30	099	63	150	96	201	C9	252	FC		
049	31	100	64	151	97	202	CA	253	FD		
050	32	101	65	152	98	203	CB	254	FE		

The browser-safe values appear in blue at the top of each column in this chart.

Hexadecimal Resources

Many resources for converting decimal RGB to hex exist on the web. There are two different options: Hex Charts, which typically show color swatches and their hex values, and Hex Converters, which allow a user to type decimal RGB values, and then offer the hexadecimal conversion in return. Those options are covered in the following sections.

Web Hex Converters

A number of sites on the web let you plug in RGB values and then generate hex code for your values on-the-fly. This can be convenient when you're working and want a quick visualization of what a certain color scheme will look like. Some sites even go so far as to accept RGB input, and then automatically output hex and HTML.

Inquisitor Mediarama's RGB-HEX Converter

http://www.echonyc.com/~xixax/Mediarama/hex.html

Test your hex color choices on-the-fly

http://www.hidaho.com/colorcenter/cc.html

Click on any color and hex numbers appear

http://www.schnoggo.com/rgb2hex.html

Browser-Safe Color JavaScript Hex Converter

http://www.hansondodge.com/colors/index.html

Hex Calculators

Some hexadecimal calculators take the RGB values you enter and convert the math automatically. After you convert your RGB colors, you are ready to use the resulting hex in your HTML code.

For Mac users, we suggest a hex calculator written by Joseph Cicinelli, called Calculator II. You can download this application by visiting http:// hotfiles.zdnet.com/ **and searching for "CalculatorII."**

Windows ships with a hex calculator, which usually is found in the Accessories group. Open the Calculator and select View:Scientific. This changes the standard calculator to a scientific calculator. Then, simply select the Hex option to start converting your RGB values.

When to Use Browser-Safe Colors?

We've reviewed the browser-safe colors, but we haven't yet explained when or how you use them. Three different types of scenarios are covered here: HTML color, illustration-type color artwork, and photographic-type color artwork.

```
<Body Text="#663300" LINK="#FF0000" VLINK="#CC6600" ALINK="#6666CC" BGCOLOR="#FFFFCC">

Sample Text

Link

Visited Link

Active Link
```

HTML color refers to programming browser-safe choices for backgrounds, text, links, and tables.

Illustration-type artwork includes line art, logos, flat-color, and cartoons.

Photographic-type artwork includes continuous-tone artwork, photographs, glows, drop shadows, and gradients.

HTML-Based Color Choices

You should always use browser-safe colors when choosing web page color schemes for backgrounds, text, or link colors. If you don't, you may be in for a rude surprise when the browser changes your colors.

This comparison demonstrates the kind of color shifting that occurs with HTML color on 8-bit systems if the colors used are not browser safe.

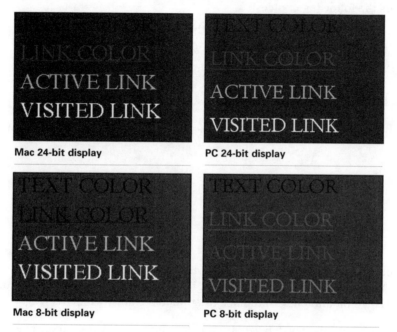

Mac 24-bit display   **PC 24-bit display**

Mac 8-bit display   **PC 8-bit display**

The exercises in this section will explain how to visualize harmonious, browser-safe schemes for HTML color using Photoshop 6.0, and how to pick browser-safe colors using various tools. Later in this chapter, you'll learn how to write HTML code to add the colors you choose to a web page.

▶ exercise

How to Load a Browser-Safe Palette into Photoshop 6.0

You'll find Photoshop's Swatches palette useful when you are choosing a browser-safe color scheme, as you will do in the next exercise. Photoshop 6.0 ships with three browser-safe Swatch sets that can be loaded into the program's Swatches palette. It's also possible to load other Swatch sets or save your own Swatch sets from a menu that drops down from the Swatches palette and offers the following choices:

Reset Swatches: Reverts the Swatches palette to the default color palette for the platform on which you're working (either the Mac or Windows palette).

Load Swatches: Appends a Swatch set of your choice to whichever swatches currently are loaded.

Save Swatches: Enables you to save your own Swatch set.

Replace Swatches: Substitutes a Swatch set of your choice for whichever swatches currently are loaded.

▶ tip

Custom Swatch Set

To create your own Swatch set, use the **Eyedropper** tool, the **Color Picker**, or the **Color palette** to select a color. Place your cursor in the Swatches palette, either on top of a color or after the last color, and click to replace or append a color (respectively).

To delete a color from the Swatch set you are creating, place your cursor over that color in the Swatches palette, and then **Command-click** (Mac) or **Control-click** (Windows) on that color. Click the arrow on the upper-right of the Swatches palette and, from the drop-down menu, choose Save Swatches. Save the new set with an .aco extension if you want it to be Windows 95/98 compatible.

To load one of Photoshop's browser-safe Swatch sets into the Swatches palette, follow these steps:

Step 1: Select **Window:Show Swatches**.

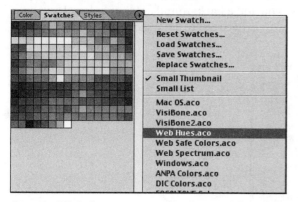

Step 2: Click the arrow on the upper-right of the Swatches palette and choose **Web Hues.aco** from the drop-down menu. (Other web palettes that ship with Photoshop 6.0 include Web Safe Colors.aco, Web Spectrum.aco, VisiBone.aco, and VisiBone2.aco.) Once you've selected a palette, a dialog box will appear asking if you want to append or replace the new Swatch set. Click **Append** if you want this palette to be added to the bottom of the current Swatches palette, and click **OK** if you want to replace the swatch set entirely.

> ▶ **Warning**
>
> ### Swatch Sets in Earlier Versions of Photoshop
>
> If you are using an earlier version of Photoshop that does not come bundled with this menu of browser-safe palettes, use the same method, only select **Load** from the menu. Browse to the browser-safe Swatch file bclut2.aco, which you'll find in the chap04 folder of the <chd2> CD-ROM. If you'd like to try a browser-safe Swatch set in which the colors are arranged by hue, value, and saturation making it easy to choose harmonious color schemes, go to http://www.lynda.com/downloads and click mouse_pad_swatches.sit (**Mac**) or mousepad.zip (**Windows**). Unstuff (Mac) or unzip (Windows) the archived file you've downloaded, and then load the resulting file into the Swatches palette.

▶ e x e r c i s e

Previsualizing Colors in Photoshop 6.0

Getting colors to work together is a very different practice from choosing individual colors that you like. A green might look great alone, but the minute you add a background color or colored text over it, the readability might suffer. To see how to work with browser-safe colors and color relationships follow these steps.

Step 1: Launch Photoshop and open the ducks.psd file from the chap04 folder of the <chd2> CD-ROM.

The first step is to identify some browser-safe colors that will work well together on a web page. One way to do that in Photoshop 6.0 is with the Swatches palette.

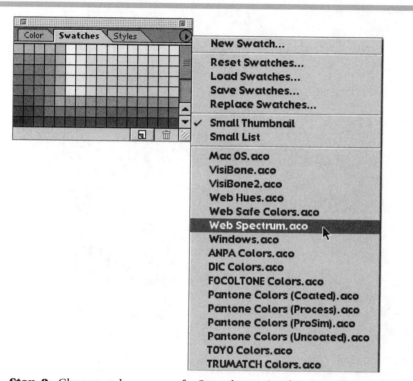

Step 2: Choose a browser-safe Swatch set in the Swatches palette, following the steps in the preceding exercise, "How to Load a Browser-Safe Swatch Palette into Photoshop."

Next you will work with Photoshop layers to choose colors. It is a great way to test and identify browser-safe color schemes for your graphics.

Step 3: Use the **Eyedropper** tool to select colors from the browser-safe Swatch set in the Swatches palette. Fill the various layers of the image to see the results of your color choices. **Note:** You must check the **Lock Transparent Pixels** feature in the Layers palette for each individual layer that you want to change.

When you've found a color combination you like, write down the hexadecimal values you'd like to use for your BODY tags (BGCOLOR, TEXT, LINK, VLINK, ALINK) and background image. There are several ways in Photoshop 6.0 to identify the hex values.

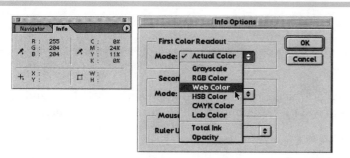

Step 4: One way to find the hex values is to select **Show Info** from the **Window** menu, which brings forth an interactive readout of color values as you touch the colors with the **Eyedropper**. Set the Info palette to display **hex values** by clicking the arrow in the upper-right corner of the Info palette, choosing **Palette Options** from the drop-down menu, and setting the First Readout Mode to **Web Color**.

Note: If you are using an older version of Photoshop that displays only RGB color values in the Info palette, write down those RGB values. Use the conversion chart in this chapter to convert the RGB values to hex.

Step 5: An alternative way to find the hex values is to place the **Eyedropper** tool over your color selection in the Swatches palette, and hold it there a few seconds. The hex number will appear.

❯ e x e r c i s e

Experimenting with Hex Color Choices

Use some of the colors you identified to color a background tile. You will need to save the resulting file as a GIF, so the colors won't shift from what you've chosen. Follow these steps to experiment with your own color choices:

Step 1: Open the tile.psd document from the chap04 folder of the <chd2> CD-ROM. Make sure to check **Lock Transparent Pixels** in order to refill all the artwork on that layer with a color of your choosing.

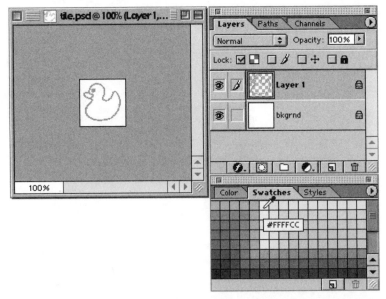

Step 2: With the **Eyedropper** tool, select the colors you chose for the tile ducks layer and the solid bkgrnd layer in the ducks.psd file. **Tip:** You can keep the tile.psd file active and eyedrop on the ducks.psd file at the same time. You can also eyedrop from the Swatches palette, assuming you've already loaded a browser-safe Swatch set as in the preceding exercise.

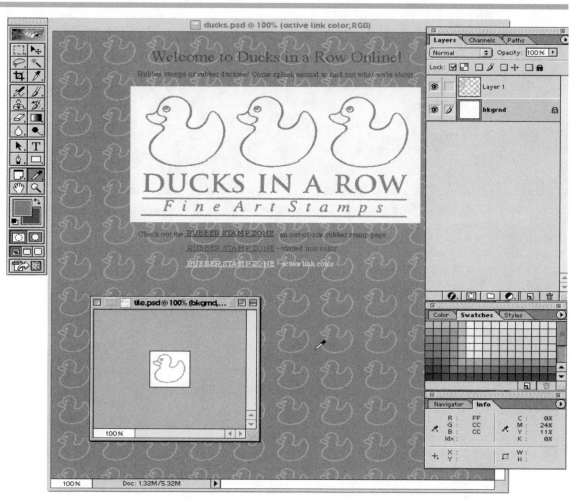

Step 3: Choose **Edit:Fill** to fill the tile.psd layers with those color choices. Make sure the layer you want to edit is selected before you fill and confirm that the Lock Transparent Pixels box on the Layers palette is checked. When you are finished, save a copy as described in the remaining steps.

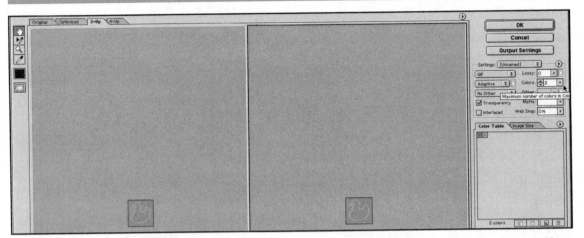

Step 4: Under **File**, select **Save for Web**. Click on the **2-Up** tab of the Save for Web window. Then select the right preview pane.

Step 5: To optimize your graphic, select **GIF** for the Format setting, **Adaptive** for the Palette setting, and **No Dither** for the Dither setting.

Step 6: For the number of colors, select **2**. Only two color chips should appear in the Color Table. Each of the color chips will have a small white diamond in its center, indicating that it is a browser-safe color. Click **OK**.

Step 7: In the **Save Optimized As** dialog box, make sure the file is named tile.gif. It's very important that there not be any spaces between the words tile and gif. The HTML will request that the file be spelled in all lowercase, so be sure to save it that way.

Step 8: Click **New Folder** and name the folder. Click **Save** to save the optimized GIF in that folder. You'll store the HTML file you will create in the same folder.

The final step is to put it all together in an HTML file that contains the hex codes for your BACKGROUND, TEXT, LINK, ALINK, and VLINK colors and that references your background image.

Step 9: Here's some HTML to copy and paste into a text editor. You only have to insert your own values into the attributes of the BODY tag. Then make sure the ylogo1.gif file, a foreground image, is in the same folder to which you save your HTML and tile.gif background image.

```
<HTML>
<HEAD>
<TITLE>Playing with Color</TITLE>
</HEAD>
<BODY BGCOLOR="#xxxxxx"
BACKGROUND="tile.gif" TEXT="#xxxxxx" LINK="#xxxxxx"
ALINK="#xxxxxx" VLINK="#xxxxxx">
<IMG SRC="ylogo1.gif">
</BODY>
</HTML>
```

Note: The Save Optimized As dialog box in Photoshop 6.0 will automatically generate an HTML file for you. If you choose this method following step 8, but before you save, change Format to **HTML and Images** from the pull-down menu. This will save the images and the HTML, as shown.

Color Pickers

You have a choice of a variety of browser-safe color pickers that are included in cross-platform web graphics and HTML authoring programs. For example, Photoshop 6.0's Color Picker can be set to display browser-safe colors by checking the Only Web Colors check box located in the lower left corner. The hex readout at the bottom of the Photoshop Color Picker offers another way to determine the hexadecimal value of a color. Experiment with the various buttons and sliders on the Color Picker to see many different arrangements of browser-safe colors that can help you pick a web-safe palette for your site. You can access the Color Picker from the foreground or background color box in the toolbar, or from the Save for Web window.

Photoshop 6.0's Color palette can also be made browser-safe, by clicking the arrow at the upper-right of the palette and choosing Web Color Sliders and Make Ramp Web Safe from the drop-down menu.

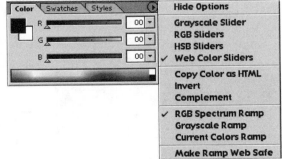

ImageReady 3.0 has a Color Picker and a Color palette that are very similar to Photoshop 6.0's.

▸ **note**

WarningCMYK/RGB Conversions

There is no perfectly accurate way to convert CMYK values to RGB. The numbers that the Pantone Internet Color Guide cites for CMYK Internet-safe values are ballpark approximations that do not yield browser-safe colors when converted to RGB. The two color spaces—RGB and CMYK—do not share common colors consistently. Some RGB colors are outside of the CMYK color gamut, and there is nothing you can adjust to create a reliable conversion method.

Illustration-Based Artwork

On 256-color computers, the web browser forces your artwork into its fixed palette. Unlike HTML-based color, which shifts non-safe colors to a new color of the browser's choice, color image files dither instead. Dithering is a process by which the computer attempts to display a color outside its color range by placing different colored dots next to one another. The colors are calculated mathematically and often look extremely unappealing.

If you use the browser-safe 216-color palette when creating illustration-based artwork, you will avoid unexpected and unwanted dithering.

Here's an example of what happens to the Ducks in a Row logo when it uses colors outside the safe range. Notice the unwanted dots? Those are caused by dithering. You usually need to avoid this dithering wherever you have areas of flat color in an illustration or line art.

If the graphic were prepared with browser-safe colors, it would not dither, regardless of which bit depth the end-viewer's system supports.

▶ e x e r c i s e

How to Check and Fix Dithering of an Image

Photoshop 6.0 and ImageReady 3.0 have features that allow you to check if your image will dither on a 256-color system.

Step 1: Open notsafe.psd from the chap04 folder of the <chd2> CD-ROM. This document uses a color that is not browser safe.

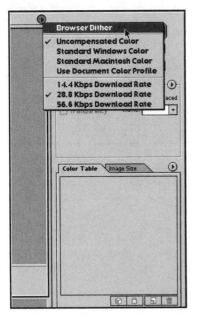

Step 2: In Photoshop 6.0 choose **File:Save for Web**. Click the arrow at the top right of the Save for Web window, and choose **Browser Dither** from the drop-down menu. This causes the image to show what the browser dither would look like.

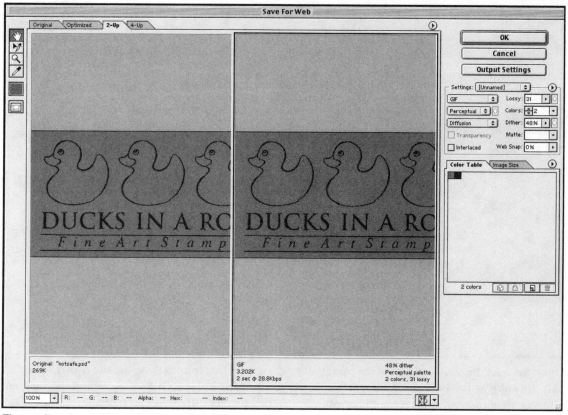

The preview shows the results of browser dither.

The preview shows the results of browser dither.

Note: This process is a little different in ImageReady 3.0. Select **View:Preview:Browser Dither**. (Alternatively, in the Optimized tab of the document window, with the **Eyedropper** tool, **Control-click** (Mac) or **right-click** (Windows), and select **Display Preview, Browser Dither** from the context menu.)

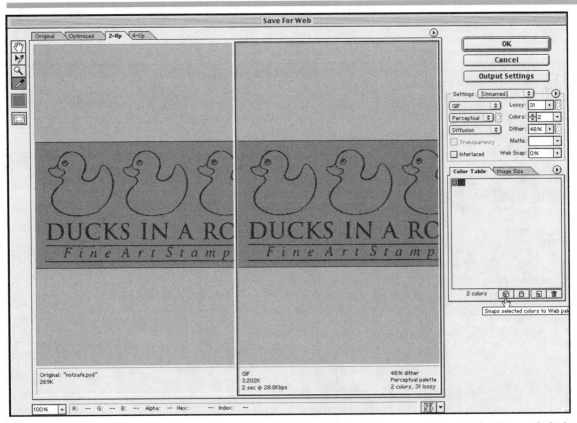

Step 3: To fix the problem (non-safe pixel colors!), use the **Eyedropper** to select the brown and click on the **cube** at the bottom of the palette. This will shift the color to become a browser-safe color (notice the diamond symbol on the swatch?) and the browser dither will go away.

Note: You should turn the Browser Dither preview feature off after you use it, or it will be on every time you optimize an image. There's nothing wrong with it being on, but you might not be able to judge photographs (that don't require browser-safe colors) as well as if it was off. To turn it off, repeat step 2, only toggle Browser Dither off.

This is a useful technique to learn, because not everyone uses a browser-safe palette when creating artwork. It is likely that you will have to convert some non-browser-safe artwork to browser-safe from time to time. Photoshop 6.0 makes that task a lot easier than it used to be. You can do the same thing in ImageReady 3.0.

▶ note

Online Graphics Service

If you don't have Photoshop, Adobe also offers graphics services to help you create web-ready images without a graphics program.

Go to http://webservices.adobe.com/optimize/main. html**, point to an image on your hard drive, and Adobe will optimize the image to the format and palette you specify.**

You can exercise even more control over online optimization at http://webservices.adobe.com/save4web.html, from which Adobe offers access to a Save for Web window much like the one in Photoshop 6.0, with detailed optimization controls. From this window, you can optimize any image on your computer and save the optimized file right back to your hard drive. If you don't have an image to start with, you can do it all from http://webservices.adobe.com/graphic/main.html. From that URL you can create a simple graphic from scratch, go directly to an online Save for Web window, and save the file to your computer.

▶ warning

Converting to Browser-Safe Doesn't Always Work!

There are times when you might have an existing color image that you want to convert to browser-safe colors. It's very rare for an image to look good when a CLUT with colors different from those used in the original image has been applied. Photoshop determines how to substitute the new colors, and it might not yield the results you expect. It's always best to create artwork with browser-safe colors first and not rely on post-processing techniques to fix existing artwork. Follow the exercises in this chapter to learn how to start with images that are created from browser-safe colors so you don't have to convert images to browser-safe colors after they've been made.

Here is the original 24-bit image, it was created in colors that were not browser-safe.

Here is that image in a web browser on an 8-bit system. Notice the unwanted dithering.

You can avoid dithering by converting the image to the 216 browser-safe colors without diffusion. However, because the computer will force the colors into a fixed palette, they may not contain colors that you would have chosen.

How to Ensure Your Artwork Stays Browser Safe

If you work with browser-safe colors when you create artwork, you still have the important task of ensuring that those colors remain browser safe during the file format conversion and saving process.

Unfortunately, files that are saved as JPEGs do not retain precise color information. The lossy compression method used by the JPEG format throws away information, and unfortunately, some of that information relates to color control. Because of this, there is no way to accurately control color using the JPEG file format.

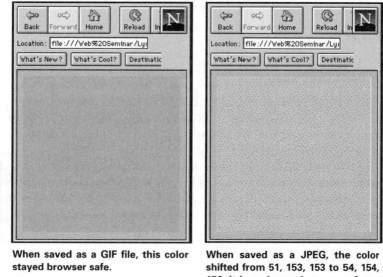

Here's an example of a solid browser-safe color with the hex readout of 51, 153, 153.

When saved as a GIF file, this color stayed browser safe.

When saved as a JPEG, the color shifted from 51, 153, 153 to 54, 154, 156. It is no longer browser safe, as evidenced by the dither when displayed in Netscape Navigator under 8-bit monitor conditions.

Chapter 2, *"First Page,"* emphasizes the point that JPEGs are not good for illustration-type graphics. Not only do they compress the graphics poorly, but they introduce artifacts into images, which alters color information.

This means that you cannot accurately match foreground GIFs to background JPEGs or foreground JPEGs to background GIFs. Even if you prepare images in browser-safe colors, they will not remain browser safe when converted to JPEG, no matter what you do. This is one more reason not to use JPEGs when dealing with flat-style illustrations, logos, cartoons, or any other graphical image that does not lend itself to unwanted dithering.

Photographic-Based Artwork

Photographic artwork is the one type of web imagery that really does not benefit from using browser-safe colors. When a photograph is displayed in a web browser on a 256-color system, the browser converts the photograph to its respective system palette. The good news is that the browser does just as good a job as you could if you had pre-built the photograph in the 216-color browser-safe palette. Let the browser do your dirty work for you! Not only will it save time, but if you create photographic artwork using thousands or millions of colors, or using a palette of adaptive colors, it will look better to end users on more modern computer systems that can display 24-bit color.

> ▶ **note**
>
> ### JPEGs Don't Use Palettes!
>
> If you are saving your photograph as a JPEG, you do not need to worry about choosing a palette for the optimized image. JPEGs don't use palettes or CLUTs; they can display any of 16.7 million colors. If you are saving your photographic image as a GIF (in order to take advantage of web transparency or GIF animation), you should use an adaptive palette. An adaptive palette is built from colors that are in the image, rather than fixed colors from an unrelated color scheme. Alternatively, you could try applying a perceptual or selective palette to photographic GIFs you are optimizing in Photoshop 6.0 or ImageReady 3.0. These new palettes are also based on colors in the original image.

Photographs viewed in 24-bit

Photographs viewed in 8-bit

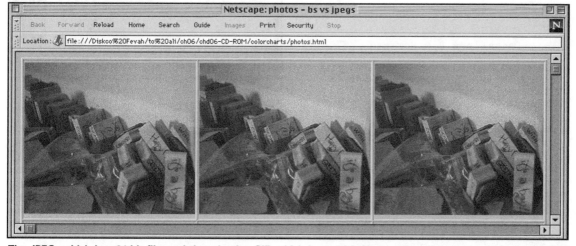

The JPEG, which is a 24-bit file, and the adaptive GIF, which is an 8-bit file based on the colors within the original image, exhibit higher quality than images forced into a fixed, outside palette (such as images saved with the browser-safe palette or a system palette). It is not necessary to convert photographic-based images to the browser-safe palette or to any 8-bit palette. The browser does its dithering dirty work, regardless of how you prepare the image. It's best to leave photographs in a 24-bit file format so that they will have the added advantage of looking better in 24-bit browser environments. JPEGs always produce the smallest file size for photographs and have the added advantage of being a 24-bit file format, which will display millions of colors in a 24-bit browser.

Adding Color to a Web Page with HTML

You learned the basics of creating colored text and backgrounds in Chapter 2, *"First Page."* Now it's time to get deeper into the HTML tags that relate to color. The following examples and exercises run you through the numerous possibilities for programming color into your HTML code.

Using Color Names Instead of Hex

You don't have to use hexadecimal numbers inside HTML color attribute tags; you can use words, too. The web offers numerous lists of color names that allegedly will work in browsers. One such list is at http://www. projectcool.com/developer/gzone/color/color_names.html.

Using any of the names inside the color attribute tag generates colored text in a web browser.

```
<HTML>
<HEAD>
<TITLE>Ducks in a Row Homepage</TITLE>
</HEAD>
<BODY TEXT="antiquewhite"
BGCOLOR="darkcyan" LINK="yellow"
VLINK="darkorange">
<H1>Welcome to Ducks in a Row
Online!</H1>
<P>Feel free to splash around...
<P><A HREF="company.html">
<IMG SRC="ylogo1.gif" BORDER="0"></A>
<P>Check out the
<A HREF="http://www.stampzone.com/">
RUBBER STAMP ZONE</A> - an out-of-site
rubber stamp page
</BODY>
</HTML>
```

Here is an example of using "antiquewhite" along with "darkcyan" as color names within the BODY tag. (This file, called clrnames.html, is in the chap04 folder on the <chd2> CD-ROM.

▶ **note**

Color Names—Not Browser Safe!

Although it might seem much easier to call a color by a name, the big problem is that very few color names are browser safe. Here's a list of the names that are cross-platform compatible:

Name	Hex
aqua	00FFFF
black	000000
blue	0000FF
cyan	00FFFF
lime	00FF00
magenta	FF00FF
red	FF0000
white	FFFFFF
yellow	FFFF00

Coloring Individual Lines of Text

You can assign specific colors to individual lines of text by using the FONT tag.

```
<HTML>
<HEAD>
<TITLE>Ducks in a Row Homepage</TITLE>
</HEAD>
<BODY TEXT="#FFFFCC"
BGCOLOR="#999966" LINK="#006699"
ALINK="#FFFF00" VLINK="#330033">
<H1><FONT COLOR="#FFFFCC">Welcome to
Ducks in a Row Online!</FONT></H1>
<P>
<FONT COLOR="#663333">Rubber stamps or
rubber duckies? Feel free to splash
around to find out what we're
about...</FONT>
<P>
<A HREF="company.html">
<IMG SRC="ylogo1.gif" WIDTH="419"
HEIGHT="219"
ALIGN="bottom"></A>
<P>
<FONT COLOR="#FFFF99">Check out
the</FONT>
<FONT COLOR="#006699">
<A HREF="http://www.stampzone.com/">
RUBBER STAMP ZONE</A></FONT>
<FONT COLOR="#FFFF99">- an out-of-site
rubber stamp page</FONT>
</BODY>
</HTML>
```

The FONT tag can contain a color attribute, which can be specified by using color names or hex numbers. It must be closed with a </FONT> tag each time you want the specific color to end.

Here are the results of using the FONT tag to insert color attributes so that individual words or letters can be colored.

Coloring Links

Link color can affect the border color around linked images or the color of linked text.

```
<HTML>
<HEAD>
<TITLE>Ducks in a Row
Homepage</TITLE>
</HEAD>
1. <BODY TEXT="#FFFFCC"
BGCOLOR="#999966" LINK="#663333"
ALINK="#FFFF00" VLINK="#330033">
<H1>Welcome to Ducks in a Row
Online!</H1>
<P>Rubber stamps or rubber duckies?
Feel free to splash around to find
out what we're about...
<P><A HREF="company.html">
2. <IMG SRC="ylogo1.gif"
BORDER="10"></A>
<P>Check out the
<A HREF="http://www.stampzone.com/">
RUBBER STAMP ZONE</A> - an out-of-
site rubber stamp page
</BODY>
</HTML>
```

The result of creating colored links. Make the border around the graphic wider with the BORDER **attribute.**

1. The LINK attribute within the BODY tag establishes the color for the linked text or graphic. The <A HREF></A> tag produces linked text.

2. The IMG SRC tag inserts an image, and the BORDER attribute enables you to set a width for the border, measured in pixels. **Note:** If you don't want a border, you can set this to BORDER=" 0" .

Adding Color to Tables

The BGCOLOR attribute works in table cells, as well as in the body of the HTML document.

```
<HTML>
<HEAD>
<TITLE>Ducks in a Row
Homepage</TITLE>
</HEAD>
<BODY TEXT=" #FFFFCC"
BGCOLOR=" #999966" LINK=" #663333"
ALINK=" #FFFF00" VLINK=" #330033">
<TABLE BORDER=1 BGCOLOR=" #663333">
<TR><TH><FONT SIZE=" 5">Welcome to
Ducks in a Row Online!</FONT>
</TABLE>
<P>Rubber stamps or rubber duckies?
Feel free to splash around to find
out what we're about...
<P><A HREF=" company.html">
<IMG SRC=" ylogo1.gif"
BORDER=" 10"></A>
<P>Check out the
<A HREF=" http://www.stampzone.com/">
RUBBER STAMP ZONE</A> an out-of-site
rubber stamp page!
</BODY>
</HTML>
```

1.
2.

Here's an example of coloring cells within a table by using the BGCOLOR attribute within the TABLE tag.

1. The TABLE tag establishes the beginning of the table command. The BORDER attribute assigns an embossed border to the table.

2. TR initiates a table row. The TH stands for table header. Everything within the TH tag is automatically bolded and centered. The BGCOLOR attribute sets a background color for the table by using hexadecimal or color names.

HTML Tags That Support Color

Here's a list of all HTML tags that may affect the color of displayed elements:

Tag	Attribute(s)	Description
BODY	BGCOLOR	Sets the colors for the document background/text/links/visited links/active links.
1. FONT	COLOR	Sets the color of the font.
BASEFONT	COLOR	Sets the color of the default font for the document.
2. TABLE	BGCOLOR	Sets the background color for the entire table.
TR2	BGCOLOR	Sets the background color for the table row.
TD2	BGCOLOR	Sets the background color for the table cell.
TH2	BGCOLOR	Sets the background color for the table heading.

1. The use of the FONT tag is depreciated in the HTML 4.0 specification (that is, the authors of the HTML spec. would rather you didn't use it) in favor of style sheets. This is wishful thinking on their part, as we can't really stop using the FONT tag until everyone updates their browsers to those that support style sheets.

2. The TABLE BGCOLOR attributes are not actually a part of the HTML specification before 4.0, although they are supported by Netscape Navigator 3.0 and later, and by MSIE 3.0 and later (so lots of folks are using them).

▶ chapter four

web color

In this chapter, you've learned how to implement color in the various elements of your web pages. Our focus was on the why of the "browser-safe" color palette, how to use the hexadecimal number system with your HTML colors, and what code elements to use for applying color to your web pages.

Some of this information may be a bit more technical than you're used to, but don't let that discourage you. Experiment with the various techniques in this chapter, and you will learn even more! Here are some guidelines to remember when working with color and the web.

- When you specify hexadecimal colors in HTML code, as for backgrounds, text, and links, always use browser-safe colors to prevent unexpected color shifts in viewers' browsers.

- Photographs should never be forced into the browser-safe palette. Photographs compress best as JPEGs, a 24-bit format that honors millions of colors. If you must save a photograph as a GIF, use a palette of colors derived from the image itself, such as the adaptive, perceptual, or selective palette in Photoshop 6.0. The same is true for other kinds of images that have substantial areas of continuous tone, such as gradients or glows.

- Illustrations and line art require browser-safe colors in areas of solid, flat color, where the dithering that results from using non-browser-safe colors can seriously interfere with the appearance of the image.

- Hybrid images, which contain both continuous tone and illustration-style artwork, need be browser safe only in areas of solid color.

"When you're hot, you're hot.
When you're not, you're not."
—Jerry Reed

Clickable
looking hot

If an image is "hot," it will send the viewer somewhere else when it's clicked. A hot button can link a viewer to another image, page, site, or external file, depending on how the link is programmed.

You can program a single image to be hot if you place it on the page using HTML tags that link to an outside URL. There are two types of hot images: those single images that are linked to one outside URL, and those single images that have been divided into regions by using an imagemap to direct viewers to multiple URLs.

When a graphic is hot, you can also refer to it as a link, hotlink, hyperlink, or interactive button. All these words describe the same thing; clicking on such an image will result in some action, usually loading a new page.

This chapter reviews the two types of hot images: linked graphics and imagemap-based graphics. You will have a chance to explore more advanced techniques that involve JavaScript rollovers, navigation bars, and frames in Chapter 14, *"Navigation."*

▶ contents

linked images
alt text
width and height info
client-side imagemaps
server-side imagemaps

Clickable

Identifying Hot Images

Images that are hot may have visual cues that differentiate them from other inline graphics. Typically, a border appears around an image that contains a link, and this border defaults to a blue color in most browsers. If your audience has had any experience on the web, they will already be trained to know that anytime they encounter a border around an image, it means that the image can be clicked as an active link.

Sometimes a hot image will not have a telltale border. In case you prefer that your hot graphic be without a border, this chapter describes how to turn the border off. The only way viewers know to click on borderless hot images is if your graphic invites them to bring their cursors closer. In most browsers, as the viewer's cursor passes over a hot spot, the cursor changes from a plain pointer to the pointing hand cursor shown here. This familiar symbol indicates, just like the border, that an image is a clickable button instead of a static graphic.

The pointing hand cursor indicates that text or graphics are "hot."

The hand symbol and blue border are both visual cues of a linked graphic.

Even if a graphic doesn't have the telltale border, the pointing hand cursor indicates that it's "hot."

Creating Linked Images and Text

Remember from Chapter 1, *"Start,"* that the IMG tag is used to insert an inline graphic on a page:

```
<IMG SRC="makingstamps.gif">
```

The result of the above code. The IMG tag inserts a graphic into the page, but it doesn't create a link.

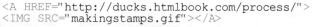

The easiest way to create a link using a graphic image is to use the IMG tag inside the <A HREF> </A> container, where you would otherwise put your anchor text. This combination of tags automatically defaults to putting a border around the graphic. The following is an example of this standard HTML code:

```
<A HREF="http://ducks.htmlbook.com/process/">
<IMG SRC="makingstamps.gif"></A>
```

The result of the above code. The combination of A HREF and IMG tags inserts a graphic with a default border and makes the graphic into a link.

Turning Off Image Borders

Sometimes that pesky blue border around an image is totally wrong for the design of your page. If you've gone to a great deal of trouble to make an irregular-shaped image float freely on a background (using techniques described in Chapter 8, *"Transparency"*), you aren't going to want to ruin the illusion by having a glaring rectangular shape around your graphic. Here's the code to eliminate the border:

```
<BODY BGCOLOR=" #FFFFCC">
<A HREF=" http://www.ducksinarow.com/
process/">
<IMG SRC=" makingstamps.gif"
BORDER=0></A>
</BODY>
```

Notice the BORDER=0 attribute in the IMG tag. This attribute tells the browser, "Don't put a border on this image when it's used as a link."

Here's an example of a linked image with no border. The border was turned off in the HTML, but the pointing finger cursor still appears when the mouse rolls over the linked image. The background color of the page matches the background color of the image, making it appear as if the image's shape is free floating. This was achieved by using the same color yellow as a BGCOLOR attribute inside the BODY tag.

Just as you can make the border disappear, you can also make it appear stronger. This code tells the browser to display a thicker border:

```
<BODY BGCOLOR=" #FFFFCC">
<A HREF=" http://www.ducksinarow.com/
process/">
  <IMG SRC=" makingstamps.gif"
BORDER=25></A>
</BODY>
```

This linked image has been programmed to have a border of 25 pixels.

Sometimes your page has a specific color theme, and the standard blue rectangle doesn't fit in. You can change the color of your borders using the LINK attribute with the BODY tag. This code changes the border color of the images, along with the color of any text links:

```
<BODY BGCOLOR=" #FFFFCC"  LINK=" #996600">
<A HREF=" http://www.ducksinarow.com/
process/">
  <IMG SRC=" makingstamps.gif"
BORDER=25></A>
</BODY>
```

This image has a different color border (still left at the astonishing 25 pixel setting!), programmed with specific hexadecimal color values. Most browsers default to using blue borders unless told otherwise.

Importance of ALT Text

Many people either use browsers that don't support inline images or have their browsers set to not display images as they surf the web. The reasons for surfing that way include physical disabilities (e.g, Braille or vocal browsers for the blind) and technological limitations (e.g, those darn images take too long to download!). For these situations, the IMG tag includes a special attribute called ALT, which you can use to specify text that will be displayed in place of the image if the image is not available for some reason.

Using our example one more time, here's where the ALT attribute would be included:

```
<BODY BGCOLOR="#FFFFCC" LINK="#996600">
<A HREF="http://www.ducksinarow.com/
process/">
<IMG SRC="makingstamps.gif"
ALT="a rubber stamp graphic."></A>
</BODY>
```

It's not necessary to put ALT text on every graphic, but always use it on essential buttons and images. ALT text can be used on static graphics as well as linked graphics.

The ALT text appears on text-based browsers and browsers on which images are turned off in the browser preferences.

The Importance of WIDTH and HEIGHT

The first thing a web browser does in preparation for displaying a web page is to download the HTML code for the page from the server. The browser then interprets the HTML in order to decide how to lay out the page. If there are images on the page, the browser must know the dimensions of each image before it can lay out the page.

The browser could make that determination by downloading each image and checking its dimensions in the image file, but that would take time, especially if the images were large. The browser's detection of image size will go much faster if you specify the WIDTH and HEIGHT of each of your graphics as attributes to the IMG tag. This ability to include WIDTH and HEIGHT in the IMG tag was introduced in Netscape Navigator 2.0 and was adopted by the HTML standards group in HTML 3.2 and later.

When you use WIDTH and HEIGHT with your IMG tags, you provide enough information for the browser to lay out your page without first downloading the associated graphics. When you use these attributes, the page displays with markers in place of the graphics until the graphics are available to display in their respective places. These attributes are supported by the latest versions of most browsers, and using them greatly speeds up the display of your web pages. Your graphics don't load any faster, but text will display before the graphics do, giving the end user the impression of a faster-loading page.

Here's how to use HEIGHT and WIDTH attributes.

```
<A HREF="http://www.ducksinarow.com/
process/">
<IMG SRC="makingstamps.gif"
WIDTH=110 HEIGHT=115
ALT="rubber stamp graphic.">
</A>
```

The values you assign to the WIDTH and HEIGHT attributes reflect the dimensions of the image measured in pixels. Most image editing programs have a feature that enables you to identify your image's size by pixel values.

To determine the image's size in Photoshop 6.0, choose Image:Image Size and view the Pixel Dimensions.

Resizing Using WIDTH and HEIGHT Info

You can even resize an image by using values that are larger or smaller than the image. The browser uses your information for the image size and reformats the image to fit. This feature can be useful at times, but be aware that when you use the browser to resize an image it will not necessarily look right. Also, if you are resizing from a large graphic to a small display size, don't expect to save time and bandwidth. The browser still has to download the entire graphic. It's almost always better to supply graphics in the correct size for display.

Here's an example of putting values larger than the true values in the `WIDTH` and `HEIGHT` attributes. This stretches the image, resulting in an image that rarely looks very good.

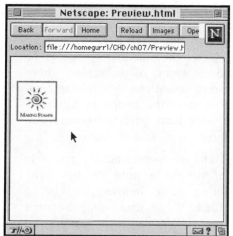

Here's an example of putting values smaller than the true values in the `WIDTH` and `HEIGHT` attributes. This shrinks the image, again resulting in an image that rarely looks good. If you want to shrink (or enlarge) your graphic, it will look best if you do so in your imaging program, not in your HTML document.

> ▶ **note**

Caching Images

It's possible to load images before they are visible in order to "cache" them, or preload them. Some people trick the browser into preloading images by specifying in the HTML that those images appear with small `WIDTH` and `HEIGHT` attributes (such as 1 pixel by 1 pixel), so they are barely visible or hidden on a part of the screen where they won't be noticed. A following page might request the image at full size, and it will load quickly because the computer has cached the image.

If you choose to preload images, it is helpful to put a note on the page explaining that images are being preloaded. Some users may become confused if they notice the excess network activity.

Aesthetics of Interlaced Graphics

If you've toured the web much, you've encountered interlaced GIFs. They're those images that start out blocky and appear less and less blocky until they come into full focus.

These examples simulate the effect of interlacing on a browser. The image starts chunky and comes into focus over time. This allows the viewer to decide whether to wait for your graphic to finish loading or click onward.

Interlacing doesn't affect the overall size or speed of a GIF. In theory, interlacing is supposed to make it possible for your viewer to get a rough idea of your visuals in order to decide whether to wait or move on before the image finishes rendering. In fact, the viewer may be forced to wait for the entire image to finish coming into focus in order to read essential information, which can be a frustrating experience. In other words, interlaced images save time only if you don't have to wait for them to finish downloading.

A Note from Lynda: My recommendation is that you do not use interlaced GIFs for important visual information that's critical to your site. An imagemap or navigation icon, for example, must be seen in order to fulfill its function. (See Chapter 14, *"Navigation,"* for more about how to make navigation icons.) Although interlaced GIFs serve their purpose on nonessential graphics, in my opinion, they only frustrate end users when used on essential graphics.

▶ e x e r c i s e

Linked Graphics Options

The chap05 folder on the <chd2> CD-ROM contains a file called imagelinks.html. In this exercise, you'll experiment with changing the code in that file to try out some of the options associated with linking graphics.

The imagelinks.html **file in a browser.**

The imagelinks.html **code in a text editor.**

Step 1: Launch a text editor and open imagelinks .html from the examples folder in the chap05 folder of the <chd2> CD-ROM.

Step 2: Change the color of the image border by adding a LINK attribute to the BODY tag and putting different hexadecimal values into that attribute. Save the file with a new name (be sure to put the .html or .htm extension at the end), and then open the changed file in your browser again.

Step 3: Change the weight of the image border by adding a BORDER attribute to the IMG tag and putting different values into that attribute. Resave the HTML document. Preview the change in the browser.

Step 4: Change the WIDTH and HEIGHT attributes in the IMG tag, and resave the HTML document. Preview the change in the browser.

Step 5: Change the ALT text message in the IMG tag. Change your browser's preferences to turn off image loading and see if your message appears. Preview the change in the browser. (**Note:** You may need to clear your browser's cache and/or restart your browser after turning off image loading before you can see the ALT text on the page!)

What Are Imagemaps?

At many web sites, you will see a list of underlined text links on a page (often referred to as a
hotlist). This is simply a list of multiple URLs
assigned to multiple text objects. Instead of
using multiple text links, however, the list of
URLs could be attached to a single image object.
Such an object is called an imagemap, which is
a fancy way of presenting a list of links. This
takes a little longer to download than a hotlist
because of the added time required for the
graphic to load. Most of the time, it's worth the
wait because imagemaps are a more convenient, visual way to present multiple choices to
your audience.

Client-Side or Server-Side Imagemap?

An imagemap contains shapes and coordinates for regions within a single image that are hyperlinked to separate URLs. There are two types of imagemaps: client-side and server-side.

A client-side imagemap contains all the information about the imagemap and is stored within the HTML document. A server-side imagemap has the same information in a slightly different format, is stored in a "map definition file" on the server, and is accessed by the server software or a separate CGI program.

- **Client-side imagemaps:** are interpreted by the browser, so they will work only with browsers that support them. Versions of Netscape Navigator since 2.0 and versions of Microsoft Internet Explorer since 3.0 support client-side imagemaps.

An advantage to client-side imagemaps is that they store information in an HTML document instead of on a server. This means the server will not get bogged down by user requests, and the performance of your imagemaps will be more responsive.

- **Server-side imagemaps:** work with all browsers, but they are more complex to set up. A server-side imagemap is accessed via CGI and requires knowledge of how the server is configured. To install a server-side imagemap, you will need to contact your server administrator (or read the server documentation if you are running your own server) to find out how the server is configured.

Another difference between client-side and server-side imagemaps is how they display data in the browser. A server-side imagemap shows the coordinates in the status line at the bottom of the screen, whereas a client-side imagemap shows the actual URL in the status bar, which is much nicer and looks like a hyperlink.

Most users prefer client-side imagemaps over server-side imagemaps; unfortunately, some older browsers don't support this feature. That's why some designers include both types of imagemaps in their documents.

`http://www.razorfish.com/bluedot/typo/menu.map?105,70`

Here's an example of a server-side imagemap display on the status line in Netscape Navigator. It shows the coordinates of the mouse cursor within the imagemap.

`http://www.cgibook.com/links.html`

Here's an example of a client-side imagemap display on the status line in Netscape Navigator. It shows the URL of the link. Much better!

▶ exercise

Create a Client-Side Imagemap in ImageReady 3.0

Step 1: Launch ImageReady 3.0 and open the navbar2.psd file from the chap05 folder of the <chd2> CD-ROM.

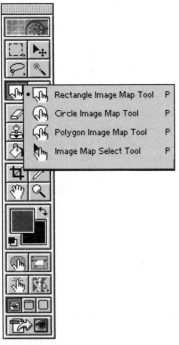

Step 2: Select the **Polygon Imagemap** tool from the toolbar.

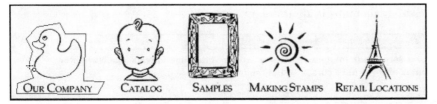

Step 3: Click around the shape of the first button area (Our Company). When you come to the end of the path, the icon will change to show a hollow circle. Click one last time, and the shape will be completed. Tip: If you need to change the shape or select it to delete it, use the Imagemap Selection tool, which is found on the toolbar with the other imagemap tools.

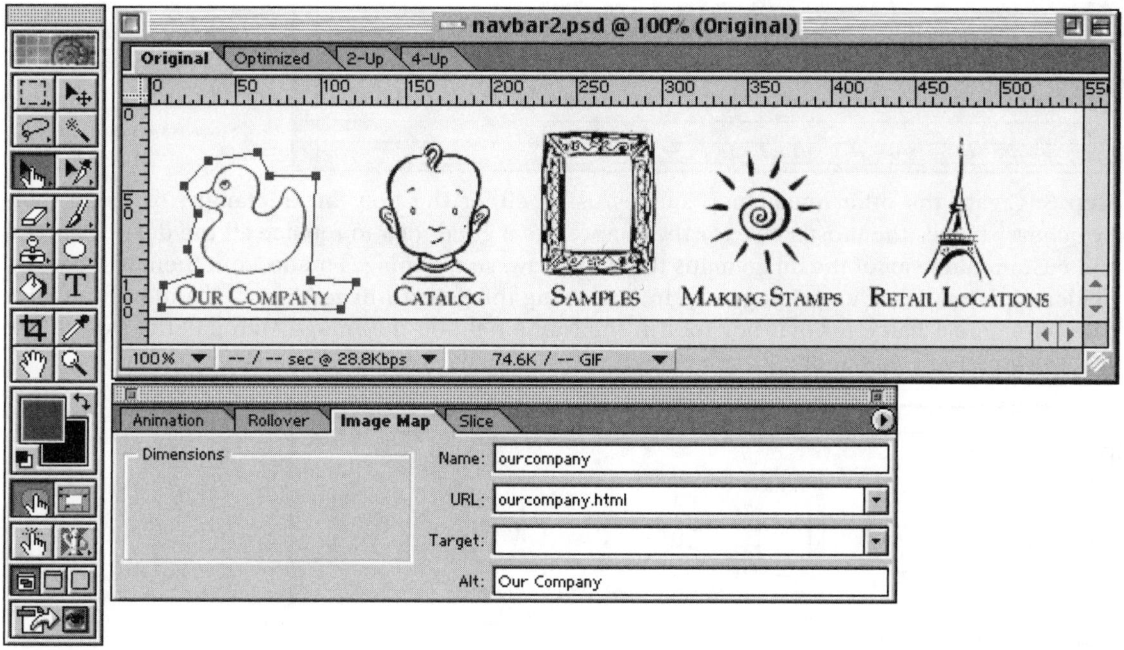

Step 4: Click the **Image Map Palette** button on the Options bar to open the **Image Map** tab. Enter a name (should never include spaces), a URL (this can be relative such as what's shown above or a full http://path name) and an ALT tag (optional, and can include spaces in the name).

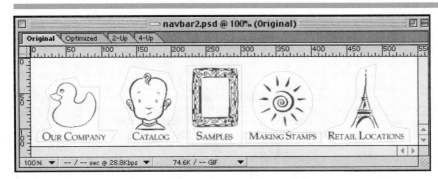

Step 5: Create the other imagemap shapes using either the polygon, rectangle, or circle tools (whichever makes the most sense for the shape). It's a good idea to replace all the default names, and custom name all of the imagemaps that you draw, so the images made from them will be easy to identify later. Select each imagemap in turn using the **Select Image Map** tool, and use the **Slice** palette to type a name for that hot spot in the **Name** field on the **Image Map** palette. Do not use spaces, uppercase letters, or special characters.

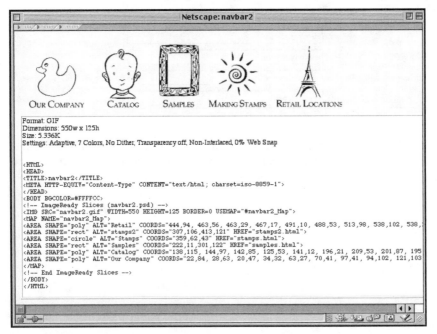

Step 6: Select **File:Preview in Browser**. In the browser, move the mouse near each of the drawings. You'll know you're over a hot spot when the cursor changes to a pointing hand.

Step 7: Click on the **Optimized** tab of the screen, and then choose some optimization parameters in the Optimize window. (**Hint:** Try **GIF**, **Adaptive** palette, **16** colors, and **No Dither**.)

Step 8: Select **File:Save Optimized As**. In the Save Optimized window, choose **Format:HTML and Images** to tell ImageReady to save all your images and write an HTML file that contains the imagemaps you created. **Note:** If you do not save the HTML, the imagemap will not work. The imagemap coordinates are stored in the HTML, not with the GIF image.

Understanding the Client-Side Imagemap Code

Creating client-side imagemaps is slightly easier than making server-side imagemaps because you do not need a CGI program or a separate map definition file (more about this later in the "Server-Side Imagemap" sections). Everything within the client-side imagemap information gets stored within the HTML. Let's analyze what's at work within the HTML.

```
1. <map name=" navbar">
2. <area shape=" rect"
3. coords=" 421,103,528,117"
4. href=" /retail.html">
   <area shape=" polygon"
   coords=" 453,95,462,77,469,55,475,21,475,55,482,81,491,98,487,98,476,86,469,89,
   461,99,453,95" href=" /retail.html">
   <area shape=" rect"  coords=" 310,103,411,120" href=" /process.html">
   <area shape=" circle"  coords=" 358,59,34" href=" /process.html">
   <area shape=" rect"  coords=" 235,103,290,117" href=" /samples.html">
   <area shape=" polygon"
   coords=" 243,14,279,16,292,16,296,28,296,76,293,95,280,97,243,96,232,95,228,65,
   231,23,232,16,243,14" href=" /samples.html">
   <area shape=" rect"  coords=" 141,104,198,119" href=" /catalog.html">
   <area shape=" rect"  coords=" 202,13,202,13" nohref>
   <area shape=" polygon"
   coords=" 157,28,166,22,172,26,174,27,189,31,194,46,190,60,193,59,201,59,195,70,
   186,79,178,86,180,90,189,98,189,101,149,100,156,92,157,86,146,78,144,74,134,61,
   139,58,144,59,139,41,144,35,157,28"
   HREF=" /catalog.html">
   <area shape=" rect"  coords=" 19,103,108,119" href=" /company.html">
   <area shape=" polygon"
   coords=" 62,36,68,47,67,57,65,62,74,61,80,52,84,48,95,59,89,83,73,95,52,96,38,
   91,33,81,37,71,46,64,45,61,34,56,33,50,40,48,44,35,62,36" href=" /company.html">
5. </map>
6. <IMG SRC=" navbar.gif" WIDTH=440 HEIGHT=116
7. BORDER=0
8. USEMAP=" #navbar">
```

1. `<map name=" navbar">`

The map name is something that you define. It must match what is used in the USEMAP attribute in the associated IMG tag.

2. `<area shape=" rect"`

This part of the code defines the shape for this region of the imagemap.

3. `coords=" 421,103,528,117"`

These are the coordinates of each defined point in the shape. Each coordinate is a pair of numbers, x,y, where x is the number of pixels from the left side of the image, and y is the number of pixels from the top of the image. A rectangle (rect) has two coordinates (four numbers): one for the upper-left corner and one for the lower-right corner; a circle (`circle`) has two coordinates (four numbers): the center and one point on the perimeter; and a polygon (`poly`) has one coordinate (one pair of numbers) for each defined point on the polygon.

4. `href="/retail.html">`

The `href` attribute contains the URL of the destination of this link.

5. `</map>`

The end tag is required to end the client-side imagemap.

6. `<IMG SRC="navbar.gif"`

This is the source URL for the image.

7. `BORDER=0`

Just like the server-side example shown later in this chapter, the `BORDER=0` attribute turns off the default blue border. It's not necessary to turn the border off, but it can ruin the illusion of irregularly shaped regions if you leave it turned on.

8. `USEMAP="#navbar">`

The `USEMAP` attribute specifies the name of the client-side imagemap file to use. The # character must always precede the map name.

▶ **note**

Imagemap Resources

Imagemap Tutorial URLs
http://www.ihip.com/

Imagemap Software Tools
(MapEdit software for Windows, Macintosh, and UNIX)
http://www.boutell.com/mapedit/

Glenn Fleishman's Server-Side to Client-Side
(Online Converter)
http://www.glenns.org/writing/convertmaps.html

Creating Server-Side Imagemaps

Server-side imagemaps are more complicated to explain than
client-side imagemaps because they tend to work differently on
different servers. Fortunately, the simplest implementation is
also the most common. According to the Netcraft survey
(http://www.netcraft.com), the Apache web server (or its deriva-
tives) is by far the most popular web server software. The method
described here will work only on servers running Apache with
the imagemap module (**mod_imap**) installed. The default
Apache installation includes this module, but some servers may
have it configured differently or otherwise disabled. Check with
your system administrator if this doesn't work on your system.

> ▶ **note**
>
> ### Do You Need an Imagemap?
>
> Carefully analyze whether you really need an imagemap
> or whether there's some other way to accomplish the
> same goal. For example, if your image is composed of rec-
> tangles, or can be seamed together by using rectangular
> shapes (or transparent irregular shapes, see Chapter 8,
> "*Transparency*"), it might be easier on your end to load
> multiple single graphics with independent links than to
> load one graphic with multiple links.
>
> You will see examples of imagemaps used on opening
> menu screens all over the web. Sometimes an imagemap
> is used even when the menu bar is composed of rectangu-
> lar shapes. Some sites do this because one image loads
> faster than multiple images. This is a valid reason to
> use an imagemap, but even so, the difficulty of
> creating and maintaining one might outweigh the
> performance increase.

The Importance of ALT Text

Using an imagemap as a navigation tool is a wonderful way to exercise your freedom of design and open the doors to more creativity. Unfortunately, it can also make life a lot more difficult for those who do not use graphical browsers.

Two classes of users will have problems with imagemaps;

- End users who browse with their image loading turned off (for speed, usually)

- End users who are using a nongraphical browser like Lynx (http://lynx.isc.org), which is designed for use on character-terminals

Here's how our current example looks on Lynx:

Lynx users don't see our imagemap.

This is what the sample page looks like in Netscape Navigator 4.0 with image loading turned off:

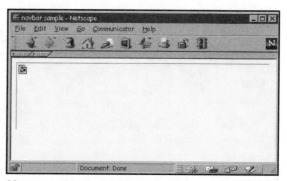

Many users browse with image loading turned off. This is what they would see on this page.

One easy way to make these pages more useful to these users, without sacrificing any design criteria, is to use the ALT attribute in our IMG tags. **Note:** MapEdit adds ALT text to the AREA tags in the client-side imagemap. We have not yet found a browser that will display this text. It would be nice, though. :-)

To add ALT text to the imagemap, simply add the ALT attribute to the IMG tag in the same way you would for any other image:

```
<A HREF="navbar.map">
   <IMG SRC="navbar.gif" WIDTH="440"
HEIGHT="116" BORDER="0"
      USEMAP="#navbar" ISMAP
ALT="Navigation Bar"></A>
```

Now it looks like this:

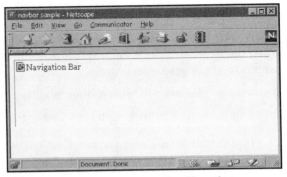

Netscape Navigator with ALT **text. Now the user may decide to load the image.**

With ALT text, it's easier to see what's on the screen in Lynx, but the user is still left wondering what to do about it.

Even though we've added ALT text, the user will still be left wondering where the links are. Our imagemap is actually active, but without any visual cues, it would be impossible (or at least difficult) for most people to use.

That's why it's such a good idea to include a simple text menu, especially on pages where all the navigation is in graphics. You can create this menu in a number of ways. (Let your imagination be your guide!) Here's one that we have used on our pages with good results. Simply add this HTML right after the imagemap:

```
<P>
[
<A HREF="/company.html">Our Company
</A> |
<A HREF="/catalog.html">Catalog
</A> |
<A HREF="/samples.html">Samples
</A> |
<A HREF="/making.html">Making Stamps
</A> |
<A HREF="/locations.html">
Retail Locations</A>
]
```

Your graphically challenged users will see this:

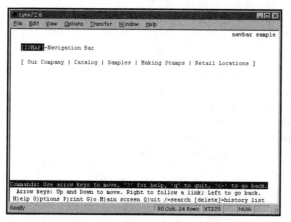

With the text menu, this page is now useable by Lynx users. They will thank you for it!

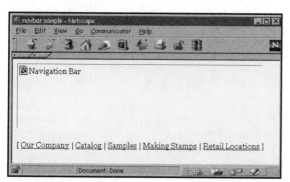

Netscape users with their graphic loading disabled will also see the menu. This may encourage them to look around a little longer. They may even decide to press the little button that loads the images!

Finally, looking at the page with images loaded, we can see that this little menu at the bottom doesn't detract from our design much at all.

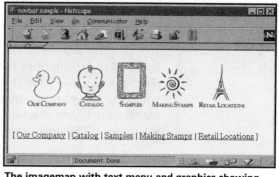

The imagemap with text menu and graphics showing.

In the end, it's really your decision. There may be sites where you will want to trade off the nongraphical audience for a certain design, but it's always a good idea to at least consider the decision. Try to find a way to accommodate as many potential users as possible, without sacrificing the look of the site.

▸ chapter five summary

Clickable

One of the coolest things about the web is the fact that
you can link viewers anywhere you want from your site.
Some of the techniques for creating linked graphics are
simple; and some, as in the case of imagemaps, are more
complex. This chapter should serve as a useful reference
for creating linked graphics and as a springboard to delve
into other HTML techniques.

6

"Well, I set my monkey on the log
And ordered him to do the Dog
He wagged his tail and shook his head
And he went and did the Cat instead
He's a weird monkey, very funky"
—Bob Dylan, I Shall Be Free No. 10, 1964

Tiles
filling the source

Tiles

▶ contents

pattern-based images
seamless patterns
size of source patterns
file formats for patterns
html for tiled images

Making full-screen, wall-to-wall graphics on the web would seem to be an impossible feat given the slow modems and itsy-bitsy phone lines most of us have to squeeze connections through. Not to mention the fact that full-screen graphics can mean one thing to a viewer using a compact laptop, and another to someone with a 21" monitor! You might think it would take way too long to download an image that fills a viewer's browser screen, and that it would be irresponsible to prepare images of this size for web graphics.

Repeated, or tiled, graphics are the answer. This chapter covers the BACKGROUND attribute for the BODY tag, which causes a single, small image to be repeated endlessly vertically and horizontally so that it fills an entire web page, regardless of size. Tiled images have the advantage of being small, so they load fast; and they include the capability to repeat over the size of any web screen. Because a small graphic loads faster than a big one, this technique works well when you need to cover a lot of real estate on a web page without incurring a lot of overhead in downloading time.

Tiling Backgrounds

The BODY BACKGROUND="URL" feature tells the browser to repeat a small graphic and turn it into a full-screen graphic. It accomplishes this effect by tiling a single image, creating a repeating image that will fill any size screen regardless of computer platform or browser area. The browser needs to load only a single source file for the pattern. Once that file is downloaded, it is repeated continuously, filling the entire web page. This saves time because the viewer has to wait only for a single, small image to download, even though the result is that the entire screen fills with an image. Repeated tiles are a great solution for creating full-screen graphics for low-bandwidth delivery systems like the web.

Bandwidth limitations aren't the only problem that tiled background patterns solve. In the past, HTML has not allowed images to be layered. If you consider that layering is a main feature of such programs as Photoshop, QuarkXpress, and PageMaker, you'll understand why this feature has been sorely missed in HTML. Cascading style sheets are an alternative solution for implementing layered images in 4.0 and later browsers (see Chapter 13, "*Style Sheets*"), but placing foreground elements over tiled background patterns is a much easier route, and one that works across browsers.

HTML allows text, links, and images to be placed on top of tiled backgrounds, making the background feature an extremely useful and economical design element. The HTML code for this tiling effect is quite simple. The real challenges are making the art look good, and controlling whether the edges of each repeated image are obvious or invisible.

The source file for a repeatable tile.

The repeated tile in a web browser.

Determining Tiled Pattern Sizes

One of the first questions to consider is how big the tiled image should be. HTML puts no restrictions on the size of a source for a background tile. The image has to be in a square or rectangle, however, because that's the native shape of any computer image.

The size of the image is entirely up to you. You should realize that the size of a tile is going to affect how many times it repeats. If a viewer's monitor is 640×80 pixels and your tile is 320×240 pixels, the image will repeat 4 times. If the tile is 20×20 pixels, it will repeat 768 times in a monitor set to 640×480 pixels.

If your tile has images that repeat on each side, it will not show visible seams, and the viewer will not know how many times the tile repeats. If the image has an obvious border around it, the border will accentuate the fact that the image is being tiled.

The size of your tile is up to you and the effect you are striving for. Be aware, however, of the contribution of your background tile to the total file size of your page. If you create a tile that takes up a lot of space, it will take the same amount of time to load as any other graphic of the same size. If need be, refer back to Chapter 3, "Speedy Graphics," for methods of minimizing file sizes.

If you use an image source that has large dimensions, it will not repeat as often. If it is large enough, it will not repeat at all. In that event, you'll lose the speed advantage of having a small image load once and automatically repeat without incurring any additional downloading time. On the other hand, if you could make a graphic large in dimensions but

not in file size, loading it in as a background image instead of a regular graphic could have its merits. We show examples of large background images later in this chapter.

Large source file and its results in a web browser.

Medium source file its results in a web browser.

Smal source file and its results in a web browser.

Full-Screen Body Backgrounds

Why would you use an image with large pixel dimensions as a tiled background, since it seems to defeat the point? The answer is because it could go behind other images and text, making a full-screen backdrop to foreground elements on your page. HTML doesn't let you easily put text or images over regular images. The simplest way around this restriction is to use a full-screen background tile.

Here's a full-screen (571×499 pixel) graphic that is only 9k. Because there are very few colors in this image, it compresses well as a GIF file.

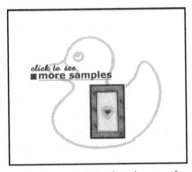

Other images are placed over the full-screen background. This is a very effective and economical use of a large background tile.

Here's an example of a 30k JPEG image used as a full-screen background in the "Making Stamps" section of the Ducks In A Row site.

With a transparent GIF of the Making Stamps logo placed over the full-screen background, this page looks rich and layered, but is not too large to download.

▸ warning

Pitfalls of Full-Screen Backgrounds

Full-screen background tiles are a neat idea, but they do present a couple of problems. For example, when you create a full-screen background, you have to make an assumption about the size of your viewers' browsers. When viewers look at these graphics on large monitors, the full-screen illusion can be broken, and you may cringe at the results.

On large monitors, the illusion of full-screen backgrounds is easily shattered.

There's no true solution to this problem. All you can do is second-guess the target size of your viewers' displays in order to plan the size of your full-screen tile. There's no foolproof way to do this. We're not saying, "Don't use full-screen backgrounds!" We're simply warning you of one of the pitfalls of this device.

Another problem with full-screen backgrounds is the difficulty of predicting exactly how their content will line up with the content of foreground images. Unfortunately, different browsers offset the vertical and horizontal placement of images by different numbers of pixels. Some designers insert special code in the BODY tag <BODY MARGINWIDTH=" 0" LEFTMARGIN=" 0" MARGINHEIGHT=" 0" TOPMARGIN=" 0"> to try to control browser offset; but this workaround does not solve the problem in all browsers. A better solution is to use a background image that is abstract and/or flexible enough to blend well with foreground elements regardless of their placement.

File Formats for Patterned Background Tiles

GIFs and JPEGs are the standard file formats for the web, and background tiles are no exception. Just remember to follow the kilobyte rule: Every kilobyte of file size can represent one second of download time to your viewer. (This is just a general estimate. Actual download time depends on a number of factors other than just file size.) The full size of the background pattern gets added to the download! If you have a background that's 60k and two images that are 10k each, the to tal file size of your page will be 80k. The background alone could add a minute of download time to your page! Tiled backgrounds that take up a lot of memory are extra annoying to your audience during download.

Be careful if you are trying to match colors of foreground and background images. The foreground image file and the background tile must both be the same file format—GIF and GIF or JPEG and JPEG—if you want the colors to match perfectly.

As usual, always save your file names in lowercase, and use the extensions .jpg or .gif to let the HTML code know what kind of image it has to load. I usually put the word "pat" somewhere in a pattern file name, just for my own reference. That way, I know what I intended to use the file for when searching for it in a text list, such as my server directory.

Seams or No Seams?

Two fundamentally different types of repeating tiles can be used for background images: seamed and seamless. This section takes a look at these two different ways to present background tiles on your web pages.

Seams

When an image has obvious seams, it looks tiled on purpose. Some web pages look great wallpapered with an obvious border. Andy Warhol shocked the art world in the 1960s and first earned his notoriety by making images of repeating soup cans on a single canvas. Video walls are often built on the power of images repeating in squares. There's nothing wrong with making patterns that have obvious borders and repeats, especially if that's what you had in mind. Making a tiled pattern with an obvious repeating border is fairly simple. Just include a border in the source file.

The source file has an obvious edge. This edge will be accentuated once the tile is repeated in a browser.

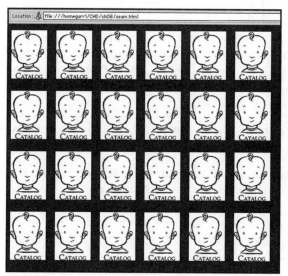

The finished tile is unmistakably repeated, with all the seams proudly showing!

No Seams, the Photoshop / ImageReady Way

"Seamless" patterns are those in which the border of the pattern tile is impossible to locate. There aren't any pros or cons to using seamless or seamed tiles; it's purely an aesthetic decision. Seamless tiles, however, are much trickier to make.

The source file for a seamless tile.

The seamless tile repeated and displayed in a web browser.

▶ e x e r c i s e

A Seamless Tile in ImageReady 3.0

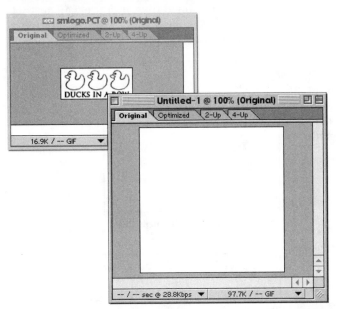

Step 1: Launch ImageReady 3.0, and open the smlogo.PCT file from the chap06 folder of the <chd2> CD-ROM. Select **File:New**, and create a new document that is 200×200 pixels with a white background. ImageReady defaults to 72 dpi, so you do not have to choose it when you set up a new image like you do in Photoshop 6.0. That's because ImageReady was developed soley for the web and Photoshop was developed for print or web.

Step 2: Click the smlogo.PCT document to make it active. Choose **Select:All**, and then **Edit:Copy**. Click the Untitled document and select **Edit:Paste**.

Tip: Whenever you paste an image into a document in ImageReady or Photoshop, it is automatically centered. Centering the graphic at this point is key to this exercise

Step 3: Click the Untitled document to ensure that it's active. Under the Filter menu, choose **Other:Offset**. In the Offset dialog box, choose **Offset by: Pixels**, and enter 100 pixels into both the Horizontal and Vertical fields. Click **OK**. Notice how the ducks logo split and was repositioned into the four corners of this document? That's exactly the goal of this exercise.

Step 4: Choose **Edit:Paste** again. A copy of the smlogo.PCT file should still be in your Clipboard and will be pasted into the center of the Untitled document one more time. Voilà! You've just created the source file for a symmetrical seamless tile.

Note: You could have completed the preceding steps in this exercise in either ImageReady 3.0 or Photoshop 6.0 (which also has an Offset filter). We chose to present this exercise in ImageReady because of what comes next. ImageReady has useful features for previewing and saving HTML background tiles that are not included in Photoshop.

Step 5: Click the **2-up** tab on the screen to observe an interactive preview of the tile as you optimize it for the web. Click on the right-hand preview pane to select that view. In the Optimize palette, choose **GIF** as the file format, **Adaptive** as the palette, **8** as the number of colors in the image, and **No Dither**.

Step 6: To identify the file as a repeating background image, select **File:Output Settings: Background**. In the Output Settings window, choose **View As:Background** and click **OK**.

Step 7: To preview the repeating background tile in a browser, select **File:Preview In** and choose a browser on your system. The preview includes information about the optimized tile and some temporary HTML code that ImageReady writes to display the browser preview.

Step 8: Return to ImageReady and make sure that the right-hand preview window is active. If you are satisfied with that preview, select **File:Save Optimized As**. In the Save Optimized window, name the optimized file smducksym.gif, choose **Format:HTML and Images** from the pull-down menu to tell ImageReady to generate an HTML file to display the tile. Click **Save**.

Step 9: Congratulations! You've created a tiling, symmetrical background. Check your hard drive for the GIF and HTML file generated automatically by ImageReady.

▶ e x e r c i s e

A Seamless Tile in Photoshop 6.0

Here is a variation on the seamless tile. You'll make this tile in Photoshop 6.0 (although it could be made in ImageReady).

Step 1: Launch Photoshop 6.0 and again open smlogo.PCT from the chap06 folder on the <chd2> CD-ROM. Select **File:New** and create a new document in Photoshop that is 200×200 pixels at 72 dpi in RGB color with a white background.

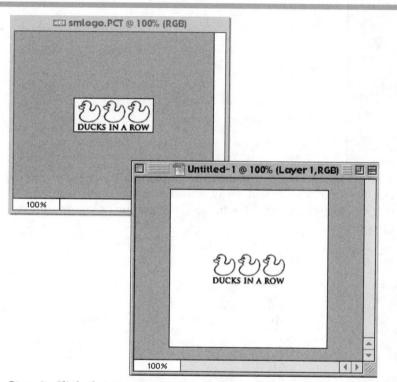

Step 2: Click the smlogo.PCT document to make it active. Choose **Select:All** and then **Edit:Copy**. Click the Untitled document and select **Edit:Paste**. As in the last exercise, the logo will be pasted into the center of the document.

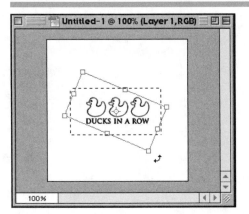

Step 3: Use the Selection Marquee tool to create a rectangular selection around the pasted logo. **Select Edit:Free Transform**. Position your cursor away from the image until you get the rotation symbol. Rotate the image clockwise, and double-click on it when you're happy with the positioning. Click off the image to deselect.

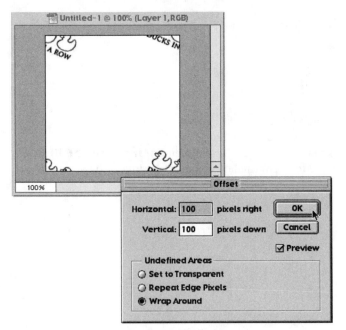

Step 4: Select **Filter:Other:Offset**. Type in Horizontal **100 pixels** and Vertical **100 pixels**. Click **OK**.

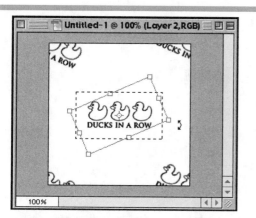

Step 5: Select **Edit:Paste** to paste another copy of the logo from the Clipboard to the center of the image. Repeat Step 3, but rotate the pasted image counterclockwise this time.

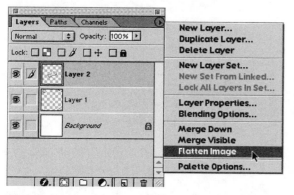

Step 6: Be sure to choose **Flatten Image** from the arrow on the top right of the Layers palette. This will put all your artwork on one layer, so that it all will be affected by the next application of the Offset filter.

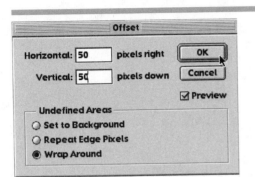

Step 7: Select **Filter:Other:Offset**. This time, enter **50 pixels** into the Horizontal and Vertical fields. Click **OK**. This creates a different offset than before.

Step 8: Open the smburst.PCT file from the chap06 folder of the <chd2> CD-ROM. Choose **Select:All** and **Edit:Copy**. Click on the seamless tile you've been working on and select **Edit:Paste**. The sunburst image will be pasted into the center, but use the Move tool to reposition it to the bottom left corner of the image as illustrated. Paste the sunburst image a second time and reposition it to the top right corner of the image as illustrated.

Step 9: Click the Untitled document on the screen and select **File:Save for Web**. Click the **2-up** tab; then click the preview window on the right. Set the optimization controls in the Save for Web window to **GIF**, **Adaptive** palette, **8** colors, and **No Dither**. Then click **OK**.

Step 10: In the Save Optimized As window, name the optimized file asym.gif and click **Save**.

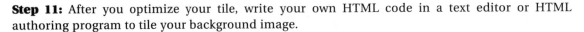

Step 11: After you optimize your tile, write your own HTML code in a text editor or HTML authoring program to tile your background image.

Step 12: Go back to the regular Photoshop editing environment and click the Untitled document. Select **File:Save** and save the source file as asym.psd.

Step 13: Write the following HTML code and save it as asym.html in the same folder as asym.gif.

```
<HTML>
<HEAD>
   <TITLE>tile test</TITLE>
</HEAD>
<BODY BACKGROUND="asym.gif">
</BODY>
</HTML>
```

Step 14: Open the finished HTML file in a browser to view the repeating background tile.

Special Effects Tiles

There are so many variations on tile making that the possible combinations of effects are unlimited. Here are some sample source files and their finished results in a browser to give you some ideas. Try your own variations. One thing to keep in mind is that the browser will load the tile from left to right or from top to bottom. If you make a wide and short tile or a narrow and tall tile, the loading process can actually look like a subtle animation of the tile painting itself into place. Unfortunately, this subtle animation effect gets tiresome after you've seen the page a couple of times.

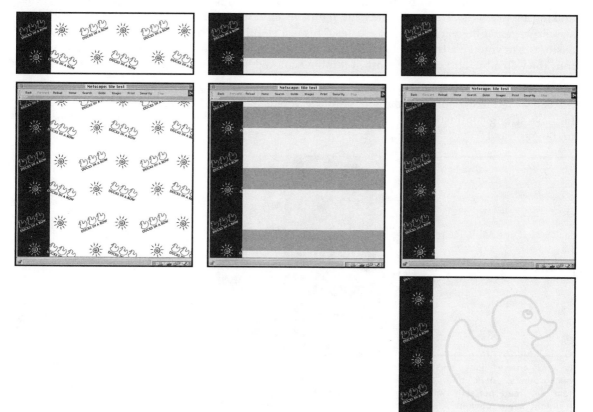

Aesthetics of Backgrounds

Always pay attention to contrast and value (lights and darks) when creating background tiles. If you have a light background, use dark type. If you have a dark background, use light type. If you are going to rely on browsers' default colors for text, links, visited links, and active links, use a light background—about the same value as the default light gray you see as the background color of most browsers. The light background ensures that the default colors of black, blue, and purple text will read against your custom background.

When you're making art for pattern tiles, try to use either all dark values or all light values. Avoid making a pattern tile with both darks and lights because neither light nor dark type will work consistently against the background it creates. This is a simple rule that can significantly improve the aesthetics of your site. Using either all dark values or all light values seems like common sense, but tour the web a bit, and you'll see lots of rainbow colored backgrounds with unreadable black type.

Make sure your images read. We don't mean your tiles should go to school to learn phonetics; instead we're talking about readability of image versus background. The examples we've shown so far have strong contrast and "read" as tiled images, but if you try to put type over them, most will no longer "read."

If you create light and faded backgrounds, dark and colored text will read perfectly. Although it might seem obvious, dark and medium value colors will read over a light background.

With a dark background, the reverse is true. It's not enough to make a cool-looking background tile—always check to make sure your type reads over it as well! If it doesn't read, make the necessary adjustments to the type or to the color or contrast of the background image. See the following exercise, "How to Color Tiles in Photoshop and ImageReady 3.0," to learn how to do this.

When the background is black and white, nothing reads well on top of it. Eventually, black type will intersect with a dark area of the background, or light text will appear on the white area. No solution can make this page work, except to redo the background tile with a better choice of colors.

▶ **note**

Specify Text Color Schemes!

Beware if you use a background image but don't specify the color of text in the HTML code! Some viewers change the text color in their browsers, and they may select a color that doesn't read well against your background!

Our recommendation: If you use a background image (or color), specify the text and link colors too. This ensures that everyone can at least read the text on your page. In fact, you may even want to specify a `BGCOLOR` so that the text on your page is readable even before the background loads.

▶ **warning**

Printing Issues

Many people print web pages instead of reading the content on screen. In older browsers, it is impossible to print a background tile. This can create readability problems in printed documents! If you use white text, for example, and the background tile doesn't print, your audience will get white text on white paper, or in other words, "nothing." One solution is to avoid pure white text on pages that you suspect might get printed. Another solution is to provide a separate "printable" page for printing and provide a link to it from the unprintable page.

▶ e x e r c i s e

How to Color Tiles in Photoshop and ImageReady

We're going to cover several different selection and recoloring techniques in this section: The first two show anti-aliased examples and the third shows an aliased example.

Anti-Aliased Example in Photoshop 6.0

Anti-aliased graphics have edges of graduating opacity, which give them a smooth appearance and can help integrate them into a composition. However, those same graduating edges can make it difficult to achieve a clean look when anti-aliased graphics are recolored. In this example you'll practice using Photoshop's Color Range tool, which is an effective way to select anti-aliased artwork for color editing. ImageReady does not have a Color Range selection feature, so you'll do this exercise in Photoshop 6.0.

Step 1: Launch Photoshop and open the antialias.pct file from the chap06 folder of the <chd2> CD-ROM.

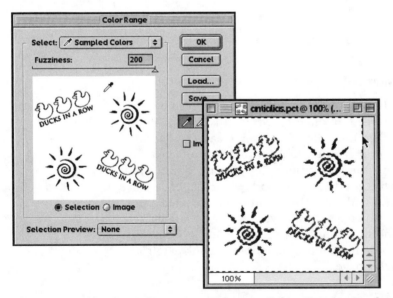

Step 2: Under the Select menu, choose **Color Range**. In the Color Range window, choose **Select:Sampled Colors** and click the leftmost Eyedropper tool. With that Eyedropper, click on the white area of the image either in the file itself or in the image preview inside the Color Range window. In the Color Range window, increase the Fuzziness slider to **200**, maximizing the range of colors selected. Click **OK**. A selection based on the white areas of the tile will appear in the file.

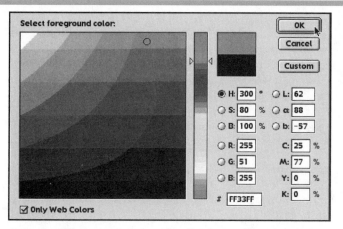

Step 3: Choose a color with which you'll recolor the selected white areas of the tile. Click the Background Color well in the toolbar to open the Color Picker. Make sure there is a check mark next to Only Web Colors. Choose a color from one of the many arrays of web-safe colors you can access by experimenting with the sliders and radio buttons in the Color Picker. **Note:** ImageReady 2.0 has a Color Picker similar to this one, except that the ImageReady Color Picker does not include controls for the print-oriented Lab and CMYK color schemes.

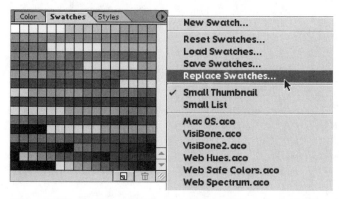

Step 4: Photoshop 6.0 has several different tools for selecting web-safe colors. Try using the Swatches feature to choose a color with which you'll recolor the line art in this tile. First, load a set of web-safe swatches that we've put together especially for web graphic designers. Click the arrow on the top right of the Swatches palette. Choose **Replace Swatches**, and then navigate to color.aco in the chap06 folder of the <chd2> CD-ROM. (Alternatively, **Replace Swatches**, and choose one of the web-safe swatches that ships with Photoshop 6.0 or ImageReady 3.0 and automatically loads.)

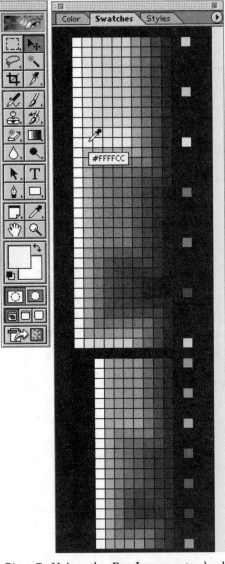

#FFFFCC

Step 5: Using the **Eyedropper** tool, click on any color chip in the Swatches palette. This color will appear in the Foreground Color well on the toolbar. **Aesthetic Tip:** This color should be of the same value (either light or dark) as the color you chose in step 3, because you'll be using the two together to recolor your background tile, over which you'll want to place readable type of a contrasting value.

Step 6: To recolor the selected white area of your tile, select **Edit:Fill**. In the Fill dialog box, choose **Use:Backround Color** and click **OK**.

Step 7: From the Select menu, choose **Inverse** to select the black line art in the tile. To recolor the line art select **Edit:Fill**, and in the Fill dialog box, choose **Use:Foreground Color**. (A useful shortcut for filling a selection with the Foreground color is **Option+Delete** on Mac, and **Alt+Delete** on Windows.) You should now have a nicely recolored tile with anti-aliased artwork.

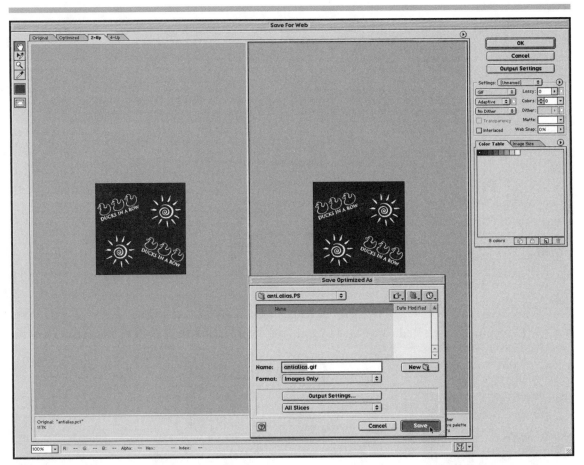

Step 8: Optimize the file in the Save for Web window, and then save it as a **GIF**. Save the source file in **PSD** format.

Step 9: Write HTML code in a text editor or HTML authoring tool to repeat the tile as a background image.

▶ exercise

Anti-Aliased Example in ImageReady 3.0

Photoshop 6.0 and ImageReady 3.0 both have a new tool, the Magic Eraser, that you can use to separate anti-aliased graphics from their backgrounds for color editing. In this example, you'll again work on antialias.pct, but this time in ImageReady. You'll use the Magic Eraser to eliminate the white background while maintaining an anti-aliased edge on the black artwork. You'll recolor the anti-aliased artwork using the Preserve Transparency feature of the Layers palette. Keep in mind that you could also do all this in Photoshop.

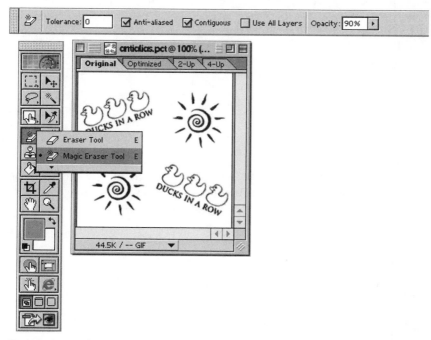

Step 1: Launch ImageReady, and open antialias.pct from the chap06 folder of the <chd2> CD-ROM.

Step 2: Click on the **Eraser** tool and from the pull-down menu select the **Magic Eraser** tool.

| ✎ | Tolerance: 0 | ☑ Anti-aliased | ☐ Contiguous | ☐ Use All Layers | Opacity: 100% ▸ |

Step 3: In the Tool Information Title Bar at the top of the screen, check the **Anti-aliased** check box. Make sure there is no check mark in the **Contiguous** check box because you want to eliminate all parts of the white background. Set the Tolerance to **0** because you only need to eliminate pure white in this example. (If you wanted to eliminate a wider range of color values, you would increase the Tolerance.)

Step 4: With the **Magic Eraser**, click in the white background area of the image. The background will magically disappear (hence the name Magic Eraser), leaving the black artwork with anti-aliased edges.

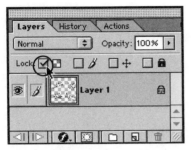

Step 5: To recolor the anti-aliased artwork, put a check mark in the **Preserve Transparency** check box on the Layers palette, choose a foreground color, and click **Option+Delete** on Mac, **Alt+Delete** on Windows. Only those pixels that are nontransparent will be recolored.

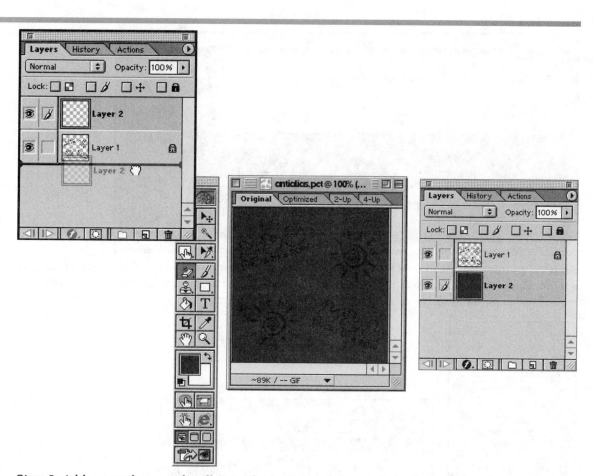

Step 6: Add a new layer and pull it to the bottom of the stack in the Layers palette. Choose a foreground color that is the same value as the recolored line art. Make sure **Preserve Transparency** is not checked, and then select **Edit:Fill Contents:Use:Foreground** to recolor all of the pixels in the new layer. You now have another recolored tile with anti-aliased graphics.

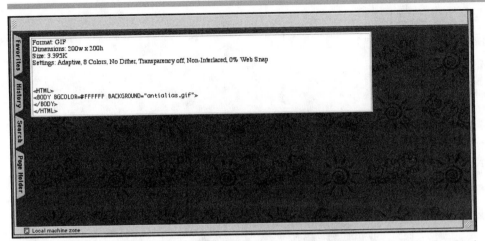

Step 7: Optimize the tile in the Optimize palette, previewing your work in the Optimized tab on the screen. Select **File:Output Settings:Background**. Set **View as: to Background image**. Preview the repeating background image directly from ImageReady to a browser.

Step 8: Save the optimized file as a **GIF** with accompanying HTML file generated by ImageReady. Save the original tile as a **PSD** file.

♦ e x e r c i s e

Aliased Example in Photoshop 6.0

When you're recoloring aliased graphics, there's no need to worry about clean edges as you must do when working with anti-aliased graphics. By nature, aliased graphics have well-defined edges, so it's easy to separate them from the background with the Magic Eraser or Magic Wand tools. In this exercise, you'll see how easy it is to use the Magic Wand on an aliased graphic. This time you'll work in Photoshop, although you could do the same thing in ImageReady.

Step 1: Launch Photoshop and open the file alias.pct from the chap06 folder of the <chd2> CD-ROM.

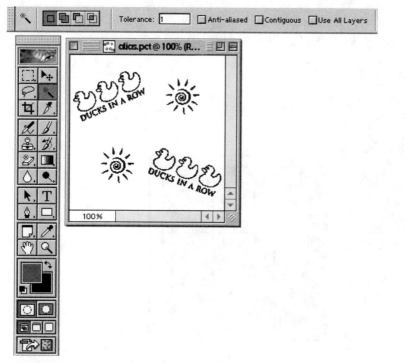

Step 2: Click the **Magic Wand** tool to define its Option settings in the Tool Information Title Bar at the top of the screen. Set the **Tolerance** to **1** and make sure there are not check marks in the Anti-Aliased or Contiguous check boxes.

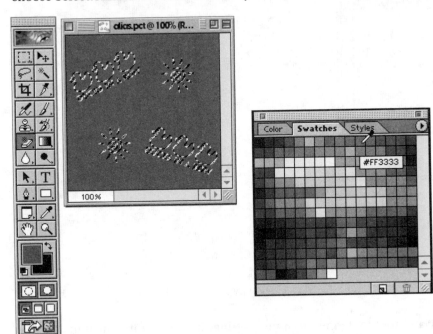

Step 3: Click on the white area of your graphic with the Magic Wand tool. Under the Select menu, choose **Select:Similar**. This will select any white areas the Magic Wand didn't capture.

Step 4: Choose a web-safe color from the Color Swatches and select **Edit:Fill**. Under the Select menu, choose **Inverse** to invert the selection.

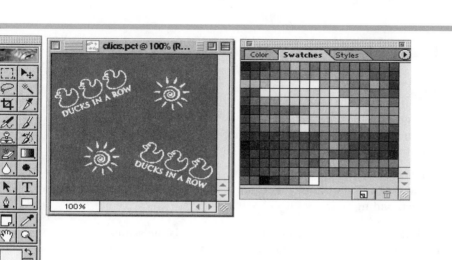

Step 5: Choose a second web-safe color of similar value and select **Edit:Fill Contents: Use:Foreground** color again (**Option+Delete** on Mac, and **Alt+Delete** on Windows.). It's that easy to recolor a tile containing aliased graphics. Choose **Select:Deselect** to deactivate the selection.

Step 6: Optimize the file as a **GIF** in the Save for Web window, save the optimized file, and save the source file. In a text editor or HTML authoring tool, write the HTML code to repeat the tile as a background image.

▶ chapter six summary

Tiles

Background tiles are a great asset to most web pages. A number of factors go into making effective tiles. Here's a list of things to remember about tiling backgrounds:

- Background tiles provide a way to fill a web page with visual content without taking up a lot of memory and downloading time.

- Choosing whether to make tiles that have visible seams is an aesthetic decision that is dependent on the content of your page.

- There is no "right" size for a background tile. The size affects the number of times the graphic repeats.

- Be sure to pay attention to the "value" (lights and darks) of your background and foreground elements. Use dark backgrounds with light text, or use light backgrounds with dark text. Don't use high-contrast source material for background tiles.

- You cannot reliably match colors between different file formats. If you are looking to match color, be sure to use a JPEG background tile with a JPEG foreground image or a GIF with a GIF.

7

Bullets & Rules

graphics & html conventions

▶ contents

html horizontal rules

custom rule artwork

html bullets

custom bullet artwork

clip art rules and bullets

The web environment has unusual limitations that don't exist in other design mediums. Web pages have no set length like printed pages do. The visual techniques and metaphors available to print designers, such as using a block of color behind text or images, changing the text color in an isolated paragraph or sidebar, or using a different screened-back image or picture frame to separate an idea or theme, are not easily replicated on the web.

It's often necessary to accept a more limited aesthetic and work with conventions that are tailored to web constraints. HTML generates limited graphics, such as rules and bullets. It's also possible to include custom graphics for more variety and originality. This chapter covers the HTML and image editing techniques used to create these small, but necessary, graphics and embellishments.

Bullets & Rules

Horizontal Rules

A horizontal rule that serves as a page divider is something you'll rarely see in print design. However, these divider lines are common in all kinds of web sites. Some dividers are embossed, some are thick, some are thin, some are colored, and some have unusual shapes. The web term for these lines is **horizontal rule**, and they are used for many things:

- Defining a page break

- Completing an idea

- Beginning a list

- Separating one picture from another

If you want to add horizontal rules to your pages, you have some options. You can use HTML code, or you can insert your own artwork to make custom horizontal or vertical rules. When all else fails, you can borrow from libraries of horizontal rule clip art.

> ▶ **note**
>
> ### Where Do Rules Come From?
>
> The term **rule** is derived from the printing and typesetting fields, where it commonly refers to a straight, unadorned line used to separate objects on a page. The most common rules seen in print are those used to separate the columns of a newspaper.

Horizontal Rules, the HTML Way

The `<HR>` tag will put an embossed line horizontally through your page at whatever point you insert it into an HTML document. This horizontal rule will stretch and contract with the width of the viewer's browser window. Horizontal rules have no set width, except to fill the horizontal distance of any browser screen. Techniques for setting a fixed width rule follow.

Here's the basic HTML horizontal rule tag:

```
<HR>
```

Here it is in the context of code:

```
Some Text
<HR>
Some More Text
```

Some Text
Some More Text

A basic horizontal rule using the `<HR>` tag.

Sometimes you might want to add room between a horizontal rule and text or an image on either side of the rule. This code will add a row of empty space above and below the rule:

```
<P>Some Text
<P>
<HR>
<P>Some More Text
```

Some Text

Some More Text

If you want to add more breathing room between your text and rules, insert a paragraph break with the `<P>` tag. That effectively puts the rule in its own paragraph.

Fancier Horizontal Rule Tags

An advanced course in horizontal rule-making would include:

- Changing the rule's width
- Changing the rule's weight (thickness)
- Changing both the rule's width and weight
- Left-aligning the rule
- Eliminating fake emboss shading

Notice that if you specify a width in an <HR> tag, the resulting horizontal rule is automatically centered. Any value you put after the = (equals) sign tells the rule how wide to be in pixels.

Here's the code instructing the rule to be 10 pixels wide:

```
<HR WIDTH=10>
```

Using a WIDTH **attribute can adjust the length of the line.**

The following code changes the weight, or thickness, of the line. This can stretch to the length of a page:

```
<HR SIZE=10>
```

When you change the SIZE **attribute, the entire line gets thicker.**

The following code changes the thickness and width at the same time. Here's an example that shows the results of code specifying that the rule be square—equal height and width.

```
<HR SIZE=25 WIDTH=25>
```

By changing the SIZE **and** WIDTH **together, you can make other rectilinear shapes like this square.**

The following code aligns the square left, and sizes it at 10 pixels high and 10 pixels wide:

```
<HR ALIGN=LEFT SIZE=10 WIDTH=10>
```

You can use alignment attributes on horizontal rules, too.

Here's the code to remove fake emboss shading!

```
<HR NOSHADE>
```

The NOSHADE **attribute creates a solid line.**

Horizontal Rules the Do-It-Yourself Way

Anything gets old when you see it too often, and horizontal rules are no exception. If you want to be a little more creative, here are some tips for creating custom artwork to design your own rules. When you create your own horizontal rule art, your artwork dictates the length, width, and height of the rule. It's a graphic like any other graphic. It can be aliased, anti-aliased, a GIF, a JPEG, interlaced, transparent, blurred, 2D, 3D—you name it. If you know how to make it, it can be a horizontal rule.

Here's the HTML code for bringing in a graphical horizontal rule:

```
<IMG SRC="your_horizontal_rule_art_here.gif">
```

Here's The Ducks In A Row site with two horizontal HTML rules.

Here's the site with custom rules; they don't have to be lines, ya know! We've included the smflowerrule.gif **file from the** chap07 **folder of the** <chd2> CD-ROM, if you'd like to try it out.

Vertical Rules

Creating vertical rules for web pages is not an easy task. Making the custom artwork is like making any other custom artwork, and all the Photoshop and ImageReady tips shared in this book should be of help.

The trick is in how to get vertical lines aligned to a web page, because there is no easy way in HTML to assign vertical columns. Learn about positioning vertical ruled lines using tables in Chapter 9, *"Alignment."*

Clip Art Rules, Too

There are many kind, generous souls on the web who lend their wares for free. Other gifted souls may charge for their art so that they can do what they're good at: satisfy you and me—and still feed themselves and their families. Clip art is a wondrous thing in a pinch, and with tools such as Photoshop, Illustrator, and Painter, there's no end to the cool ways you can personalize clip art files. Make sure the images are royalty-free if you are going to modify them. Some authors have stipulations that must be honored. Read the licensing agreements and readmes! Here are some clip art collections that we think are really cool:

Gifs R Us—Jay Boersma's prolific collection:
http://www.ecn.bgu.edu/users/gas52r0/Jay/art.html

Yahoo search for clip art:
http://www.yahoo.com/Computers_and_Internet/ Graphics/Clip_Art/

Bullets

You'll see plenty of pages with diverse information on the web, but lists of one type or another are needed universally. List items can appear indented with numbers or preceded by icons known as **bullets**. Bullets on the web can look like standardized solid circles in front of text, or they can include custom artwork that looks more typical of a CD-ROM or magazine page layout. Creating custom bullets is similar to creating custom horizontal rules. Basically, any artwork that you're capable of creating is a candidate for bullet art.

When designing bulleted lists for the web, you can choose from either HTML bullets or image-based bullets. HTML bullets are created by using tags that identify the type of list you are creating; such bullets appear as basic circles or squares. Image-based bullets are those you generate from clip art or your own artwork, and they can be used to enhance a list or provide added functionality, such as links. The next section shows you how to create both HTML and image-based bullets, including several variations on both themes.

Creating HTML Bulleted Lists

Using HTML-based bullets is certainly less work than creating your own custom artwork, and it is sometimes most appropriate from a design standpoint. A simple and clean design, without a lot of custom artwork, can be most effective. There will be many instances when an HTML-based bullet or indent will do the job more effectively than custom bullet artwork.

To create a list with solid circle bullets, use the UL (Unordered List) tag. Individual lines are designated with the LI (List Item) tag. The UL element is a container, and it requires an end tag. The LI element is also a container, but its end tag is optional. Here's the code:

```
<UL>
<LI> The first thinga-dingy
<LI> The second thinga-dingy
<LI> The third thinga-dingy
</UL>
```

Using the "unordered" list tags , and "list item" tags produces this result:

- The first thinga-dingy
- The second thinga-dingy
- The third thinga-dingy

The results of using UL and LI.

Lists can be nested by nesting UL elements. The following code uses an additional UL tag to create a bulleted list nested within another bulleted list:

```
<UL>
<LI> The first thinga-dingy
<LI> The second thinga-dingy
<LI> The third thinga-dingy
  <UL>
  <LI> More types of thinga-dingies
  <LI> Yet More types of thinga-
  dingies
  <LI> Even more types of thinga-
  dingies
  </UL>
<LI> Fourth thinga-dingy
</UL>
```

- The first thinga-dingy
- The second thinga-dingy
- The third thinga-dingy
    - More types of thinga-dingies
    - Yet More types of thinga-dingies
    - Even more types of thinga-dingies
- Fourth thinga-dingy

You can nest bulleted points by nesting multiple UL tags and close /UL tags.

You can link items in your list to other pages or sites by using the anchor A HREF tag within an ordered list or an unordered list. The following code shows how to use anchor tags to include links within a bulleted list:

```
<UL>
<LI> <A HREF="http://www.domain.com">
The first thinga-dingy.</A>
<LI> <A HREF="http://www.domain.com">
The second thinga-dingy.</A>
<LI> <A HREF="http://www.domain.com">
The third thinga-dingy.</A>
</UL>
```

Including links within a list is a matter of using link tags within lists. The results look like this:

- The first thinga-dingy
- The second thinga-dingy
- The third thinga-dingy

The items in your list can be straight text or hypertext by changing a few tags.

Creating Ordered and Definition Lists

At times, you may not want your lists to be preceded by bullets. When creating a list of steps to be followed in order, for example, using numbers instead of bullets will help get your point across. Such numbered lists are called ordered lists. Likewise, lists such as glossaries can appear with indents instead of bullets or numbers. These lists are known as definition lists.

To make a list that automatically generates numbers in front of its items, use the OL (Ordered List) tag. The following lines of code show how to use OL to produce a numbered list:

```
<OL>
<LI> The first thinga-dingy
<LI> The second thinga-dingy
<LI> The third thinga-dingy
</OL>
```

Using the "ordered list" would automatically generate numbers, instead of bullets in front of each "list item":

1. The first thinga-dingy
2. The second thinga-dingy
3. The third thinga-dingy

The OL tag generates ordered (numbered) lists.

If you want to indent items in a list without a bullet, you may want to use a DL (Definition List) tag instead of creating an ordered list or unordered list. You use the DT tag for the flush-left items and the DD tag for the indented items, as shown in the following code:

```
<DL>
<DT>
Thingy Dingies
<DD>The first thinga-dingy
<DD>The second thinga-dingy
<DD>The third thinga-dingy
</DL>
```

Thingy Dingies
   The first thinga-dingy
   The second thinga-dingy
   The third thinga-dingy

Using the DL definition list tags creates indented lists.

If you want to change the shape of automatically generated bullets, you can use the TYPE=circle, TYPE=square, or TYPE=disc attributes, as shown in the following code:

```
<UL>
<LI TYPE=circle>Circle-shaped Bullet
<LI TYPE=square>Square-shaped Bullet
<LI TYPE=disc>Disc-shaped Bullet
</UL>
```

○ Circle-shaped Bullet
□ Square-shaped Bullet
● Disc-shaped Bullet

You can use the TYPE attribute to change the shape of HTML-generated bullets.

Alphabetical and Roman Ordered Lists

You can also organize your ordered lists by using alphabetic and Roman numerals for bullets. You can do this by adding the variations shown in the following table:

Attribute	List Type	Example
Type=1	Numbers	1,2,3
Type=A	Uppercase Letters	A,B,C
Type=a	Lowercase Letters	a,b,c
Type=I	Uppercase Roman	I,II,III
Type=i	Lowercase Roman	i,ii,iii

An example of several types of HTML-generated bullets.

The following code shows variations of the TYPE attribute, which produces these results:

```
<OL>
<LI TYPE=1> Thingy One
<LI TYPE=1> Thingy Two
<LI TYPE=1> Thingy Three
<P>
<LI TYPE=A> Thingy One
<LI TYPE=A> Thingy Two
<LI TYPE=A> Thingy Three
<P>
<LI TYPE=a> Thingy One
<LI TYPE=a> Thingy Two
<LI TYPE=a> Thingy Three
<P>
<LI TYPE=I> Thingy One
<LI TYPE=I> Thingy Two
<LI TYPE=I> Thingy Three
<P>
<LI TYPE=i> Thingy One
<LI TYPE=i> Thingy Two
<LI TYPE=i> Thingy Three
</OL>
```

Button Clip Art

You'll find clip art for buttons all over the World Wide Web. Clip art buttons follow the same rules as custom bullet art. Use the `IMG SRC` tag if you want to use the button for decoration only. Add the anchor `A HREF` tag if you want the artwork to link elsewhere. Clip art typically already exists in GIF or JPEG web file formats, and if not, you can use Photoshop to convert its format. Bullets can be abstract shapes, such as dots and cubes, or representative icons that have symbolic meaning.

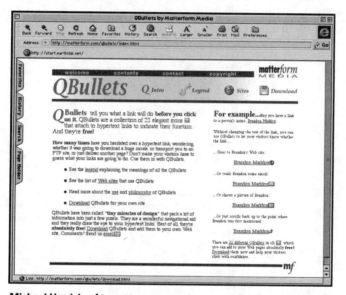

Michael Herrick, of http://www.matterform.com, **has invented something called QBullets (after cue-bullet), or bullets that cue you to their hint or function. These buttons are part of a proposed interface standard that his site discusses in detail.**

Creating Custom-Made Bullets

If you want to use bullets that show more creativity than the basic square or circle, or if you need added linking functionality, you can create custom-made bullets. Custom-made bullets can be ornamental, such that their sole purpose is to decorate the beginning of a list item. They can also be functional in that they serve as icons that link you to another page or site.

If you plan to make your own artwork or use clip art for buttons, you'll need to use different HTML tags to make the art behave as you want. For visual enhancement only, use the IMG tag to place image-based bullets at the front of a list, as shown in the following code example. You won't use the OL or the UL tags because the image itself is creating both the bullet and the indent. Note that you do have to put a BR (Line Break) tag at the end of each list item to tell the browser to jump to a new line for the next entry in the list. The BR tag isn't necessary when working with the OL or UL tags because it's a built-in part of the list functionality.

```
<HTML>
<HEAD>
<TITLE>ducks process</TITLE>
</HEAD>
<BODY BGCOLOR="#FFFF99">
<IMG SRC="process.gif">
<P><IMG SRC="littleduck.gif">
Joan designs the artwork
<BR>
<IMG SRC="littleduck.gif">
It's sent out to get made
into molds
<BR>
<IMG SRC="littleduck.gif">
The designs are produced
on big sheets of rubber
<BR>
<IMG SRC="littleduck.gif">
The sheets are cut apart
and glued onto wood
<BR>
<IMG SRC="littleduck.gif">
The stamp design is printed
on the wood blocks
</BODY>
</HTML>
```

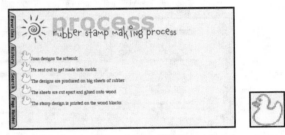

Here is the result of the HTML code shown on the left. Notice how the ducks are crowded next to the text? You can fix this by changing the source graphic. Adding more space to the right of the original graphic will push the text to the right in the HTML document.

There's more space between the bullets and the text because the source graphic is wider. This is a big improvement! Be sure to read Chapter 9, *"Alignment,"* to learn other techniques to control text and image alignment.

▶ e x e r c i s e

Changing Bullet Size in Photoshop 6.0

In this exercise, you will experiment with varying the alignment of graphic bullets in an HTML document by changing the size of the bullet artwork.

Step 1: Make a new folder on your hard drive and copy the following files from the chap07 folder on the <chd2> CD-ROM into your new folder: bullet.html, littleduck.gif, and process.gif.

Step 2: In a browser, open the bullet.html file from the new folder on your hard drive. Notice the amount of horizontal and vertical spacing between the bullets and the lines of text.

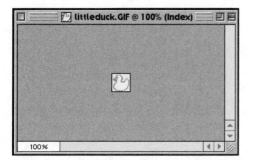

Step 3: In Photoshop, open the littleduck.gif file from the new folder on your hard drive.

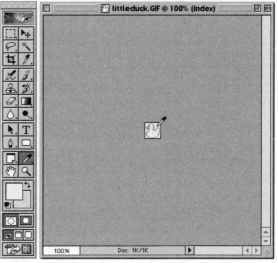

Step 4: Select the Eyedropper tool from the toolbar, and then **Option-click** (Mac) or **Alt-click** (Windows) when you're on the background color of littleduck.gif. That color will appear in the Background Color well on the toolbar.

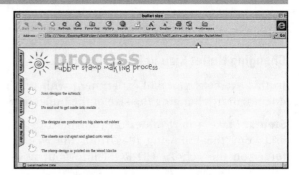

Step 5: Select **Image:Canvas Size** and enter new dimensions into the Width and Height fields (try **40** and **40**, respectively). Click the bottom-left square of the Anchor diagram to set the position from which the Canvas Size will expand.

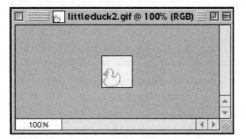

Step 6: Resave littleduck.gif into the new folder on your hard drive by choosing **File:Save**. Make sure that folder also contains the bullet.html file.

Step 7: In your browser, reload the bullet.html file. Notice the additional horizontal and vertical space between the bullets and lines of text.

Linked Bullets

If you want to use bullets as icons to link to another site or page, use the anchor A HREF tag, as shown in the following code example. Linked images typically have a blue border around them. To eliminate that border on a bullet, add the BORDER=0 attribute inside the IMG tag. Note the pointing hand cursor on the company link in the following illustration. Your viewer's cursor will change to this hand when gliding over a linked image to let the viewer know the image is a link.

```
<HTML>
<HEAD>
<TITLE>ducks process</TITLE>
</HEAD>
<BODY TEXT="#333300" BGCOLOR="#FFFF99"
LINK="#330000">
<IMG SRC="siteview.gif">
<P><A HREF="catalog.html">
<IMG SRC="littlecat.gif"
BORDER=0></A>catalog
<P><A HREF="process.html">
<IMG SRC="littleproc.gif"
BORDER=0></A>process
<P><A HREF="company.html">
<IMG SRC="smcomp.gif"
BORDER=0></A>company
<P><A HREF="retail.html">
<IMG SRC="smretail.gif"
BORDER=0></A>retail locations
<P><A HREF="samples.html">
<IMG SRC="smsamp.gif"
BORDER=0></A>samples
</BODY>
</HTML>
```

This demonstrates the use of the anchor A HREF tag to link the buttons to URLs. The BORDER=0 attribute was used to turn off the default borders around the linked graphics, creating a seamless effect. The only way an end user would know to click on the buttons would be to pass the cursor over the illustrations.

▶ chapter seven summary

Bullets & Rules

Working with bullets, and rules on the web is a lot less straightforward than using them in a text or print document. It requires a mixture of programming and design skills. The contents of this chapter are summarized here:

- Horizontal rules and bullets can be added using either HTML or custom graphics. Graphics take longer to download, but they can add a lot more originality to a page design.

- It can be useful to create buttons and bullets that mean something, rather than those that just exist for decoration. Refer to Michael Herrick's Matterform page at http://www.matterform.com for ideas. Or better yet—create your own ideas!

8

"The secret of ugliness consists not in irregularity, but in being uninteresting."
—Ralph Waldo Emerson (1803–82)

Transparency
look, no matte lines

▶ **contents**

transparency tricks
matching backgrounds
clean transparency
transparency software

A technique called **masking** is commonly used in computer graphics to make artwork appear in irregular shapes rather than squares and rectangles. In web design, the term masking is often referred to as "transparency" because transparent GIFs are the most prevalent means of creating a masking effect. Creating transparency mostly involves using image editing techniques, making it more a web graphics process than a function of HTML.

This chapter covers transparency techniques in Photoshop and ImageReady. We'll look at the common pitfalls of and solutions to making clean transparent GIFs, and we'll examine PNG transparency, a new format that is not yet supported by most browsers but that holds the promise of becoming a superior masking method. We'll also investigate graphic processes such as anti-aliasing, aliasing, masking, and alpha channels.

A computer image file, by definition, is automatically saved in a rectangle. Way too much artwork on the web is in the shape of rectangles—buttons, pictures, splash screens, menu bars—ugh! Mastering transparency is the only escape!

Transparency

Transparency Tricks

There are two types of transparency: One requires true masking, and the other involves trickery. The trickery method is the easiest, so let's study it first.

Let's say you make a graphic of a circle and want it to look as if it's free-floating. When you create the circle, make its background the same color as your web page. When you put the elements together in HTML, there should be no obvious rectangular border. However, there is a snag. Getting foreground and background images on the web to match in color takes an extra bit of education. This chapter reviews how to set exact background colors (assuming your end viewer has not changed his or her preferences to override color choices) using two HTML-based techniques. One involves using hexadecimal code to set a specific background color; the other involves setting up the HTML to display a repeating background tile of a solid color. You'll learn step by step how to execute these techniques. Then you'll learn how ImageReady 3.0 can help you do them.

Result in browser

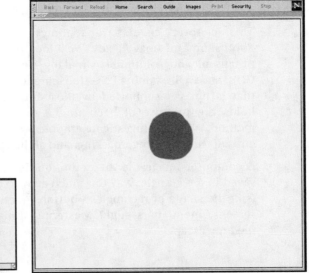

Source file

You can easily create the illusion of irregularly shaped images by making the edges of foreground artwork the same color as the background of your web page.

▶ **note**

Color Preferences in Browsers

It's kind of scary for web designers who count on the background colors they pick to support an illusion of irregularly shaped images, because viewers can set their browsers to override the colors designers specify!

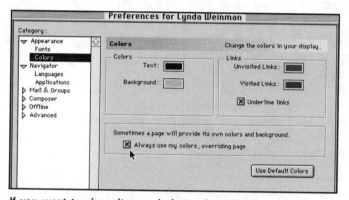

If you want to view sites as designers intended them to be seen, make sure that "Always use my colors, overriding page" is unchecked in your Netscape preferences and that "Allow page to specify colors" is checked in your Internet Explorer preferences.

▶ **note**

JPEG or GIF?

Your images and tiled background patterns may be saved as either JPEGs or GIFs. If you are going to use a solid background image and want it to match your solid foreground image, you must use either a JPEG background and JPEG foreground or a GIF background and a GIF foreground; otherwise, color shifting will occur.

◗ e x e r c i s e

Creating Background Color the Hex Way

This technique was covered in Chapter 4, *"Web Color,"* but will be reviewed here in the context of transparency. This first example demonstrates how to create a background in HTML using the BGCOLOR attribute of the BODY tag and how to place on that background artwork that simulates irregularity (as described in the section "Transparency Tricks"). This technique works especially well on images that include anti-aliasing, soft edges, glows, or drop shadows.

Step 1: First you'll use Photoshop to identify the hexadecimal value of the background of a piece of artwork. Launch Photoshop 6.0 and open the floatduck.gif file from the chap08 folder of the <chd2> CD-ROM.

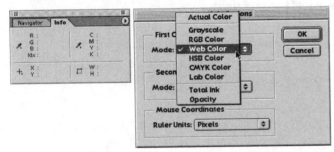

Step 2: Click the **Info tab** to bring the Info palette to the foreground. (If you can't find it, select **Window:Show Info**.) Click the arrow at the top right of the Info palette and choose **Palette Options**. In the Info Options window, choose **Web Color** for the First Color Readout Mode.

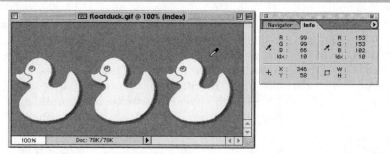

Step 3: Choose the **Eyedropper** tool from the toolbar and move it over the green background of floatduck.gif on the screen. The hexadecimal value of this RGB color (#999966) will be displayed on the left side of the Info palette.

Step 4: Next, in a text editor write the following HTML. This code sets the web page background to green by specifying that color's hexadecimal code #999966, and it places the foreground image floatduck.gif on top of that background.

```
<HTML>
<HEAD>
<TITLE>transparency trick!</TITLE>
</HEAD>
<BODY BGCOLOR="#999966">
<CENTER>
<IMG SRC="floatduck.gif">
</CENTER>
</BODY>
</HTML>
```

Step 5: Save the HTML document as floatduck.html.

Step 6: Open floatduck.html in a browser to view the final result. With this technique, you do not need transparency software to achieve the illusion of transparency.

Background Color Using Solid Patterns

Another way to color the background of a page is to create a solid color tile and then reference that tile in the BACKGROUND attribute of the BODY tag. The BODY BACKGROUND tag is more commonly used with a tile containing artwork, as in the examples provided in Chapter 6, "Tiles." However, the BACKGROUND attribute will take even a solid color tile and repeat it to fill an entire web page.

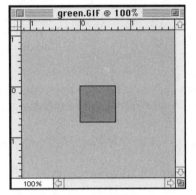

Here's an example of a small GIF file that is filled with the same solid green used in the last hexadecimal-based example.

For instructions on how to make images repeat as tiles, refer to Chapter 6. In this exercise, you're using the same HTML technique that Chapter 6 described in detail, but your source image for the repeating tile is a solid color instead of an image. As this tile is repeated over the page, it will produce a solid background identical in appearance to the background created by the hexadecimal method described in the last exercise.

You can actually use both the BGCOLOR and BACKGROUND attributes inside the same BODY tag, which is the safest course of action to ensure that the background will match the foreground image. Here's an example of the code:

```
<HTML>
<HEAD>
<TITLE>transparency trick.2</TITLE>
</HEAD>
<BODY BGCOLOR="#999966"
BACKGROUND="green.gif">
<CENTER>
<IMG SRC="floatduck.gif">
</CENTER>
</BODY>
</HTML>
```

❯ exercise

Creating Background Color in ImageReady 3.0

You may be surprised to learn that ImageReady 3.0 will write some HTML code for you, including code that specifies a background color or a background image. You can take advantage of this feature when you are trying to create the illusion of irregularly shaped artwork by matching a color in a foreground image to a web page background. Here's how it's done in ImageReady:

Step 1: Launch ImageReady 3.0 and, again, open floatduck.gif from the chap08 folder of the <chd2> CD-ROM. Select the **Eyedropper** in the toolbar, and then move the cursor over the green background of the image on the screen and click. This will cause that color to appear in the Foreground Color well on the toolbar.

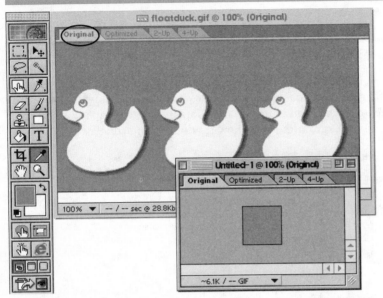

Step 2: Now make a small tile of the same color. Select **File:New** and create a document 50×50 pixels. Working in the Original tab, click **Option-delete** (Mac) or **Alt-delete** (Windows) to fill that file with the foreground color.

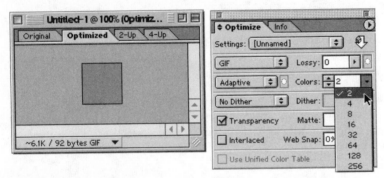

Step 3: In the Optimize palette, choose **GIF**, **Adaptive** palette, **2** colors, and **No Dither**. Select **File:Save Optimized As,** and then save the file on your hard drive as greentile.gif.

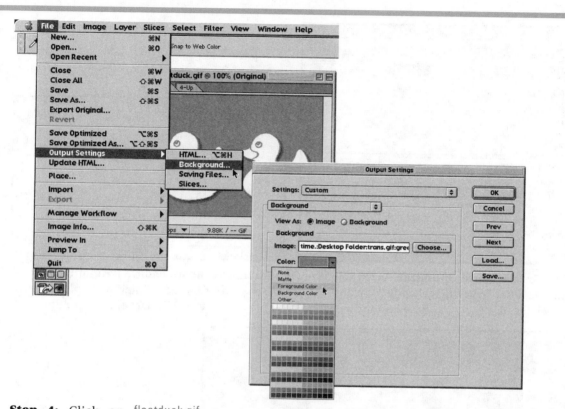

Step 4: Click on floatduck.gif on your screen to make it active. Select **File:Output Settings:Background**. In the Output Settings window, choose **View As:Image**. Click the **Choose** button next to the Background Image field and navigate to greentile.gif on your hard drive. Click the arrow next to the Color field and choose **Foreground Color**. Click **OK**.

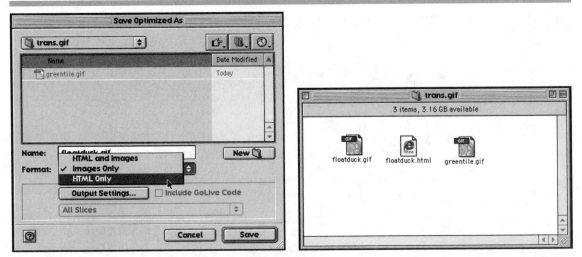

Step 5: Select **Save Optimized As**. In the Save Optimized As window, choose **Format:HTML and Images**. Click **Save**. ImageReady 3.0 will save floatduck.gif to your hard drive and write plus save an HTML file, floatduck.html, based on the selections you made in the HTML Background window.

The final result viewed in a browser gives the illusion that the foreground image is not rectangular.

Transparent GIFs

If transparent GIFs are an unfamiliar term to you, don't worry. We know of no common application for transparent GIFs other than the web, so they're relatively new to everyone. Transparent GIFs are used to create the illusion of irregularly shaped images by assigning one color in an image to be invisible. This process is also called masking.

Transparency is assigned when the file is saved. A variety of software applications enable you to save and define transparency, and we'll cover several of them in this chapter. When working with transparent GIFs, there are two things to keep in mind: first, how to make art properly for one-color transparency, and second, how to use the programs that let you save the artwork in this file format.

When to Use Transparent Artwork

We recommend using transparent GIFs (and PNGs, but more on this later in the chapter) only on web pages that have patterned background tiles, because you can more easily create the illusion of transparency against solid colors by using the trickery techniques we just covered. Establishing transparency in a GIF or PNG adds extra steps to production, so there's no reason to do that when there's an easier way.

The reason we recommend making foreground images transparent over patterned background tiles is that you can't reliably match the position of a foreground image to that of a background tile with only standard HTML. (This problem is described in more detail in Chapter 9, *"Alignment."*) If you want to put irregularly shaped artwork over patterned backgrounds, you'll have to use transparency.

You can try to align a foreground image with a pattern to the identical background pattern, but they won't line up. And to make matters worse, the alignment is different on a Mac and Windows!

Note: We used the same artwork in the BACKGROUND and IMG SRC attributes but intentionally reversed the color in the foreground image to accentuate the offset alignment problem. On a Mac, most browsers introduce an 8-pixel offset on the upper and left sides of the foreground image, and on Windows there is a 10-pixel offset. This makes it impossible to align a foreground to a background in the cross-platform web environment.

Making Clean Transparent GIF Artwork

The key to producing effective transparent GIFs is to ensure that your artwork is produced correctly. We need to begin by going through a short primer on aliased versus anti-aliased artwork. Anti-aliasing is the process of blending around the edges of a graphic to hide the jagged square pixels it is made of.

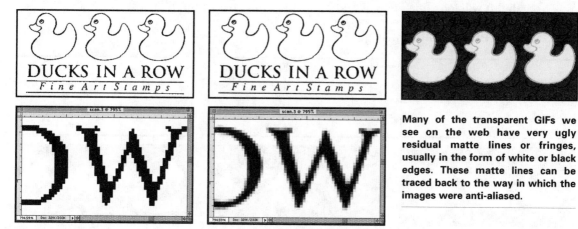

Many of the transparent GIFs we see on the web have very ugly residual matte lines or fringes, usually in the form of white or black edges. These matte lines can be traced back to the way in which the images were anti-aliased.

Anti-aliasing is the process by which one color and shape blends into another in order to hide the jagged, square-pixel nature of computer-generated graphics.

For web graphics, anti-aliasing is not always the best approach. The anti-aliased blended edge is precisely what causes matte line or "fringing" problems once the graphic is converted to a transparent GIF. Because GIF transparency masks only one color out of an image, the semi-opaque colors along the blended edge of anti-aliased artwork remain attached to the graphic.

Aliased graphics, despite their jagged edges, make clean, transparent GIFs with well-defined edges that do not have residual matte lines when placed on web page backgrounds.

This doesn't mean that you can't use anti-aliased graphics on your site. As you'll learn, proper matting techniques can eliminate the dreaded fringes. Just be aware of what causes the problem, and be willing to take a few extra steps to avoid it.

Glows, Soft Edges, and Drop Shadows with GIF Transparency

Because of the problems anti-aliasing introduces, artwork with glows, soft edges, and drop shadows can look awful as transparent GIFs. One popular solution is to build this kind of artwork against roughly the same color background you plan to use as your web page background. The artwork will look terrible when you make it, but it will look fine once placed against the final background in a web browser.

GIF Transparency Compositing

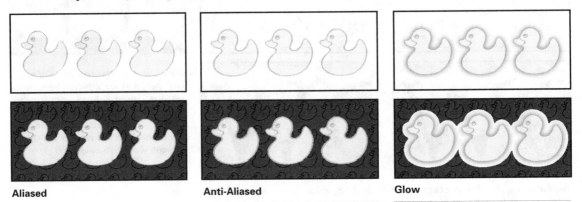

Aliased   **Anti-Aliased**   **Glow**

When the different examples of edges are made into transparent GIFs using 1-color transparency, did you notice how every example except the aliased version picked up the background color against which the image was made, which created an unwanted white rim around the graphic? That's because the images with soft edges picked up parts of the white color against which they were created. This caused an unsightly problem, which is commonly called a halo, fringe, rim, or matte line.

Making clean transparent artwork with no fringes around the edges involves setting the background color to the primary color of the pattern on which the art will be placed in HTML. This example shows the anti-aliased ducks against green.

This example shows the ducks with a glow against green. Setting the background color to green will avoid the fringing problem once the artwork is set on top of a green patterned background in the HTML file.

When the transparency is set, the files look pretty terrible. They won't look good until they are laid over their target green background. By preparing the files this way, you will correct their predisposition to favor any other color.

The end result looks quite acceptable now. The glow is beautiful, and there are no more matte lines!

HTML for Transparent GIFs

The HTML for transparent GIFs is identical to the HTML for any other type of GIF or JPEG. The IMG SRC tag is all you need. For an unlinked transparent GIF graphic, the HTML code looks like this:

```
<IMG SRC="transgif.gif">
```

For a linked transparent GIF graphic, the HTML is this:

```
<A HREF="http://www.destination_domain_name.com">
<IMG SRC="transgif.gif" BORDER="0"></A>
```

Transparent GIF Software

There are lots of popular software packages that support GIF transparency; however, it is impossible to cover all of them in this book. On the next few pages; we include instructions for creating transparent GIFs in ImageReady 3.0 and Photoshop 6.0.

▶ e x e r c i s e

Creating a Transparent GIF in ImageReady 3.0

ImageReady 3.0 is a great tool for creating transparent images for the web. The following is a step-by-step explanation of how to create a transparent GIF in ImageReady. The procedure in Photoshop 6.0 is very similar, as you'll see in the next example.

Step 1: In ImageReady 3.0, open the 3ducks.pct file from the chap08 folder of the <chd2> CD-ROM. Select the **Magic Eraser** tool (the eraser with the asterisk). In the Tool Information Title Bar at the top of your screen, put a check mark in the **Anti-Aliased** check box. Set the Tolerance to **0** and uncheck **Contiguous**. Click the **Original** tab so you can work on the source file.

Step 2: Click on the white background of the image on the screen with the **Magic Eraser** to erase the white pixels, leaving the graphic with an anti-aliased edge. **Note:** You cannot create transparency in a GIF unless the source file has transparent pixels.

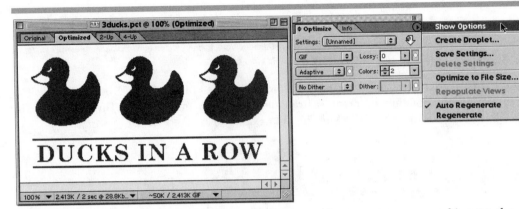

Step 3: Click on the **Optimized** tab on the screen so that you are now working on the optimized file. Click on the Optimize palette to bring it to the foreground. (If you cannot find that palette, select **Window:Show Optimize**.) Click the arrow at the top right of the Optimize palette and choose **Show Options** from the drop-down menu. This will expand the Optimize palette, making the transparency controls accessible.

Step 4: In the Optimize palette, put a check mark in the **Transparency** check box. Set the other optimization controls to **GIF**, **Adaptive** palette, **8** colors, and **No Dither**.

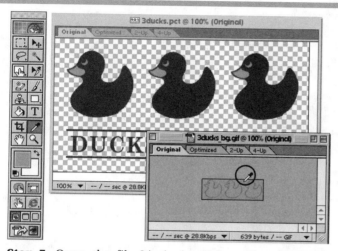

Step 5: Open the file 3ducks_bg.gif from the chap08 folder of the <chd2> CD-ROM. This is the background tile for the web page you are making. With the **Eyedropper** tool, click on a yellow area of 3ducks_bg.gif to fill the Foreground Color well on the toolbar with that color. You can now close the background tile.

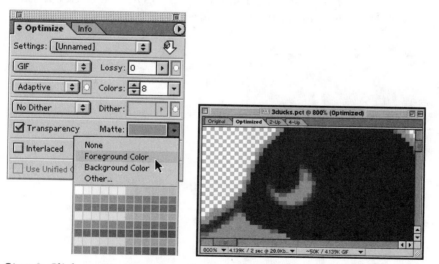

Step 6: Click on 3ducks.pct to make that file active. In the Optimize palette, click the arrow on the Matte field and choose **Foreground Color**. This will set the matte to the yellow you just sampled from the background tile so that the anti-aliased edges of the graphics will blend with the predominant color in the patterned web page background. If you zoom in on the image, in the Optimized mode, you'll see the yellow matte lines around the edges of the graphics.

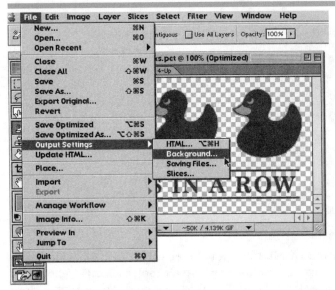

Step 7: Select **File:Output Settings:Background**. Choose **View As:Image**. Click the **Image:Choose** button and navigate to 3ducks_bg.gif in the chap08 folder of the <chd2> CD-ROM. Click **OK**. Click the arrow next to **Color** and choose **Matte** to set the background color behind the background tile to yellow.

Step 8: Select **File:Preview In**. Notice that your transparent graphic has the illusion of a non-rectangular shape and that its anti-aliased edges appear to blend in with the background pattern.

Step 9: Select **File:Save Optimized As** to save 3ducks.gif and an accompanying HTML file generated by ImageReady (3ducks.html).

▶ e x e r c i s e

Creating a Transparent GIF in Photoshop 6.0

Creating a transparent GIF in Photoshop 6.0 is almost identical to creating one in ImageReady 3.0, with two exceptions. First, Photoshop does not have the ability to display a preview of a foreground image against a tiling background like ImageReady does. Second, in Photoshop, you'll optimize the transparent GIF in a special interface, the Save for Web window, rather than from a palette as in ImageReady. Here's how it's done in Photoshop.

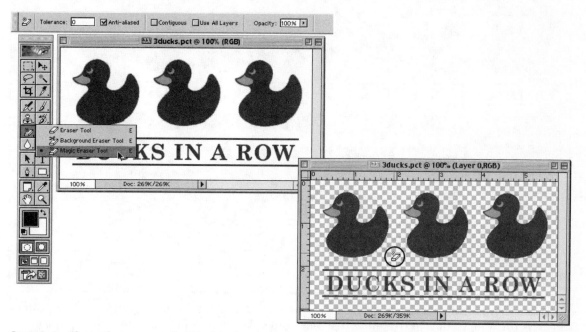

Step 1: In Photoshop, open the file 3ducks.pct from the chap08 folder of the <chd2> CD-ROM. In the Tool Information Title Bar at the top of your screen, set the Magic Eraser to **Anti-Aliased** and uncheck **Contiguous**. Click on the white background of the image to make the original source file transparent. **Tip:** You cannot make changes to the original file in the Save for Web window.

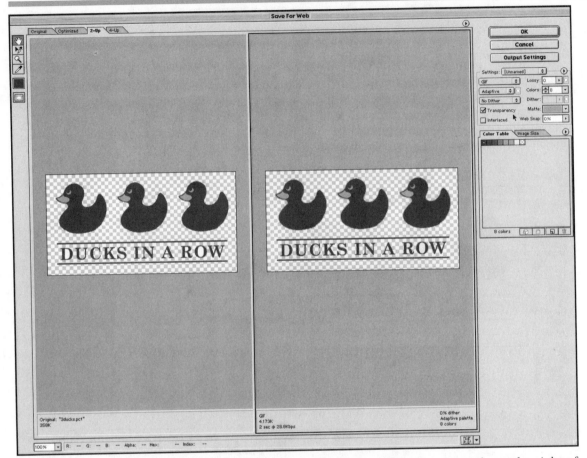

Step 2: Select **File:Save for Web**. Click the **2-Up** tab. Set the optimization controls on the right of the Save for Web window to **GIF**, **Adaptive** palette, **8** colors, and **No Dither**. Be sure to put a check mark in the **Transparency** check box.

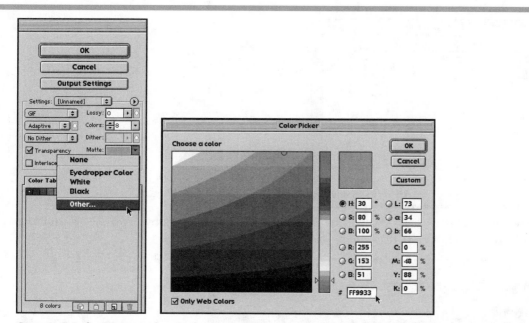

Step 3: Set the **Matte** color to the orange hue that is the predominant color in the background tile 3ducks_bg.gif. Before you do this, make sure you know the hex code of that color. (Hint: #FF9933.) Choose **Other** from the **Matte** field and type that hex code into the color picker that opens.

Step 4: Click **OK** in the Save for Web window. From the Save Optimized As window, save the optimized transparent GIF as 3ducks.gif in a new folder on your hard drive.

Step 5: In a text editor, write the following HTML code:

```
<HTML>
<HEAD>
<TITLE>transparency.pshop</TITLE>
</HEAD>
<BODY BGCOLOR="#FF9933" BACKGROUND="3ducks_bg.gif">
<CENTER>
    <IMG SRC="3ducks.gif">
</CENTER>
</BODY>
</HTML>
```

Step 6: Save this HTML as 3ducks.html in the same folder as 3ducks.gif. Copy 3ducks_bg.gif from the chap08 folder of the <chd2> CD-ROM to the same folder.

To view the final results, open 3ducks.html **in a web browser.**

PNG Transparency

The PNG file format has a sensational masking feature, which unfortunately isn't supported fully in any of the popular browsers at the time of this writing. It allows you, in an 8-bit image, to create a mask with up to 256 levels of transparency. No other file format has ever allowed this! What it means is that very small 8-bit (and lower) files can be generated with varying levels of translucency (unlike GIF, which only has one level of masking: on or off).

Unfortunately, at the time this chapter was written, no tools for Mac or Windows existed to save a PNG file with 8-bit transparency. And as of early 2000, existing browsers (with the possible exceptions of Internet Explorer 5.0 for Macs and Netscape 6.0 for Linux) did not fully support PNG's features. An example of PNG transparency is in the "PNG Alpha-Channel Transparency" section of Chapter 3, *Speedy Graphics.*" Here are some URLs with further information about the PNG format:

The PNG Home Page:
http://www.libpng.org/pub/png/

The PNG Specification at W3C:
http://www.w3.org/TR/REC-png-multi.html

▶ chapter eight summary

Transparency

This chapter covered the complexities of creating transparency for the web. Here's a summary of key points:

- If you create artwork against solid colors and match the same solid color to your web page background, you can fake transparency. This method is just as effective as creating a transparent GIF, but it's a lot easier! We recommend using transparent GIFs only when you want to put an irregularly shaped image on top of a patterned background tile.

- If you create transparent artwork with anti-aliased edges, it will be predisposed to work with the background it was created against. This often causes unwanted fringing or halos around transparent artwork.

- Creating aliased edges is the key to making transparent artwork look good against any background color or pattern. Create artwork with aliased tools to avoid anti-aliased edges.

- PNG transparency is much better than GIF transparency, but there is currently insufficient browser and tool support to implement it on anything but experimental web pages.

"It's not wise to violate rules until you know how to observe them."
—T. S. Eliot

Alignment
bossing pixels around

▶ **contents**

text alignment tags
graphic alignment tags
html tables
coloring tables
spacing text with tables
complex tables

If you are used to laying out graphics and text in other media, even other computer-based media, you will find a unique challenge in HTML's alignment capabilities—or its lack thereof.

Because of the web's unique distributed environment, in which you have no idea what disparate types of systems your page will be viewed on, HTML was not originally equipped to align the various elements on a page. The original HTML had no facility for text alignment, tables, or even inline images, let alone a method of sizing and aligning them.

Fortunately, that has changed significantly. It's still common to hear web publishers complain about their lack of control over the final display properties of a given page; however, the situation is rapidly improving.

As you read this chapter, keep in mind that alignment in HTML is not an easy issue. You are dealing with a lot of variables over which you have no control. Many of your efforts in this area will be more of a compromise than you are probably used to. Absolute control over layout is not possible with pure HTML, but it's more than possible to create pages that will look great on a variety of platforms.

Text Alignment Tags

In its simplest form, aligning text is a matter of controlling how a paragraph flows from one line to the next. For example, the paragraphs in this book are aligned on the left sides of each line relative to the margins on the page. This is called left-justified text.

HTML gives us the ability to center or align text against the left or right margins. Beginning with HTML 4.0, justified alignment is also available. The 4.0 versions of Netscape Navigator and MS Internet Explorer support full justification. HTML supports text content anywhere within a document. In fact, HTML treats most content as text, including inline graphics. However, in order to control the appearance of text, it must be within some sort of container that specifies the desired attributes. The most common container for text is the paragraph element (the P tag).

Examples of text justification options: left, right, middle, and justified (left and right).

Using P to Align Text

The P tag is used to place a block of text within a paragraph. Normally, the purpose for this is to apply vertical spacing between paragraphs as a visual cue. You can also use paragraphs to specify horizontal alignment for your text, using the ALIGN attribute.

For example, to create a paragraph of text, you could enclose it in P and /P like this:

```
<P> Ducks In A Row products represent
a unique concept in rubber stamping.
Our original designs created by Joan
Farber, internationally recognized
illustrator, are unlike anything found
in the stamp market today. </P>

<P>Joan Farber is a freelance illustra-
tor, designer, fine artist, and teacher
who has done work for such notable
companies as American Express, CBS
Records, Redken, MCI, Cosmopolitan,
Playboy and Vogue Magazines. With her
early roots as a fashion illustrator,
Joan has developed a style of illustra-
tion which has become popular in recent
years, utilizing a skillfully calli-
graphic brush stroke which brings an
elegance and sophistication to any
image. </P>

<P>Because the style of art throughout
the catalog is consistent, any of the
designs may be used together side by
side or superimposed, making the possi-
bilities for personal expression bound-
less. </P>
```

In practice, the end tag (/P) is rarely necessary, so you don't see it very often. We use it here only to show that P creates a container with both a beginning and an end. By default, most browsers will display paragraphs of text left-aligned—that is, with a ragged-right margin.

Here's what the code on the left looks like in Netscape Navigator:

Ducks In A Row products represent a unique concept in rubber stamping. Our original designscreated by Joan Farber, internationally recognized illustrator, are unlike anything found in the stamp market today.

Joan Farber is a freelance illustrator, designer, fine artist, and teacher who has done work for such notable companies as American Express, CBS Records, Redken, MCI, Cosmopolitan, Playboy and Vogue Magazines. With her early roots as a fashion illustrator, Joan has developed a style of illustration which has become popular in recent years, utilizing a skillfully calligraphic brush stroke which brings an elegance and sophistication to any image.

Because the style of art throughout the catalog is consistent, any of the designs may be used together side by side or superimposed, making the possibilities for personal expression boundless.

The default left alignment of text in Netscape Navigator.

If you want different alignment, you must specify it. The P tag may be used with the ALIGN attribute:

```
<P ALIGN="RIGHT">

Ducks In A Row products represent a
unique concept in rubber stamping. Our
original designs created by Joan
Farber, internationally recognized
illustrator, are unlike anything found
in the stamp market today.</P>
```

With the ALIGN="RIGHT" attribute, the paragraph is displayed with the right side aligned and the left side ragged.

> Ducks In A Row products represent a unique concept in rubber stamping. Our original designscreated by Joan Farber, internationally recognized illustrator, are unlike anything found in the stamp market today.

A paragraph in Netscape with `ALIGN="RIGHT"`.

The `ALIGN` attribute can also be set to `CENTER` or `JUSTIFY`. The `CENTER` alignment will center each line in a paragraph.

> Ducks In A Row products represent a unique concept in rubber stamping. Our original designscreated by Joan Farber, internationally recognized illustrator, are unlike anything found in the stamp market today.

A paragraph in Netscape with `ALIGN="CENTER"`.

The `JUSTIFY` alignment will align both sides to their margins.

> Ducks In A Row products represent a unique concept in rubber stamping. Our original designscreated by Joan Farber, internationally recognized illustrator, are unlike anything found in the stamp market today.

A paragraph in Netscape with `ALIGN="JUSTIFY"`.

The usefulness of this setting is somewhat reduced by the way it is implemented. In order to justify both margins, spaces are inserted between words, but not between letters. This results in lines of text like the second-to-last line in our example. The spaces between the words are so large they really detract from the overall value of the technique.

The `ALIGN="JUSTIFY"` setting exaggerates a long-time problem with the Netscape browser: The right margin is larger than the left. This is true in all versions of the Netscape browser, but it's much more noticeable with justified text. Using style sheets and/or frames, it is possible to overcome this limitation (more about those techniques in Chapters 13, *"Style Sheets,"* and 14, *"Navigation"*), but with the simple justified paragraph, it's pretty obvious that the margins don't match.

Another important point to mention is that these margins are defined by the width of the browser. This means that if someone has their browser window maximized to the width of the screen, the lines of type will be quite long. It's also possible to use the `ALIGN="JUSTIFY"` setting with tables to limit the width of text lines. We'll cover this technique later in this chapter.

Using DIV to Align Blocks of Text

More often than not, when you want to apply a specific alignment to a paragraph, you will want to apply that alignment to more than one paragraph at a time. That's what the DIV tag is for.

The DIV tag is a container, and it requires an end tag. By using DIV, you are effectively saying, "Apply this alignment from here to there." Here's an example:

```
<DIV ALIGN=" CENTER">

<P> Ducks In A Row products represent
a unique concept in rubber stamping.
Our original designs created by Joan
Farber, internationally recognized
illustrator, are unlike anything found
in the stamp market today.
<P>Joan Farber is a freelance illustra-
tor, designer, fine artist, and teacher
who has done work for such notable
companies as American Express, CBS
Records, Redken, MCI, Cosmopolitan,
Playboy and Vogue Magazines. With her
early roots as a fashion illustrator,
Joan has developed a style of illustra-
tion which has become popular in recent
years, utilizing a skillfully calli-
graphic brush stroke which brings an
elegance and sophistication to any
image.

<P>Because the style of art throughout
the catalog is consistent, any of the
designs may be used together side
by side or superimposed, making the
possibilities for personal expression
boundless.

</DIV>
```

The DIV tag can be used with any of the ALIGN values that work with paragraphs—CENTER, LEFT, RIGHT, or JUSTIFY.

Ducks In A Row products represent a unique concept in rubber stamping. Our original designscreated by Joan Farber, internationally recognized illustrator, are unlike anything found in the stamp market today.

Joan Farber is a freelance illustrator, designer, fine artist, and teacher who has done work for such notable companies as American Express, CBS Records, Redken, MCI, Cosmopolitan, Playboy and Vogue Magazines. With her early roots as a fashion illustrator, Joan has developed a style of illustration which has become popular in recent years, utilizing a skillfully calligraphic brush stroke which brings an elegance and sophistication to any image.

Because the style of art throughout the catalog is consistent, any of the designs may be used together side by side or superimposed, making the possibilities for personal expression boundless.

Use the DIV tag to align a block of paragraphs.

CENTER

Netscape first introduced the CENTER tag with version 1.1 of the Navigator browser (long before the DIV tag, was invented). Because Navigator was the browser of choice for the vast majority of web users, the CENTER tag was quickly adopted by others, and it is now supported by virtually all browsers in common use on the Net. With the introduction of the DIV tag, the CENTER tag was supposed to go away, and in fact it's still considered "obsolescent" in the HTML specifications. In technical terms, <CENTER> is just an alias for <DIV ALIGN=" CENTER">.

We don't expect CENTER to go away anytime soon, so feel free to use it. It's convenient. The browser developers, especially Netscape, appear to have a lot more respect for the needs of the marketplace than they do for the needs of the people who write the specifications. Whether you feel that's a good thing or a bad thing (there are plenty of arguments for each of those opinions), the fact is that CENTER is here to stay.

As you can see from this example, <CENTER> has exactly the same effect as <DIV ALIGN=" CENTER">:

```
<CENTER>

<P> Ducks In A Row products represent
a unique concept in rubber stamping.
Our original designs created by Joan
Farber, internationally recognized
illustrator, are unlike anything found
in the stamp market today.

<P>Joan Farber is a freelance illustra-
tor, designer, fine artist, and teacher
who has done work for such notable
companies as American Express, CBS
Records, Redken, MCI, Cosmopolitan,
Playboy and Vogue Magazines. With her
early roots as a fashion illustrator,
Joan has developed a style of illustra-
tion which has become popular in
recent years, utilizing a skillfully
calligraphic brush stroke which brings
an elegance and sophistication to
any image.

<P>Because the style of art throughout
the catalog is consistent, any of the
designs may be used together side
by side or superimposed, making the
possibilities for personal
expression boundless.

</CENTER>
```

The text formatting capabilities of HTML are indeed limited. There is no way to adjust leading, character or word spacing, kerning, or even the size of the text. In Chapter 13, *"Style,"* we will discuss how you can overcome some of these shortcomings with CSS style sheets, but even then it's good to remember that the web was not designed as a presentation medium. It will take some more time for the medium itself to catch up with its potential.

Ducks In A Row products represent a unique concept in rubber stamping. Our original designs created by Joan Farber, internationally recognized illustrator, are unlike anything found in the stamp market today.

Joan Farber is a freelance illustrator, designer, fine artist, and teacher who has done work for such notable companies as American Express, CBS Records, Redken, MCI, Cosmopolitan, Playboy and Vogue Magazines. With her early roots as a fashion illustrator, Joan has developed a style of illustration which has become popular in recent years, utilizing a skillfully calligraphic brush stroke which brings an elegance and sophistication to any image.

Because the style of art throughout the catalog is consistent, any of the designs may be used together side by side or superimposed, making the possibilities for personal expression boundless.

Use the CENTER tag to center a block of paragraphs.

Graphic Alignment Tags

When we discuss aligning graphics on the page, it's important to first understand that HTML considers a graphic object (the IMG tag) to be part of the text stream. That's right; as far as HTML is concerned, graphics are part of the text, unless you tell it to do something special. For example, notice how Netscape renders this HTML:

```
<HEAD>
<TITLE> Graphic Alignment </TITLE>
</HEAD>
<BODY BGCOLOR="white">

<P>This paragraph has a small
<IMG SRC="ducky.gif">
graphic in the middle of it.

</BODY>
</HTML>
```

A graphic is considered part of a paragraph.

As you can see, the graphic was inserted directly in the paragraph along with the text. This is what is meant by "inline" graphics. The graphic itself is in line with the stream of text in the paragraph.

Notice also that the bottom of the graphic lines up with the baseline of the text. This is typical for most browsers.

IMG ALIGN Attribute

If you want the inline image to align differently (relative to the line of text it is on), you must supply an `ALIGN` attribute:

`ALIGN="BOTTOM"` Aligns the bottom of the image with the baseline (default).

`ALIGN="MIDDLE"` Aligns the middle of the image with the baseline.

`ALIGN="TOP"` Aligns the top of the image with the top of the tallest object on the line.

Here's what each of the inline image alignment types looks like in Netscape Navigator:

The `ALIGN="BOTTOM"` **attribute.**

```
<HEAD>
<TITLE> Graphic Alignment </TITLE>
</HEAD>
<BODY BGCOLOR="white">

<P>This paragraph has a small
<IMG SRC="ducky.gif" ALIGN="BOTTOM">
graphic in the middle of it.

</BODY>
</HTML>
```

The `ALIGN="MIDDLE"` **attribute.**

```
<HEAD>
<TITLE> Graphic Alignment </TITLE>
</HEAD>
<BODY BGCOLOR="white">

<P>This paragraph has a small
<IMG SRC="ducky.gif" ALIGN="MIDDLE">
graphic in the middle of it.

</BODY>
</HTML>
```

The `ALIGN="TOP"` **attribute.**

```
<HEAD>
<TITLE> Graphic Alignment </TITLE>
</HEAD>
<BODY BGCOLOR="white">

<P>This paragraph has a small
<IMG SRC="ducky.gif" ALIGN="TOP">
graphic in the middle of it.

</BODY>
</HTML>
```

Floating Graphics

You can also align a graphic to one side or the other and have text wrap around that graphic. This is done with the floating-type ALIGN values: RIGHT and LEFT. Consider this example:

```
<HTML>
<HEAD>
<TITLE>Ducks In A Row Company
Information</TITLE>
</HEAD>
<BODY BGCOLOR="white">

<P><IMG SRC="joan.jpg"
ALIGN="LEFT">Joan Farber is a freelance
illustrator, designer, fine artist and
teacher who has done work for such
notable companies as American Express,
CBS Records, Redken, MCI, Cosmopolitan,
Playboy and Vogue Magazines. With her
early roots as a fashion illustrator,
Joan has developed a style of illustra-
tion which has become popular in recent
years, utilizing a skillfully calli-
graphic brush stroke which brings an
elegance and sophistication to any
image.

</BODY>
</HTML>
```

Joan Farber is a free-lance illustrator, designer, fine artist and teacher, who has done work for such notable companies as American Express, CBS Records, Redken, MCI, Cosmopolitan, Playboy and Vogue Magazines. With her early roots as a fashion illustrator, Joan has developed a style of illustration which has become popular in recent years, utilizing a skillfully calligraphic brush stroke which brings an elegance and sophistication to any image.

By using ALIGN=" LEFT" **, the image aligns to the left side of the page, and the text wraps around it.**

In this example, the inline image is a photo of the person we're talking about in the text. So we actually want the text to flow around the image. Here's what using ALIGN="RIGHT" looks like in the browser:

Joan Farber is a free-lance illustrator, designer, fine artist and teacher, who has done work for such notable companies as American Express, CBS Records, Redken, MCI, Cosmopolitan, Playboy and Vogue Magazines. With her early roots as a fashion illustrator, Joan has developed a style of illustration which has become popular in recent years, utilizing a skillfully calligraphic brush stroke which brings an elegance and sophistication to any image.

By using ALIGN="RIGHT"**, the image floats to the right.**

In HTML parlance, the LEFT and RIGHT values for the ALIGN attribute tell the browser to "float" the image to the right or left side of the text. This is a distinct behavior from that of the TOP, BOTTOM, and MIDDLE values, which apply to the image as an inline text element.

Now and then you may wonder if you can use ALIGN="RIGHT" and ALIGN="MIDDLE" for the same image. No, you cannot use the same attribute more than once in the same element. But stay tuned to this chapter for the "Tables for Graphics" section, and you'll see how you can accomplish the same effect.

Insert a Line Break with BR

You are probably already familiar with the BR tag at this point, but you may not be aware that it has some peculiarities when used with floating images. Let's take a quick look at those peculiarities, so that you know how to break lines when you need to.

First, let's consider this small piece of HTML:

```
<P><IMG SRC="ducky.gif">
Line one
<BR>Line two
<BR>Line three
```

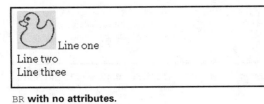

BR **with no attributes.**

Notice that the image is part of the paragraph. This is the normal behavior for an inline image. Notice that the BR tags break the lines of text, but the "Line one" text is inline with the image. That's because the text and the image are part of the same paragraph. Now let's see what happens if we add ALIGN="LEFT" to the IMG tag:

```
<P><IMG SRC="ducky.gif" ALIGN="LEFT">
Line one
<BR>Line two
<BR>Line three
```

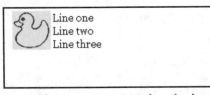

IMG **with** ALIGN="LEFT" **makes the image "float" to the left.**

When we add ALIGN="LEFT" to an IMG tag, the image floats to the left, leaving the paragraph text to wrap around it. Now the BR tag no longer brings the text out under the image; instead, it breaks the text but leaves it next to the image. This is the behavior with a floating (as opposed to inline) image.

The BR tag has an attribute called CLEAR that allows you to force the text to clear the floating image. For example, use CLEAR="LEFT" to force a text break below an image floating on the left:

```
<P><IMG SRC="ducky.gif" ALIGN="LEFT">
Line one
<BR>Line two
<BR CLEAR="LEFT">Line three
```

BR **with** CLEAR="LEFT".

Use CLEAR="RIGHT" to force a text break below an image floating on the right:

```
<P ALIGN="RIGHT">
<IMG SRC="ducky.gif" ALIGN="RIGHT">
Line one
<BR>Line two
<BR CLEAR="RIGHT">Line three
```

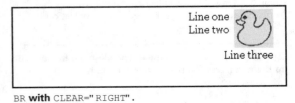

BR **with** CLEAR="RIGHT".

You can also use CLEAR=" ALL" to force a break below images on both sides:

```
<P ALIGN=" CENTER">
<IMG SRC=" ducky.gif"  ALIGN=" RIGHT">
<IMG SRC=" ducky.gif"  ALIGN=" LEFT">
Line one
<BR>Line two
<BR CLEAR="ALL">Line three
```

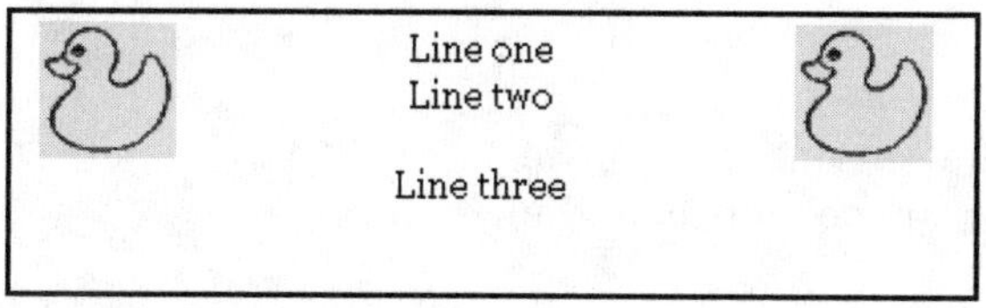

BR **with** CLEAR=" ALL".

The BR tag can be a little confusing when you are using it with floating images. As a rule of thumb, it can't hurt to just get into the habit of using CLEAR=" ALL" anytime you want the break to go below an image.

Image Gutters

Did you notice that when we wrapped text around the duck image, there was a space between the image and the text? This space is called a gutter. It is controlled with the VSPACE and HSPACE attributes to the IMG tag.

```
<P><IMG SRC="ducky.gif" ALIGN="LEFT"
HSPACE="0">
Line one
<BR>Line two
<BR>Line three
```

Notice that by setting the HSPACE to zero, we have eliminated all the space between the image and the text.

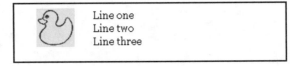

IMG **with** HSPACE="0".

On the other hand, it is also possible to create extra space by increasing the value of HSPACE. (The default value is 3 for most browsers.)

```
<P><IMG SRC="ducky.gif" ALIGN="LEFT"
HSPACE="25">
Line one
<BR>Line two
<BR>Line three
```

In this case, we have increased the horizontal gutter to 25 pixels.

IMG **with** HSPACE="25".

Notice that 25 pixels have been added to both sides of the image, this may not be what you want. To add 25 pixels of space to only one side, apply the trick described in the following section.

The Single-Pixel GIF Trick—Part I

Let's say that, for design purposes, you want 25 pixels of gutter only on the right side of the duck. You can't do that with the normal HSPACE attribute. Instead, you have to get creative.

First, some background: When you supply WIDTH and HEIGHT attributes to the IMG tag, the browser will display the graphic at the specified height and width, regardless of the original size of the image. If the image was that size in the first place, that's fine. This will actually speed up the display of the page (see Chapter 3, *"Speedy Graphics"*). On the other hand, if the graphic is not those dimensions, the browser will stretch (and/or shrink) the graphic to fit the dimensions specified by HEIGHT and WIDTH. Why would you want to do that?

The trick is to use a 1 pixel by 1 pixel GIF file, with the color of the pixel set to transparent. Then you can stretch that GIF to whatever size you want for the explicit purpose of creating space! You can use this trick to create horizontal space or vertical space. This example uses the blank.gif file from the chap09/1pixel folder of the <chd2> CD-ROM to create the one-sided gutter for us:

```
<P><IMG SRC=" ducky.gif"  WIDTH=" 50"
HEIGHT=" 50"  HSPACE=" 0"  ALIGN=" LEFT" >
  <IMG SRC=" blank.gif"  WIDTH=" 25"
HEIGHT=" 50"  HSPACE=" 0"  ALIGN=" LEFT" >
Line one
<BR>Line two
<BR>Line three
```

Creating a gutter with a single-pixel transparent GIF.

Watch for the single-pixel GIF Trick—Part II later in this chapter.

HTML Tables

Unless you are dealing with a strictly textual site, you will likely want somewhat more freedom to express your design than what is available with the HTML that we have discussed so far. Fortunately, most current browsers support HTML tables.

Using tables, it is possible to display tabular data, create columns of text, precisely position various elements of your design, and solve many other HTML design problems.

The HTML Tables specification has been around in various forms since early 1995. Since that time, it has undergone many changes and transformations, and it continues to change with the HTML 4 specification. This chapter documents those features of tables that work with the widest variety of browsers. What is documented here, unless otherwise specified, works in Netscape Navigator versions 2.0 and later, as well as all the browsers that are designed to be compatible with it. That includes at least 90% of all browsers.

Table Basics

In its simplest form, a table is useful for organizing data into rows (horizontal) and columns (vertical). For example:

```
<TABLE>
  <TR>
    <TD> Ducks In A Row products rep-
    resent a unique concept in rubber
    stamping.

    <TD> Our original designs created
    by Joan Farber, internationally
    recognized illustrator, are unlike
    anything found in the stamp market
    today.

    <TD> Joan Farber is a freelance
    illustrator, designer, fine
    artist, and teacher who has done
    work for such notable companies as
    American Express, CBS Records, ...
</TABLE>
```

The TABLE element is a container, so it requires both the start tag and the end tag. Everything in between is part of the table. The TR tag (also a container, but the end tag is optional) designates the beginning of a row (horizontal), and each of the TD tags (also containers with optional end tags) marks the beginning of a column (vertical). Because there are one TR and three TD tags, this table contains one row and three columns.

Ducks In A Row products represent a unique concept in rubber stamping.	Our original designs created by Joan Farber, internationally recognized illustrator, are unlike anything found in the stamp market today.	Joan Farber is a freelance illustrator, designer, fine artist, and teacher who has done work for such notable companies as American Express, CBS Records, ...

A simple table example.

The table itself becomes the size of all the elements it contains. If the elements within the table are not of a fixed size, the table gravitates to the size of the window in which it is displayed, and gives equal space to each of the elements in the table. It's easier to see what a table is doing if you turn on its borders with the BORDER attribute in the TABLE tag:

```
<TABLE BORDER>
  <TR>
    <TD> Ducks In A Row products rep-
resent a unique concept in rubber
stamping.

    <TD> Our original designs created
by Joan Farber, internationally recog-
nized illustrator, are unlike anything
found in the stamp market today.

    <TD> Joan Farber is a freelance
illustrator, designer, fine artist,
and teacher who has done work for such
notable companies as American Express,
CBS Records, . . .
</TABLE>
```

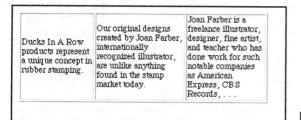

A table with the BORDER **attribute.**

You may have noticed that the columns do not line up at the top. That's because the default behavior is for each column to vertically align to the middle. This can be controlled with the VALIGN attribute for either the TR (to apply it to a whole row) or TD (for column-only) tags. Here's the same table with VALIGN in both the TR and TD elements:

```
<TABLE BORDER>
  <TR VALIGN="TOP">
    <TD> Ducks In A Row products
represent a unique concept in rubber
stamping.
      <TD VALIGN="BOTTOM">
          Our original designs created
by Joan Farber, internationally recog-
nized illustrator, are unlike anything
found in the stamp market today.

    <TD> Joan Farber is a freelance
illustrator, designer, fine artist,
and teacher who has done work for such
notable companies as American Express,
CBS Records, . . .
</TABLE>
```

We used VALIGN="TOP" in the TR element to align all the cells in the row to the top. We also used VALIGN="BOTTOM" in the second TD to align only that cell to the bottom. So, the first and third columns are top-aligned, and the second column is bottom-aligned.

Ducks In A Row products represent a unique concept in rubber stamping.	Our original designs created by Joan Farber, internationally recognized illustrator, are unlike anything found in the stamp market today.	Joan Farber is a freelance illustrator, designer, fine artist, and teacher who has done work for such notable companies as American Express, CBS Records, . . .

Using VALIGN **to vertically align table cells.**

Sometimes, you may want headings for your different columns. You can do this with the TH element. TH works just like TD, except it displays the cell in a bold heading style.

Partnership	Design	Bio
Ducks In A Row products represent a unique concept in rubber stamping.	Our original designs created by Joan Farber, internationally recognized illustrator, are unlike anything found in the stamp market today.	Joan Farber is a freelance illustrator, designer, fine artist, and teacher who has done work for such notable companies as American Express, CBS Records, . . .

A table with TH **cells for headings.**

Finally, a caption for the entire table can sometimes help to identify it on the page.

```
<TABLE BORDER>
  <CAPTION> <BIG> About The Company
</BIG> </CAPTION>
  <TR>
    <TH> Partnership
    <TH> Design
    <TH> Bio
  <TR VALIGN="TOP">
    <TD> Ducks In A Row products rep-
resent a unique concept in rubber
stamping.

    <TD> Our original designs created
by Joan Farber, internationally recog-
nized illustrator, are unlike anything
found in the stamp market today.

    <TD> Joan Farber is a freelance
illustrator, designer, fine artist, and
teacher who has done work for such
notable companies as American Express,
CBS Records, . . .
</TABLE>
```

The CAPTION element works a lot like TITLE, but for a table. The text in the CAPTION is displayed above the table by default and uses the default font for text. Here we used BIG to make it larger.

About The Company		
Partnership	**Design**	**Bio**
Ducks In A Row products represent a unique concept in rubber stamping.	Our original designs created by Joan Farber, internationally recognized illustrator, are unlike anything found in the stamp market today.	Joan Farber is a freelance illustrator, designer, fine artist, and teacher who has done work for such notable companies as American Express, CBS Records, . . .

The table with a caption.

If you prefer that the caption display at the bottom of the table, you can use ALIGN="BOTTOM" in the CAPTION element, like this:

```
<CAPTION ALIGN="BOTTOM"> <BIG> About
The Company </BIG> </CAPTION>
```

Partnership	Design	Bio
Ducks In A Row products represent a unique concept in rubber stamping.	Our original designs created by Joan Farber, internationally recognized illustrator, are unlike anything found in the stamp market today.	Joan Farber is a freelance illustrator, designer, fine artist, and teacher who has done work for such notable companies as American Express, CBS Records, . . .
About The Company		

The caption with ALIGN="BOTTOM".

Coloring and Spacing in Tables

Let's remove the border from the table and experiment with color for identifying the different cells in the table. To start with, we'll use the BGCOLOR attribute for the whole table to see what happens:

```
<TABLE BGCOLOR=" #FFFFCC">
<TR>
    <TH> Partnership
    <TH> Design
    <TH> Bio
  <TR VALIGN=" TOP">
    <TD> Ducks In A Row products rep-
resent a unique concept in rubber
stamping.

    <TD> Our original designs created
by Joan Farber, internationally recog-
nized illustrator, are unlike anything
found in the stamp market today.

    <TD> Joan Farber is a freelance
illustrator, designer, fine artist, and
teacher who has done work for such
notable companies as American Express,
CBS Records, . . .
</TABLE>
```

Here, we took out the BORDER attribute and put in a BGCOLOR attribute instead. The BGCOLOR attribute works exactly the same way as the BGCOLOR attribute to the BODY tag, which we have used quite a bit already.

Partnership	Design	Bio
Ducks In A Row products represent a unique concept in rubber stamping.	Our original designs created by Joan Farber, internationally recognized illustrator, are unlike anything found in the stamp market today.	Joan Farber is a freelance illustrator, designer, fine artist, and teacher who has done work for such notable companies as American Express, CBS Records, . . .

The table with the BGCOLOR attribute.

When used with the TABLE element, the BGCOLOR attribute sets a default background color for the entire table.

You probably noticed that the space between the cells is not colored. We'll show you how to control—or remove—spaces a bit later.

We can also use the BGCOLOR attribute with the TR element to set the background color of a row, and with the TD element to set the background color for an individual cell.

```
<TABLE BGCOLOR=" #FFFFCC">
  <TR BGCOLOR=" #CCCCFF">
    <TH> Partnership
    <TH> Design
    <TH> Bio
  <TR VALIGN=" TOP">
    <TD> Ducks In A Row products
represent a unique concept in rubber
stamping.

    <TD BGCOLOR=" #CCFFFF">
        Our original designs created
by Joan Farber, internationally recog-
nized illustrator, are unlike anything
found in the stamp market today.

    <TD> Joan Farber is a freelance
illustrator, designer, fine artist,
and teacher who has done work for such
notable companies as American Express,
CBS Records, . . .
</TABLE>
```

Here we set the color for an entire row (the row with the headings in it) and for an individual cell (the middle one in the second row). All the other cells are the default color, set in the TABLE tag.

Partnership	Design	Bio
Ducks In A Row products represent a unique concept in rubber stamping.	Our original designs created by Joan Farber, internationally recognized illustrator, are unlike anything found in the stamp market today.	Joan Farber is a free-lance illustrator, designer, fine artist, and teacher, who has done work for such notable companies as American Express, CBS Records, . . .

The BGCOLOR attribute in rows and cells.

Space Between Table Cells

The space between the table cells is controlled by the CELLSPACING attribute in the TABLE tag. By setting CELLSPACING to zero, you can remove all the space between the cells of your table.

Let's start by setting CELLSPACING and BORDER to zero for our example (the rest of the code remains the same):

```
<TABLE BGCOLOR=" #FFFFCC" BORDER=" 0"
CELLSPACING=" 0">
```

This removes all the space from between the cells of our table.

Partnership	Design	Bio
Ducks In A Row products represent a unique concept in rubber stamping.	Our original designs created by Joan Farber, internationally recognized illustrator, are unlike anything found in the stamp market today.	Joan Farber is a free-lance illustrator, designer, fine artist, and teacher, who has done work for such notable companies as American Express, CBS Records, . . .

Our example with CELLSPACING=" 0".

Notice that this example leaves all the text jammed up against the edges of the cells. You can adjust the space inside the cell borders with the CELLPADDING attribute.

```
<TABLE BGCOLOR=" #FFFFCC" BORDER=" 0"
CELLSPACING=" 0" CELLPADDING=" 5">
```

Partnership	Design	Bio
Ducks In A Row products represent a unique concept in rubber stamping.	Our original designs created by Joan Farber, internationally recognized illustrator, are unlike anything found in the stamp market today.	Joan Farber is a free-lance illustrator, designer, fine artist, and teacher, who has done work for such notable companies as American Express, CBS Records, . . .

The table with CELLSPACING=" 0" **and** CELLPADDING=" 5".

This gives a little breathing room for the text inside the cells.

This technique can be nicely applied to columnar-type data, giving you some design flexibility that would otherwise be difficult without using large graphics files:

```
<TABLE BGCOLOR=" #FFFFCC" BORDER=" 0"
CELLSPACING=" 0" CELLPADDING=" 6">
   <TR><TD>
     You will find designs in our
catalog which cover a vast array
of categories:
   <TR><TD BGCOLOR="" #CCCC99">
floral images
   <TR><TD> humor
   <TR><TD BGCOLOR=" #CCCC99">
holiday stamps
   <TR><TD> border designs
   <TR><TD BGCOLOR=" #CCCC99">
decorative imagery
</TABLE>
```

In this decorative table, we use a separate row for each element of the list. **Remember:** You need both a TR and a TD to create a row. In this example, we used a BGCOLOR attribute in the TABLE tag as a default and then changed the color in every other row.

You will find designs in our catalog which cover a vast array of categories:
floral images
humor
holiday stamps
border designs
decorative imagery

A decorative table for listing options.

You can create many other interesting designs by using tables. Hopefully, we've given you enough tools to be able to experiment on your own, and use your creativity.

▶ **warning**

The BORDER Attribute in Netscape

There is a bug in the Netscape implementation of tables that goes all the way back to the first version of Netscape that supported tables (Navigator version 1.1). According to the specification, a table that has CELLSPACING set to 0 should have no space between the cells. In the Netscape browser, there is still space if you have not explicitly set BORDER=" 0".

The default value of the BORDER attribute should be zero, but it's not in Netscape Navigator. Even though the border is not rendered, it still takes up space unless you set it to zero. Other browsers may emulate this behavior.

Tables for Spacing

Another common use for tables is to create accurate spacing. By using HEIGHT and WIDTH attributes in the TABLE and TR tags, it is possible to position text and graphics precisely on the page.

Margins in HTML

It is possible to precisely position elements on the page relative to one another. However, it is not always possible to position objects accurately relative to the edge of the screen. Most browsers (including Netscape's and Microsoft's) have various margins on the page, which differ from version to version and platform to platform. The only way around this limitation is to use frames (which can be set to have zero margins), but that solution prevents those members of your audience without a frames-capable browser from viewing your site. (For instructions on how to align text and images using frames, check out Chapter 14, *"Navigation."*)

For these reasons, we recommend that you accept the variable margins in your design, if possible, and instead use tables to precisely align objects relative to one another. This approach has worked well for many web sites.

The HEIGHT and WIDTH attributes can be used in the TABLE tag to fix the minimum height and width of the entire table. Keep in mind that if you use any elements that are larger than these minimums, your table will expand accordingly.

```
<TABLE BORDER="0" CELLSPACING="0"
BGCOLOR="#00CCCC"
   WIDTH="200" HEIGHT="200">
   <TR><TD ALIGN="CENTER"> 200×200
Table
</TABLE>
```

In this table, we have specified a width of 200 pixels and a height of 200 pixels. The table has only one cell, and that cell has the text "200 ×200 Table" in it. To help us see the size of the table visually, we have given it a cyan background color. We set the BORDER and CELLSPACING attributes to 0 so that the cell itself will fill all the space of the table.

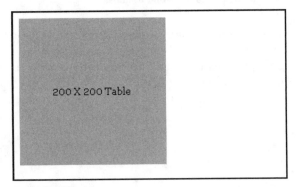

A 200 X 200 table.

Spacing Text with Tables

Tables are commonly used to create space so that text doesn't flow all the way across the page.

```
<TABLE BORDER="1" CELLSPACING="0"
CELLPADDING="8" WIDTH="350">
  <TR>
    <TD HEIGHT="50"><BR>
    <TD>
  <TR>
    <TD WIDTH="50">
    <TD WIDTH="300" BGCOLOR=#FFFF99>
      <P> Joan Farber is a freelance
illustrator, designer, fine artist,
and teacher who has done work for such
notable companies as American Express,
CBS Records, Redken, MCI, Cosmopolitan,
Playboy and Vogue Magazines.
</TABLE>
```

This table has two rows. The first row exists only to create a 50-pixel high margin to keep the text away from the top of the window. The BR tag is there to give the cell content; otherwise, it won't take up any space. The second row sets the spacing of the table: The first column is 50 pixels wide to provide space to the left of the text. The second column contains the text itself (on a nice duck-yellow background), and it will be 50 pixels down and 50 pixels across from the left margin. The text is in a cell that is 300 pixels wide, no matter how wide the window is opened. This keeps the text from becoming one long line across somebody's huge screen.

We left the border on so you could see the table layout. Normally, you would turn it off with BORDER="0".

A table used to create space for text.

You could easily use this same table to create another space for an image to accompany the text.

```
<TABLE BORDER="0" CELLSPACING="0"
CELLPADDING="8" WIDTH="500">
  <TR>
    <TD HEIGHT="50"><BR>
    <TD>
  <TR>
    <TD WIDTH="50">
    <TD WIDTH="300" BGCOLOR="#FFFF99">
      <P> Joan Farber is a freelance
illustrator, designer, fine artist,
and teacher who has done work for such
notable companies as American Express,
CBS Records, Redken, MCI, Cosmopolitan,
Playboy and Vogue Magazines.
      <TD WIDTH="150"><IMG
SRC="joan2.jpg" WIDTH="118"
HEIGHT="127">
</TABLE>
```

We have added the image to the table in its own cell. Be careful, however, because the width of the table is equal to the sum of all the cells.

Joan Farber is a free-lance illustrator, designer, fine artist and teacher, who has done work for such notable companies as American Express, CBS Records, Redken, MCI, Cosmopolitan, Playboy and Vogue Magazines.

The table can be used to align different types of objects, including text and graphics.

In the advanced tables department, you may sometimes want to have a table with cells that span more than one row or column. If this seems strange to you, feel free to skip the next section.

Tables with Odd Numbers of Cells

The cells in HTML tables can, for many reasons, span more than one column or row at a time. In this section, we will show you how to construct such tables. If you take your time with each of these examples—and experiment with them freely—you may find them good for hours of fascinating fun!

```
<TABLE BORDER=" 0"  CELLSPACING=" 0"
BGCOLOR=" #00CCCC"
     WIDTH=" 200"  HEIGHT=" 200">
  <TR>
     <TD WIDTH=" 50"  HEIGHT=" 50"
     BGCOLOR=" #CCCC00"  ALIGN=" CENTER">
        50×50
     <TD WIDTH=" 150"  HEIGHT=" 50"
BGCOLOR=" #999900"  ALIGN=" CENTER">
        150×50
  <TR>
     <TD WIDTH=" 200"  HEIGHT=" 150"
     COLSPAN=" 2"  ALIGN=" CENTER">
        200×150 <BR>  COLSPAN=" 2"
</TABLE>
```

In this example, the table itself is set to 200×200, and there are three cells. The first row has two cells, and the second row has one. In the first row, the first cell has a width of 50 pixels and a height of 50 pixels. The second cell is 150 pixels wide and 50 pixels high. They each have a different background color so you can see what's going on.

But the second row has something new. Notice the COLSPAN=" 2" attribute in the TD element. This tells the browser that the cell takes up two columns. **Important:** In HTML tables, every row must take up the same number of columns, and every column must take up the same number of rows. If your first row has two columns, but the second row has only one, the browser will definitely do something unpredictable! So, if you want a cell to span more than one column, you need to tell the browser which cell it's going to be! You do this with the COLSPAN attribute.

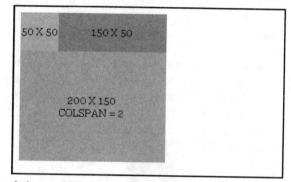

A three-celled table with COLSPAN.

Likewise, you can have a cell span more than one row. You do this with the ROWSPAN attribute.

```
<TABLE BORDER=" 0"  CELLSPACING=" 0"
WIDTH=" 200"  HEIGHT=" 200">
  <TR>
     <TD WIDTH=" 100"  HEIGHT=" 200"
     ROWSPAN=" 2"  BGCOLOR=" #CCCC00"
     ALIGN=" CENTER">
        100×200 <BR>  ROWSPAN=" 2"
     <TD WIDTH=" 100"  HEIGHT=" 50"
     BGCOLOR=" #00CCCC"  ALIGN=" CENTER">
        100×50
  <TR>
     <TD WIDTH=" 100"  HEIGHT=" 150"
BGCOLOR=" #999900"  ALIGN=" CENTER">
        100×150
</TABLE>
```

In the table below, there is a cell that spans two rows. The first row has two columns, a 100×200 cell and a 100×50 cell. Notice that the first cell has ROWSPAN=" 2" in the first TD element. This means that the cell will also be part of the next row! So the second row has only one cell in it (100×150), and that cell is positioned in the second column because a cell from the previous row occupies the first column.

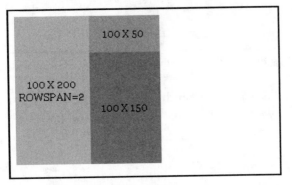

100 X 50

100 X 200
ROWSPAN=2

100 X 150

A three-celled table with ROWSPAN.

We know that this aspect of tables can be confusing. It requires that you consider your design carefully and usually draw a map. The tables shown with numeric markings in them represent the sorts of drawings Bill makes when he plans complex tables. This makes it a lot easier to code the tables when it's time for that.

Tables for Graphics

Another common use for tables is to reassemble large images that have been broken apart into smaller individual files. There are a number of reasons to cut apart and reassemble a large graphic:

- Some parts of the graphic may compress best in one file format, and some may compress best in another file format. This is often the case with hybrid images that contain continuous tone photographs and flat color illustration.

- Perhaps you want to animate part of the graphic (animating a large file takes up a lot more space than animating a small file).

- You can reduce the viewer's wait time. Because some of the images will download before others, the viewer won't have to wait for an entire large image to download before experiencing part of the page.

- Multiple images appearing at different intervals can produce an interesting effect in itself.

- You may want to create interactive rollovers in parts of a large graphic. Rollovers can occur locally (for example, a button may change color when the viewer moves the mouse over the area of the button) or remotely (an image may appear in one area when the viewer presses a button in another area). Cutting a large graphic into individual images will allow you to program such interactive effects.

Prior to the introduction of programs like ImageReady, which are oriented specifically to making web graphics, breaking apart and reassembling a large image was a labor intensive, inexact, piece-by-piece process. However, once you try slicing graphics in Photoshop or ImageReady, you may never do it the old-fashioned way again.

9

> **▶ e x e r c i s e**

Slicing an Image in Photoshop 6.0

It's possible to cut apart an image in Photoshop 6.0 or ImageReady. This is usually done if you want to optimize different parts of an image with different compression formats, or if you want some regions of an image to contain rollovers or animations.

Step 1: Copy the chap09 folder from the <chd.2> CD-ROM to your hard drive, launch Photoshop 6.0 and open the cutapart.psd file in the chap09 folder of the chd2> CD-ROM.

Step 2: Using the Slice tool from the toolbar, drag a region around the word "process." The type in this graphic would best be optimized as a GIF, while the other regions would be best optimized as JPEG. The first step to accomplishing this is to create a "slice" around the areas you want to isolate for different compression settings. This will cut the image into three pieces, as Photoshop creates cuts not just where you sliced the one image, but automatically creates slices for the remaining regions. These slices are always in square or rectangular pieces. Because of this, Photoshop has to make two slices for the remaining regions, because it can't make an irregularly shaped slice.

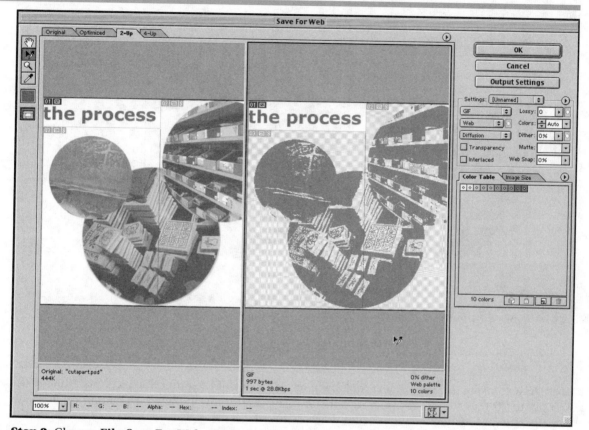

Step 3: Choose **File:Save For Web**. Using the Slice Select tool, click first on the region with the type in it. Change the settings to the **GIF** format with the setting you see above.

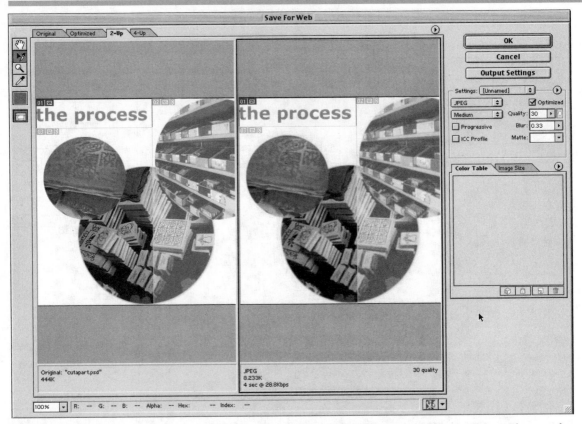

Step 4: Next, using the **Slice Select** tool again, click on one of the other **Slice** regions. Change the settings to **JPEG** as you see above. Notice that both of the remaining slices take on the compression settings you just created. That's because they are linked.

Photoshop automatically links slices that are created automatically by the program. Since you created the slice around the words "**the process**," Photoshop knew that the top, left region was a "**user-based slice**," meaning that you, the user, created it. The other slices are called "auto-slices," because the program created them automatically.

Note: Auto-slices are always linked, meaning if you change the compression setting of one, the others will inherit the change.

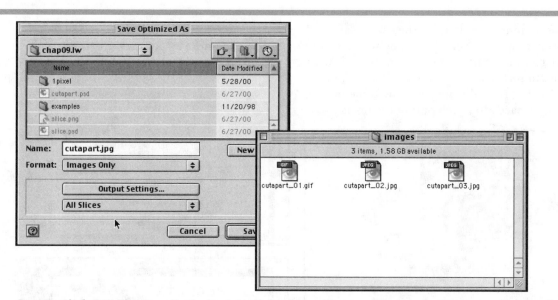

Step 5: Click **OK**. The Save Optimized As dialog box will open. Change the Format to **Images Only**, navigate to the chap09 folder and click **Save**. This will save three files into a new folder called images. Notice that one is a **GIF** and the others are **JPEGs**.

The next section will describe how to write the code to put the large image back together using tables. You can use our naming scheme, or you can create your own and modify the HTML to work with your names.

Piecing the Artwork Back Together

Now that you've cut the large image into individual files, you'll need a way to display it on a page as if it were in one piece. A table will provide the perfect container for holding all the pieces of the image in place in a browser. Using the techniques you've already learned in this chapter, it's relatively easy to create the table to display this compound graphic. There are three rows and three columns, so piecing the image back together is just a matter of building the table, right?

First, let's look at the wrong way to do this:

```
<TABLE BORDER=0 CELLSPACING=0
CELLPADDING=0>
```

```
<TR>
<TD><IMG SRC=" images/cutapart_01.gif">

<TD ROWSPAN=2>
<IMG SRC=" images/cutapart_02.jpg">
<TR>
<TD><IMG SRC=" images/cutapart_03.jpg">
</TABLE>
```

Earlier, you learned that the TD and TR elements have optional end tags. This is true, but when an end tag is optional in HTML, it only means that the browser is able to guess where the end of the element should be. In most cases, that guess is good enough, but in some cases it may not be. This is one of those cases where guessing won't work.

Unless told otherwise, the browser will terminate a table cell at the beginning of the next cell or at the end of the current row or table. In this case, because the TD or TR following each TD is on the next line, the browser may insert a space after each part of the image!

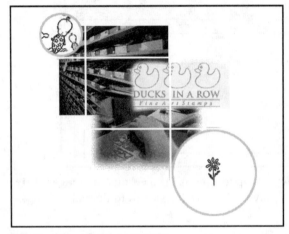

A table with non-terminated TDs.

Now, let's look at the right way to piece the image back together:

```
<TABLE BORDER=0 CELLSPACING=0
CELLPADDING=0><TR>
<TD><IMG
SRC="images/cutapart_01.gif"></TD>
<TD ROWSPAN=2>
<IMG SRC="images/cutapart_02.jpg">
</TD><TR>
<TD><IMG SRC="images/cutapart_03.jpg">
</TD>
</TABLE>
```

In this HTML, we told the browser to terminate the cell immediately after the image with no space between the image and the end of the cell. The result is a perfectly clean rendering of the image, with no seams and no spaces.

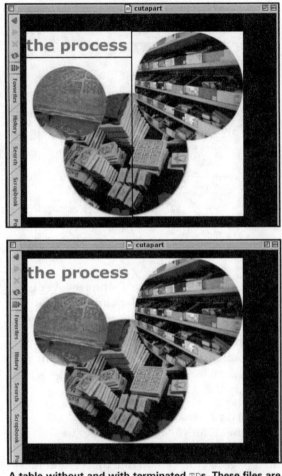

A table without and with terminated TDs. These files are called cutapart_bad.html and cutapart_good.html **are available to review in the** chap09 **folder of the <chd2> CD-ROM.**

Piecing together an image can leave you a lot of room to create dynamic content. You can have different words over parts of an image for different pages, animate parts of an image, or change it in any number of ways. Understanding how tables work will help you design these pages more freely as a part of your web design repertoire.

Table Tricks and Tips

Tables don't have to be large and complex to be useful. In fact, once you understand the basics of tables, you will find them useful for a number of little things.

The Single-Pixel GIF Trick—Part II

Ever wanted to add a little vertical space to a page? Maybe add a little air before a graphic? One way to do it is with the single-pixel GIF. We showed you earlier how to use it to add horizontal space, but it can also be used to add vertical space.

```
<IMG SRC="blank.gif" WIDTH=" 1"
HEIGHT=" 50"><BR>
This is 50 pixels down.
```

The disadvantage of using a GIF for adding space is that, although the GIF itself is small, it requires a whole new connection to download it, and that can slow your page down. And if for some reason that download fails, you could get a broken-image icon on the page instead of the pretty little blank space you wanted.

As an alternative, here's a little table that works just as well:

```
<TABLE><TR><TD HEIGHT=" 50"></TABLE>
This is 50 pixels down.
```

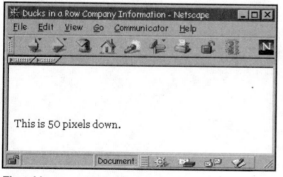

The table-spacer at work!

Just change the 50 to another number for a different amount of space. A lower number will create less space, and a higher number will yield more.

The table has several distinct advantages over the GIF: The table is part of the HTML, so if the page loads at all, the space will be there. Because there is no GIF to download, there is one less thing to go wrong. The table is only about 35 bytes; even the smallest GIF is larger than that.

Bulleted List

Do you sometimes get tired of the UL tag?
Want some new bullets? Create your own!
Here's a small table to do it with:

```
<TABLE>
    <TR><TD><IMG SRC="bull1.gif">
        <TD> Each item in the list can
be either very, very long; meandering
with interminably circumlocutory rumi-
nations,
    <TR><TD><IMG SRC="bull1.gif">
        <TD> Or they can be short.
    <TR><TD><IMG SRC="bull1.gif">
        <TD> To the point.
    <TR><TD><IMG SRC="bull1.gif">
        <TD> Succinct.
</TABLE>
```

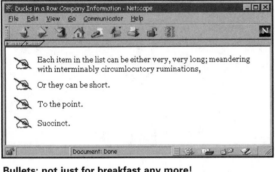

Bullets: not just for breakfast any more!

Center an Object on the Page

Here's a simple table for centering an object
both vertically and horizontally on the page.
This technique is really useful for a splash
screen ("entrance tunnel" in web-speak).

```
<TABLE WIDTH="100%" HEIGHT="100%">
    <TR VALIGN="MIDDLE"
ALIGN="CENTER"><TD>
        <A HREF="home.html">
<IMG SRC="ducky.gif" BORDER="0"></A>
</TABLE>
```

Keep your hands and arms inside the vehicle...

Vertical Rules

Here's a technique for making vertical rules by using a table. The advantage of this technique is that the line will automatically extend to the height of the text. There are other methods for creating vertical rules using the HR tag or a single-pixel GIF, but those techniques do not automatically fill the space. Another advantage the table method has over the GIF method is that it does not require an extra file to download.

```
<BODY BGCOLOR=" #FFFFCC">

<TABLE CELLSPACING=" 10" CELLPADDING=" 0"
BORDER=" 0">
   <TR VALIGN=" TOP"><TD>

     <P>
     We have seen several ways to make
vertical rules, all of which must use
a table, and most of which also use
another element—like a single-pixel
GIF—that adds bandwidth and is prone
to problems.

   <!— this cell is the vertical rule —
>
   <TD BGCOLOR=" Black" WIDTH=" 1"><BR>
   <TD>

     <P>
     This technique uses a one-pixel-
wide table cell, with a dark background
color for the rule itself. It's low
in calories and Good-Webkeeping&reg;
Approved!

</TABLE>
```

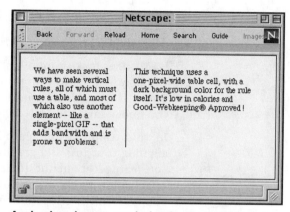

A simple, elegant, vertical rule made from a few recycled electrons.

This technique uses a single-pixel-wide table cell with a dark background for the rule itself. As a side effect of it being a table cell, the rule will automatically grow or shrink to the size of the table no matter how the user's browser is configured, which ensures that it will always extend to the height of the tallest column.

9

▶ chapter nine summary

Alignment

HTML does make it more difficult to align your work than you may be used to with print or other multimedia work. But it is possible to make great-looking web pages if you understand the tools at your disposal.

In this chapter, you learned a lot of techniques for aligning your text and graphics, but even more valuable, you learned about the tools at your disposal. Let your imagination guide you a little, and you will find a lot of opportunity buried in the limitations of HTML.

In the next chapter, we'll talk more about text, type, and the options you have for controlling typography on the web.

"It isn't writing at all, it's typing."
—Truman Capote, 1959

Typography
overcoming the limits

▶ **contents**

html-based typography
web fonts
font embedding
leading techniques

Typography is an incredibly powerful visual design medium, but good typography requires much more control than HTML easily affords. HTML is about display flexibility and cross-platform distribution of information. Typography is about precise control and variety. This chapter will clue you in to the many techniques available to trick and coerce HTML into generating pages with typographic control.

There's a lot of change afoot in the web type world. We'll examine some of the different web typog-raphy options—from HTML tags and attributes, to using images that contain bitmapped type treatments, to new font embedding proposals.

Typography

Limited Choices

Until now, most web publishers and designers have lived in a chocolate-and-vanilla typographical world. Web browsers have defaulted to using two basic typefaces: a proportional-spaced serif font for standard text and a monospaced (or fixed-space) font for code.

A serif is the small stroke (sometimes called the fiddly bit) at the end of the main strokes of letterforms.

Sans serif fonts have no serifs (sans means "without" in French).

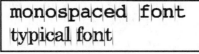

Monospaced fonts are typefaces in which each character takes the same amount of width. Standard typefaces have varying widths.

Welcome to Ducks in a Row Online!

This example depicts the default serif font display in Netscape Navigator 4.0 on a Macintosh.

Welcome to Ducks in a Row Online

This example depicts a monospaced font—also typical of the generic web.

Generic type on web pages is the easiest form of typography to program and view, so we will first focus on HTML defaults for creating typographic effects on the web.

HTML Type Versus Graphical Type

There are basically two kinds of typographical elements on the web (or the printed page, for that matter): body type and headline type. Body type, often referred to as body copy, composes the bulk of the written text. Body type is typically smaller and contains the majority of the written content of a web page. Headline type is typically larger and is used to quickly draw the viewer's eye, help define a page break, and/or organize multiple ideas.

This example demonstrates the difference between body and headline type.

You can make body and headline type a couple of different ways on the web. The first way we'll examine involves using HTML's specialized font tags and attributes.

HTML-Based Typography

The advantages of using HTML for most body-type needs are obvious. First of all, the memory and download time required for using native text is much lower than that used for graphics. Many sites are text-intensive, and using HTML-based type is the only choice to present large quantities of written information in a timely and efficient manner.

The following examples demonstrate how to use type tags.

Headings: A few ways to size type.

```
<H3>Welcome to Ducks in a Row!</H3>
<H4>Welcome to Ducks in a Row!</H4>
<H5>Welcome to Ducks in a Row!</H5>
```

> ### Welcome to Ducks In A Row!
>
> ## Welcome to Ducks In A Row!
>
> #### Welcome to Ducks In A Row!

Bold: Two ways to make type bold.

```
<P> Rubber <B>STAMPS</B>
<P> Rubber <STRONG>STAMPS</STRONG>
```

> Rubber **STAMPS**
>
> Rubber **STAMPS**

Italics: Two ways to italicize type.

```
<P> Rubber <I>STAMPS</I>
<P> Rubber <EM>STAMPS</EM>
```

> Rubber *STAMPS*
>
> Rubber *STAMPS*

▶ note

More on Typographic Tags

Are you wondering why there are two tags that do the same thing for bold and italic? Although they may appear to be the same tag disguised with different names, they do not actually do the same thing. Here is the difference...

The B tag tells the browser to display the text in a bold face, and the I tag tells it to display the text in an italicized face.

The STRONG tag tells the browser that this text should be read in a strong voice. For visual browsers, that usually means to use a boldfaced type. For an audio browser (perhaps for the blind), it tells the browser to speak the text in a stronger voice, louder, deeper, and more forcefully. Likewise, the EM tag tells the browser to emphasize that part of the text, perhaps with a raised pitch in the voice. EM text is normally rendered in italics on a visual browser.

We recommend that you use STRONG and EM tags where possible, so your pages are more accessible to the visually impaired.

Preformatting: Preformatted text usually shows up in Courier or monospaced type, unless the end user's font preferences have been changed (more on this later.) When you use the PRE tag, the formatting appears exactly as you type it. Here's the code.

```
<PRE>      Rubber STAmPs are
c     o    l
check
out                       [ !]

our


selection..............</PRE>
```

```
              Rubber STAmPs are
c     o    l
check
out                       [ !]

our


selection..............
```

Blinking Text: Use with caution! Many end viewers find this tag to be very annoying.

```
<BLINK> flash news!</BLINK>
```

Note: The blinking tag cannot be viewed in a book since it is a dynamic effect. To check out this example, open the blink.html file from the chap10 folder of the <chd2> CD-ROM. For a refreshingly artistic use of this tag, check out http://www.jodi.org.

Changing Font Sizes: Font sizes can be changed by using the two tags, <FONT SIZE> and </FONT>. To see a list of the different sizes and how they will appear in your browser, visit:

http://ncdesign.kyushuid.ac.jp/html/Normal/font.html

Here's how it works:

```
Do you <FONT SIZE=5>like</FONT> your
rubber stamps?
```

Do you **like** your rubber stamps?

Caps and Small Caps: Here's the code for caps and small caps.

```
<FONT SIZE=4>C</FONT>APS
<FONT SIZE=4>F</FONT>UN
```

CAPS FUN

Small Caps: Use the following for small caps.

```
<FONT SIZE=1>SMALL CAPS </FONT>
<BR>REGULAR CAPS
```

SMALL CAPS
REGULAR CAPS

Centering Text: Text can be centered by using the CENTER tag. Use the following code.

```
<CENTER>
I'm in the middle...
</CENTER>
```

I'm in the middle...

HTML Font Choices

Chances are, the person looking at your web page is using the default settings for whatever browser he or she is viewing the page from. Most browsers default to using a Times Roman font. We've seen sites that include instructions to the viewer to change their default font to some other typeface. We wish them luck! We know very few web navigators who would take the time to change their settings to see an individual page. If you want your HTML type to be something other than Times Roman, don't count on asking your viewer to change his or her web browser settings as a fool-proof method. In fact, we would imagine an extremely low percentage of viewers would actually act on the suggestion. As an alternative, try the FONT FACE tag described next.

Font Face Attribute

If you want your audience to see your body copy in a font other than their default font settings, you can use a relatively new attribute to the FONT tag, which is written as FONT FACE.

The FONT FACE element enables you to specify which font your text will be displayed in. The catch is that your end user must have the font you specify installed in their system. There is no danger in using this tag, however, because if they don't have the requested font, the browser will use their default font settings. They are no worse off than if you hadn't used <FONT FACE> in the first place!

Here is some sample code which demonstrates how to use FONT FACE.

```
<FONT FACE=" helvetica, arial"> TESTING,
</FONT> one, two, three
```

> TESTING, one, two, three

Notice that two fonts were specified in the above example. This simply tells the browser to try Helvetica first, and if that's not found, try Arial. You can list as many alternatives as you want here. If it can't find any of them, it will just use the default font.

To add size variation, add the size attribute:

```
<FONT FACE="helvetica, arial" SIZE=5>
TESTING, </FONT> one, two, three
```

> TESTING, one, two, three

To change the color, add the color attribute:

```
<FONT FACE="helvetica, arial" SIZE=5
color=" #CC3366"> TESTING,
</FONT> one, two, three
```

> TESTING, one, two, three

> ▶ **note**
>
> ### Experiment with Type
>
> Open the ducks.txt file from the chap10 folder of the <chd2> CD-ROM. It's an example of some different type treatments based on what's been covered so far. Try your hand at creating a variation on this theme, incorporating some of the tags and attributes we've just reviewed.

Which Fonts?

If you choose to use FONT FACE in your HTML, you might be curious to know which native fonts ship on Macs and Windows.

PC	Mac
Arial	Helvetica
Courier New	Courier
Times New Roman	Times

Newer versions of Windows 95 ship with two other very special and wonderful fonts called Verdana and Georgia (see the section on these font families later in this chapter).

Microsoft has made a huge effort to increase the number of font styles by offering a free web fonts package for Mac and Windows owners to download:

http://www.microsoft.com/typography/fontpack/default.htm

Even though Microsoft offers the free web fonts package to Mac and Windows users, the odds are most of your web audience won't know about the offer or take the time to install fonts that don't ship on their system. For that reason, it's safest to go with the basic fonts that ship with every Mac and Windows. Still, there's no harm in requesting a font that your end user doesn't have, because the worst penalty is they'll see your text in their default font setting.

Web Type Blues

Although we often think of the web as a graphical medium, most of the information we see is in text. In fact, most of the information available throughout human history is text. The ability to read and write is probably right up there with the domestication of the cat as one of the top ten hallmarks of civilization.

In the past few hundred years, the art of typography has made tremendous strides. The pioneering work of typographic artists such as Johannes Gutenberg, Claude Garamond, William Caslon, Eric Gill, and Jan Tschichold have contributed to the advance of civilization by making our text more readable and more enjoyable to read. Yet all that progress is in danger of being rendered worthless as the information age finally fulfills its promise of delivering the combined knowledge of humanity to our collective desktop in a poorly rasterized version of Times Roman.

One problem with type on the web is that the typefaces available were designed for print, not screen delivery. To look good on the screen, fonts should be hinted (extra information about how to display them at lower resolutions), have enough space between the letters, and have enough of an x-height (the height of a lowercase "x" relative to a capital "X") to be readable at the smaller sizes. These criteria are often very different from the criteria used in designing fonts for print.

Digital type is generally not well hinted for the screen. Letters often touch each other, making them hard to read, especially in very small sizes (9 pt. and below). Serifs help readability when printed at high resolution, but actually interfere with readability on the screen. Italics are even more problematic and are almost illegible in many sizes and on many platforms.

If we are going to get a wider range of choices for type on the web, it's not just a matter of being able to display different fonts—it's a matter of creating fonts from the ground up that are designed for the screen. Microsoft has taken a leadership role in this endeavor by hiring renowned type designer Matthew Carter (ITC Galliard, Snell Roundhand, Charter, and Bell Centennial, the font used in phone books) to develop two screen-based font families for web use.

Verdana and Georgia

Matthew Carter's first two fonts for Microsoft, Verdana and Georgia, are part of a larger web font library that Microsoft distributes for free (http://www.microsoft.com/typography/web/fonts/). Looking at the differences between these font families and the default font families offers a primer on which features work better for screen-based typography. Georgia and Verdana were designed with a larger x-height (the height of the lowercase letter "x"). Letter combinations such as "fi," "fl," and "ff" were designed clearly so they do not touch; uppercase characters are a pixel taller than their lowercase counterparts at key screen sizes to add extra readability. The spacing between characters is much looser, making it easier to scan quickly.

Compare Georgia to Times New Roman. Georgia reads beautifully, even at small sizes.

Compare Verdana to MS Sans. Verdana reads beautifully, even at small sizes.

It took Matthew Carter two years to create these typefaces, for which he was probably paid handsomely. By giving these fonts away, Microsoft is doing both a service and a disservice to the web community. On one hand, the community gets immediate use of these sorely-needed fonts (and an excellent example of how to design fonts for screen-use). On the other hand, by giving away the fonts, they are making it much more difficult—perhaps impossible—for other font designers who don't have the resources of a multi-billion dollar corporation to practice their craft and sell their fonts to this lucrative market.

Arial

Ducks in a Row

From the inspired partnership of Laurel Dekker and Joan Farber, comes a unique concept in rubber stamping. Our original designs created by Joan Farber, an internationally recognized illustrator, are unlike anything found in the stamp market today.

Joan Farber is a free-lance illustrator, designer, fine artist and teacher, who has done work for such notable companies as American Express, CBS Records, Redken, MCI, Cosmopolitan, Playboy and Vogue Magazines. With her early roots as a fashion illustrator, Joan has developed a style of illustration which has become popular in recent years, utilizing a skillfully calligraphic brush stroke which brings an elegance and sophistication to any image.

Because the style of art throughout the catalog is consistent, any of the designs may be used together side by side or superimposed, making the possibilities for personal expression boundless.

You will find designs in our catalog which cover a a vast array of categories, from floral images to humor, holiday stamps, border designs and decorative imagery for all around use.. You, as the stamping artist will be the one to create original art works from these designs, and nothing pleasures us more than to see the beautiful and original ways in which our designs are being used.

Throughout the catalog you will find some helpful hints on some of the usages and techniques to enjoy your stamps, but we're sure that you as the stamping artist can teach us a thing or two! One thing for certain, the possibilities are endless!

Verdana

Ducks in a Row

From the inspired partnership of Laurel Dekker and Joan Farber, comes a unique concept in rubber stamping. Our original designs created by Joan Farber; an internationally recognized illustrator, are unlike anything found in the stamp market today.

Joan Farber is a free-lance illustrator, designer, fine artist and teacher, who has done work for such notable companies as American Express, CBS Records, Redken, MCI, Cosmopolitan, Playboy and Vogue Magazines. With her early roots as a fashion illustrator, Joan has developed a style of illustration which has become popular in recent years, utilizing a skillfully calligraphic brush stroke which brings an elegance and sophistication to any image.

Because the style of art throughout the catalog is consistent, any of the designs may be used together side by side or superimposed, making the possibilities for personal expression boundless.

You will find designs in our catalog which cover a a vast array of categories, from floral images to humor, holiday stamps, border designs and decorative imagery for all around use.. You, as the stamping artist will be the one to create original art works from these designs, and nothing pleasures us more than to see the beautiful and original ways in which our designs are being used.

Throughout the catalog you will find some

Times

Ducks in a Row

From the inspired partnership of Laurel Dekker and Joan Farber comes a unique concept in rubber stamping. Our original designs created by Joan Farber an internationally recognized illustrator are unlike anything found in the stamp market today

Joan Farber is a free-lance illustrator, designer, fine artist and teacher, who has done work for such notable companies as American Express, CBS Records, Redken, MCI, Cosmopolitan, Playboy and Vogue Magazines With her early roots as a fashion illustrator, Joan has developed a style of illustration which has become popular in recent years, utilizing a skillfully calligraphic brush stroke which brings an elegance and sophistication to any image

Because the style of art throughout the catalog is consistent, any of the designs may be used together side by side or superimposed, making the possibilities for personal expression boundless

You will find designs in our catalog which cover a a vast array of categories, from floral images to humor, holiday stamps, border designs and decorative imagery for all around use You, as the stamping artist will be the one to create original art works from these designs, and nothing pleasures us more than to see the beautiful and original ways in which our designs are being used

Throughout the catalog you will find some helpful hints on some of the usages and techniques to enjoy your stamps, but we're sure that you as the stamping artist can teach us a thing or two One thing for certain, the possibilities are endless

Georgia

Ducks in a Row

From the inspired partnership of Laurel Dekker and Joan Farber comes a unique concept in rubber stamping. Our original designs created by Joan Farber an internationally recognized illustrator are unlike anything found in the stamp market today

Joan Farber is a free-lance illustrator, designer fine artist and teacher who has done work for such notable companies as American Express CBS Records Redken MCI Cosmopolitan Playboy and Vogue Magazines With her early roots as a fashion illustrator, Joan has developed a style of illustration which has become popular in recent years, utilizing a calligraphic brush stroke which brings an elegance and sophistication to any image

Because the style of art throughout the catalog is consistent any of the designs may be used together side by side or superimposed making the possibilities for personal expression boundless

You will find designs in our catalog which cover a a vast array of categories from floral images to humor holiday stamps border designs and decorative imagery for all around use You as the stamping artist will be the one to create original art works from these designs and nothing pleasures us more than to see the utiful and original ways in which our designs being used

Throughout the catalog you will find some helpful hints of the usages and techniques to enjoy your stamps but we're tha as the stam artist can teach us or One thing for certain the possibilities are endless

Compare Arial to Verdana and Times to Georgia, and we think you'll agree that the Matthew Carter's fonts are superior. His fonts print nicely as well.

Embedding Options

Wouldn't it be cool if you could specify a certain font and have it automatically download and apply itself to your page without the end user needing to install anything? Netscape and Microsoft are both offering "font embedding" in version 4.0 of their browser software releases.

Unfortunately for us, Netscape and Microsoft are duking it out in the type arena and are each offering different embedded font technologies. It makes a web designer's job very difficult to have to make decisions between which specification to support.

TrueDoc

Netscape is supporting TrueDoc font files, which were developed by Bitstream, a major supplier of digital type (http://www.bitstream. com). The idea is that fonts will be downloaded along with an HTML page, the same way as GIF and JPEG images are. A browser that can display TrueDoc font files will render the fonts on the screen (or on a printer). Browsers that cannot display TrueDoc fonts will use alternative fonts on the user's system.

If you are creating web pages and want to use TrueDoc dynamic fonts, you will need a TrueDoc-enabled authoring tool that will generate a PFR (Portable Font Resource) file that the browser can link to using FONT FACE or CSS (Cascading Style Sheets). TrueDoc requires that fonts are generated with a CSR (Character Shape Recorder) and rendered with a CSP (Character Shape Player). Many manufacturers of authoring tools are licensing this technology, including Macromedia, Corel, Sausage, SoftQuad, and InfoAccess.

TrueType Embedding and OpenType

Microsoft was originally pushing TrueType Embedding (http://www.microsoft.com/truetype/ embed/embed.htm) for its Explorer browser, then switched gears and publicized a newly formed alliance with former type competitor Adobe, and started promoting a new format jointly developed called OpenType(http://www.adobe. com/asn/developer/opentype/). Since OpenType isn't available yet, Microsoft was only able to offer TrueType embedding when this chapter was written.

TrueType Embedding does not support Type1 fonts, the more popular format among graphic designers, which utilizes PostScript. Unfortunately, tools that support authoring TrueType Embedding are Windows-only, making Mac developers (still the highest population of web designers) unable to author this type of content.

Aliasing Versus Anti-Aliasing

Most digital artists prefer the way anti-aliasing looks, but anti-aliasing is not always the best technique for screen-based typography.

Very small type actually looks worse and quite mushy if it's anti-aliased. If you look at other examples of very small type that is displayed on computer screens (HTML type, the type on your computer desktop, and the type in a word processor), you will see that none are anti-aliased. This is because very small type sizes (12 pt. and below) do not look good anti-aliased.

Anti-aliasing at small point sizes tends to look mushy and is hard to read.	Type at small point sizes (12 pt and below) looks better without anti-aliasing

This anti-aliased small type looks bad.   **This aliased HTML type looks much better.**

▶ warning

TrueDoc Anti-Aliasing Defaults

We find it difficult to read anti-aliased fonts at small sizes, and this appears to be a built-in feature of the TrueDoc font embedding technology. Good hinting for raster displays will help alleviate this problem. We look forward to more typefaces becoming available with good hinting for computer displays. It's also rumored that future versions of TrueDoc will allow anti-aliasing to be disabled by the end user viewing a web page.

▶ tip

Resources for Typography

Digital Type Design Guide: The Page Designer's Guide to Working with Type
Authors: Sean Cavanaugh and Ken Oyer
Publisher: Hayden Books
ISBN: 1568301901

The Non-Designer's Type Book
Author: Robin Williams
Publisher: PeachPit Press
ISBN: 0201353679

Stop Stealing Sheep & Find Out How Type Works
Authors: Erik Spiekermann and E.M. Ginger
Publisher: Adobe Press
ISBN: 0672485435

▶ definitions

Type Standards

Your eyes might be glazing over just about now with all these standards and document types. Here's a handy definition list:

OpenType: A standard for font embedding established by Microsoft and Adobe.

TrueDoc: A standard for font embedding established by Bitstream.

TrueType: A type format developed by Apple as an alternative to PostScript for computer di plays.

Type1: A type format developed by Adobe for print usage.

PostScript: A page description language developed for printing type and graphics.

Graphics-Based Typography

Using graphics instead of HTML for text is where you get the chance to flash your type design aesthetic for the world to see. You'll be able to use any font your heart desires and add special effects to it, such as drop shadows, glows, and blurs. A great advantage to using this technique is that your end users will not have to own the font you used or have it installed on their system. Because it's a graphic, it shows up like any other graphic, regardless of what system your site is viewed on.

Earlier chapters demonstrated some techniques we recommend you use with your text-based graphics. Using transparency and solid colors that match the background color of your page are two processes in particular that can be employed in combination to achieve some of the effects described here.

The HTML to Place Your Text Graphics

Placing graphics on a web page is addressed in depth in Chapter 7, *"Bullets & Rules,"* and Chapter 14 *"Navigation."* The basic way to insert a graphic on a page is to use the IMG tag. Here's how to put the drop shadow artwork, created earlier, on a page.

```
<HTML>
<IMG SRC="dropshad.jpeg">
</HTML>
```

If you want to link the drop shadow image to another source, add an anchor tag to the above image like this:

```
<HTML>
<A HREF="http://www.domain.com">
<IMG SRC="dropshad.jpeg"></A>
</HTML>
```

See Chapter 5, *"Clickable,"* for more about combining links with graphics.

Leading Techniques

Leading is the term used to describe the space between lines of type. In professional typesetting circles, programs like PageMaker and QuarkXPress allow you to easily specify leading settings. Raw HTML doesn't have any leading control. Ah, but there are tricks, and we shall share them with you!

Trick 1: Use the paragraph tag (see leadingp.html inside the chap10 folder of the <chd2> CD-ROM):

```
<HTML>
<HEAD>
<TITLE>Paragraph Leading</TITLE>
</HEAD>
<BODY BGCOLOR=" #ffffff">
<CENTER>
<IMG SRC=" logo.jpg" WIDTH=" 419"
HEIGHT=" 108">
<P><FONT FACE=GEORGIA SIZE=+1>Ducks
In A Row products represents a unique
concept in
<P> rubber stamping.
Our original designs, created by
<P> internationally recognized
illustrator Joan Farber, are
<P>unlike anything found in the
stamp market today.</FONT></CENTER>
</BODY>
</HTML>
```

Ducks In A Row products represents a unique concept in

rubber stamping. Our original designs, created by

internationally recognized illustrator Joan Farber, are

unlike anything found in the stamp market today.

Trick 2: You can use the single-pixel GIF trick.

- Create a document in Photoshop that is 1 pixel by 1 pixel. Make it transparent or color it the same as your background page. Alternatively, you can use the white.gif file from the chap10 folder of the <chd2> CD-ROM.

- Using the VSPACE attribute, specify your leading with pixels. **Note:** You can experiment with changing the VSPACE attribute in the singlep.html file from the chap10 folder on the <chd2> CD-ROM.

```
<HTML>
<HEAD>
<TITLE>Paragraph Leading</TITLE>
</HEAD>
<BODY BGCOLOR=" #ffffff">
<CENTER>
<IMG SRC=" logo.jpg" WIDTH=" 419"
HEIGHT=" 108"><P><FONT FACE=GEORGIA
SIZE=+1>Ducks In A Row products
represent a unique,<BR><IMG
SRC=" white.gif" VSPACE=10>
concept in rubber stamping. Our
original designs, created
<BR><IMG SRC=" white.gif" VSPACE=10>
by internationally recognized
illustrator Joan Farber, are
<BR><IMG SRC=" white.gif" VSPACE=10>
unlike anything found in the stamp
market today.</FONT></CENTER>
</BODY>
</HTML>
```

Ducks In A Row products represent a unique,
concept in rubber stamping. Our original designs, created
by internationally recognized illustrator Joan Farber, are
unlike anything found in the stamp market today.

Trick 3: Use the PRE tag for preformatted text. Note: The pre.html file is located inside the chap10 folder of the <chd2> CD-ROM.

```
<HTML>
<HEAD>
<TITLE>Paragraph Leading</TITLE>
</HEAD>
<BODY BGCOLOR="#ffffff"><CENTER>
<IMG SRC="logo.jpg" WIDTH="419"
HEIGHT="108"> <PRE><FONT FACE=GEORGIA
SIZE=+1>
Ducks In A Row products represent a
unique concept in rubber stamping. Our
original designs created by Joan
Farber, internationally recognized
illustrator,  are unlike anything found
in the stamp market today.

</FONT></CENTER>
</BODY>
</HTML>
```

Trick 4: Use a graphic and set the leading in a program like Photoshop. The following HTML file is called pshop.html and is located inside the chap10 folder of the <chd2> CD-ROM.

```
<HTML>
<HEAD>
<TITLE>Photoshop Leading</TITLE>
</HEAD>
<BODY BGCOLOR=white>
<CENTER>
<IMG SRC="logo.jpg" WIDTH="419"
HEIGHT="108">
<BR><IMG SRC="lead.gif" ALT="Ducks In
A Row represents a unique concept in
rubber stamping. Our original designs
created by Joan Farber, internationally
recognized illustrator, are unlike
anything found in the stamp market
today.">
<BR CLEAR=ALL>
</CENTER>
</BODY>
</HTML>
```

Ducks In A Row products represent a unique concept
in rubber stamping. Our original designs created
by Joan Farber, internationally recognized illustrator,
are unlike anything found in the stamp market today.

Ducks In A Row products represent a unique concept
in rubber stamping. Our original designs created
by Joan Farber, internationally recognized illustrator,
are unlike anything found in the stamp market today.

There are some basic disadvantages to each of these techniques. The first two, using paragraphs and single-pixel GIFs between lines of text, assume that users have not changed their default font size (some people make it much larger, especially if they have vision problems), and have their browser windows open as wide as yours. If either of those assumptions are not true, your line breaks will be different and you may end up with widows, lines of text with only one word on them.

The example that uses the PRE tag assumes that the browser will allow you to change the font inside the PRE container. Some browsers don't allow that.

Finally, the example that uses a graphic for the text is inefficient. Make sure that your graphic is as small as possible (in terms of file size) so that it will download quickly. Of course, users who use text-only browsers, or have graphic loading turned off, will not see your text at all. Be sure to use ALT text with this one, as we have done in our example pshop.html, located in the chap10 folder of the <chd2> CD-ROM.

▶ note

Unreliable Leading Methods

Bill is probably not the only person who hates HTML leading techniques that introduce space by manually breaking the lines of text. He recommends that you avoid them if at all possible and use CSS instead. (See Chapter 13, *"Style Sheets,"* to learn how to lead with CSS.)

When you use the techniques presented here, you will probably go to a lot of trouble to get the lines to break just where you want them to. Then, if all goes well, you will put your masterpiece of faux typesetting up on the web for all to see, and herein lies the problem.

Type on the web is not all the same size. Variations in screen sizes, operating systems, browser settings, and available fonts all conspire to change the actual size of the type displayed on the screen. The end result is that your lines will break in other places, and you will end up with something that looks like the image below and never know it!

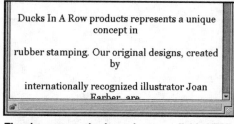

The above example shows how unreliable HTML leading is. It manually breaks your lines of text.

▶ note

Type Facts

Upper and Lowercase: Originally, lead type was kept in wooden "type cases." The capital letters were typically kept in the "upper case" because they were used less frequently, and the "lower case" was used for the more common small letters.

Leading: Indicates the amount of vertical space between lines of text. This spacing was created by inserting lead slugs in between lines of type. The term remains with us, even though lead type is hardly used anymore.

Cold Type: A photographic process of typesetting, developed before electronic typesetting.

Hot Type: Original lead-type presses referred to setting "hot" type. The lead had to be hot for the letterform casts to be made.

Electronic Typesetting: Setting type with computers and typesetting machines that render the type via software instead of photographic or physical methods.

Indent Techniques

Creating indents in HTML is most often done with tables. The following file is called indtable.html and is located inside the chap10 folder of the <chd2> CD-ROM:

```
<HTML>
<HEAD>
    <TITLE>Table Indents</TITLE>
</HEAD>
<BODY BGCOLOR="ffffff">
<IMG SRC="logo.jpg">
<TABLE WIDTH="450" BORDER="0"
HEIGHT="129">
<TR>
<TD WIDTH="124" HEIGHT="105"></TD>
<TD WIDTH="335">Ducks In A Row products
represent a unique concept in
<P> rubber stamping. Our original
designs, created by
<P> internationally recognized
illustrator Joan Farber,  are
<P> unlike anything found in the
stamp market today.</TD></TR>
</TABLE>
</BODY>
</HTML>
```

You can also create indents by using invisible graphics or single-pixel GIFs and the HSPACE attribute. The following file is called gifindent.html and is located inside the chap10 folder of the <chd2> CD-ROM:

```
<HTML>
<HEAD>
    <TITLE>Table Indents</TITLE>
</HEAD>
<BODY BGCOLOR="ffffff">
<IMG SRC="logo.jpg">
<P>
<IMG SRC="white.gif" HSPACE=45>Ducks
In A Row products represent a unique
<P><IMG SRC="white.gif" HSPACE=45>
concept in rubber stamping. Our
original designs,
<P><IMG SRC="white.gif" HSPACE=45>
created by internationally recognized
illustrator Joan Farber, are
<P><IMG SRC="white.gif"
HSPACE=45>unlike anything found in
the stamp market today.
</BODY>
</HTML>
```

Digital Font Foundries

Today there are tens of thousands of PostScript and TrueType fonts available to personal computer users. It's a great benefit to be able to view and order fonts online, especially during those late nights when you're designing something that's due the next day and you need a specific font you don't yet own. If you're looking for new fonts, check out these URLs:

House Industries

http://www.houseind.com/

Letraset Online

http://www.letraset.com/letraset/

Handwriting Fonts

http://www.execpc.com/~adw/

Fonthead Design

http://www.fonthead.com

Emigre

http://www.emigre.com

Interesting Typography-Based URLs

Razorfish's Amazing Site: Typographic

Teaches the principles of type using hypertext at its best. Oh, and a little Shockwave, animated GIF action, plus an amazing type glossary!

http://www.subnetwork.com/typo/
http://www.subnetwork.com/typo/glossary/

Typofile

An online magazine devoted to type techniques and technology. This site has lots of great tutorials and essays about typography.

http://www.will-harris.com/type.htm

Paul Baker Typographic, Inc.

A short presentation on basic typography that includes the use of spacing, leading, choosing a typeface, etc.

http://www.pbtweb.com/typostyl/typostyl.htm

Just van Rossum and Erik van Blokland

Acclaimed type designers work from their homes in The Hague (Netherlands). Their goal is to create typefaces that do more than the usual fonts. They create animations, music, typography, web sites, and graphic design also. Be sure to read their rant on embedded fonts.

http://www.letterror.com/LTR_About.html

Type-Centric Bookstore
Educational articles.

http://www.fontsite.com/

Type Glossary
Excellent (and funny).

http://www.microsoft.com/truetype/glossary/content.htm

▶ **chapter ten summary**

Typography

Typography on the web is challenging because controls that typographers want are nonexistent in HTML. This chapter covers a few good tricks that will help you break through the limits of HTML:

- HTML offers limited control over typography. Even so, it's important to know all the tags and learn to combine them for visually interesting type design.

- You can use images of type on web pages, just like images of anything else. This helps break up the predictability of HTML type.

- Using the PRE tag provides you with more control over typographic spacing. It enables you to create interesting alignment.

- Visit digital type foundries for a rich selection of fonts and type tips.

"Reality leaves a lot to the imagination."
—John Lennon

Planning
ideas and metaphors

▶ **contents**

mind maps

determining goals

determining navigation

determining art direction

metaphors

flowcharting

You may be wondering why we're talking about site planning in the middle of this book instead of at the beginning. We've waited until now to offer this chapter, because we think it's important for you to understand some of the capabilities of HTML and web design before trying to figure out how to storyboard and plan a site. It's hard to plan something you've never done before.

This chapter walks you through the planning and art direction process for the Ducks In A Row sample site profiled in this book. It documents some of the methods we used when planning this and other web sites. As you read this chapter, keep in mind that there is no one "correct" or "right" way to plan a web site. As with most things, there are many ways to approach the same task. Each site is different, and different methods and rules will apply on an individual basis. Our goal in this chapter is to share the way we have worked in order to help you develop your own site planning techniques.

Planning

Looking Ahead

Once you've finished learning what this book has to teach, take some time to plan your own web site before you get started. There are many approaches to building a web site, some more effective than others. Some people prefer to launch an HTML editor and start making pages, without thinking through the site structure beforehand. Others start a small web site, not realizing that it might grow into something much bigger in the future. Creating a web site is different from any other kind of publishing, and most likely you've never planned for anything like this before.

Organizing Your Site

One of the features of the World Wide Web that makes it so attractive is how easy it is for users to jump from one train of thought to another as they surf the web. One could say that the disorganization of the web is what makes it work!

How do you organize a web? Indeed, how do you organize something that by its very nature is unorganized? In 1974, psychologist and mathematician Tony Buzan (then editor of *Mensa* magazine) invented a method of note-taking called Mind Maps as a means of organizing another inherently unorganized web of information, the human brain.

Mind Maps

In mind mapping, you start taking notes on a subject in the middle of a page by writing a word or two that represents the overall theme of your notes. Then you add, in a pattern radiating outward from the center, key words and pictures that represent related ideas. You connect each thought to the thought that preceded it with lines or arrows.

Mind mapping techniques are very valuable in designing and organizing web sites. In fact, there are those who claim that the concept of hypertext was based on the concept of mind mapping. All hyperbole aside, the two concepts are very similar.

We find mind mapping techniques useful for generating the first cut of a web site layout. From there, it's easy to refine, expand, and integrate to get the final blueprint for the site.

Below is the mind map we made when we started to lay out the Ducks In A Row web site.

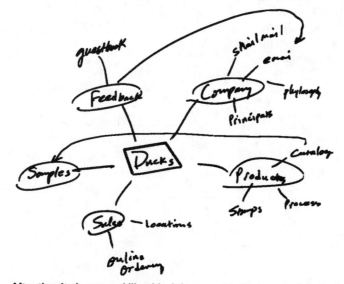

After the site is mapped like this, it becomes easier to organize—both logically and physically—on the server.

▶ **note**

Resources for Getting Organized

Pete Russell
A description of mind maps.
http://www.peterussell.com/mindmap1.html

The Buzan Centre
Mind mapping software.
http://www.buzancentre.com/software.html

Inspiration Software Inc.
A commercial site offering Inspiration 6, another
interesting software tool for organizing thoughts
and developing ideas.
http://www.conceptmapping.com/

Web Navigation: Designing the User Experience
Author: Jennifer Fleming
Editor: Richard Koman
Publisher: O'Reilly & Associates
List Price: $34.95

Ducks In A Row Goals

When we approached the principals at DIAR (Ducks In A Row) with the idea of creating a web site for them, we talked about their goals and how a web site might further those goals. Determining the GOALS of the site is the first stage of web design. Here's what we concluded from these early conversations:

- A web site could be a great way for Ducks In A Row to achieve better visibility, without the expense of advertising in magazines.

- The site could provide a means for potential rubber stamp buyers to locate retail outlets that sell DIAR stamps. We were specifically told not to create an online retail catalog because Ducks In A Row is a wholesaler of rubber stamps; the company does not sell its products at a retail level.

- The site could be an opportunity to promote the retailers that carry DIAR stamps.

- The site could serve an educational purpose—to illustrate the process of making rubber stamps.

- The site could contain a gallery to inspire viewers to make great looking designs with DIAR rubber stamps.

Once we were aware of these goals, we were able to categorize the main content areas of the DIAR site:

- **Our Company:** An area to profile the company and its principals

- **Catalog:** An area to show some of the DIAR stamp catalogs

- **Samples:** A gallery of designs made with DIAR rubber stamps

- **Process:** An area to profile the rubber stamp creation process

- **Retail Locations:** An area on the site where people could locate retail outlets that stock DIAR rubber stamps

Because we didn't want to take up a lot of room with each icon, it was important to settle on one- or two-word descriptions of each navigational element.

Art Direction

Before starting the project, we looked carefully at the existing catalogs and promotional materials (called collateral in marketing-speak) that the Ducks In A Row company had already created. Their catalogs were printed with one color on colored paper, and they provided more elaborate, handmade color samples to their retail outlets for in-store displays. For the web site design, we chose to borrow and expand on the design direction that the company already had set.

We looked first at Ducks In A Row catalogs to get an idea of what their existing design direction was.

We thought the stamps themselves would work well throughout the site as icons and artistic elements. Even though ducks come in a variety of colors, the word "rubber" in rubber stamps and "ducks" from Ducks In A Row made us think of rubber duckies. This triggered the idea to use yellow as a unifying color throughout the site. A bright yellow could be overbearing, so we arrived at a muted yellow color (using the browser-safe color chart) as the dominant color.

To us, these rubber stamps were sophisticated and classy—a departure from typical rubber stamps that might be kitsch or campy. To emphasize the difference between these stamps and other rubber stamp designs, we chose colors that were muted and subdued, rather than bright and saturated.

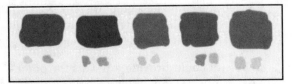

This color chart helped us limit the palette in order to make the site feel unified and consistent. Reddish browns, muted greens, deep blues, and mauves were chosen, because they work well against the light yellow theme. We alternated these color themes throughout the site to add variety while maintaining continuity.

We felt that overt drop shadows and 3D effects, such as beveled buttons and specular highlights, were inappropriate for the subject matter of this site. The stamp designs were flat, so there seemed to be no reason to throw dimensional effects into the artwork.

We added headlines to the pages so that our audience would always know where they were on the site. We chose to work with a classical sans serif font (Gill Sans) and offset it with a handwritten font (Chauncy Snowman) to lend a friendlier, more homemade feeling to the site.

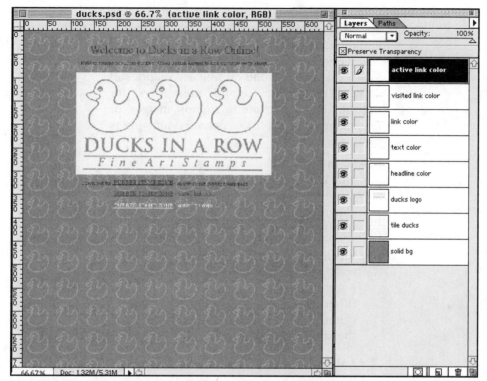

Creating a layered Photoshop document can help you experiment with a design direction and allow you to make multiple versions of a site to show a client.

These decisions were all made in advance of making any artwork. We created a layered Photoshop document that allowed us to try out designs and colors and show them to our client before we went forward with production or went live with the site. This layered document is called ducks.psd and can be found in the chap11 folder of the <chd2> CD-ROM.

Metaphors

It's often helpful when planning a site to draw up a list of metaphors. Webster's dictionary defines metaphor as "a figure of speech in which one thing is spoken of as if it is another." Visual metaphors build on free associations of objects or ideas. Helpful metaphors for web building can relate to sounds, images, or movement. Here's a list of potential metaphors for Ducks In A Row:

- **Sounds**
  quack
  water
  paper folding
  splashing

- **Visual**
  water splashing
  water ripples
  rubber ducks
  yellow
  the actual stamps

- **Animation**
  pond ripples
  stamps animating on and off
  ducks swimming

A list like this can feed you ideas while you create your animations, sounds, rollovers, navigation, and images.

Flowcharting

Flowcharting is a useful way to plan the navigational structure of the site. There are many ways to create a flowchart of a site—from scribbles on a napkin or chalkboard, to index cards, to computer software. Margaret Gould Stewart, creative director at http://www.tripod.com, described her storyboarding process at a web design conference. She uses index cards, each of which represents a page in the site. She spreads the cards out on a table or floor, organizing and reorganizing them to visualize the navigational structure of the site. When she is finished, she gives the same cards to other members of her team to see if they come up with a different structure. This process allows her to get valuable input from others and ensures that all the possible navigation choices have been explored.

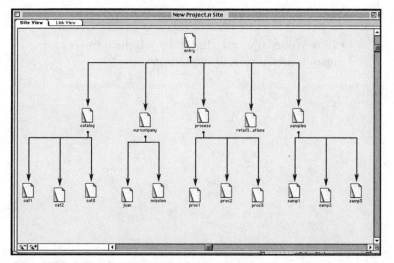

Some HTML editors, such as Adobe GoLive (pictured above) and Macromedia Dreamweaver, help you set up the site structure in flowcharting windows. If you use these products, they automatically generate HTML pages that are linked with the proper hierarchy and can be viewed like this, as a map.

▶ chapter eleven summary

Planning

Planning a site is important to its overall aesthetic continuity and navigational success. This chapter has outlined some of the techniques we use when approaching a new site design.

Here's a handy checklist to follow when planning a site:

- Determine the goals of the site.

- Document the goals and share them with your client and/or partners.

- Identify the different sections of the site.

- Determine the art direction of the site—colors, layout, metaphors, and typefaces.

Organization
absolutely relative

▶ **contents**

site anatomy

absolute URLs

relative URLs

server-side includes

If you are planning a site of any substantial size—with say, 10 or more different files—it's a good idea to organize the site so you can find things when you need to work with them.

It's common to start a web site small, with a couple of .html files and a few .gif files, and then add some here and tack something else on there. Before long you have hundreds of files all in one folder, and you haven't got a clue what they all are!

Some of the files may no longer be in use; some of them may be older versions of files that are still in use.But you don't know, and it doesn't really matter because everything works just fine.

And then the fateful day comes when you save a new file with the name of an old file and poof!, you've got trouble in River City! You thought that was an old version of something, but it was actually a page that you had spent hours getting just right, and now you're going to have to do it all over again!

Keeping it organized can help a lot.

Organization

Simplicity Versus Chaos

Some may argue that it's far simpler to keep everything in one folder, and indeed it is—at least for the person putting it there. But can you also argue that it's easier in the long run? When you come back a year (or even just a week) from now to update that site with 387 different files in one folder, will that be easy? Expedience belies chaos.

On the other hand, let's say you put all the images in one folder called images, all the files for the company information page in a company folder, all the files used for the personal biographies in a folder called people, and so on. Now each folder has a dozen or so files, and it's easier to keep them straight.

Not only does this make the maintenance of the site easier, but it becomes easier to share files—images, for instance—between different parts of the site. This process is only difficult if we start the site without organization in mind. If we start the site with all the files in one folder, then we will have a much harder time getting it organized later.

This is not to say that there is any one right way to organize your site files. What is important is that you decide on a structure that works for you and for anyone else who maintains the site, that you implement that structure from the beginning, and that you stick with that structure. Organization and consistency are the watchwords of a usable site.

What's in a Name?

The location of each object on the World Wide Web can be described with a URL (**U**niform **R**esource **L**ocator). A URL is an address in a specific format that can uniquely identify an individual object on the web.

The purpose of a URL is to describe to a computer precisely how to ask for an object that resides on another computer somewhere on the Net. A URL is like a sophisticated address or phone number, in that it tells your computer exactly where to find that particular object.

The Parts of a URL

A URL has a number of different parts. Referring to the diagram below, you can see that a complete URL can have scheme, host, port, path, parameters, query, and fragment parts. In practice, though, a URL almost never uses all of them at once.

scheme:	//host	:port	/path	:parameters	?query	#fragment

This is the most common form of a URL.

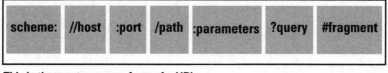

http://www.htmlbook.com/examples/url.html

1   2   3   4

The parts of a URL.

- The first part (http://) is called the **scheme**. That's a fancy way of saying that this is the protocol that the browser will use to ask the server for a file. In this case (as in most), the HTTP protocol will be used to retrieve the object.

- The second part (www.htmlbook.com) is called the **host**. This is the name (or it can be the IP address) of the server (host computer) that holds the object you want. Many web browsers will accept just the host part and connect you to that machine using HTTP (the protocol used by web servers). For example, you could access our site by typing http://www.htmlbook.com, or you could type just the host part, www.htmlbook.com, and most browsers would still find our site. If you use the host-only feature, remember that it is a shortcut on the part of the browser, and is not a proper URL.

- Finally, the last part (/examples/url.html) is the **path** to the object on that particular server. The path consists of directories (or folders) and the file name itself. In this case, the directory is /examples and the file name is url.html. Directories are separated by slashes (/) by convention, probably because that's how you do it on UNIX, and the web was developed on UNIX.

Absolute and Relative URLs

When you specify a URL, such as http://www. host.com/thatpage.html, you are telling the browser everything it needs to know to find that object on the web, including the protocol to use (http), the host to contact (www.host.com), and the absolute (exact) path to the object on that host (/thatpage.html).

There are times, however, when it may be more useful to refer to the location of an object relative to the location of the last object you requested. For example, if a web page needs to refer to a graphic file that will be displayed on the same page, it's useful to use a notation that says "get this other file from the same place (the same server, protocol, folder, etc.) where you got the page that requested that file." That way, when you move the page to another server, or even another folder on the same server, you don't need to update all the URLs in all the HTML files. A relative URL, like newpage.html, is the simplest way to accomplish this goal.

- An **absolute** URL is a complete URL that specifies the exact location of the object on the web, like this:

    http://www.htmlbook.com/examples/url/ url.gif

- A **relative** URL gives the location of the object relative to the location of the page that contains the URL, like this:

    url.gif

Let's look at an example of the code for a page using an absolute URL in context.

```
<HTML>
<HEAD>
<TITLE> URL Example </TITLE>
</HEAD>
<BODY BGCOLOR=white>

<H1> The Parts of a URL </H1>
<IMG SRC="http://www.htmlbook.com/
examples/url.gif">
<P> A URL has a number of different
parts. Referring to the diagram, you
can see that a complete URL can have
scheme, host, port, path, parameters,
query, and fragment parts. In prac-
tice, though, a URL almost never
uses all of them at once.
</BODY>
</HTML>
```

1. Notice the IMG tag, which specifies an image using an absolute (complete) URL. However, it is much more convenient—and more common —to use a relative (partial) URL like this: <IMG SRC="url.gif">

    By definition, the SRC attribute must always contain a URL, but it can be a relative URL. In this case, when the browser sees url.gif, it knows to look in the same folder, on the same server, as where it got the page that contains the URL.

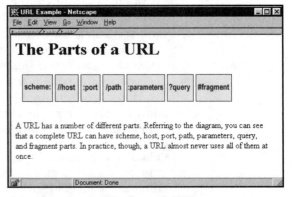

A browser showing The Parts of a URL page.

Paths in Relative URLs

Remember that the part of the URL after the **host** part is called the **path** part. It can include a path of directories that will lead to the specific file that has the object you want.

Paths in a relative URL describe the location of the object on the server in a hierarchical directory structure. Each level of the hierarchy is separated by a slash (/) character in the relative URL. This directory structure is, for all intents and purposes, the same sort of structure as the folders or directories on a Mac, Windows, or UNIX system. Though you may be more accustomed to using a colon (:) or a reverse slash (\) to separate levels of folders in your OS, the concepts involved are the same.

When the browser encounters a relative URL in a file, it uses the location of the HTML file that contains the reference as a base URL. The browser builds a full URL by combining the relative URL with the base URL.

By definition, a base URL must be an absolute URL, including the name of the file at the end. (That's just because the URL specification treats the path part, including the file name, as a single unit.) In practice, however, the file name part is discarded, and the relative URL is attached in its place.

For example, let's use the document at http://www.htmlbook.com/examples/url/ex2.html as a base URL and url.gif as a relative URL:

- **Base URL:** http://www.htmlbook.com/examples/url/ex2.html

- **Relative URL:** url.gif

- **Resulting URL:** http://www.htmlbook.com/examples/url/url.gif

In order to build the resulting URL, the browser first discards the file name part of the base URL, which leaves http://www.htmlbook.com/examples/url/. For the purposes of this discussion, we'll call this the base URL path (there is no official name for it, as the URL specification doesn't deal with this part separately). Then it appends the relative URL, effectively replacing the file name that was just removed. The resulting URL is effectively the concatenation of the base URL—minus the file name—and the relative URL.

Relative URL Examples

In order to help you visualize what happens when you use relative URLs, we've prepared a few examples using two files: a base file called ex2.html and a graphic file, url.gif.

The following diagrams show where the graphic file will be found, using various relative URLs:

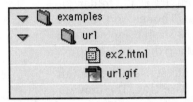

`<IMG SRC="url.gif">` **will find the** url.gif **file in the current** base **folder.**

Base URL:

http://www.htmlbook.com/examples/url/ex2.html

Relative URL:

url.gif

Resulting URL:

http://www.htmlbook.com/examples/url/url.gif

The relative URL is simply pasted onto the base URL path.

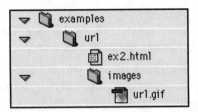

`<IMG SRC="images/url.gif">` **will find the** url.gif **file in the images folder, under the** url **folder.**

Base URL:

http://www.htmlbook.com/examples/url/ex2.html

Relative URL:

images/url.gif

Resulting URL:

http://www.htmlbook.com/examples/url/images/url.gif

The relative URL is simply pasted onto the base URL path.

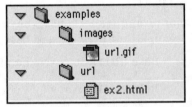

`<IMG SRC="../images/url.gif">` **will find the** url.gif **file in the** images **folder one level above the current folder.**

Base URL:

http://www.htmlbook.com/examples/url/ex2.html

Relative URL:

../images/url.gif

Resulting URL:

http://www.htmlbook.com/examples/images/url.gif

Two dots together in place of a directory name is a special case, meaning "go up one level." If the path begins with two dots (..), the path will start one directory higher than the current one.

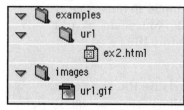

`<IMG SRC="/images/url.gif">` **will find the** url.gif **file in the** images **folder at the root level of the web site.**

Base URL:

http://www.htmlbook.com/examples/url/ex2.html

Relative URL:

/images/url.gif

Resulting URL:

http://www.htmlbook.com/images/url.gif

If the relative URL begins with a slash (/), the entire path part of the base URL is replaced with the relative URL.

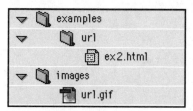

From ex2.html, `<IMG SRC="../../images/url.gif">` **will find the** url.gif **file in the** images **folder two levels above the current folder.**

Base URL:

http://www.htmlbook.com/examples/url/ex2.html

Relative URL:

../../images/url.gif

Resulting URL:

http://www.htmlbook.com/images/url.gif

Taking the (..) concept one step further, (../../) means "go up two directories."

▶ tip

Convert a Relative URL

If you are still a little confused about how relative URLs work, don't despair! Bill wrote a CGI program that converts relative URLs to absolute URLs so that you can get a better feel for how this all works. To use our converter go to http://www.htmlbook.com/examples/url/conv-url.cgi.

Here's how it works:

> **Convert a Relative URL**
>
> Because the resulting URL is derived from a base URL and a relative URL, this program requires both.
>
> Base URL: `http://www.htmlbook.com/examples/url/ex1.html`
>
> Relative URL: `url.gif`
>
> [Convert]   [Start Over]

Step 1: First enter the base and relative URLs in the form fields, and then press **Convert**.

> **Result**
>
> The base URL was: **http://www.htmlbook.com/examples/url/ex1.html**
> The relative URL was: **url.gif**
> The resulting URL is: **http://www.htmlbook.com/examples/url/url.gif**

Step 2: The result shows up on the next page. This program should give you more confidence to use relative URLs in your own pages.

Relative URLs as Links

You can also use relative URLs as links. For example, if your page is at http://www.htmlbook.com/examples/url/ex3.html, you could have a relative link to ex4.html without having to type the entire URL:

```
<A HREF="ex4.html">Over Here!</A>
```

The browser would then apply the rules it uses for relative URLs and treat the link as if you had typed http://www.htmlbook.com/examples/url/ex4.html as a complete URL.

Here's an example that uses a few different types of relative URLs.

```
<HTML>
<HEAD>
<TITLE> Relative URL Link Example </TITLE>
</HEAD>
<BODY BGCOLOR=white>

<H1> Relative URL Links </H1>

<P> This page is at http://www.htmlbook.com/examples/
url/ex3.html
</P>

<TABLE WIDTH=400><TR><TD>
Run your mouse cursor over the links below, and see
what they look like in your status bar. Can you see
how the browser completes the URL for you?
</TABLE>

<UL>
  <LI><A HREF="ex4.html">Over Here!</A> ex4.html
  <LI><A HREF="company/index.html">
Over there.</a> company/index.html
  <LI><A HREF="bios/">Yonder./</a> bios/
  <LI><A HREF="../">Somewhere . . .
</a>   ../
  <LI><A HREF="images/url.gif">. . . else.</A>
images/url.gif
</UL>

<P>
<HR>
&copy; 1997 Lynda and Bill Weinman

</BODY>
```

Below the screen shot of the Relative URL Links page on the next page are separate screen shots of the status line as the cursor is passed over each link. (The status bar shows the full URL for each of the links.) This page is available as http://www.htmlbook.com/examples/url/ex3.html on the <chd2> web site, so you can see it run on your system.

Relative URL Links

This page is at http://www.htmlbook.com/examples/url/ex3.html

Run your mouse cursor over the links below, and see what they look like in your status bar. Can you see how the browser completes the URL for you?

- Over Here! ex4.html
- Over there. company/index.html
- Yonder./ bios/
- Somewhere . . . . ./
- . . . else. images/url.gif

The relative URL links page.

http://www.htmlbook.com/examples/url/ex4.html

http://www.htmlbook.com/examples/url/company/index.html

http://www.htmlbook.com/examples/url/bios/

http://www.htmlbook.com/examples/

http://www.htmlbook.com/examples/url/images/url.gif

The status bar for each of the links on the page.

▶ **note**

URL Resources

Relative URL Specification
http://www.w3.org/Addressing/rfc1808.txt

The URL Specification
(does not include relative URLs)
http://www.w3.org/Addressing/URL/Overview.html
http://www.w3.org/Addressing/rfc1738.txt

The CGI Book, by Bill Weinman
Chapter 4, "Understanding URLs"

By understanding how relative URLs work, you can organize your site more flexibly and make it easier to maintain, as well as easier to navigate. By using relative URLs throughout your site, you can create a site that is well-organized, and have it still work when you move the site from one machine to another.

Say, for example, you build your site on your local machine at home or in your office. But when you are ready to put the site up on the Net, you have to move it to another machine. By using relative URLs, you can ensure that the links on your site still work when you move it to your web server.

Directory Structure

Now that you have a good understanding of how relative URLs work, it will be much easier to organize your site into various directories according to a logical plan. In fact, it will even be easier to change the structure of your site, if you should be so inclined in the future.

The structure of the directories should roughly match the layout of the site. In other words, if you have a section of the site about "Company," you can put that section in a directory called company; you can use a directory called sales for your "Sales" section, and so on.

If one of your sections has other branches, like "Products" in our example below, you may want to use other subdirectories under the products directory.

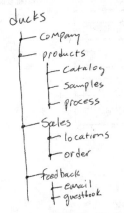

A sample directory layout for the Ducks In A Row site.

Above we chose to put each of the major sections in its own folder, and we further separated sections into subsections, where we felt they were still too complex. This organization allows us to deal with each section's complexity as distinct from the others, while sharing those elements of the site that are in common.

Repeating Elements

In dealing with the commonalties of different parts of the site, you will find yourself using exactly the same HTML in many places. For example, you may have a common menu, or a common BODY tag that you use over and over again. Not only is it inconvenient to have to continually rewrite the same bit of code, but it's prone to error when you eventually need to make changes.

For example, let's say you have a common BODY tag that you want to use throughout your site.

```
<BODY BGCOLOR="#FFFFCC" TEXT="#663333"
LINK="#006699" VLINK="#006699">
```

This creates a nice color scheme with a yellow background, brown lettering, and teal links. But, six months or a year from now, you may find yourself tired of it. But in order to change it, you have to find all the places you used it and replace the code throughout your site!

When you do decide to change it, what are the odds that you'll miss a page here and a page there? Then some visitors who find those less-used pages will see the old color scheme, while the rest of the site uses the new!

One solution to this problem is to consolidate the repeating elements of the site into one place. We can do this with a technique called Server-Side Includes.

Server-Side Includes

The term **Server-Side I**ncludes (SSI) refers to the ability of a web server to merge various files together into one file, while serving an HTML file. The concept of file inclusion is probably not entirely foreign to you because most word processors have similar capabilities.

For example, if your word processor has templates for creating certain types of documents, or if it can merge-print a form letter from a database, these are file includes in the same way that SSI is for web servers.

▶ **note**

SSI Resources

NCSA SSI Tutorial
http://hoohoo.ncsa.uiuc.edu/
docs/tutorials/includes.html

The CGI Book
http://www.cgibook.com/
http://www.cgibook.com/chap08

▶ **note**

Potential SSI Problems

Some web servers, especially those with many users on them, have some SSI capabilities turned off—or have disabled SSI entirely—for security reasons. If so, you will have to ask your system administrator to enable it for you.

Some other servers may use such a radically different paradigm that these examples may not work at all! The problem is that there's no standard for SSI. Most web servers use the SSI specification that was developed for the NCSA server (one of the original web servers, developed at the University of Illinois). The server that we use is called Apache. It's a free server based on the original NCSA code, and it's by far the most popular server on the Internet as of this writing. Most other servers, including Netscape's servers, also use this same SSI model.

If you find that these examples don't work on your server, ask your system administrator for the proper syntax for including files on your server. It may be one of those servers that just works differently.

▶ note

File and Folder Names

On many systems—especially if you are using an NCSA-derived server, like Apache or Netscape—you can name your files anything that you want to and put them in whatever folder you want to.

On some web servers, you are required to use the `.shtml` extension for any HTML documents that use SSI. On our web server, since we use SSI on all our pages, we chose to configure the server to accept SSI in files with the `.html` extension. So, all of our pages use `.html`.

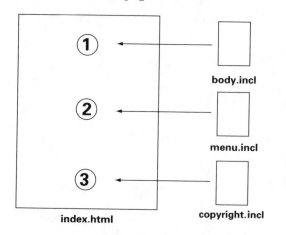

body.incl

menu.incl

index.html   copyright.incl

For the included files, you can usually use whatever file name extension that you want to. We end our file names with the `.incl` extension so that we can easily distinguish between full HTML files and included files that aren't otherwise a full page.

We also chose to put all of our included files in a separate folder called incl. That allows us to use a consistent syntax for including the files throughout the site.

How SSI Works

On many web servers, in order to use SSI you must name your file with the `.shtml` extension instead of `.html`. Your system may differ, though, so check with your system administrator for the correct requirements. The examples in this book use the `.html` extension because we have configured our server to use SSI with all the pages on our site.

SSI has a number of different features. Depending on your server, you can use SSI to include files, run external programs, display server parameters, and more! Most of those features are outside of the scope of this book. For this book, we will concentrate on using SSI to help organize and manage a complex web site. For information on other SSI features, see Chapter 8 of *The CGI Book* or consult your server documentation.

The Ducks In A Row home page.

SSI commands are embedded in HTML comments (`<!-- this is an HTML comment -->`) so that they won't display in the browser if, for some reason, the server fails to intercept them. The format of an SSI command is like this:

```
<!--#include virtual="filename" -->
```

The pound sign (#) introduces the keyword (`include`) so that the server knows to interpret the rest of the comment. The keyword `virtual` tells the server to treat the file name as a relative path instead of an absolute file path. (SSI also allows the keyword `file` instead of `virtual`, but it is far more complicated to use, and we don't recommend it.) The space after the file name is required, and no space is allowed before the pound sign.

For the Ducks In A Row site, we created a separate folder called `include` for all of our included files. We named the included files with the .incl extension so that we could easily distinguish them from complete HTML files. For example, the index.html file from the site looks like this:

```
   <HTML>
   <HEAD>
      <TITLE>Ducks in a Row Homepage</TITLE>
   </HEAD>
1. <!--#include virtual="/include/body.incl" -->

   <P ALIGN=CENTER>
   <BR CLEAR=ALL>

   <!-- Logo -->
   <A HREF="sitemap.html">
   <IMG SRC="/images/ylogo1.gif"
       ALT="Ducks in a Row Logo"
       BORDER=0    WIDTH=419 HEIGHT=219></A>

   <TABLE><TR><TD HEIGHT=20></TABLE>
   <!-- for spacing -->
2. <!--#include virtual="/include/menu.incl" -->

   <TABLE><TR><TD HEIGHT=20></TABLE>
   <!-- for spacing -->
3. <!--#include virtual="/include/copyright.incl" -->
   </BODY>
   </HTML>
```

This brings in all the elements from the `include` directory, and the server sends the fully assembled HTML page to the browser.

1. By using SSI for the BODY tag, our common menus, and the copyright elements, we were able to reduce the size of our HTML files and create a consistent look with a minimum of effort. The include file for the BODY tag, /include/body.incl, looks like this:

```
<BODY BGCOLOR="#FFFFCC" TEXT="#663333"
LINK="#006699" VLINK="#006699"
```

This allows for a consistent color scheme across the site without having to keep track of different pages.

2. The SSI file for the menu /include/menu.incl looks like this:

```
<!-- menu include -->
<map name="navbar">
<area shape ="polygon" alt="Our Company"
coords="84,58,83,64,78,72,67,78,59,79,53,79,46,77,39,72,37,
67,41,59,44,56,46,54,46,51,43,50,37,47,35,43,38,43,4241,46,
32,50,30,55,29,58,30,62,34,64,37,63,42,63,46,60,48,63,52,70,
52,73,47,74,43,78,40,83,46,84,52
" href="/company/">
<area shape="polygon" alt="Catalog"
coords="122,67,126,69,129,70,131,74,122,80,122,82,156,82,
156,79,147,74,147,71,152,67,154,64,154,61,158,60,159,55,
162,52,162,48,159,48,157,51,158,43,158,33,152,26,140,24,
139,20,135,20,130,26,122,28,117,38,117,47,111,50,111,54,
115,57,117,61,120,63
" href="/products/">
<area shape="rect" alt="Samples" coords="187,15,236,79"
href="/samples/">
<area shape="circle" alt="Making Stamps" coords="287,51,28"
href="/making.html">
<area shape="polygon" alt="Retail Locations"
coords="390,81,381,61,378,41,377,13,374,13,372,41,367,62,
357,81"
href="/sales/">
<area shape="rect" coords="21,82,98,97" href="/company/">
<area shape="rect" coords="113,83,166,96" href="/products/">
<area shape="rect" coords="186,81,236,96" href="/samples/">
<area shape="rect" coords="244,81,325,95"
href="/making.html">
<area shape="rect" coords="332,81,419,96" href="/sales/">
<area shape="rect" nohref>
</map>

<P ALIGN=CENTER>
<IMG SRC="/images/navbar.gif"
   WIDTH="440" HEIGHT="116" BORDER="0" USEMAP="#navbar">
<BR CLEAR=ALL>
<FONT FACE="verdana,helvetica,arial">
<SMALL><STRONG>
[
<A HREF="/company/">Company</A> |
<A HREF="/catalog/">Catalog</A> |
<A HREF="/samples/">Samples</A> |
<A HREF="/process/">Making Stamps</A> |
<A HREF="/locations/">Retail Locations</A>
```

```
]
<BR>[
<A HREF="/feedback/">Feedback</A>
<!--#if expr="\"$DOCUMENT_URI\" != \"/index.html\"" -->
  <A HREF="/">Home</A>
  <!--#if expr="$HTTP_REFERER" -->
    | <A HREF="<!--#echo var="HTTP_REFERER" -->">Back</A>
  <!--#endif -->
<!--#endif -->
]
</STRONG></SMALL></FONT></P>
<!-- end menu include -->
```

With that menu include, we can use a complex menu, with imagemaps and a text menu, without having to duplicate all that code on each page.

3. The include file for the copyright notice, /include/copyright.incl, looks like this:

```
<!-- copyright include -->
<CENTER>
<!-- outer table -->
<TABLE BORDER=0 CELLSPACING=0 CELLPADDING=0
BGCOLOR=#663333>
  <TR><TD>

    <!-- inner table -->
    <TABLE BORDER=0 CELLPADDING=4 CELLSPACING=1
    WIDTH=100% BGCOLOR="#FFFFCC">
      <TR><TD ALIGN=CENTER ROWSPAN=2>
        <FONT SIZE=-2 COLOR="#006699"
        FACE="verdana,helvetica,arial">
        &copy 1997-2001</FONT></TD>
      <TD>
        <FONT SIZE=-2 COLOR="#006699"
        FACE="verdana,helvetica,arial">
        Ducks In A Row, Inc.</FONT></TD>
      <TR><TD>
        <FONT SIZE=-2 COLOR="#006699"
        FACE="verdana,helvetica,arial">
        <A HREF="http://www.lynda.com/">Lynda</A> &
        <A HREF="http://www.weinman.com/wew/">Bill</A>
        <A HREF="http://www.weinman.com/">
        Weinman</A></FONT></TD>
      </TR>
    </TABLE>      <!-- end inner table -->

  </TD></TR>
</TABLE>   <!-- end outer table -->
</CENTER>
<!-- end copyright include -->
```

This is a nice-looking nested table with a discreet 1-pixel outline. Again, the use of SSI allows us to use this level of complexity without having to duplicate it across the site.

12

‣ chapter twelve summary

Organization

Organizing your web site is more than just designing an attractive and functional interface. It means deciding how the site best breaks down and using the tools that HTML provides, such as relative URLs, to keep it all manageable.

In this chapter, you learned how to use relative URLs and Server-Side Includes to keep your site organized and manageable at the same time.

13

Style Sheets

*"My spelling is Wobbly.
It's good spelling but it Wobbles,
and the letters get in the wrong places."
—A. A. Milne (1882–1958)*

Style Sheets

control at last

▶ **contents**

redefining your tags

cascading style sheets

formatting text

absolute positioning

When you've been writing HTML for a while, you'll start wishing that it could do a few more tricks. Wouldn't it be nice, for instance, if you could adjust the spaces between lines? Wouldn't it be nice if you could create shortcuts for some common formatting operations? Wouldn't it be nice if you could position a graphic right up against the upper-left corner of the browser window? Style sheets are the Tooth Fairy for a lot of these wishes.

A **style sheet** is a collection of templates, or styles, that apply to various parts of your document and describe the way it gets rendered. Style sheets have been available in all the major word processing programs for quite some time.

Early in the development of HTML and the web, designers and programmers started asking for a form of style sheets that could be applied to HTML documents. A number of different proposals were fielded, and one proposal, **C**ascading **S**tyle **S**heet (CSS), was implemented. There are other style sheet specifications, but CSS is the form that has been accepted, and all the major browser vendors are working hard to adopt it.

Cascading Style Sheets

The **C**ascading **S**tyle **S**heets (CSS) specification is the form of style sheets recommended by the **W**orld **W**ide **W**eb **C**onsortium (W3C) as appropriate for use with HTML. It is also the form that is being deployed by the two major browser manufacturers, Netscape and Microsoft.

Unfortunately for those of us who would like to really use CSS, it is implemented neither completely nor consistently enough in either of the major browsers for us to use CSS with any confidence. With that in mind, the intent of this chapter is to show you how CSS works and what its potential is, so that you will be familiar with it when it eventually becomes ready for prime time.

Therefore, we urge you to read this chapter with this caveat emptor: The details of CSS will almost certainly change somewhat before the dust settles. The basic principles will almost certainly not change. Treat what you learn in this chapter as a preview of things to come, and experiment with it, but don't be surprised if it works differently in later versions of your favorite browser. (We conducted our tests using Netscape Navigator 4 and Microsoft Internet Explorer 4 , and we have only included examples that work the same between the two.)

The scope of this chapter is to show you generally what style sheets are going to be able to do. The scope of this chapter is not to show you all the details of CSS because most of it doesn't work today and is subject to a lot of change before it does work. Or spoken more simply, "Your mileage may vary."

> ### ▶ note
>
> #### External Style Sheets
>
> External style sheets are convenient for situations when you may want to apply a set of styles across a number of different documents. For example, you could create an external style sheet that defines a color scheme for your web site, including a background image, fonts and sizes for headings and paragraphs, etc. Then whenever you want to change the look of your site, you simply update the external style sheet and—voilà—your site is updated! For more details about linking external style sheets, see the documentation at:
>
> **W3C**
> http://www.w3.org/TR/WD-style#intro

How CSS Style Sheets Work

A CSS style sheet is a type of document that is used by a web browser to redefine the properties of the various elements and tags in the HTML.

The style sheet document may be contained within the HTML document, or it may be in a separate file on the server. An internal style sheet is one that's contained within the HTML document. An external style sheet is stored in a separate file on the server, allowing one style sheet to be used for a whole group of HTML documents. In the future, you may also be able to specify a style sheet with your favorite settings in your browser and have it apply to pages without style sheets, or even override some style sheets on some pages.

For our purposes, we will work with internal style sheets. Just keep in mind that there are other ways to do this.

For the first few examples, we use a page from the Ducks In A Row site, which explains how the rubber stamps are used. First, here's what the page looks like in plain old ordinary HTML. If you want to follow along, you can find this page as css1.html in the chap13 folder on the <chd2> CD-ROM:

```
<HEAD>
<TITLE>CSS Examples</TITLE>
</HEAD>
<BODY BGCOLOR="#FFFFCC" TEXT="#663300"
LINK="#006699" VLINK="#006699">
<H1>Working with Ducks in a Row
Stamps</H1>
<P>
Because the style of art throughout
the catalog is consistent, any of the
designs may be used together side by
```

side, or superimposed, making the possibilities for personal expressi on boundless.
```
<P>
You will find designs in our catalog
which cover a vast array of categories,
from floral images to humor, holiday
stamps, border designs and decorative
imagery, for all around use. You, as
the stamping artist will be the one
to create original art works from
these designs, and nothing pleasures
us more than to see the beautiful and
original ways in which our designs
are being used.
<P>
Throughout the catalog you will find
some helpful hints on some of the uses
and techniques to enjoy your stamps,
but we're sure that you as the stamping
artist can teach us a thing or two! One
thing for certain, the possibilities
are endless!
</BODY>
```

Working with Ducks in a Row Rubber Stamps

Because the style of art throughout the catalog is consistent, any of the designs may be used together side by side, or superimposed, making the possibilities for personal expression boundless.

You will find designs in our catalog which cover a vast array of categories, from floral images to humor, holiday stamps, border designs and decorative imagery, for all around use. You, as the stamping artist will be the one to create original art works from these designs, and nothing pleasures us more than to see the beautiful and original ways in which our designs are being used.

Throughout the catalog you will find some helpful hints on some of the uses and techniques to enjoy your stamps, but we're sure that you as the stamping artist can teach us a thing or two! One thing for certain, the possibilities are endless!

Document: Done

Sample page without CSS.

13

Adding a Style Sheet

One major concern when using style sheets, especially today when only the very latest browsers understand them, is making sure that older browsers can still view pages that use them.

Using our example, we'll add a style sheet to a page by using the STYLE tag. We can hide the style sheet from older browsers by putting comment tags around everything within the STYLE container. Here's what that looks like in the HEAD section of our current example (this file is css2.html in the chap13 folder on the <chd2> CD-ROM):

```
<HEAD>
<TITLE>CSS Examples</TITLE>

<STYLE TYPE=" text/css">
<!--

H1 {
    font-family: Verdana
    }

-->
</STYLE>
</HEAD>
```

Because the style sheet itself is enclosed in HTML comments, browsers that don't understand the STYLE tag are prevented from displaying the style sheet in the browser window. Browsers that do understand the style sheet will ignore the comment tags and apply the style sheet to the page.

Let's pretend we're an older browser, so we can see why we don't get confused by the style sheet here. We're merrily reading through the file (top-to-bottom), and we get to the STYLE tag. Since we don't know what it is, we just ignore it (that's one of the rules of HTML: Ignore the tags you don't understand). Then we get to the comment beginning (<!--), and we become blind to everything until we see the comment ending (-->), so none of the style sheet syntax is noticed by us at all! Now we see the end tag for the STYLE element (</STYLE>), which we ignore, and we can merrily continue as if nothing happened.

We'll look at the style sheet itself more closely in a moment, but right now let's see what a new browser and an older browser do with it. First, here's a screen shot of this page in Netscape Navigator 4, which understands simple CSS style sheets:

Working with Ducks in a Row Rubber Stamps

Because the style of art throughout the catalog is consistent, any of the designs may be used together side by side, or superimposed, making the possibilities for personal expression boundless.

You will find designs in our catalog which cover a vast array of categories, from floral images to humor, holiday stamps, border designs and decorative imagery, for all around use. You, as the stamping artist will be the one to create original art works from these designs, and nothing pleasures us more than to see the beautiful and original ways in which our designs are being used.

Throughout the catalog you will find some helpful hints on some of the uses and techniques to enjoy your stamps, but we're sure that you as the stamping artist can teach us a thing or two! One thing for certain, the possibilities are endless!

css2.html **in Netscape Navigator 4.**

Working with Ducks in a Row Rubber Stamps

Because the style of art throughout the catalog is consistent, any of the designs may be used together side by side, or superimposed, making the possibilities for personal expression boundless.

You will find designs in our catalog which cover a vast array of categories, from floral images to humor, holiday stamps, border designs and decorative imagery, for all around use. You, as the stamping artist will be the one to create original art works from these designs, and nothing pleasures us more than to see the beautiful and original ways in which our designs are being used.

Throughout the catalog you will find some helpful hints on some of the uses and techniques to enjoy your stamps, but we're sure that you as the stamping artist can teach us a thing or two! One thing for certain, the possibilities are endless!

Here's what css2.html **looks like in Netscape Navigator 3, which does not understand style sheets.**

H1 (font-family: Verdana)

Working with Ducks in a Row Rubber Stamps

Because the style of art throughout the catalog is consistent, any of the designs may be used together side by side, or superimposed, making the possibilities for personal expression boundless.

You will find designs in our catalog which cover a vast array of categories, from floral images to humor, holiday stamps, border designs and decorative imagery, for all around use. You, as the stamping artist will be the one to create original art works from these designs, and nothing pleasures us more than to see the beautiful and original ways in which our designs are being used.

Throughout the catalog you will find some helpful hints on some of the uses and techniques to enjoy your stamps, but we're sure that you as the stamping artist can teach us a thing or two! One thing for certain, the possibilities are endless!

Here's what some of your users may see in css2.html **if you don't hide your style sheet with comment tags.**

As you can see, browsers that don't understand the style sheets ignore them because of the comment tags. When you add a style sheet to an HTML document, it's always a good idea to use the comment tags inside the STYLE element so that older browsers won't display the style sheet.

The Anatomy of a CSS Style Sheet

Now that you know how to add a style sheet to a document, let's take a quick look at the style that we defined in this document.

1.
```
<STYLE TYPE=" text/css">
<!--

H1 {
   font-family: Verdana
   }

-->
</STYLE>
```

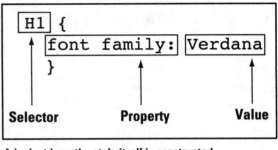

A look at how the style itself is constructed.

1. The STYLE element is a container that goes in the HEAD section of your HTML document. The TYPE attribute specifies the type of style sheet being used, which in this case is CSS. The STYLE element can contain any number of different styles. This style element contains one style, it applies to the H1 tag, changing its font to Verdana.

The first part of the style is called the **selector**. The selector specifies where the style should be applied. In this case, the selector is H1, indicating that this style should be applied to the text in all H1 tags in this document.

The curly braces ("{ "and"} ") enclose the body of the style. Within the body of the style are lines with properties and values. The word on the left side of the colon is called a property, and the right side is the value assigned to the property. In this example, the font-family property is given the value, Verdana, which effectively tells the browser to use the Verdana font for H1 elements in this document.

You can specify more than one property in a single style, and they needn't be in any particular order. If you need to specify more than one property in a style, you must end each one with a semicolon (;) character. For example,

```
H1 {
   font-family: Verdana;
   font-size: 24px;
   }
```

Working with Ducks in a Row Rubber Stamps

Because the style of art throughout the catalog is consistent, any of the designs may be used together side by side, or superimposed, making the possibilities for personal expression boundless.

You will find designs in our catalog which cover a vast array of categories, from floral images to humor, holiday stamps, border designs and decorative imagery, for all around use. You, as the stamping artist will be the one to create original art works from these designs, and nothing pleasures us more than to see the beautiful and original ways in which our designs are being used.

Throughout the catalog you will find some helpful hints on some of the uses and techniques to enjoy your stamps, but we're sure that you as the stamping artist can teach us a thing or two! One thing for certain, the possibilities are endless!

css3.html: Both font-family and font-size properties.

You can also specify more than one style in a single style sheet. This style sheet has styles for both H1 and P elements:

```
H1 {
   font-family: Verdana;
   font-size: 24px;
   }

P {
   font-family: Georgia;
   font-size: 18px;
   }
```

Working with Ducks in a Row Rubber Stamps

Because the style of art throughout the catalog is consistent, any of the designs may be used together side by side, or superimposed, making the possibilities for personal expression boundless.

You will find designs in our catalog which cover a vast array of categories, from floral images to humor, holiday stamps, border designs and decorative imagery, for all around use. You, as the stamping artist will be the one to create original art works from these designs, and nothing pleasures us more than to see the beautiful and original ways in which our designs are being used.

Throughout the catalog you will find some helpful hints on some of the uses and techniques to enjoy your stamps, but we're sure that you as the stamping artist can teach us a thing or two! One thing for certain, the possibilities are endless!

css4.html: Styles for both H1 and P in the same style sheet.

Now that you know the basic format for adding a style sheet to a document, instead of showing you the whole STYLE section for each change we make, the rest of our examples will just concentrate on the individual style that we're working on.

Type and Measurements

Before we discuss CSS measurement units for text, it's important to understand the terminology used in measuring type.

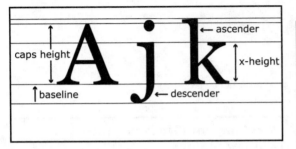

Back in the days when "setting type" meant a physical activity handled by skilled professionals with leaded type and wooden typecases, the body size of a type referred to the actual size of the metal block on which the letter was formed. This is a size somewhat larger than any of the measurable dimensions of the printed letters, though not by any specific ratio. There is no analogous measurement in electronic type, so when we refer to a "twelve-point" typeface, a certain amount of ambiguity cannot be resolved.

Let's look at some measuring units. The table below lists the English name, the CSS name, and a short description for each measurement unit.

English	CSS	Description
Pixel	px	A pixel is the distance from one dot to the next on a computer screen (pixel literally means picture element).
Point	pt	A point is 1/72 inch. How many pixels depends on the resolution of your screen, but it is one pixel on 72 dpi systems.
Pica	pc	12 points.
Em	em	The "body size" of the font. That is, if the font size is 12 points, one em is 12 points.
En	en	1/2 em.
x-height	ex	The height of a lower-case "x".
Inch	in	The length of the thumb of King Henry VIII.
Centimeter	cm	1/100 meter.
Millimeter	mm	1/1,000 meter.

If you wanted to display the word "Quack" in 3-inch type, you could use this HTML:

```
<HTML>
<HEAD>
<STYLE TYPE=" text/css">
P {
    font-size: 3in;
    font-family: Garamond;
    font-style: italic;
    }
</STYLE>
</HEAD>
<BODY BGCOLOR=WHITE>
<P ALIGN=CENTER> Quack
</BODY>
</HTML>
```

Because most web-based graphics are a fixed number of pixels wide and a fixed number of pixels high, we recommend that you use pixel measurements most of the time. That way, you can always be sure that your page will look more-or-less uniform relative to the size of the graphics on the page.

quack.html: Quack in 3-inch letters.

As we go through the chapter, you will see more uses for these measurements.

Text-Related Properties

CSS defines a number of different properties for working with text. You have already seen the `font-family` property that we used in our last example. This property lets you specify a particular font family, either by name (like Verdana) or by generic type (like sans-serif).

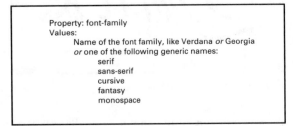

You can also give a list of values (separated by commas) for `font-family`. For example,

```
H1 {
    font-family: Verdana, Helvetica,
sans-serif
    }
```

In that case, the system would try to use `Verdana`, or if that's not available, `Helvetica`; otherwise, it will use whatever sans-serif font is available.

Another useful text-related property is `line-height`. This property affects the space between lines, also called leading, after the strips of lead used to provide the spaces between lines of metal type.

```
Property: line-height
Values:
    number
    default
Sets the amount of space between lines of text
```

The line-height is measured from the baseline of one line to the baseline of the next. The special value default will set the line-height to the default of the browser, which is probably about the same as 1.2em.

```
P {
    font-family: Georgia;
    font-size: 12px;
    line-height: 1.5em;
}
```

This will set the line-height to 1.5em. Remember: 1em is the same as the font-size, so 1.5em is one-and-a-half times the body size of the type.

Working with Ducks in a Row Rubber Stamps

Because the style of art throughout the catalog is consistent, any of the designs may be used together side by side, or superimposed, making the possibilities for personal expression boundless.

You will find designs in our catalog which cover a vast array of categories, from floral images to humor, holiday stamps, border designs and decorative imagery, for all around use. You, as the stamping artist will be the one to create original art works from these designs, and nothing pleasures us more than to see the beautiful and original ways in which our designs are being used.

Throughout the catalog you will find some helpful hints on some of the uses and techniques to enjoy your stamps, but we're sure that you as the stamping artist can teach us a thing or two! One thing for certain, the possibilities are endless!

css5.html: **A line-height of 1.5em.**

Selectors

So far, we've been using the selector to specify what tag the style will apply to, but the selector can do more than that! You can also use the selector to apply to only some instances of a particular tag.

For example, what if you wanted every paragraph except the first to have an indent on the first line.

```
P {
    font-family: Georgia;
    font-size: 12px;
    line-height: 1.5em;
    text-indent: 1.5em;
    }
```

The `text-indent` property indents just the first line of a paragraph. Our P style now has a 1.5em indent for the first paragraph. Now we add another style with a class selector like this:

```
.first {
    text-indent: 0;
    }
```

A class selector always starts with a dot (.). Now you can use the CLASS attribute in your HTML to apply that style in addition to the existing style on the paragraph tag:

```
<P CLASS="first">
Because the style of art throughout
the catalog is consistent, any of the
designs may be used together side by
side, or superimposed, making the pos-
sibilities for personal expression
boundless.
```

The result is like this:

Working with Ducks in a Row Rubber Stamps

Because the style of art throughout the catalog is consistent, any of the designs may be used together side by side, or superimposed, making the possibilities for personal expression boundless.

You will find designs in our catalog which cover a vast array of categories, from floral images to humor, holiday stamps, border designs and decorative imagery, for all around use. You, as the stamping artist will be the one to create original art works from these designs, and nothing pleasures us more than to see the beautiful and original ways in which our designs are being used.

Throughout the catalog you will find some helpful hints on some of the uses and techniques to enjoy your stamps, but we're sure that you as the stamping artist can teach us a thing or two! One thing for certain, the possibilities are endless!

---

css6.html: Look no single-pixel GIFs!

The potential of this for simplifying web sites and reducing bandwidth is truly exciting! It used to be that you needed to trick HTML into indenting your paragraphs and adding space between the lines by using single-pixel transparent GIFs. Now you can do it with style sheets!

The SPAN Tag

Sometimes you will want to apply a style to some text that doesn't otherwise fit into standard HTML categories, like STRONG or EM. You may even want several different types of emphasis within one paragraph. The new SPAN tag applies formatting that you define to small parts of text, without affecting the way the text is rendered in browsers that don't understand style sheets.

Using the SPAN tag with class selectors, you can create effects that are much more complex than using straight HTML. Suppose you want to be able to highlight certain types of references using a combination of a different font, bold weight, and a different color. Without style sheets, you may decide that it's just too much trouble to put this in each instance:

```
<FONT FACE="Footlight MT Light"
SIZE="+1"
    COLOR="#6699CC"><STRONG>
  text
</STRONG></FONT>
```

With a style sheet, you can specify all that stuff just once:

```
.high {
   font-family: Footlight MT Light;
   font-size: large;
   color: #6699CC;
   font-weight: bold;
   }
```

And then, each time you want to use this formatting, you just use the SPAN tag. The SPAN tag doesn't do anything at all by itself. It's only purpose is to apply a style to a span of text. Here's an example:

```
<P CLASS="first">
Because the style of art throughout
the catalog is consistent, any of the
designs may be used together side by
side, or superimposed, making the
possibilities for <SPAN CLASS="high">
personal expression</SPAN> boundless.
<P>
You will find designs in our catalog
which cover a vast array of categories,
from floral images to humor, holiday
<SPAN CLASS="high">stamp</SPAN>s,
border designs and decorative imagery,
for all around use. You, as the
<SPAN CLASS="high">stamp</SPAN>ing
artist will be the one to create
<SPAN CLASS="high">original art</SPAN>
works from these designs, and nothing
pleasures us more than to see the
```

```
beautiful and original ways in which
our designs are being used.
<P>
Throughout the catalog you will find
some helpful hints on some of the uses
and techniques to enjoy your
<SPAN CLASS="high">stamp</SPAN>s,
but we're sure that you as the
<SPAN CLASS="high">stamp</SPAN>ing
<SPAN CLASS="high">artist</SPAN>
can teach us a thing or two! One
thing for certain, the possibilities
are endless!
```

Working with Ducks in a Row Rubber Stamps

Because the style of art throughout the catalog is consistent, any of the designs may be used together side by side, or superimposed, making the possibilities for **personal expression** boundless.

You will find designs in our catalog which cover a vast array of categories, from floral images to humor, holiday **stamp**s, border designs and decorative imagery, for all around use. You, as the **stamp**ing artist will be the one to create **original art** works from these designs, and nothing pleasures us more than to see the beautiful and original ways in which our designs are being used.

Throughout the catalog you will find some helpful hints on some of the uses and techniques to enjoy your **stamp**s, but we're sure that you as the **stamp**ing **artist** can teach us a thing or two! One thing for certain, the possibilities are endless!

css7.html: Simple highlighting with SPAN **and** CLASS.

Absolute Positioning

Graphic designers have long complained that it's not possible to absolutely position a graphic on a page using HTML. CSS has a solution to that problem. Let's look at one more type of selector—the ID—and a few new properties:

```
1.    #smduck1 {
2.        position: absolute;
3.        top: 0px;
4.        left: 0px;
5.        z-index: 1;
          }
```

1. `#smduck1 {`

The `ID` selector always begins with a hash mark (#) and must be unique within the document. That means that you can only define it once, and can only use it once (see the sidebar, "ID vs. CLASS"). It works almost exactly like the class selector (`.`), but is usually used for absolute positioning of objects on a page, where only one object will have any single position.

2. `position: absolute;`

The `position` property can be either absolute or relative. Use absolute for objects that you want to have at a specific position on the page and relative for objects that you want to position relative to wherever they would have otherwise fallen. We used absolute positioning in this example to position the graphic at a specific point on the page. We'll see an example of relative a little later.

3. `top: 0px;`
4. `left: 0px;`

The `top` and `left` properties are used to position the object. These measurements are absolute measurements—from the top-left corner of the screen—with no padding. This style will place the graphic in the absolute upper left-hand corner of the screen.

5. `z-index: 1;`

Objects that are put on the screen with absolute positioning can be laid on top of each other. The `z-index` property tells the browser which objects should be on top of (or under) other objects. Higher-numbered objects will overlay lower-numbered objects.

Here's a page that uses the style we just defined:

```
<HTML>
<HEAD>
<TITLE>Absolute Positioning:
    Simple</TITLE>
<STYLE>

#smduck1 { position: absolute; }
top: 0px; left: 0px; }
</STYLE>
<BODY>
```

1.
```
<DIV ID="smduck1">
<IMG SRC=revgreentile.gif
    WIDTH=50 HEIGHT=50></DIV>

</BODY>
</HTML>
```

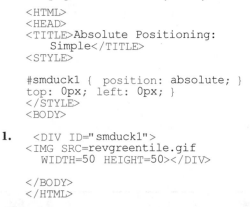

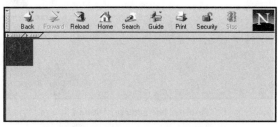

css-abs1.html: That GIF is right up against the corner!

1.
```
<DIV ID=" smduck1">
<IMG SRC=revgreentile.gif
    WIDTH=50 HEIGHT=50></DIV>
```
Notice the use of the `DIV` element that encloses the `IMG`. The `DIV` tag has a new attribute called `ID`, which is used to specify the selector in the style. The `DIV` element is necessary to make the absolute positioning work.

The little image in the example on the previous page is 50×50 pixels in size, so we should be able to lay another one right on its lower right-hand corner by positioning it 50 pixels in and down:

```
<HEAD>
<TITLE>Absolute Positioning:
Simple</TITLE>
<STYLE>

#smduck1 { position: absolute; top:
0px; left: 0px; z-index: 0; }
#smduck2 { position: absolute; top:
50px; left: 50px; z-index: 0; }

</STYLE>

<BODY BGCOLOR=" #999966"
BACKGROUND="greentile.gif">

<DIV ID=" smduck1">
<IMG SRC=revgreentile.gif
   WIDTH=50 HEIGHT=50></DIV>
<DIV ID=" smduck2">
<IMG SRC=revgreentile.gif
   WIDTH=50 HEIGHT=50></DIV>

</BODY>
```

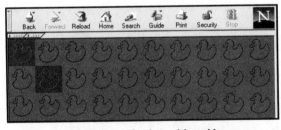

css-abs1a.html: **Another perfectly positioned image.**

In this example, we also added a 50×50 tiled background so that you can better see the perfect alignment of the images against a repeating background.

> ♦ **note**
>
> ### ID vs. CLASS
>
> On the surface, the ID and CLASS selectors seem so similar that it makes us wonder why there are two different methods for the same thing!
>
> As best we can determine, the only difference is that it is considered an error to use the same ID selector more than once. Validation engines—and some future browsers—may flag errors on duplicate ID selectors.

> ♦ **note**
>
> ### DIV and Absolute Positioning
>
> According to the specification, you should be able to forgo the DIV tag and use the ID attribute directly in the IMG tag, but the current crop of browsers will not perform absolute positioning without the DIV tag. This is one of those areas that will likely change in the next generation of browsers.

Layering Text and Images

By extending these same techniques to a mixture of text and graphics, we are able to create a nice effect that requires very little bandwidth. This example is a little complex, but keep in mind that we've already seen all the techniques involved.

Let's first take a look at the result, and then see what it takes to do this.

css-abs2.html: Overlapping text and a simple graphic make a nice splash page.

This example is basically just 20 copies of the text "ducks in a row" using the Verdana font and a number of different overlapping browser-safe colors, covered with a black oval cutout duck and one more "ducks in a row" in black.

```
<HTML>
<HEAD>
<TITLE>Absolute Positioning: Complex</TITLE>

<STYLE TYPE="text/css">
```

1.
```
H1 {
  font-family: verdana;
  font-weight: bold;
  font-size: 52px;
  color: black;
  }
```

2.
```
H2 {
  font-family: verdana;
  font-weight: bold;
  font-size: 32px;
  }
```

3.
```
#words1 {
  position: absolute;
  top: 50px;
  left: 50px;
  z-index: 1;
  }
```

4.
```
#words2 {
  position: absolute;
  top: 60px;
  left: 90px;
  z-index: 2;
  }
```

5.
```
.ovalduck {
  position: absolute;
  top: 35px;
  left: 30px;
  }
```

6.
```
.ducktitle {
  position: absolute;
  top: 130px;
  left: 0px;
  }
```

7.
```
.duck1 { color: #999900; }
.duck2 { color: #FFCC00; }
.duck3 { color: #FF9933; }
.duck4 { color: #FF6633; }
.duck5 { color: #FF9933; }
```

8.
```
#w00 { position: absolute; top: 112px; left: 52px; }
#w01 { position: absolute; top: 24px; left: 45px; }
#w02 { position: absolute; top: 95px; left: 62px; }
#w03 { position: absolute; top: 142px; left: 138px; }
#w04 { position: absolute; top: 128px; left: 74px; }
#w05 { position: absolute; top: 63px; left: 122px; }
#w06 { position: absolute; top: 79px; left: 36px; }
```

```
#w07 { position: absolute; top: 158px; left: 29px; }
#w08 { position: absolute; top: 83px; left: 146px; }
#w09 { position: absolute; top: 42px; left: 12px; }
#w10 { position: absolute; top: 112px; left: 52px; }
#w11 { position: absolute; top: 24px; left: 45px; }
#w12 { position: absolute; top: 95px; left: 62px; }
#w13 { position: absolute; top: 142px; left: 138px; }
#w14 { position: absolute; top: 128px; left: 74px; }
#w15 { position: absolute; top: 63px; left: 122px; }
#w16 { position: absolute; top: 79px; left: 36px; }
#w17 { position: absolute; top: 158px; left: 29px; }
#w18 { position: absolute; top: 83px; left: 146px; }
#w19 { position: absolute; top: 42px; left: 12px; }

</STYLE>

</HEAD>
<BODY BGCOLOR="#FFFFCC" TEXT="#663333" LINK="#006699"
VLINK="#006699">
```

9.
```
<DIV ID="words1">
<H2 CLASS="duck1"><SPAN ID="w00">ducks in a row</SPAN></H2>
<H2 CLASS="duck2"><SPAN ID="w01">ducks in a row</SPAN></H2>
<H2 CLASS="duck3"><SPAN ID="w02">ducks in a row</SPAN></H2>
<H2 CLASS="duck4"><SPAN ID="w03">ducks in a row</SPAN></H2>
<H2 CLASS="duck5"><SPAN ID="w04">ducks in a row</SPAN></H2>
<H2 CLASS="duck1"><SPAN ID="w05">ducks in a row</SPAN></H2>
<H2 CLASS="duck2"><SPAN ID="w06">ducks in a row</SPAN></H2>
<H2 CLASS="duck3"><SPAN ID="w07">ducks in a row</SPAN></H2>
<H2 CLASS="duck4"><SPAN ID="w08">ducks in a row</SPAN></H2>
<H2 CLASS="duck5"><SPAN ID="w09">ducks in a row</SPAN></H2>
</DIV>
```

10.
```
<DIV ID="words2">
<H2 CLASS="duck5"><SPAN ID="w10">ducks in a row</SPAN></H2>
<H2 CLASS="duck1"><SPAN ID="w11">ducks in a row</SPAN></H2>
<H2 CLASS="duck4"><SPAN ID="w12">ducks in a row</SPAN></H2>
<H2 CLASS="duck2"><SPAN ID="w13">ducks in a row</SPAN></H2>
<H2 CLASS="duck3"><SPAN ID="w14">ducks in a row</SPAN></H2>
<H2 CLASS="duck5"><SPAN ID="w15">ducks in a row</SPAN></H2>
<H2 CLASS="duck1"><SPAN ID="w16">ducks in a row</SPAN></H2>
<H2 CLASS="duck4"><SPAN ID="w17">ducks in a row</SPAN></H2>
<H2 CLASS="duck2"><SPAN ID="w18">ducks in a row</SPAN></H2>
<H2 CLASS="duck3"><SPAN ID="w19">ducks in a row</SPAN></H2>
</DIV>
```

11.
```
<DIV CLASS="ovalduck">
<IMG SRC="blackoval.gif" width=269 height=136>
<H1><SPAN CLASS="ducktitle">ducks in a row</SPAN></H1>
</DIV>

</BODY>
</HTML>
```

The HTML file is only 3k and the GIF is only 900 bytes! There are no techniques used here that you haven't already seen in this chapter:

1.
```
H1 {
    font-family: verdana;
    font-weight: bold;
    font-size: 52px;
    color: black;
    }
```
This defines the style for the H1 element, used for the black "ducks in a row" on the top.

2.
```
H2 {
    font-family: verdana;
    font-weight: bold;
    font-size: 32px;
    }
```
This defines the base style that is used for all the overlapping "ducks in a row" strings.

3.
```
#words1 {
    position: absolute;
    top: 50px;
    left: 50px;
    z-index: 1;
    }
```
This defines the **ID** used for the first layer of words in [9].

4.
```
#words2 {
    position: absolute;
    top: 60px;
    left: 90px;
    z-index: 2;
    }
```
This defines the ID used for the second layer of words in [10].

5.
```
.ovalduck {
    position: absolute;
    top: 35px;
    left: 30px;
    z-index: 3;
    }
```
This defines the position used for the black oval duck image and black type in [11].

6. `.ducktitle {`
   `position: absolute;`
   `top: 130px;`
   `left: 0px;`
   `}`

This positions the title relative to the image in [11].

7. `.duck1 { color: #999900; }`
   `.duck2 { color: #FFCC00; }`
   `.duck3 { color: #FF9933; }`
   `.duck4 { color: #FF6633; }`
   `.duck5 { color: #FF9933; }`

These classes define colors for the overlapping "ducks in a row" strings.

8. `#w00 { position: absolute; top: 112px; left: 52px; }`
   `#w01 { position: absolute; top: 24px; left: 45px; }`
   `#w02 { position: absolute; top: 95px; left: 62px; }`
   `#w03 { position: absolute; top: 142px; left: 138px; }`
   `#w04 { position: absolute; top: 128px; left: 74px; }`
   `#w05 { position: absolute; top: 63px; left: 122px; }`
   `#w06 { position: absolute; top: 79px; left: 36px; }`
   `#w07 { position: absolute; top: 158px; left: 29px; }`
   `#w08 { position: absolute; top: 83px; left: 146px; }`
   `#w09 { position: absolute; top: 42px; left: 12px; }`
   `#w10 { position: absolute; top: 112px; left: 52px; }`
   `#w11 { position: absolute; top: 24px; left: 45px; }`
   `#w12 { position: absolute; top: 95px; left: 62px; }`
   `#w13 { position: absolute; top: 142px; left: 138px; }`
   `#w14 { position: absolute; top: 128px; left: 74px; }`
   `#w15 { position: absolute; top: 63px; left: 122px; }`
   `#w16 { position: absolute; top: 79px; left: 36px; }`
   `#w17 { position: absolute; top: 158px; left: 29px; }`
   `#w18 { position: absolute; top: 83px; left: 146px; }`
   `#w19 { position: absolute; top: 42px; left: 12px; }`

These are all the positions for the "ducks in a row" strings.

9. `<DIV ID="words1">`
    `<H2 CLASS="duck1"><SPAN ID="w00">ducks in a row</SPAN></H2>`
    `<H2 CLASS="duck2"><SPAN ID="w01">ducks in a row</SPAN></H2>`
    `<H2 CLASS="duck3"><SPAN ID="w02">ducks in a row</SPAN></H2>`
    `<H2 CLASS="duck4"><SPAN ID="w03">ducks in a row</SPAN></H2>`
    `<H2 CLASS="duck5"><SPAN ID="w04">ducks in a row</SPAN></H2>`
    `<H2 CLASS="duck1"><SPAN ID="w05">ducks in a row</SPAN></H2>`
    `<H2 CLASS="duck2"><SPAN ID="w06">ducks in a row</SPAN></H2>`
    `<H2 CLASS="duck3"><SPAN ID="w07">ducks in a row</SPAN></H2>`
    `<H2 CLASS="duck4"><SPAN ID="w08">ducks in a row</SPAN></H2>`
    `<H2 CLASS="duck5"><SPAN ID="w09">ducks in a row</SPAN></H2>`
`</DIV>`

There are two layers of overlapping strings, and this is the first one. The `DIV` element is used to position the block absolutely on the page. Each of the `SPAN` elements position an individual string within the block. The `H2` elements have the font and size for the strings, and the `duck1-5` classes have the varying colors.

Since we didn't use the `z-index` property, the layering occurs in the same order that the text appears in the HTML file. You only need to use `z-index` when you want to specify a particular order. In this example, we don't really care about the order of the layers, as long as they're layered.

10.   `<DIV ID="words2">`
    `<H2 CLASS="duck5"><SPAN ID="w10">ducks in a row</SPAN></H2>`
    `<H2 CLASS="duck1"><SPAN ID="w11">ducks in a row</SPAN></H2>`
    `<H2 CLASS="duck4"><SPAN ID="w12">ducks in a row</SPAN></H2>`
    `<H2 CLASS="duck2"><SPAN ID="w13">ducks in a row</SPAN></H2>`
    `<H2 CLASS="duck3"><SPAN ID="w14">ducks in a row</SPAN></H2>`
    `<H2 CLASS="duck5"><SPAN ID="w15">ducks in a row</SPAN></H2>`
    `<H2 CLASS="duck1"><SPAN ID="w16">ducks in a row</SPAN></H2>`
    `<H2 CLASS="duck4"><SPAN ID="w17">ducks in a row</SPAN></H2>`
    `<H2 CLASS="duck2"><SPAN ID="w18">ducks in a row</SPAN></H2>`
    `<H2 CLASS="duck3"><SPAN ID="w19">ducks in a row</SPAN></H2>`
`</DIV>`

This works exactly like [9] and gets overlapped on top of it to provide a more random appearance than just one layer of 10 strings.

11.
```
<DIV CLASS="ovalduck">
<IMG SRC="blackoval.gif" width=269 height=136>
<H1><SPAN CLASS="ducktitle">ducks in a row</SPAN></H1>
</DIV>
```

Finally, the oval duck and the black letters are layered on top of the rest, using the classes from [5] and [6] a couple pages back.

As we said, this is a complex example that applies all the elements we have learned in this chapter so far. It's intended to demonstrate the power of style sheets, but it is not really intended for a production web site. There are still too few browsers that understand CSS, and we believe that the specification will change significantly before it is really ready for widespread use.

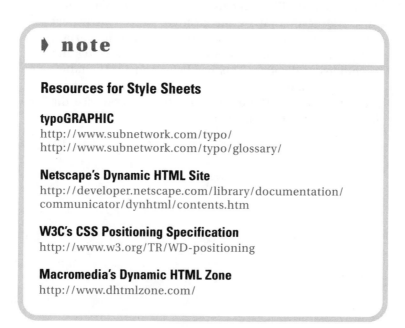

▶ **note**

Resources for Style Sheets

typoGRAPHIC
http://www.subnetwork.com/typo/
http://www.subnetwork.com/typo/glossary/

Netscape's Dynamic HTML Site
http://developer.netscape.com/library/documentation/
communicator/dynhtml/contents.htm

W3C's CSS Positioning Specification
http://www.w3.org/TR/WD-positioning

Macromedia's Dynamic HTML Zone
http://www.dhtmlzone.com/

▶ chapter thirteen summary

Style Sheets

CSS style sheets are going to be a very powerful mechanism for enhancing the presentation quality of text on the web. Though not ready for prime time yet, there is good reason to believe that CSS will become a useable feature of mainstream browsers in the not-so-distant future.

Using CSS, you will be able to format your text in manners much closer to that of the printed page, and expect your layouts to work consistently—within certain limits—across platforms, browsers, and differing sizes and resolutions of displays. This has been a major limitation for designers of web sites until now, but the fairy godmother of web standards is finally letting us see the light at the end of the mixed metaphor.

"Wherever you, go, there you are."
—Buckaroo Banzai

Navigation
take me to your leader

▶ **contents**

frames

frames aesthetics

navbar aesthetics

thumbnails

fragments

Creating navigation for a web site is one of the most complex undertakings of web publishing. As much as image and HTML editor manufacturers like to tout "easy-to-author-web-pages/graphics" products, there is no easy way to design or execute navigation. This is one of the uncharted frontiers of web publishing, and you will likely find it the most challenging aspect of creating any new site.

You are faced with many decisions when you are creating site navigation. For example: Will your audience have current web browsers? If not, how will you ensure that visitors with older browsers can easily maneuver your site? Should you make two versions of your site, such as a frames and a no-frames version? Do you want to rely on graphical icons or text to describe categories? Have you included measures that make it possible to access the rest of your site from all areas of your site? Do you have "back" buttons on all your pages? Have you given thought to integrating the style of your site with navigational buttons and graphics?

This chapter gives us the opportunity to share the graphics and programming techniques we used for designing the navigation for the Ducks In A Row site.

Frames

Netscape introduced the concept of frames with version 2 of the Navigator browser to satisfy designers' needs for more sophisticated navigation. The initial implementation left much to be desired, and in some ways even made navigation harder; but by the time version 3 came along, most of the deficiencies had been addressed, and frames were here to stay. Now frames are part of the HTML 4 specification. The basic frames specification works with Netscape Navigator versions 2+ and Microsoft Internet Explorer versions 3+, and is being incorporated into the latest WYSIWYG editors and site-management systems.

Frames are considered by many to be a navigational godsend, and by others, a navigational nightmare. The principle behind frames is that they offer the ability to have regions of a web page change, while other regions remain stationary. Before frames, every page of HTML had to be separate. If you had a navigation bar at the bottom of each page on your site, clicking it would cause the entire screen to redraw, loading a completely new page. Frames offer the ability to have a fixed navigation bar that never refreshes. Clicking a frames-based navigation bar can launch other documents on your screen while the navigation bar itself remains unchanged.

Many people hate frames, with good reason. It's hard to bookmark a page within a framed site, because the location that the browser bookmarks is that of the framed site, not of the individual pages. Also, it's confusing to print a page that's nested inside frames. There are workarounds for all these problems, but they require extra effort from your end viewer.

On the other hand, there are times when you have a lot of information to display or simply a lot of different pages on a similar topic in your site, and you want your main navigational elements to remain available to your users. Being able to keep one or more parts of the screen still while the user scrolls through other parts is a technique long available to designers of multimedia, but only recently available on the web.

How Frames Work

The basic model of HTML frames revolves around the concept of framesets. A **frameset** is a container for frames, which are really just windows into other HTML documents. You can think of each frame as almost a separate browser, which shares common buttons and controls with the main window. Let's take a look at a simple example; then we'll get into all the bells and whistles a little later. This document is in the chap14 folder of the <chd2> CD-ROM as frames1.html.

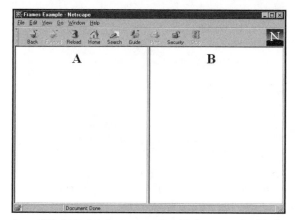

frames1.html: **A simple document with frames.** a.html **is in the left frame, and** b.html **is in the right frame.**

1. `<HTML>`
   `<HEAD>`
   `<TITLE> Frames Example </TITLE>`
   `</HEAD>`
2. `<FRAMESET COLS="*,*">`
3. `<FRAME SRC="a.html">`
   `<FRAME SRC="b.html">`
4. `</FRAMESET>`

   `</HTML>`

1. The outside container of the document is still the HTML element, just like in any other HTML.

2. The FRAMESET container is an element that goes after the HEAD element, and is still inside of the HTML container. The COLS attribute specifies the number of columns (vertical divisions) and the widths of those columns (more about this later). The asterisks (*) mean to evenly divide the space. This value ("*,*") means to use two equally spaced columns. Use ROWS instead of columns to get horizontally divided frames.

3. The actual FRAME tags go within the FRAMESET container. These define the frames themselves. The SRC attribute specifies the HTML document to display inside the frame. In our example, a.html and b.html are the two HTML documents, one of which appears in each frame.

4. The FRAMESET element must be terminated with the </FRAMESET> tag, or your page will not load.

The file a.html (in the chap14 folder of the <chd2> CD-ROM) looks like this:

```
<BODY BGCOLOR=White>
<H1 ALIGN=CENTER> A </H1>
</BODY>
```

And b.html (surprise!) looks like this:

```
<BODY BGCOLOR=White>
<H1 ALIGN=CENTER> B </H1>
</BODY>
```

We will use several files like this as we explain the capabilities of frames in this chapter.

▶ **note**

Support for Older Browsers

Because there is no BODY in a frames document, and in fact, there is no content at all outside of the FRAMESET and FRAME tags, a browser that doesn't understand frames will see nothing but a blank screen!

The solution to this is to use the special NOFRAMES element. Any content within NOFRAMES will not be displayed on frames-supporting browsers, but will be displayed on older browsers.

```
<HTML>
<HEAD>
<TITLE> Frames Example </TITLE>
</HEAD>

<FRAMESET COLS="*,*">
    <FRAME SRC="a.html">
    <FRAME SRC="b.html">
</FRAMESET>

<NOFRAMES>
    <P>
    This site uses frames. If you are
    seeing this message, your web
    browser does not support frames.
    You can still see what we have to
    offer, although without the navi-
    gation advantages of frames, by
    using these links:

    <UL>
       <LI> <A HREF="a.html">Document
       A</A>
       <LI> <A HREF="b.html">Document
       B</A>
    </UL>

</NOFRAMES>
</HTML>
```

The content within the NOFRAMES element will be displayed by browsers that don't understand frames, so they will know what to do. The file to the left is available in the chap14 folder of the <chd2> CD-ROM as frames1a.html.

What browsers without frames capability will see.

Of course, you could instead display an entire web page with alternate content for frames-challenged browsers.

(...Frames (...Within Frames))

"Well now," you may ask. "If a frame is just a window with another HTML document in it, what prevents me from (place wild idea here)?" And we answer, "Absolutely anything you can do with a normal HTML document can be done in a frame." In fact, a frame can even have more frames inside of it!

If we take the previous example and use a frames document in place of b.html, we get more frames in our "**B**" frame:

frames2.html:

```
<HTML>
<HEAD>
<TITLE> Frames Example </TITLE>
</HEAD>

<FRAMESET COLS="*,*" >
  <FRAME SRC="a.html">
  <FRAME SRC="b2.html">
</FRAMESET>

</HTML>
```

b2.html:

```
<FRAMESET ROWS="*,*">
   <FRAME SRC="c.html">
   <FRAME SRC="d.html">
</FRAMESET>
```

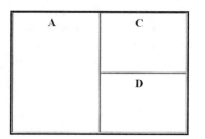

frames2.html: **The right-side document is another frameset.**

There is, however, an easier way to accomplish this same task. You can nest another FRAMESET within your existing FRAMESET. When you nest frames like this, it's a good idea to put comments in the code so that you can keep track of which frame is which:

frames3.html:

```
<HTML>
<HEAD>
<TITLE> Frames Example </TITLE>
</HEAD>

<!– cols for vertical divisions –>
<FRAMESET COLS="*,*" >

  <!– left frame –>
  <FRAME SRC="a.html">

  <!– right frame is another frameset
  –>
  <!– rows for horizontal divisions –>
  <FRAMESET ROWS="*,*">
    <!– top frame –>
    <FRAME SRC="c.html">
    <!– bottom frame –>
    <FRAME SRC="d.html">
  </FRAMESET>

</FRAMESET>

</HTML>
```

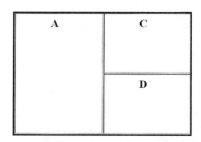

frames3.html: **Looks just like the last one!**

This example accomplishes exactly the same thing as frames2.html, but it does so with one less file. This is the preferred way to nest frames. This version also uses comments to explain what each FRAME and FRAMESET is for. Using comments makes it easier to figure out what you did when you come back and look at your code sometime later.

Adjusting the Size of Frames

As you learned earlier, the ROWS and COLS attributes to the FRAMESET tag take values that define the size of the frame. So far, we have been using the default sizes, "*,*".

You can adjust the sizes of the frames by using values instead of the asterisks, and the values can be either numbers (for the number of pixels) or percentages (for a percentage of the remaining space). In this example, the leftmost frame is 90 pixels wide, and the top right frame is 33% of the height of the screen. The bottom right frame fills out the remaining space.

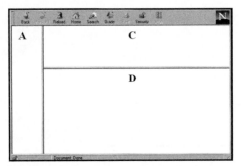

frames4.html: **These frames are specific sizes.**

frames4.html:

```
<HTML>
<HEAD>
<TITLE> Frames Example </TITLE>
</HEAD>

<!- cols for vertical divisions ->
1. <FRAMESET COLS=" 90,*" >

   <!- left frame ->
   <FRAME SRC=" a.html">

   <!- right frame is another
   frameset ->
   <!- rows for horizontal divisions
   ->
```

```
2. <FRAMESET ROWS=" 33%,*">
       <!- top frame ->
       <FRAME SRC=" c.html">
       <!- bottom frame ->
       <FRAME SRC=" d.html">
   </FRAMESET>

</FRAMESET>

</HTML>
```

1. In this first frameset, the COLS attribute specifies a number, instead of the default asterisk, for the first column. When you use a plain number, this indicates pixels. The asterisk for the second column means "use the rest of the available space."

2. The inner frameset specifies ROWS, and the first number is expressed as a percentage. This means "use 33% of the available space."

As you design your site, keep in mind that percentage values will change as the browser is resized, and pixel values will not. If you have a frame that holds a single graphic (like a title bar or an imagemap), you will probably want to use a specific pixel size for that frame so that it doesn't change size when the user changes the size of his or her browser. If a frame is going to hold text or other variable-size information, you may prefer to use a percentage, or even the asterisk. We'll show examples from DIAR later in this chapter.

Borderless Frames

You can remove the borders from your frames by simply adding the attribute BORDER=0 to your outermost FRAMESET tag.

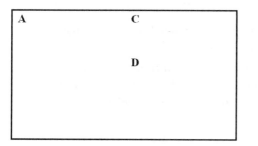

frames5.html: **Borders: Be gone!**

```
    <!— cols for vertical divisions —>
1.  <FRAMESET COLS=" 90,*"  BORDER=0>

      <!— left frame —>
      <FRAME SRC=" a.html">

      <!— right frame is another frame-
      set —>
      <!— rows for horizontal divisions
      —>
      <FRAMESET ROWS=" 33%,*">
        <!— top frame —>
        <FRAME SRC=" c.html">
        <!— bottom frame —>
        <FRAME SRC=" b.html">
      </FRAMESET>

    </FRAMESET>
```

1. The BORDER=0 attribute is used with the outermost FRAMESET tag to turn off the borders for all the frames on the page. With the borders off and the BGCOLOR of all the frames the same, it becomes impossible to tell where one frame starts and the next frame ends. That can be a nice effect for some purposes, but you may want to have a distinction without the borders.

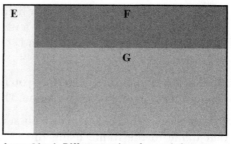

frames6.html: **Different colors for each frame.**

An effective way to distinguish between frames is using a different BGCOLOR for adjacent frames. In this example, we have used three different HTML files. This technique often creates a nicer aesthetic than the borders, and it gives you more flexible use of your space.

You can also use a background tile in any of your frames by using the BACKGROUND attribute in the BODY tag of the frame's HTML document. In the next example, we used a background tile for the lower-right frame.

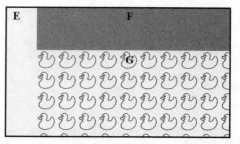
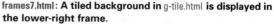

frames7.html: **A tiled background in** g-tile.html **is displayed in the lower-right frame.**

In this interesting case, the color of the left frame and the background color of the tile used in the lower-right frame blend such that the tile appears to run out of ducks on the left!

Navigating Frames

Frames can be a wonderful tool for helping your visitors navigate your site. Using frames, you can put your menus and imagemaps in fixed areas of the screen, keeping them from moving and scrolling as the content of the other frames changes.

When using frames for navigation, you need to create links in one frame that cause documents to load in another frame. These are called **targeted links**.

To create a targeted link, you must first make up a name for your frame, and assign that name to the frame using the NAME attribute in the FRAME tag. This is the name that you will use later to identify the frame in the TARGET attribute of an anchor tag.

frames8.html:

```
<HTML>
<HEAD>
<TITLE> Frames Example </TITLE>
</HEAD>

<!– cols for vertical divisions –>
<FRAMESET COLS="90,*" BORDER=0>

   <!– left frame –>
1. <FRAME SRC="menu.html" NAME=left>

   <!– right frame is another frameset –>
   <!– rows for horizontal divisions –>
   <FRAMESET ROWS="33%,*">
      <!– top frame –>
2. <FRAME SRC="f.html" NAME=upper>
         <!– bottom frame –>
3. <FRAME SRC="g.html" NAME=lower>
   </FRAMESET>

</FRAMESET>

</HTML>
```

1/2/3   Notice the NAME attributes in the FRAME tags. This allows you to assign a name to each of your frames so you can target the frames in your links. The name can be anything you want it to be, but it's best to stick to letters and numbers to avoid compatibility problems with future browsers. To target a particular frame, use the TARGET attribute in the anchor tag when you create your link. For example, this link would load a new page in the frame named "lower":

```
<A HREF="a.html" TARGET="lower"> The "A" page</A>
```

As an example, we'll load this page in the left frame:

links1.html:

```
<BODY BGCOLOR=" #FFFFCC'>
<H1 ALIGN=CENTER> Links </H1>

<A HREF=" a.html"  TARGET=" lower"> The " A"  page</A><BR>
<A HREF=" b.html"  TARGET=" lower"> The " B'  page</A><BR>
<A HREF=" c.html"  TARGET=" lower"> The " C'  page</A><BR>
<A HREF=" d.html"  TARGET=" lower"> The " D'  page</A><BR>

</BODY>
```

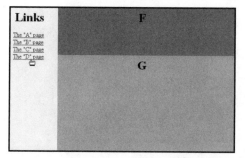

frames8.html with links1.html **loaded in the left frame.**

The target frame is the frame named "lower," which is the frame with the g.html file in it. Now, we'll click on a link, and the new file will replace the lower frame:

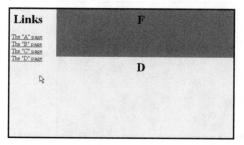

After clicking on the D link, the d.html **file will replace the lower frame.**

Scrollbars in Frames

When the content of a frame becomes larger than the size of the frame—either because the content is too long or the users have shrunk their browser window—scrollbars appear to allow the user to access all the content of the frame.

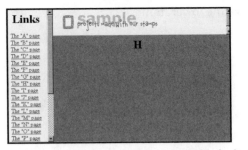

frames9.html **with** links2.html, **a longer list of links loaded in the left-hand frame.**

There may be times when you don't want a scrollbar to appear, even if the content is too large for the frame. For example, consider this screen:

frames10.html: **The image at the top is too big for its frame.**

In this case we have a titleish image in the top frame, which extends beyond the bottom of the frame. The image actually looks fine in the frame, but the scrollbar on the right is really unnecessary.

We can get rid of that scrollbar by using the SCROLLING=NO attribute to the FRAME tag:

```
<HTML>
<HEAD>
<TITLE> Frames Example </TITLE>
</HEAD>

<!– cols for vertical divisions –>
<FRAMESET COLS="130,*" BORDER=0>

<!– left frame –>
<FRAME SRC="links2.html" NAME=left>

<!– right frame is another frameset –>
<!– rows for horizontal divisions –>
<FRAMESET ROWS="75,*">
    <!– top frame –>
    <FRAME SRC="titlebar.html"
NAME=titlebar SCROLLING=NO>
        <!– bottom frame –>
        <FRAME SRC="h.html" NAME=lower>
    </FRAMESET>

</FRAMESET>

</HTML>
```

1. The SCROLLING=NO attribute forces the frame to keep the scrollbar off at all times, even if the content is too big for the frame.

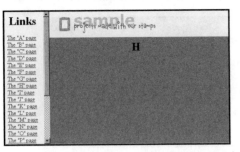

frames10a.html: **Voilà! Zee scrollbar ees vamoose!**

Margins in Frames

Because your frames will sometimes consist of only one graphic, it can be convenient to position the graphic right up against the edge of the frame. Normally, there are both vertical and horizontal margins on the frames. If we temporarily use a contrasting color for the background of the title bar, you can see the margins around the window:

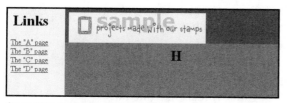

frames11.html **with** titlebar2.html: **There is an unwanted margin around the image.**

You can remove the margins with the MARGINHEIGHT and MARGINWIDTH attributes from the FRAME tag:

```
<HTML>
<HEAD>
<TITLE> Frames Example </TITLE>
</HEAD>

<!- cols for vertical divisions ->
<FRAMESET COLS="130,*" BORDER=0>

  <!- left frame ->
  <FRAME SRC="links1.html"
  NAME=left>

  <!- right frame is another frame-
set ->
  <!- rows for horizontal divisions
->
  <FRAMESET ROWS="67,*">
    <!- top frame ->
    <FRAME SRC="titlebar2.html"
    NAME=titlebar
      SCROLLING=NO
    MARGINHEIGHT=0 MARGINWIDTH=0>
    <!- bottom frame ->
    <FRAME SRC="h.html" NAME=lower>
  </FRAMESET>
```

1.

```
</FRAMESET>

</HTML>
```

1. The MARGINHEIGHT and MARGINWIDTH attributes adjust the margins in the frame. Setting them to zero should remove the margins entirely, but Netscape Navigator (versions 3 and 4) always leaves one pixel.

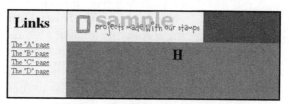

frames11a.html: **With the contrasting background, you can clearly see the one-pixel margin Netscape leaves behind.**

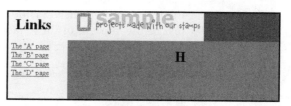

frames11a.html: **Microsoft Internet Explorer 4.0 and later do not reserve the one-pixel margin.**

Of course, the extra pixel of margin is not critical, because your page will still look right when you match the background color.

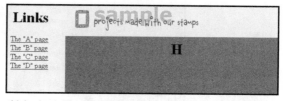

titlebar.html: **The top frame looks great even in Netscape with the matching seamless** BGCOLOR.

Aesthetics of Frames

We used frames extensively in the Catalog and Sample areas of the DIAR site because we had a lot of images to display. Frames worked well as a navigation device to load thumbnail previews that create a visual directory to our larger image libraries. (A section called "Making Thumbnails and Small Graphics" follows later in this chapter.)

One disadvantage to using frames is that it divides the real estate on your web page into smaller pieces. Many web publishers and visitors are already frustrated by small screen space, so dividing the screen into smaller sections runs the risk of being more of an irritant than an enhancement to a site.

In order to make our frames feel less confining, we worked with color relationships that unified the page. Even though this page is divided into four separate frame regions, it feels like one page instead of four disjointed parts pieced together. We paid a great deal of attention to visual continuity as well as color. We matched the icons and type used inside the frames to the aesthetics of the rest of the site. All of these factors made our use of frames less annoying than other examples we see on the web.

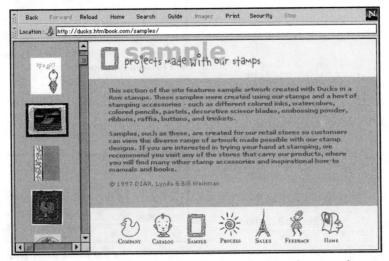

Working with color relationships and visual continuity make our web page feel unified.

> ## ▶ note
>
> ### Do People Scroll?
>
> Lynda once visited the offices of HotWired (http://www.hotwired.com) to meet with her friend Mike Kuniavsky, who heads their research efforts for interface design. There, he set up a video camera to tape the response of test users who had never navigated the HotWired site before. One of the most startling results of his videotaped studies was that the test users almost never scrolled beyond the initial screen that appeared, even if the screen contained essential navigation information lower on the page. Many respondents didn't even realize there was more to the page than what they saw, despite the vertical scrollbars. Moral of the story? Be careful with key navigational graphics. Don't make the end users work hard to figure out the navigation to your site. Make it easy for them to know where they are and how to get where they want to go, and make key navigation text and/or graphics appear within their browser windows without requiring scrolling.

Size Considerations

When you're developing your web site, it's important to think about the size of the browser window and the resulting size relationships of images. The starting point is to establish who your audience is, and from what size displays you think they will be viewing the web. While many designers have large monitors, most average web visitors have smaller displays. The most common monitor size is 13" or 14". Most people who have average size displays have them set to 800×600.

Netscape Navigator and Microsoft Internet Explorer open in a narrow window on Macintoshes, and fill the screen on Windows. If a web page is bigger than the browser window on which it is displayed, scrollbars automatically appear to signal to the end user that the page is larger than what is visible. Here are some sample browser configurations on a standard 640×480 display.

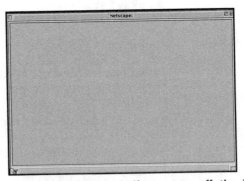

Macintosh Maximized: If you turn off the icons in Netscape Navigator and maximize the browser window to its fullest, the available space for your web page will be 624×400 pixels.

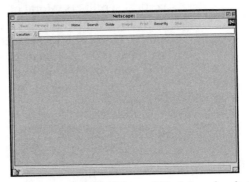

Macintosh with Small Icons: This is how Lynda typically conforms her Netscape Navigator browser, which yields available space of 634×324 pixels.

Macintosh Default: In Netscape Navigator with large icons turned on, the default size is 382×324 pixels.

What happens on a 640×480 display if you make a graphic that is 800 pixels wide? It will require the end user to scroll horizontally to see the graphic. What happens if you make a graphic that is longer than the browser window? Vertical scrollbars will appear.

There are no standard guidelines for the size of navigational graphics, only educated guesses about what is practical and what isn't. We believe it's prudent to create essential navigation elements so they can be seen within 800×600 displays, and for some audiences 640×480 displays, without requiring the end viewer to scroll his or her browser window.

This directive is easier said than done. If you're designing for an audience that still uses 800×600 browsers, it's a good idea to set your monitor to 800×600 before you begin creating navigation graphics. This will ensure that there will be a one-to-one size relationship between your artwork as it is created and as it will be viewed. In the case of frames, it can be helpful to mock up the navigation artwork in a Photoshop document that matches the size of the browser window. We recommend that if you are designing for an 800×600 audience, you set up your graphic template so it's no wider than 780 and no higher than 450 pixels. We have set up an empty Photoshop template of that size for you as browser.psd, located in the chap14 folder of the <chd2> CD-ROM. This empty document should be a good starting point for designing navigational graphics, to ensure that your graphics don't end up too big for a 640×480 display.

Size Considerations Navbars/Frames

Now that you've seen the different size browser windows, let's look at some of the size issues inherent in our Ducks In A Row site design. Lynda uses a 17" monitor on her Macintosh system, which is a fairly typical size setup for many professional designers. Since the majority of the web audience will be on 13" monitors, however, Lynda's setup gave her a false sense of size security that proved wrong when we went live with the DIAR site. Mistakes are best when they're someone else's, so you get to benefit from our hard lessons by understanding where we went awry.

The first navbar we made was constructed while we were writing earlier chapters of this book. It was good enough to show as an example for learning about imagemaps, but the example we made was taken out of context of its true home on our site. Because of this, Lynda made the navbar without thinking about future size constraints.

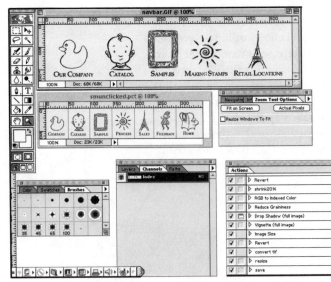

On Lynda's 17" monitor, the navbar.gif **shown at the top of this screen seemed like a reasonable size.**

At 640×480 this bottom navbar looks like it's a transplant from the Land of the Giants site.

After Lynda reduced the bottom navbar, it fit much better in scale to the 640×480 window.

By switching her monitor to 640×480, it was obvious that the top navbar was way too large for our target audience of viewers, whom we suspected would be surfing on systems set to 640×480 pixels. The lower navbar shows the corrected file, and the next screen shot shows it in context of the frames.

After Lynda got the size of the navbar corrected, it was time to design our framesets for the Sample and Catalog sections of our site. This time, Lynda and Bill readjusted their monitor's resolutions to 640×480 in order to previsualize how the target web audience would view the site.

Moral of the story? Design at the resolution you're planning to publish for. If you want your site to look good at 640×480, for a better reality check switch your monitor to that resolution while you're designing graphics for the site.

This example looked great on a 640×480 display.

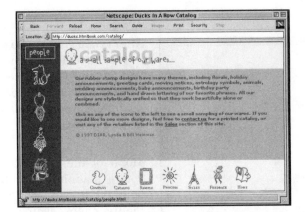

In our Catalog section, we chose a different frames navigation technique. The opening page looks similar to the opening screen of the Sample section.

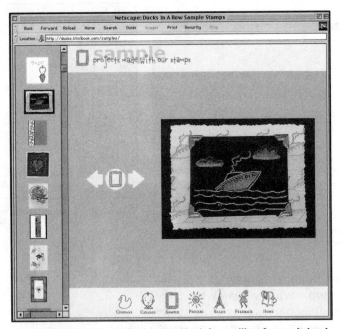

Once a thumbnail is clicked inside the left scrolling frame, it loads the larger version of the sample into the middle frame of the right frameset. Notice how scrollbars appear on the right that weren't there before?

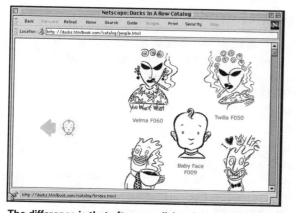

The difference is that after you click a thumbnail in the left frame, a new window appears with the result, rather than the artwork loading into the middle frame, as in the Sample section of the site. This was accomplished in the HTML with `TARGET=_top` in the anchor tag.

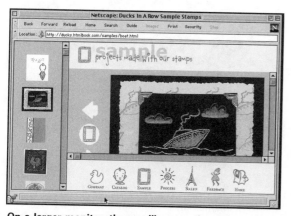

On a larger monitor, the scrollbars on the right would not appear. Bill created the HTML to ensure that the top, left, and bottom frames were fixed sizes. The right middle frame was set to asterisk (*), which fills the remaining size of the browser window on any size monitor, large or small.

Making Thumbnails and Small Graphics

If you've never heard the term "thumbnail" before, in web-speak it refers to a small graphic that links to a larger graphic. Using thumbnails is common practice on web sites, because graphics that are small in dimensions and file size typically load much faster than graphics that are large in dimensions and file size. We created a lot of thumbnail graphics that link to larger graphics in the Catalog and Sample sections of the DIAR web site.

It's actually a lot trickier to create small graphics than large ones. You'll find that you will resize your artwork over and over in Photoshop, and that quality management will be critical. A good rule of thumb is to save master documents of key graphics, preferably in large sizes, so you can work from copies instead of originals. It will always yield higher quality to shrink a computer image than to enlarge it. The moral of the story? Scan large and reduce—never enlarge raster images such as scans or GIFs or JPEGs.

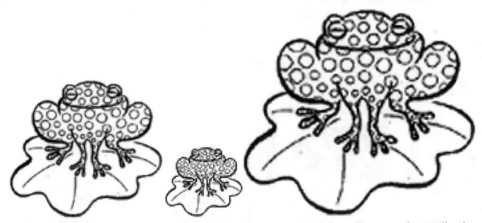

The original scanned image (to the left) is 100%, and it looks fine. The same image (in the middle) is reduced 50% and sharpened with the Photoshop Sharpen filter. The same image again (to the right) is enlarged 150% and even with sharpening filters, this image is soft and lacks good quality.

Fragments

One final navigation technique that's effective when you have lots of information on one page is the HTML fragment. An HTML **fragment** is a separately addressable section of a web page that you access with a special URL part called a fragment.

To create a fragment on a web page, you enclose a section of your page in an anchor element (the A tag) using a NAME attribute to assign a name to it. As an example, we have a text version of the list of retail outlets for the Ducks In A Row rubber stamps at http://ducks. htmlbook. com/sales/locations.html on the DIAR web site. We fragmented the file based on individual states. Here's the entry for Texas:

```
<A NAME=" TX">
<H2>TX</H2> [  <A HREF=" #top">Top</A> ]

    <P><STRONG>Stamp De Ville</STRONG>
    <BR>1014 S. Broadway Suite 100
    <BR>Carrollton TX
<STRONG>75006</STRONG>

    <P><STRONG>Stamp Asylum</STRONG>
    <BR>201 Coit Rd. #165
    <BR>Plano TX <STRONG>75075</STRONG>

    <P><STRONG>Imprints</STRONG>
    <BR>4912 Camp Boyle Blvd.
    <BR>Fort Worth TX
<STRONG>76107</STRONG>

    <P><STRONG>Iconography</STRONG>
    <BR>P.O. Box 130090
    <BR>Houston TX
<STRONG>77219</STRONG>

</A>
```

Now that you have the fragment set aside, you will want a way to link directly to it. For that purpose, you can use a special extension to the URL called the fragment.

▶ **tip**

Frames Resources

Netscape's Basic Frames Tutorial
http://home.netscape.com/assist/
net_sites/frames.html

Bruce Heavin's Portfolio
http://www.stink.com/bruce/

A URL with a Fragment

The fragment part of the URL identifies a fragment of a page. So, if you wanted to link to the TX fragment that we just created, you would use the URL http://ducks.htmlbook.com/sales/locations.htlm#TX. This will cause a browser to display the page starting with the top of the fragment.

fragment identifier

http://ducks.htmlbook.com/sales/locations.html#TX

host　　　　　　　**path**　　**fragment**

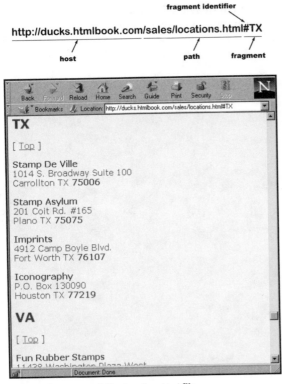

The TX **fragment of the** locations.html **file.**

At the top of our locations page, we have a list of states with a link to a fragment of the page for each state.

Links to each of the state fragments.

Just as you can use a relative URL to link to another file on the same web site, you can link to a fragment by itself when it's in the same file.

In this case, we used fragment links in the HREF attributes to our anchor tags to link to each U.S. state (or Canadian province) where a customer can find a store that sells DIAR's rubber stamps.

```
<P> [
<A HREF="#AK">AK</A>       |
<A HREF="#AZ">AZ</A>       |
<A HREF="#Alberta">Alberta</A>    |
<A HREF="#CA">CA</A>       |
<A HREF="#CO">CO</A>       |
<A HREF="#CT">CT</A>       |
<A HREF="#FL">FL</A>       |
<A HREF="#GA">GA</A>       |
<A HREF="#IA">IA</A>       |
<A HREF="#IL">IL</A>       |
<A HREF="#KY">KY</A>       |
<A HREF="#MA">MA</A>       |
<A HREF="#MD">MD</A>       |
<A HREF="#MI">MI</A>       |
<A HREF="#MN">MN</A>       |
<A HREF="#MO">MO</A>       |
<A HREF="#NH">NH</A>       |
<A HREF="#NJ">NJ</A>       |
<A HREF="#NM">NM</A>       |
<A HREF="#NV">NV</A>       |
<A HREF="#NY">NY</A>       |
<A HREF="#OH">OH</A>       |
<A HREF="#OK">OK</A>       |
<A HREF="#OR">OR</A>       |
<A HREF="#PA">PA</A>       |
<A HREF="#RI">RI</A>       |
<A HREF="#SC">SC</A>       |
<A HREF="#TN">TN</A>       |
<A HREF="#TX">TX</A>       |
<A HREF="#VA">VA</A>       |
<A HREF="#WA">WA</A>       |
<A HREF="#WI">WI</A>       ]
```

Finally, one important navigational detail: Whenever you have a long page, it's very important to have a link back to the top of the page. This page lists over 130 different retail outlets, so a user could easily get lost in it all.

To accomplish this, we created a fragment at the top of the page, and we called it top:

```
<A NAME="top">
<!- Logo ->
<IMG SRC="/images/ylogo1.gif"
    ALT="Ducks in a Row Logo"
    BORDER=0
    WIDTH=419 HEIGHT=219>
<H1>List of Retail Stores</H1>
</A>
```

Then, next to every individual state heading, we inserted a link back to #top.

```
<H2>TX</H2> [  <A HREF="#top">Top</A> ]
```

This makes it easy for a user to get back to the top of the page—like a little electronic trail of bread crumbs. Now the users can find their way home!

▶ chapter fourteen summary

Navigation

In print, no one gives much thought to navigation issues, though they are present there, too. Most people intuitively know how to flip pages, use a table of contents, or find a reference in an index. The web has an unspoken navigation language that is still being defined, and since hyperlinks can transport your end users without them even knowing where they're going, it's a huge challenge to design intuitive navigation.

Frames and fragments are among many navigational devices (including hyperlinks, imagemaps, rollovers, button graphics, and others) that can either enhance or detract from the navigability of your site. Now that you've studied these two new techniques, your navigation design choices are wider. Given how difficult navigation issues are, it's best to understand when and why to use techniques like frames and fragments. We've covered the nuances of both navigation methods, and filled you in on the design decisions related to choosing one, the other, or none of the above!

*"Is that a real poncho,
or is that a Sears poncho?"*
—*Frank Zappa*

Rollovers
enhancing navigation

▶ **contents**

rollover graphics
javascript rollovers
rollover exercises
dhtml

Web browsers have introduced a few preset conventions to indicate that an image or text is "hot," such as underlined text, colored borders around images, and the appearance of a hand cursor. Artists and web publishers can make their own protocols for how graphics or text will look when a rollover is triggered, which allows for much greater personalization of web site design than standard HTML provides.

Any number of things can be programmed to happen when a viewer interacts with a "hot" graphic or text. It's common to see the hot object itself change appearance, as with the highlighting rollover examples in this chapter. Another object can appear on the same page, like the pointer in the pointing rollover example in this chapter. Or a floating window could pop up, or an animation could begin playing. Almost any action you can program in JavaScript can be triggered by a rollover.

When Lynda and Bill were preparing for this chapter, the idea of writing about rollovers excited both of us—but for different reasons. Lynda saw it as an opportunity to write about techniques for creating the rollover graphics, and Bill saw the opportunity to write about JavaScript techniques for creating the rollover effects.

Because you will need the graphics before you can use the JavaScript, we have put Lynda's section first. If you find that the other order works better for you, feel free to jump ahead.

Creating Rollover Graphics

The traditional way to create a rollover was to produce the artwork for each state of a rollover in a graphics program like Photoshop, and then to program the rollover effects by writing your own JavaScript and including it in your HTML file. As web graphics programs like ImageReady and Fireworks evolve, you have more options for creating rollovers. These applications not only give you tools to create rollover artwork; they also can write JavaScript and HTML to make your rollovers functional. In the following exercises, we'll show you a number of alternatives for creating rollover graphics in Photoshop, ImageReady, and Fireworks, with and without built-in functionality.

You might wonder whether or not we recommend that you write your own JavaScript or use the code that ImageReady or Fireworks generates. Bill and Lynda would probably disagree on this.

From Lynda's Perspective

Tools like ImageReady make it easy for non-JavaScript programmers to create rollovers. The code works, though it isn't as elegant or well-crafted as someone's hand-coded JavaScript. You'll never meet a programmer who "likes" the code that an automatic code generator like ImageReady or Fireworks produce. Regardless, in Lynda's view, not everyone cares whether the code looks good or is compact; sometimes it's a great convenience and time saver to have an application like ImageReady to write the code automatically.

However, the purpose of this book is to learn HTML and JavaScript, so with that in mind, she recommends that you still complete the JavaScript programming exercises in this chapter so you can, at minimum, understand how to read JavaScript and troubleshoot problems with it. Now, for Bill's turn on his soapbox.

From Bill's Perspective

As Lynda predicted, this programmer does not like the JavaScript that comes out of Image-Ready. It's fine for quickly validating your work (though I don't really find it quick or easy), but for a production environment you will do much better with code that is designed for your particular application.

The code that is generated by the graphic design programs is generalized. That's because it was written to work in a very broad set of circumstances. Because of that it tends to be much larger than it needs to be, and that means that there are a lot of things that can go wrong that don't otherwise have anything to do with your particular application.

The basic function of a rollover is to swap one graphic with another as a reaction to some event (e.g. the mouse moved over a certain area, so replace this graphic with that one). In this chapter you will find a piece of JavaScript code that does just that, and only that. We also present examples of how to use it in several different circumstances.

Personally, I find this easier than implementing the code from the graphics program. I just keep a copy of the JavaScript in a file, and paste it in to whatever HTML piece I am working on.

As Lynda said, it's entirely up to you. Even if you use the JavaScript from the graphics program, you will benefit from reading and understanding the code presented here.

♦ exercise

ImageReady 3.0 Rollover Techniques

ImageReady 3.0 is a great tool for making rollovers. ImageReady can not only slice artwork, it can also create the necessary JavaScript required for rollovers in the HTML it outputs. In this exercise, you'll learn to slice artwork, create rollover states, and output the results.

Step 1: Launch ImageReady 3.0, and open the file icons.psd from the chap15 folder of the <chd2> CD-ROM.

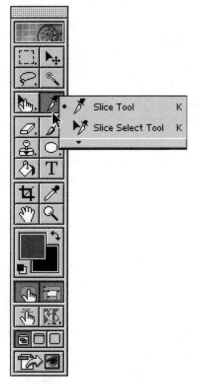

Step 2: Using the **Slice** tool, drag a region around each button, like shown above. This will number each region automatically. If you want to adjust the shape of the slice, use the **Slice Select** tool to select the slice, then adjust the handles. When you're happy with the shape and position of each slice, use the Slice Select tool to select slice01.

Step 3: Click on the **Slice palette** button at the top of the Options Bar. This will bring the Slice tab forward. Enter a name that relates to the slice. ImageReady assigns default names, but they aren't meaningful, so we prefer to give them a custom slice name. Again, names should not contain spaces, capital letters, or special characters.

> ▶ **note**
>
> ### The Slicing Process
>
> What happens when you slice a file in ImageReady? The program prepares to save the contents of each slice as an individual GIF or JPEG, and, at your option, to write an HTML file containing a table to reassemble the individual images. Notice that each time you draw a slice, some additional slices are also drawn. The purpose of these extra slices is to fill in the rectangular layout of the underlying HTML table.

Creates new rollover state

Step 4: Now you'll create your rollover states. With the company slice still selected, click on the **Rollover** tab. You'll see a thumbnail of the Normal state of the **Company** icon. Click the **Duplicate Slice** icon at the bottom of the Rollover palette to create an Over state for the company icon.

Step 5: Make sure that the company layer is selected. Click the **Layer Effects** icon (*f*) and select **Color Overlay** from the popup menu. The company slice should turn red!

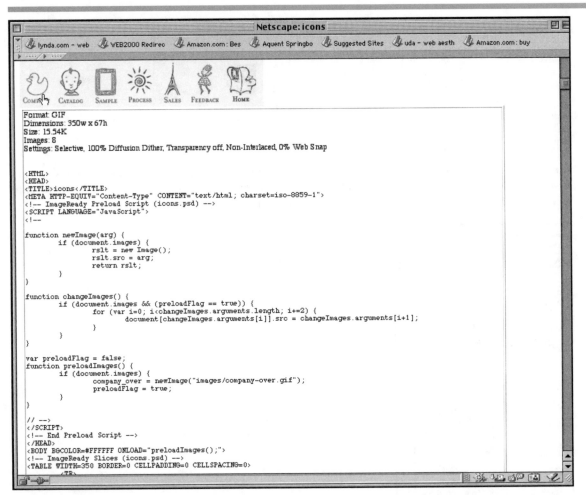

Step 6: Click back and forth between the **Normal** state and **Over** states in the Rollover palette to see the company rollover work. To preview the rollover in a browser, select **File:Preview In**, and choose a browser. If the preview doesn't look good, go to the step 8 to optimize the company slice, and then try previewing.

Step 7: Repeat steps 3 (but change the slice to the next icon), 4 (make sure the correct layer is selected!), 5, and 6 for each of the slices in your navigation bar to create a rollover for each icon.

Step 8: You can optimize your slices one at a time by selecting a slice, clicking the **Optimized, 2-Up** or **4-Up** tab, and setting the optimization controls for that slice in the Optimize palette. In cases like this, in which the content of all slices is similar, you can save time by optimizing a linked group of slices.

Step 9: Shift-click all the slices, and select **Slices:Link Slices**. Then click on any of the linked slices, and choose your optimization settings in the **Optimize** palette. Keep in mind that when you optimize any slice, the graphics for all of the rollover states in that slice are optimized the same way.

Step 10: Select **File:Save** to save the **.PSD** source file with its slices. This is the file you'll come back to if you need to make changes to your rollovers.

Step 11: Select **File:Save Optimized As** to save your optimized images for the web. In the Save Optimized dialog box, click the **New Folder** icon and name the folder rollover3. Choose **Format: Images Only**. Choose **All Slices**. This tells ImageReady to save an individual image file for each rollover state in each slice (a total of 14 GIFs in this case). You can program these images to act as rollovers by creating your own HTML file containing JavaScript that you write yourself.

Step 12: Alternatively, you can have Image-Ready write an HTML file for you that contains JavaScript to make your images into working rollovers, as well as a table to hold the images in place. Choose **Format:HTML and Image** in the Save Optimized dialog box. When you're done, click **Save**.

▶ **note**

Rollover Possiblilities

ImageReady can create rollovers by memorizing any of three Layers features: **Layer Effects** (as in this example), **Layer Opacity** (which you manipulate with the opacity slider on the Layers palette), and **Layer Visibility** (which you control with the eye icons on the Layers palette). Experiment with each to create a variety of rollover effects.

JavaScript for Rollovers

You may prefer to write your own JavaScript rollover code instead of relying on a program like ImageReady to write it for you. If you used a graphics program to create rollover graphics without accompanying JavaScript and HTML, you'll need to create some code to make your rollovers work. This section of the chapter covers JavaScript techniques you can integrate into your HTML code to enable your rollovers to function.

There are three types of rollovers that we've encountered on the web. We've named them **"pointing,"** **"highlighting,"** and **"slideshow."** These names are not intended to imply that you must use these types of rollovers for certain purposes; your personal creativity will determine that! These names are used here only to distinguish one from the other.

Bill has written a single JavaScript program that handles all three of these types of rollovers. In the next few pages, we will show how you can create rollovers using this program, simply by modifying a few parts of the example files we have provided on the CD-ROM.

• **Pointing rollover:** This is the kind in which there is an image that seems to follow your mouse as you pass it over a set of links. Normally used with a small arrow and a long list of links, this type of rollover uses one image for the pointer and a blank image for swapping out.

• **Highlighting rollover:** This is the most common type. As your mouse passes over a set of images, each image is replaced by a "highlighted" version. Of course, you can put whatever you want in the image—there is no law that it must be a highlighted version of the same image.

• **Slideshow rollover:** This is the least commonly used, but we love the effect. (We used a slideshow rollover for the Catalog page on the DIAR site.) With this type of rollover, as the mouse passes over the links, images are replaced in a single location on the screen—like the word "people" at the top of the image. The effect is somewhat like a slide show.

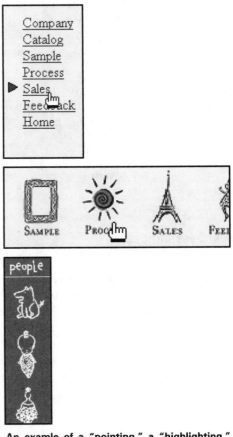

An examle of a "pointing," a "highlighting," and a "slideshow" rollover.

Pointing Rollover

The Pointing rollover is the easiest type of rollover to implement. All you need is a small pointing image, and a corresponding blank image that is the same size and background color as the pointing image.

Two GIF files are needed for the Pointing rollover effect. The left image is called blank.gif, and the right image is called smarrow.gif. Both files are included in the images folder in the chap15 folder of the <chd2> CD-ROM.

Using Bill's program, you can make a custom Pointing rollover by replacing the example images shown below with any two images that are equal to each other in dimensions. This will enable you to create your own Pointing rollover effects, without having to learn to write the JavaScript yourself. In this example, we have used a small arrow (14×14 pixels) for the pointer, and a flat white GIF in the same size for the blank image.

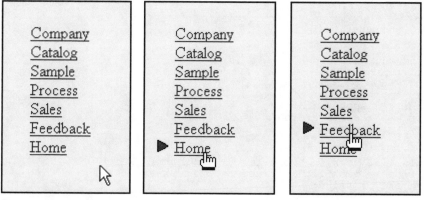

The pointing rollover in action.

Here's the HTML code that creates the Pointing rollover effect (pointing.html in the chap15 folder on the CD-ROM):

```
<HTML>
<HEAD>
<TITLE> Pointing Rollover Example </TITLE>
```
1. `<SCRIPT LANGUAGE="JavaScript">`
2. `<!--`

3.
```
// Bill Weinman's Generic Rollover Engine
// (c) 2000 William E. Weinman
//
// http://bw.org/
//
```

```
// This program is free software. You may modify and distribute
it
// as long as you include this notice in all copies.
//
// No other rights are granted. This program is not "public
domain".
//
```

4. `okay = false;   // wait until variables are initialized`

5. `var preload = new Array (`

```
//////////////////////////////////////////////////
// list all your images here.
// Remember: No comma after the last image!
//

   "images/smarrow.gif", "images/blank.gif"

//
// you shouldn't need to modify anything
// below this line
//////////////////////////////////////////////////

   );
```

6.
```
// find out what browser this is
with(navigator) {
   code = appCodeName;
   app = appName;
   version = appVersion;
   iver = parseInt(version);
   ua = userAgent;
   }

// this will work in "Mozilla" 3+ (includes MSIE 4)
if ( code == "Mozilla" && iver >= 3 )   okay = true;
else { okay = false; }

if(okay) {
   // compile the RegExp because we use it a lot
   var re = new RegExp();
   re.compile("[ \\/.:\\-\\s]", "g");

   // preload the images
   for (var i = 0; i < preload.length; i++) {
     i_preload(preload[ i] );
     }
   var preloaded = true
   }

// take a filename and make a legal variable name from it
function iname (img)
{
var s = img.replace(re, "_");
return s;
}
```

```
// preload the images
function i_preload(img)
{
if(img) {
   var imgn = iname(img);
   eval(imgn + " = new Image()");
   eval(imgn + ".src = '" + img + "'");
   }
return true;
}
```

7.
```
// swap entry function
function swap (name, image)
{
if(!okay) return true; // just leave unless okay

// don't try to do this before the preloading is finished
if(preloaded) document.images[ name] .src = image;
return true;
}

// ->
</SCRIPT>

</HEAD>
<BODY BGCOLOR=" white">

<TABLE><TR><TD HEIGHT=10></TABLE> <!- spacer ->

<TABLE><TR><TD WIDTH=40><TD>
   <!- List of Links starts here ->
```
8.
9.
```
   <IMG NAME=" i1" SRC=" images/blank.gif">
   <A HREF="" onMouseOver=" swap('i1', 'images/smarrow.gif')"
      onMouseOut=" swap('i1', 'images/blank.gif')">Company</A><BR>
   <IMG NAME=" i2" SRC=" images/blank.gif">
   <A HREF="" onMouseOver=" swap('i2', 'images/smarrow.gif')"
      onMouseOut=" swap('i2', 'images/blank.gif')">Catalog</A><BR>
   <IMG NAME=" i3" SRC=" images/blank.gif">
   <A HREF="" onMouseOver=" swap('i3', 'images/smarrow.gif')"
      onMouseOut=" swap('i3', 'images/blank.gif')">Sample</A><BR>
   <IMG NAME=" i4" SRC=" images/blank.gif">
   <A HREF="" onMouseOver=" swap('i4', 'images/smarrow.gif')"
      onMouseOut=" swap('i4', 'images/blank.gif')">Process</A><BR>
   <IMG NAME=" i5" SRC=" images/blank.gif">
   <A HREF="" onMouseOver=" swap('i5', 'images/smarrow.gif')"
      onMouseOut=" swap('i5', 'images/blank.gif')">Sales</A><BR>
   <IMG NAME=" i6" SRC=" images/blank.gif">
   <A HREF="" onMouseOver=" swap('i6', 'images/smarrow.gif')"
      onMouseOut=" swap('i6', 'images/blank.gif')">Feedback</A><BR>
   <IMG NAME=" i7" SRC=" images/blank.gif">
   <A HREF="" onMouseOver=" swap('i7', 'images/smarrow.gif')"
      onMouseOut=" swap('i7', 'images/blank.gif')">Home</A><BR>
   <!- List of Links ends here ->
</TABLE>

</BODY>
</HTML>
```

1. `<SCRIPT LANGUAGE="JavaScript">`

This is where we tell the browser that we are using JavaScript. If the browser understands JavaScript, it will use the next part of the document as JavaScript code up to the `</SCRIPT>` end tag.

2. `<!--`

Some browsers don't understand the `SCRIPT` element at all, and we want to make sure they don't display the JavaScript (they may think it's HTML!). We put the content of the `SCRIPT` element in an HTML comment (between `<!--` and `-->`). This causes browsers that don't understand JavaScript to ignore the code, and those that do understand the JavaScript to go ahead and use it.

3. `// Bill Weinman's Generic Rollover Engine`
   `// (c) 2000 William E. Weinman`

JavaScript comments are introduced with a pair of slashes (`//`). Everything following the pair of slashes, to the end of the line, is ignored by the browser.

4. `okay = false;   // wait until variables are initialized`

One of the most common problems with JavaScript programs is that it is extremely difficult to ensure that one part of the program runs before another. The result of this problem is often seen as a page that "works most of the time," but not all of the time.

This line of code cures that problem. It initializes a special variable that instructs the rest of the program to remain idle until it knows everything is okay. By having this as the very first line of JavaScript in the HTML file, you can be sure that it will be initialized before anything else happens.

5. `var preload = new Array (`

```
/////////////////////////////////////////////////
// list all your images here.
// Remember: No comma after the last image!
   //

   "images/smarrow.gif", "images/blank.gif"
```

```
//
// you shouldn't need to modify anything
// below this line
/////////////////////////////////////////////////

    );
```

One common reason that some rollover techniques don't work well is that they do not load all the necessary images from the server at the same time the page loads. This part of the program takes a list of images that it will load from the server all at once, so that the images can swap quickly when you use the rollovers.

If you don't list your images here, the rollovers will still appear to work when you run on your local system, but your visitors will have trouble when they connect from far away.

```
"images/smarrow.gif", "images/blank.gif"
```

This is the only part of the code that you will ever need to modify. Just list your images here, putting the relative URL for each image within quotation marks, and separating them with commas. Do not put a comma at the end of the list.

6.
```
// find out what browser this is
with(navigator) {
   code = appCodeName;
   app = appName;
   version = appVersion;
   iver = parseInt(version);
   ua = userAgent;
   }
// this will work in "Mozilla" 3+ (includes MSIE 4)
    if ( code == "Mozilla" && iver >= 3 )  okay = true;
        else { okay = false; }
```

This is the part where we determine if the browser is capable of running the rollovers. Unfortunately, some browsers claim to have enough functionality to run the rollovers when, in fact, they do not (e.g. early versions of Internet Explorer). We need to prevent those browsers from running the code so that they don't display error messages to the user.

This code will accept all browsers that report a "Mozilla" version of 3 or greater. That includes Netscape 3.0 and above, as well as Internet Explorer 4.0 and above.

7.
```
// swap entry function
function swap (name, image)
{
if(!okay) return true; // just leave unless okay

    // don't try to do this before the preloading is finished

    if(preloaded) document.images[ name] .src = image;
    return true;
    }
```
This is what's called the "entry point" for the program. The rest of the program is initialization and support for this part. This is the part that is called from the HTML to actually swap the images.

8.
```
<IMG NAME=" i1"  SRC=" images/blank.gif">
```
In order to swap the images in place on the page, the browser needs to know precisely which image you want swapped. In other words, the images involved need to have unique names. You name an image with the NAME attribute to the IMG tag.

In this document we name the images i1, i2, etc. through i7. It is also worth mentioning that the blank image is used in the SRC attribute. This is the image that will display before any mouse movement triggers the rollover effect. So this should be the image you want for the "normal" state of display.

9.
```
<A HREF=""  onMouseOver=" swap('i1',  'images/smarrow.gif')"
            onMouseOut=" swap('i1',
 'images/blank.gif')">Company</A><BR>
```
Finally, we use the onMouseOver and onMouseOut attributes (also called events by the object-oriented programming crowd) to make the browser call the JavaScript whenever a mouse is passed over the link.

The onMouseOver and onMouseOut attributes are special "script" attributes that contain script language as their value instead of HTML. In this case we use the script attributes with the A tag to cover mouse movements that happen in the space occupied by the link on the screen. The actual Javascript calls are like this:
```
swap('i1',  'images/smarrow.gif')
```
The name of the function being called is "swap". This same function is used for all the different types of rollovers (because they all swap images). The arguments to swap are the name of the image to replace (from the NAME attribute of the IMG tag) and the relative URL of the image to swap in its place. (Make sure that the URL is listed in the JavaScript to be preloaded!)

▶ e x e r c i s e

Make Your Own Pointing Rollover

In this exercise, you will create a pointing rollover using your own pointing graphic.

Step 1: Create a pointing graphic for the rollover.

Step 2: Create a blank graphic that is filled with the same color as the background of your pointing graphic, and has the same dimensions as your pointing graphic.

Step 3: Create a folder called rollover on your local hard disk, and place both your images into it.

Step 4: Copy the pointing.html file from the chap15 folder on the <chd2> CD-ROM to your local rollover folder.

Step 5: Open your local copy of pointing.html in your favorite text editor.

Step 6: Find the following line:

```
"images/smarrow.gif",
"images/blank.gif"
```

. . . and change it to list the graphics that you made in steps 1 and 2. In other words, if your graphics are named pointer.gif and yellow.gif, then you would use:

```
"pointer.gif", "yellow.gif"
```

You don't need to use the path part of the file names because your images are in the same directory as your HTML file.

Step 7: Now edit the list of links at the end of the pointing.html file. For each link, change SRC="images/blank.gif" to the name of your blank image. For example, if your blank image is called yellow.gif you would use SRC="yellow.gif" for your graphic.

Step 8: For each link, place the URL to which you want to link inside the quotation marks of the HREF="" attribute.

Step 9: If you need more links, go ahead and add them. Be sure to add images and links in equal numbers, and be sure to increment the IMG NAME attribute for each link as well. For example, the code to add one more link would look like this:

```
<IMG NAME="i8" SRC="yellow.gif">

  <A HREF="" onMouseOver="swap('i8',
  'arrow.gif')"
     onMouseOut="swap('i8',
     'yellow.gif')">Home</A><BR>
```

Notice that i8 is the next name after i7, and that it goes in three places: in the IMG NAME attribute, and in the two JavaScript swap calls. For more links, use i9, i10, i11, etc...

Step 10: Now, open pointing.html in a browser, and your rollovers should work fine! Go ahead and edit the rest of the file to your liking. Feel free to rename pointing.html to whatever suits its purpose on your site.

Slideshow Rollover

The slideshow rollover is the next level in complexity, and is probably the least used (or the least overused?) of the three major types of rollovers. For this type of rollover, you use one image for each link, plus a default image—which doesn't need to be blank—for the state in which the mouse is not over any of the links.

For the DIAR catalog page, we wanted to use a vertical navigation bar in a frame along the left side of a page. We chose to use a single shifting image at the top of the bar that changes as the mouse rolls over each icon.

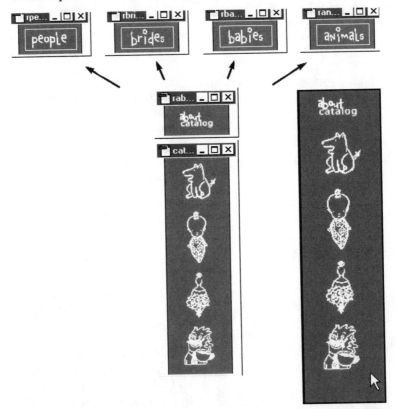

The vertical navigation bar for the DIAR catalog page, is shown to the left with each of the images used for the slideshow rollover on top of the navigation bar. To the right is the catalog page navigation bar in action, with the slideshow rollover at the top.

The HTML for the Slideshow rollover is on the <chd2> CD-ROM as navcatalog.html in the chap15 folder. Here's the code:

```
<HTML>
<HEAD>
<TITLE> Slideshow Rollover Example  </TITLE>

<SCRIPT LANGUAGE="JavaScript">
<!--

// Bill Weinman's Generic Rollover Engine
// (c) 2000 William E. Weinman
//
// http://bw.org/
//
// This program is free software. You may modify and distribute it
// as long as you include this notice in all copies.
//
// No other rights are granted. This program is not "public domain".
//

okay = false;  // wait until variables are initialized

var preload = new Array (
```

1.
```
/////////////////////////////////////////////////
// list all your images here.
// Remember: No comma after the last image!
//

  "images/catalog/rabout.gif", "images/catalog/ranimals.gif",
  "images/catalog/rbabies.gif, "images/catalog/rbrides.gif",
  "images/catalog/rpeople.gif"

//
// you shouldn't need to modify anything
// below this line
/////////////////////////////////////////////////

  );

// find out what browser this is
with(navigator) {
  code = appCodeName;
  app = appName;
  version = appVersion;
  iver = parseInt(version);
  ua = userAgent;
  }

// this will work in "Mozilla" 3+ (includes MSIE 4)
if ( code == "Mozilla" && iver >= 3 )  okay = true;
else { okay = false; }

if(okay) {
```

```
    // compile the RegExp because we use it a lot
    var re = new RegExp();
    re.compile("[\\/.:\\-\\s]", "g");

    // preload the images
    for (var i = 0; i < preload.length; i++) {
      i_preload(preload[i]);
    }
    var preloaded = true
  }

// take a filename and make a legal variable name from it
function iname (img)
{
var s = img.replace(re, "_");
return s;
}

// preload the images
function i_preload(img)
{
if(img) {
  var imgn = iname(img);
  eval(imgn + " = new Image()");
  eval(imgn + ".src = '" + img + "'");
  }
return true;
}

// swap entry function
function swap (name, image)
{
if(!okay) return true; // just leave unless okay

// don't try to do this before the preloading is finished
if(preloaded) document.images[name].src = image;
return true;
}

// ->
</SCRIPT>


<BASE TARGET="_top">

</HEAD>
<BODY BGCOLOR="#990000" text="WHITE">
```

2. `<map name="caticons">`
3. `<area shape="polygon" alt="Animals"`
```
   coords="22,22,24,25,28,26,27,30,30,32,32,33,26,38,27,45,32,48,
   27,50,27,54,29,55,30,64,38,62,45,63,56,64,51,54,57,50,60,48,60,
   44,60,40,68,34,66,29,62,29,59,34,52,26,51,17,48,8,47,6,44,11,
   39,5,39,11,21,18" href="animals.html"
        onMouseOver="swap('rollover',
        'images/catalog/ranimals.gif')"
        onMouseOut="swap('rollover', 'images/catalog/rabout.gif')">
```

```
        <area shape="polygon" alt="Babies"
        coords="39,64,25,63,36,78,27,81,27,85,26,91,28,97,33,104,27,
        117,28,120,31,121,35,133,36,145,52,146,51,130,51,120,57,116,
        48,106,51,101,52,93,54,84,51,77,51,75,56,64" href="babies.html"
            onMouseOver="swap('rollover',
            'images/catalog/rbabies.gif')"
            onMouseOut="swap('rollover',
 'images/catalog/rabout.gif')">
        <area shape="polygon" alt="Brides"
        coords="43,146,32,145,36,161,37,165,39,170,33,176,30,185,24,
        186,24,189,23,194,27,198,29,202,33,206,32,218,54,218,50,208,
        52,200,57,200,54,194,59,191,53,183,50,175,44,170,50,165,46,
        158,58,147" href="brides.html"
            onMouseOver="swap('rollover',
            'images/catalog/rbrides.gif')"
            onMouseOut="swap('rollover',
            'images/catalog/rabout.gif')">
        <area shape="polygon" alt="People"
        coords="37,218,30,218,35,227,27,237,26,243,23,246,25,250,25,
        258,20,267,19,276,52,276,52,273,55,269,60,269,61,262,58,259,
        57,258,58,255,56,254,63,251,56,246,59,243,57,239,61,235,61,
        231,56,231,59,224,49,228,49,218" href="people.html"
            onMouseOver="swap('rollover',
            'images/catalog/rpeople.gif')"
            onMouseOut="swap('rollover',
            'images/catalog/rabout.gif')">
        <area shape="default" nohref>
    </map>

    <TABLE BORDER="0" CELLSPACING="0" CELLPADDING="0">
4.  <TR><TD><A HREF="content.html"><IMG NAME="rollover"
        SRC="images/catalog/rabout.gif" WIDTH="85" HEIGHT="40"
        BORDER="0"></A></TD>
        <TR><TD><A HREF=""><IMG SRC="images/catalog/caticons.gif"
        WIDTH="85" HEIGHT="290" BORDER="0"
        usemap="#caticons"></A></TD>
    </TABLE>

    </BODY>
    </HTML>
```

The JavaScript for this page is exactly the same as it was for the pointing rollover (because all it really has to do is swap images!), so we won't repeat the detail for that part, except to mention the list of images to preload.

1.
```
//////////////////////////////////////////////////
// list all your images here.
// Remember: No comma after the last image!

//

   "images/catalog/rabout.gif", "images/catalog/ranimals.gif",
   "images/catalog/rbabies.gif", "images/catalog/rbrides.gif",
   "images/catalog/rpeople.gif"

//
// you shouldn't need to modify anything
// below this line
//////////////////////////////////////////////////
```

Here we list the images to preload for the rollovers. This is exactly what we did in the previous example, but with the correct images for this page.

2. `<map name="caticons">`

In this example, we have used the rollovers with an imagemap. The concepts are the same as with individual images.

3.
```
<area shape="polygon" alt="Animals"
coords="22,22,24,25,28,26,27,30,30,32,32,33,26,38,27,45,32,48,
27,50,27,54,29,55,30,64,38,62,45,63,56,64,51,54,57,50,60,48,60,
44,60,40,68,34,66,29,62,29,59,34,52,26,51,17,48,8,47,6,44,11,
39,5,39,11,21,18" href="animals.html"
            onMouseOver="swap
         ('rollover', 'images/catalog/ranimals.gif')"
              onMouseOut="swap('rollover',
               'images/catalog/rabout.gif')">
```

In the `AREA` tag, we use the `onMouseOver` and `onMouseOut` attributes to call the JavaScript, just like in an anchor (`A`) tag.

4.
```
<TR><TD><A HREF="content.html"><IMG NAME="rollover"
   SRC="images/catalog/rabout.gif" WIDTH="85" HEIGHT="40"
   BORDER="0"></A></TD>
```

And finally, the image location is created with the `IMG` tag and named with the `NAME` attribute.

As you can see, the principals are exactly the same as in the Pointing rollover example. The only real difference is that the slideshow rollover uses one location for all the image swapping activity, so all the JavaScript swap calls use the same image name, "rollover."

▶ e x e r c i s e

Make Your Own Slideshow Rollover

In this exercise, you will use your own graphics to create a Slideshow rollover. For simplicity's sake, we will use text links instead of an imagemap. If you prefer to use images for your links, you certainly can. If you want to use an imagemap, the previous example will serve as a guide. We suggest, however, that you do this simplified exercise first to get a feel for how it all works.

Step 1: Create a series of graphics to use for the rollovers. Be sure to make them all the same width and height.

Step 2: Create a default graphic in the same dimensions as the rollover graphics. The default graphic will be visible until the user rolls over one of the links; then the default graphic will be replaced with the corresponding rollover graphic. This graphic must also be the same dimensions as those you made in step 1.

Step 3: Create a folder called rollover on your local hard disk and place your images in the folder.

Step 4: Copy the slideshow.html file from the chap15 folder on the <chd2> CD-ROM to your local rollover folder.

Step 5: Open your local copy of slideshow.html in your favorite text editor.

Step 6: Find the line that says:

```
"images/smarrow.gif",
"images/blank.gif"
```

. . . and change it to list the graphics that you made in steps 1 and 2. In other words, if your graphics are named image1.gif, image2.gif, and image3.gif, then you would use:

```
"image1.gif",
"image2.gif",
"image3.gif"
```

You don't need to use the path part of the file names because your images are in the same directory as your HTML file.

Step 7: Now edit the list of links at the end of the slideshow.html file. For each link, change the onMouseOver="swap('rollover', 'images/image1.gif')" to use the filename of the image you want to appear for that link. For example, if the image for a particular link is called red.gif, use onMouseOver="swap ('rollover', 'red.gif')" for that link.

Also make sure that the onMouseOut graphic matches your default image.

Step 8: For each link, place the URL to which you want to link inside the quotation marks of HREF="".

Step 9: If you need more links, go ahead and add them. Be sure to use the right image name in the swap call for each link, and be sure that each image is specified in the list described in step 6. For example, the code to add one more link would look like this:

```
<A HREF="http://www.over.there.com/"
    onMouseOver="swap('rollover',
    chartreuse.gif')"
    onMouseOut="swap('rollover',
    'default.gif')">Over
    There!</A><BR>
```

Step 10: Finally, find the line that says:

```
<IMG NAME="rollover"
SRC="images/blank.gif">
```

...and change the "images/blank.gif" to the default graphic you created in step 2. This is the default graphic that will display when a mouse is not over any of the links. Be sure to remove the "images/", unless you actually have your graphics files in a folder called images. For example, if your default graphic is named default.gif, write your line like this:

```
<IMG NAME="rollover"  SRC="default.gif">
```

Step 11: Now, open slideshow.html in a browser, and your rollovers should work! Go ahead and edit the rest of the file to your liking. Feel free to rename slideshow.html to whatever suits its purpose on your site.

Highlighting Rollover

The Highlighting rollover is the most common of the three, and it's also the most complicated to produce. This is the type of rollover in which a highlighted version of a graphic appears when a mouse is rolled over that graphic.

Two pieces of artwork—one normal and one highlighted—are provided for each position. As an example, let's use the main menu that we used throughout the DIAR site:

The main menu for the DIAR site required 14 separate pieces of art. For each of the seven positions, there was one normal (top row) and one highlighted (bottom row).

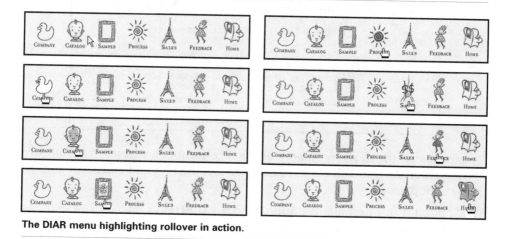

The DIAR menu highlighting rollover in action.

Highlighting Rollover File Naming Convention

To keep track of which image goes where, it is useful to devise a convention for naming the images and files. In our examples we have chosen to name the files with a suffix of "-off" for the normal images, and "-on" for the highlighted images. Using this convention, each of the files are named as shown here:

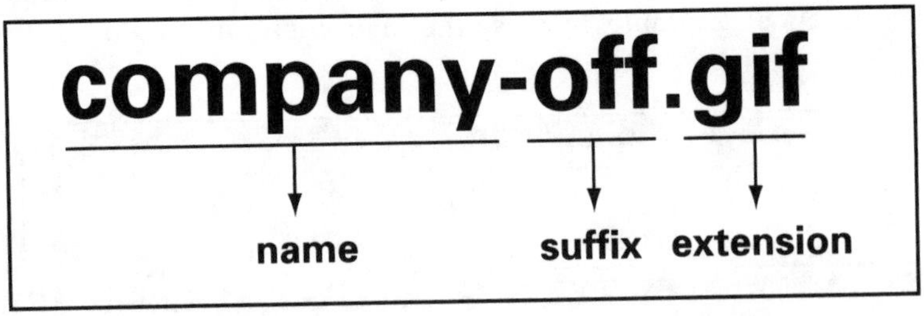

company-off.gif

name   **suffix** **extension**

Image Name	Normal File Name	Highlighted File Name
company	company-off.gif	company-on.gif
catalog	catalog-off.gif	catalog-on.gif
sample	sample-off.gif	sample-on.gif
process	process-off.gif	process-on.gif
sales	sales-off.gif	sales-on.gif
feedback	feedback-off.gif	feedback-on.gif
home	home-off.gif	home-on.gif

Because there are so many images and image locations to keep track of, this convention makes it much easier to keep track of the files and make sure they go in the right places.

The HTML for this example is on the <chd2> CD-ROM as highlighting.html in the chap15 folder. The code looks like this:

```
<HTML>
<HEAD>
<TITLE> Highlighting Rollover Example </TITLE>

<SCRIPT LANGUAGE="JavaScript">
<!--

// Bill Weinman's Generic Rollover Engine
// (c) 2000 William E. Weinman
//
```

```
// http://bw.org/
//
// This program is free software. You may modify and distribute
it
// as long as you include this notice in all copies.
//
// No other rights are granted. This program is not "public
domain".
//

okay = false;   // wait until variables are initialized

var preload = new Array (
```

1.
```
////////////////////////////////////////////////////////////
// list all your images here.
// Remember: No comma after the last image!
//

   "images/company-on.gif",    "images/company-off.gif",
   "images/catalog-on.gif",    "images/catalog-off.gif",
   "images/sample-on.gif",     "images/sample-off.gif",
   "images/process-on.gif",    "images/process-off.gif",
   "images/sales-on.gif",      "images/sales-off.gif",
   "images/feedback-on.gif",   "images/feedback-off.gif",
   "images/home-on.gif",       "images/home-off.gif"

//
// you shouldn't need to modify anything
// below this line
////////////////////////////////////////////////////////////

   );

// find out what browser this is
with(navigator) {
  code = appCodeName;
  app = appName;
  version = appVersion;
  iver = parseInt(version);
  ua = userAgent;
  }

// this will work in "Mozilla" 3+ (includes MSIE 4)
if ( code == "Mozilla" && iver >= 3 )   okay = true;
else { okay = false; }

if(okay) {
  // compile the RegExp because we use it a lot
  var re = new RegExp();
  re.compile("[\\/.:\\-\\s]", "g");

  // preload the images
  for (var i = 0; i < preload.length; i++) {
    i_preload(preload[i]);
    }
  var preloaded = true
  }
```

```
// take a filename and make a legal variable name from it
function iname (img)
{
var s = img.replace(re, "_");
return s;
}

// preload the images
function i_preload(img)
{
if(img) {
  var imgn = iname(img);
  eval(imgn + " = new Image()");
  eval(imgn + ".src = '" + img + "'");
  }
return true;
}

// swap entry function
function swap (name, image)
{
if(!okay) return true; // just leave unless okay

// don't try to do this before the preloading is finished
if(preloaded) document.images[ name] .src = image;
return true;
}

// ->
</SCRIPT>

</HEAD>
<BODY BGCOLOR="#FFFFCC">

<TABLE><TR><TD HEIGHT=20></TABLE> <!- spacer ->

<CENTER>
  <TABLE><TR>
    <!- List of Links starts here ->
```
2.
```
  <TD><A HREF=""
        onMouseOver=" swap('company', 'images/company-on.gif')"
        onMouseOut=" swap('company', 'images/company-off.gif')">
      <IMG NAME=company SRC=" images/company-off.gif"
        BORDER=0></A></TD>
    <TD><A HREF=""
        onMouseOver=" swap('catalog', 'images/catalog-on.gif')"
        onMouseOut=" swap('catalog', 'images/catalog-off.gif')">
      <IMG NAME=catalog SRC=" images/catalog-off.gif"
        BORDER=0></A></TD>
    <TD><A HREF=""
        onMouseOver=" swap('sample', 'images/sample-on.gif')"
        onMouseOut=" swap('sample', 'images/sample-off.gif')">
      <IMG NAME=sample SRC=" images/sample-off.gif"
        BORDER=0></A></TD>
    <TD><A HREF=""
        onMouseOver=" swap('process', 'images/process-on.gif')"
        onMouseOut=" swap('process', 'images/process-off.gif')">
```

```
        <IMG NAME=process SRC="images/process-off.gif"
           BORDER=0></A></TD>
     <TD><A HREF=""
        onMouseOver="swap('sales', 'images/sales-on.gif')"
        onMouseOut="swap('sales', 'images/sales-off.gif')">
        <IMG NAME=sales SRC="images/sales-off.gif"
           BORDER=0></A></TD>
     <TD><A HREF=""
        onMouseOver="swap('feedback' 'images/feedback-on.gif')"
        onMouseOut="swap('feedback', 'images/feedback-
           off.gif')">
        <IMG NAME=feedback SRC="images/feedback-off.gif"
           BORDER=0></A></TD>
     <TD><A HREF=""
        onMouseOver="swap('home', 'images/home-on.gif')"
        onMouseOut="swap('home', 'images/home-off.gif')">
        <IMG NAME=home SRC="images/home-off.gif"
           BORDER=0></A></TD>
   <!- List of Links ends here ->
   </TABLE>
  </CENTER>

  </BODY>
  </HTML>
```

Again, the JavaScript for this page is exactly the same as it was for the Pointing and Slideshow rollovers (because all it really has to do is swap images!). So we won't repeat the detail for that part, except to mention the list of images to preload.

1. `///////////////////////////////////////////////////`
```
// list all your images here.
// Remember: No comma after the last image!
//

   "images/company-on.gif",    "images/company-off.gif",
   "images/catalog-on.gif",    "images/catalog-off.gif",
   "images/sample-on.gif",     "images/sample-off.gif",
   "images/process-on.gif",    "images/process-off.gif",
   "images/sales-on.gif",      "images/sales-off.gif",
   "images/feedback-on.gif",   "images/feedback-off.gif",
   "images/home-on.gif",       "images/home-off.gif"

//
// you shouldn't need to modify anything
// below this line
///////////////////////////////////////////////////
```

Here we list the images to preload for the rollovers. This is exactly what we did in the previous examples, but with the correct images for this page.

2.
```
<TD><A HREF=""
    onMouseOver="swap('company, 'images/company-on.gif')" |
    onMouseOut="swap('company', 'images/company-off.gif')">
  <IMG NAME=company SRC="images/company-off.gif"
    BORDER=0></A></TD>
```

Each of the links looks like this. It's quite a bit more complicated than the other types of rollovers, so let's analyze it bit-by-bit:

In this case the A element encloses the image. That's because the image is used for the link as well as for the visual cue. The IMG tag has a NAME attribute, which names the image for use by the swap function. In this case the name is company. It will be different for each name.

The onMouseOver attribute calls the swap function with the image name (company) and the relative URL for the highlighted image (images/company-on.gif). Likewise, the onMouseOut attribute calls the swap function with the same image name and with the relative URL for the normal image (images/company-off.gif).

Finally, the IMG tag is used to create the image space on the screen. The NAME attribute specifies the name of the image location (company), and the SRC attribute specifies the relative URL for the normal image (images/company-off.gif).

> ## ▸ warning
>
> ### Blank Images
>
> Both the Pointing and Slideshow types of rollovers can use a blank image for the default state. Do not use a transparent GIF for your blank image. On some systems (Windows for example), the transparent GIF will replace another image, and on other systems (Macs for example), the transparent GIF may have no effect or may even distort the image instead.

▶ e x e r c i s e

Make Your Own Highlighting Rollover

In this exercise, you will use your own graphics and create a Highlighting rollover with them.

Step 1: Create a series of graphics to use for the rollovers. Although all the graphics don't have to be the same size, each normal and highlighted pair do need to be precisely the same size. Name the files by using the -on and -off convention described in the earlier section "Highlighting Rollover File Naming Conventions."

Step 2: Create a folder called rollover on your local hard disk, and place your images in that folder.

Step 3: Copy the highlighting.html file from the chap15 folder on the <chd2> CD-ROM to your local rollover folder.

Step 4: Open your local copy of highlighting.html in your favorite text editor. Find the part of the file that looks like this:

```
"images/company-on.gif",
"images/company-off.gif",
"images/catalog-on.gif",
"images/catalog-off.gif",
"images/sample-on.gif",
"images/sample-off.gif",
"images/process-on.gif",
"images/process-off.gif",
"images/sales-on.gif",
"images/sales-off.gif",
"images/feedback-on.gif",
"images/feedback-off.gif",
"images/home-on.gif",
"images/home-off.gif"
```

. . . and replace the parts inside the quotes with the names of your graphics files.

Step 5: Note: It is very important that you pay extra attention to this step, or your rollover will not work! Edit the list of links at the end of the highlighting.html file. For each link, change the

```
onMouseOver="swap('feedback',
'images/feedback-on.gif')"
```

to reflect the name of the image and the location of the file.

Now do the same thing for the onMouseOut attribute. Be sure to use your -on graphic for onMouseOver, and your -off graphic for onMouseOut. Finally, change the NAME and SRC attributes of the IMG tag to match the name for your graphic and the URL for the normal version.

Step 6: For each link, place the URL to which you want to link inside the quotation marks of the HREF="" attribute.

Step 7: If you need more links, go ahead and add them. Be sure to use the right image name in all the relevant places for each link, and be sure that each image is identified in the list in step 4. For example, the code to add one more link would look like this:

```
<TD><A HREF=""
    onMouseOver="swap('dino',
    'images/dino-on.gif')"
    onMouseOut="swap('dino',
    'images/dino-off.gif')">
    <IMG NAME=dino
    SRC="images/dino-off.gif"
    BORDER=0></A></TD>
```

Step 8: Now, open highlighting.html in a browser, and your rollovers should work! Go ahead and edit the rest of the file to your liking. Feel free to rename highlighting.html to whatever suits its purpose on your site.

Extra Rollover Example

One of the most common questions we get about rollovers is "How can I use more than one type of rollover on a page?"

On the CD-ROM in the chap15/combination folder you will find one further example called combination.html. It contains complete examples of all three types of rollovers, including a set of links that use all three at once. After you have done all the examples in this chapter, it should be relatively easy for you to read and understand the combination example on your own.

▶ **note**

DHTML for Navigation

JavaScript plays an important role in a new type of web multimedia called Dynamic HTML. DHTML is a loosely defined term that describes enhancements to standard HTML such as animation, sound, rollovers, and better control over typography. These enhancements are achieved by combining various types of existing technologies, such as JavaScript, **CSS** (**C**ascading **S**tyle **S**heets), and an object model, which allows you to treat ActiveX controls and plug-ins as objects within a document that can be manipulated by CSS and JavaScript.

What this means to the end user is that pages created with DHTML will include a new level of dynamic content. With DHTML, it's possible to accurately position artwork and type, animate HTML elements like GIFs and JPEGs, and create custom navigation more akin to CD-ROMs than the web. Not only could you include rollovers in DHTML, but the artwork for the rollovers could animate, include

♦ **note**

Cont... DHTML for Navigation

custom scrollbar graphics, or let the end user move parts of your interface pieces around the screen.The huge challenge of DHMTL is the same challenge that faces any web developer—browser and platform differences. Some JavaScripts work on Netscape and not on Explorer. ActiveX works on Windows versions of Explorer, but not Mac versions. If you delve into the nitty gritty, it's horrifying to discover what works where and what doesn't. You literally could spend all your time testing tags and browsers, and forget about ever making any web content at all.

Another drawback of DHTML is that it requires 4.0 browsers in order to be viewed. In our opinion, this makes it available to too narrow an audience to serve many sites' purposes. Also, you may be frustrated by the long download wait time on most DHMTL sites. That's because everything in DHTML works on the client side, so all the code and the graphics have to download before anything can be seen. This is both a drawback and a feature. After the artwork and elements are downloaded, DHTML sites are wicked fast, because everything they need to run is on your hard drive.

If you want to see a really exciting example of DHTML in action, visit http://www.dhtmlzone.com/, and click on the Tutorial section. Launch the SuperFly demo, designed by Akimbo Design (http://www.akimbodesign.com/) and witness the next level of web navigation. Each screen in this demo includes a tutorial that explains how the page was constructed.

Unfortunately, DHTML knows no standards yet, so competing methods for creating this type of content abound between the warring browserlords. Netscape and Microsoft have pledged future support for a standard that is currently being decided by the W3C (**W**orld **W**ide **W**eb **C**onsortium), but we've all heard that one before. Meanwhile, life goes on without standards, as usual.

For a visual DHTML design tool, visit http://www.dreamweaver.com/. Dreamweaver is Macromedia's latest web authoring tool, and a free tryout demo is available to Mac and Windows web developers. It boasts the ability to write cross-browser compatible DHTML, design CSS layouts without coding by hand, and create JavaScript animations with a graphical interface.

♦ chapter fifteen summary

Rollovers

Rollovers are a valuable technique for inviting people to press on a link, or for informing them of what they will find on the other end of the link. In this chapter, we covered rollovers from both the design and the programming sides. If you use these techniques, you should be well-equipped to design and implement rollovers on your web sites.

We have identified three categories of rollovers:

- Pointing rollovers

- Slideshow rollovers

- Highlighting rollovers

However, we must admit that we have seen plenty of rollovers that don't fit neatly into these three categories, so we have included an example that uses a combination of rollovers all at once. We have not seen any rollovers that we couldn't implement in one or some combination of these methods.

"He gains everyone's approval who mixes the pleasant with the useful."
—Horace, Roman Poet ca. 13 BC

Forms
collecting information

▶ **contents**

elements
widgets
form examples
tables
cgi

The ability to interact with users is one of the most fundamental uses for computers and networks. The ability to ask questions and collect responses is, in turn, one of the most fundamental ways to interact with users.

HTML provides the ability to create forms, text boxes, radio buttons, and other graphical devices for interacting with users and gathering information. If you want to ask for a name and email address, take a survey, run a guestbook, or just get feedback on your web site, you are going to have to use forms.

Forms

The FORM Element

To create a form on your page, you must start with the FORM element. The FORM element is the main container for all your forms. Here's a simple example of the FORM element. This file is form-1.html in the chap16 folder on the <chd2> CD-ROM:

```
<HTML>
<HEAD>
<TITLE> Example Form </TITLE>
</HEAD>

<BODY BGCOLOR=white>

<H1> A Sample Form </H1>

<FORM>
Your Name: <INPUT TYPE=text>
</FORM>

</BODY>
</HTML>
```

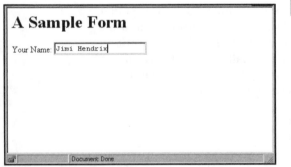

form-1.html: **A simple form.**

Above is a simple form that asks for the user's name. It uses the INPUT tag with TYPE=text to create a text box for typing a response.

The FORM element is also where you will tell the form how to transmit the data. We will cover that later in the section, "How Can I Use the Data?"

Widgets

Each of the graphical devices for collecting data are called **widgets** (some people call them controls, but we think it's more fun to call them widgets). The text box is just one type of widget that you can create in your forms.

There are two basic categories of widgets: those that work with the INPUT tag and those that have their own tags. First, let's look at the various INPUT types:

```
<INPUT TYPE=text NAME=name>
```

> Textbox

The text box is the basic field for typing in a line of text.

```
<INPUT TYPE=password NAME=name>
```

> ✶ ✶ ✶ ✶ ✶ ✶ ✶

The password box works exactly like the text box, except it obscures the typing so that people can't watch over the user's shoulder to learn their password.

```
<INPUT TYPE=checkbox NAME=name>
```

Checkbox ☑

The check box is used for yes/no type of input.

```
<INPUT TYPE=radio NAME=name VALUE=value>
```

Radio Button ○ ◉ ○

The radio button is used for multiple-choice input. Only one radio button in a set can be on at one time.

```
<INPUT TYPE=submit NAME=name>
```

The submit button is used to send the form to the server.

```
<INPUT TYPE=reset>
```

The reset button resets the form to its default values.

```
<INPUT TYPE=hidden NAME=name VALUE=value>
```

The hidden field is used to pass information on to the server without displaying it on the page. It's mostly used by programmers for state-management. If that makes no sense to you, then you don't need this widget.

```
<INPUT TYPE=image NAME=name SRC=send.gif>
```

send!

The image type is an alternative to the submit button. It lets you use an image rather than a button for submitting the form to the server. It will accept all the same attributes as the IMG tag.

```
<INPUT TYPE=button>
```

The button widget is a button that doesn't do anything. It's currently only used for JavaScript. When browsers start supporting the new forms capabilities in HTML 4, this widget will become very useful.

```
<SELECT>
  <OPTION> Option 1
  <OPTION> Option 2
  <OPTION> Option 3
  <OPTION> Option 4
  <OPTION> Option 5
</OPTION></SELECT>
```

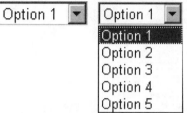

The select box is another type of multiple-choice input widget. Use it for lists that are too long for radio buttons.

```
<TEXTAREA>
  Some Default Text
</TEXTAREA>
```

The text area is for typing long amounts of text, good for things like guestbooks and email forms.

Some additional widgets that are part of the new HTML 4.0 specification can be found in the Reference section. Unfortunately, we can't show those to you today because there are no browsers that support them yet.

The Feedback Form

One obvious use for forms on the Ducks In A Row site is for the feedback page. Here's an example of a simple feedback page for the DIAR site:

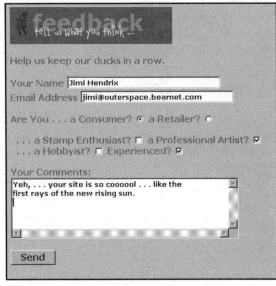

form-2.html: A simple feedback page.

```
<HTML>
<HEAD>
<TITLE> Ducks In A Row Info Form
</TITLE>
</HEAD>

<BODY TEXT=" #666633"
BGCOLOR=" #CCCC99"  LINK=" #990000"
     VLINK=" #990000">
```
1. `<FONT FACE="Verdana,Helvetica,Arial">`
```
<B>
<IMG SRC=" feedback.gif"
ALT=" Feedback">
<P>Help us keep our ducks in a row.
```

2. `<FORM>`

3. `Your Name <INPUT TYPE=text NAME=name><BR>`
```
Email Address
<INPUT TYPE=text NAME=email><BR>

<P>
```
4. `Are You . . . a Consumer?`
```
<INPUT TYPE=radio
NAME=custtype VALUE=consumer>
          a Retailer?
<INPUT TYPE=radio
NAME=custtype VALUE=consumer><BR>
<P>
```
5. `  . . . a Stamp`
```
Enthusiast? <INPUT TYPE=checkbox
NAME=enthusiast>
     a Professional Artist?
<INPUT TYPE=checkbox NAME=artist><BR>
  . . . a Hobbyist?
<INPUT TYPE=checkbox NAME=hobbyist>
     Experienced? <INPUT TYPE=check
box NAME=hendrixfan>

<P>Your Comments:<BR>
```
6. `<TEXTAREA NAME=comments ROWS=5 COLS=30></TEXTAREA>`

7. `<P><INPUT TYPE=submit VALUE=" Send">`
```
</FORM>

</B></FONT>

</BODY>
</HTML>
```

1. `<FONT FACE="Verdana,Helvetica,Arial">` `<B>`

We used the `FONT` tag because we like the Verdana typeface for the uniform look of this site. Given the color scheme of this page, using the `B` tag helps the text be more readable. Notice that even the form fields are affected by the `FONT` tag.

This is a new behavior for forms in the 4.0 browsers, and it's welcome. Later, in the "Using Tables with Forms" section of this chapter, we'll show you how you can take advantage of this feature to make your forms more pleasant to use.

2. `<FORM>`

The `<FORM>` element marks the beginning of the forms. Later in this chapter, we will add the attributes to get it to call the CGI program. It's a good idea to use the `<FORM>` tag without any attributes while you're in the process of laying out the page. You can always add the attributes when you're ready to start testing the CGI.

3. `Your Name`
`<INPUT TYPE=text NAME=name><BR>`
`Email Address`
`<INPUT TYPE=text NAME=email><BR>`

We used the `INPUT` tag with `TYPE=text` for the text boxes. The `NAME` attribute identifies an individual widget for the CGI program that will process the form. It's important that you make up a unique name for each widget on a page.

4. `Are You . . . a Consumer?`
`<INPUT TYPE=radio NAME=custtype`
`VALUE=consumer>`
`          a Retailer?`
`<INPUT TYPE=radio NAME=custtype`
`VALUE=consumer><BR>`

These are radio buttons. Groups of radio buttons are considered one widget, so only one radio button in a group is allowed to be on at one time. All the radio buttons in the group use the same value for their `NAME` attributes.

That's what puts them in the same group. In the case of the radio button, the `VALUE` attribute is used to distinguish one button from another, within a group. Both of these radio buttons use the same `NAME`, so that puts them in the same group. The `VALUE` attributes are different, so you will be able to tell which one was pushed.

5. `  . . . a Stamp Enthusiast?`
`<INPUT TYPE=checkbox NAME=enthusiast>`
`      a Professional Artist?`
`<INPUT TYPE=checkbox`
`NAME=artist><BR>`
`  . . . a Hobbyist?`
`<INPUT TYPE=checkbox`
`NAME=hobbyist>`
`          Experienced?`
`<INPUT TYPE=checkbox`
`NAME=hendrixfan>`

Check boxes are not grouped, so each one has its own `NAME`.

6. `<TEXTAREA NAME=comments ROWS=5`
`COLS=30></TEXTAREA>`

The `TEXTAREA` widget provides a space for the user to type comments.

7. `<P><INPUT TYPE=submit VALUE=" Send">`

And, finally, the `Submit` widget is used to make a button that sends the form. The `VALUE` attribute is used to label the button.

Using Tables with Forms

The next problem with our form is that it's not very nicely aligned. It would be a lot better—even easier to use—if the various elements of the form were lined up better.

To solve this problem, we use HTML tables. We must warn you, however, that putting your forms into tables does limit your audience somewhat. Older browsers, especially early versions of the AOL browser, cannot see forms in tables. We think that's a bug that borders on criminality, but it's true nonetheless.

This is one area where we suggest to go ahead and do it anyway, because there are few things that can benefit more from the use of a table than a form. And for the record, the amount of your audience today that won't be able to use the form is probably a small fraction. But do be aware of the problem, and if your form is for a truly mass audience, make sure you have an alternative non-table form available.

There is a new behavior for forms in the 4.0 browsers that we really like. Now you can change the font of the characters inside the form widgets! This gives you, the designer, another layer of control over the way your pages look and feel. Unfortunately, combined with the use of tables, it can make the page much more complex.

The reason is that the TABLE element is not valid content for the FONT element. That means that you cannot put a table within a FONT container and expect the contents of the table to use that font. If you do, you will find that all the text in the table is just in the default font. Why did they design it that way? Only God and a few brainiacs on the HTML committee know for sure, but it gives us pains in the lower lumbar area. Fortunately, there's an elegant solution.

form-3.html: **The same form with tables.**

Because only the 4.0 browsers use the FONT tags for formatting form fields, it seems that this is one place we can get away with using a style sheet. Here's a version of the above table that uses a style sheet to format the table (this is form-4.html in the chap16 folder on the <chd2> CD-ROM):

```
<HTML>
<HEAD>
<TITLE> Ducks In A Row Info Form
</TITLE>

<STYLE TYPE=" text/css">
<!-

P,TD,SPAN {
    font-family: Verdana,Helvetica,Arial;
    font-size: 14px;
    }

.text {
    font-weight: bold;
    font-size: 16px;
    }

.label {  font-weight: bold }
.form {  font-weight: normal }

->
</STYLE>
</HEAD>

<BODY TEXT=" #666633" BGCOLOR=" #CCCC99"
LINK=" #990000" VINK=" #990000">

<IMG SRC=" feedback.gif" ALT=" Feedback">
<P CLASS=text>Help us keep our ducks
in a row.

<FORM>
<TABLE>
  <TR>
    <TD CLASS=label>
        Your Name
    <TD CLASS=form>
      <INPUT NAME=Name TYPE=TEXT>
```

```
<TR>
   <TD CLASS=label>
      Email Address
   <TD CLASS=form>
      <INPUT NAME=Email TYPE=TEXT>


<TR>
   <TD CLASS=label>
      Are You
   <TD CLASS=label>
      <SPAN CLASS=label>
         Consumer <INPUT TYPE=RADIO
NAME=Retail VALUE="Consumer" CHECKED>
         Retail Store <INPUT TYPE=RADIO
NAME=Retail VALUE="Store">
            <BR>
         Stamp Enthusiast
<INPUT TYPE=CHECKBOX NAME="Enthusiast">
         Professional Artist
<INPUT TYPE=CHECKBOX
NAME="ProArtist"><BR>
         Hobbyist <INPUT TYPE=CHECKBOX
NAME="Hobbyist">
         Experienced? <INPUT
TYPE=CHECKBOX NAME="HendrixFan">
      </SPAN>
<TR>
   <TD CLASS=label>
      Other
      </FONT></B>
   <TD CLASS=form>
      <INPUT NAME=Other TYPE=TEXT>


  <TR VALIGN=TOP>
     <TD CLASS=label>
        Comments
     <TD><SPAN CLASS=form>
        <TEXTAREA COLS=30 ROWS=5
NAME=message WRAP=HARD></TEXTAREA>
        </SPAN>
  <TR><TD HEIGHT=20>
  <TR><TD>
     <TD CLASS=label><INPUT TYPE=submit
VALUE=" Send! ">

</TABLE>

</FORM>

</BODY>
</HTML>
```

There were a few places where the form field didn't pick up the formatting of the style, but we were able to solve those by using the SPAN tag. This will probably work a lot better in the 5.0 browsers, but for now using the SPAN tag in a few spots is far better than the plethora of FONT tags of the previous version. If this code is confusing to you, turn to Chapter 13, *"Style Sheets,"* where SPAN and CSS are thoroughly explained.

form-4.html: Tables with a style sheet—look great!

The IMAGE Type

Our form is almost finished, but we need to fix one more aesthetic problem. That "send" button is all wrong. Let's use an image instead, shall we?

The image conforms much more to the look of the page. This is accomplished by replacing the line,

```
<TD CLASS=label><INPUT TYPE=submit
VALUE=" Send! ">
```

with this line:

```
<TD><INPUT TYPE=image NAME=submit
SRC=" send.gif" BORDER=0>
```

Be aware that when you use an image for a sub-mit button, the cursor does not change to a pointing finger as it does with an image hyper-link. So your graphic must be compelling. It must say "push me!" in the clearest of visual cues. For this image, we chose a subtle border to go along with the word "send!" Whatever you decide on, you may want to test it on a naïve user to make sure that it communicates the "push me" message clearly.

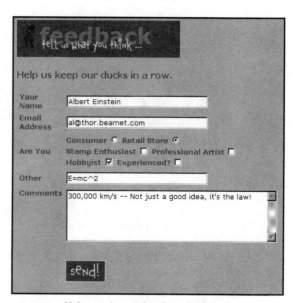

form-5.html: **Using an image for the submit button.**

How Can I Use the Data?

Now that you have a form, you are probably wondering: When someone types information into my form, how does it get to me? The answer to this question goes beyond the realm of HTML because it requires CGI programs written in any number of programming languages.

HTML forms require the cooperation of several different systems in order to work. Forms use HTTP (the **H**yper**T**ext **T**ransport **P**rotocol, used by web servers to communicate with web browsers) to carry information to the server; and forms require the use of a CGI (the **C**ommon **G**ateway **I**nterface) program to process the information on the server and interact with the user.

It is possible to use forms without a CGI program, but all the available ways to do it require certain browsers, which must be configured a certain way in order to work. You can use JavaScript, but that eliminates all but the most current browsers, and it still doesn't allow you to actually collect data from the user. You can use mailto URLs, but that also eliminates all but the latest versions of browsers. Both of these alternatives require that the end user's browser is configured to send email, which many are not.

In order to make this information more useful for you, Bill has written a generic CGI program called mailform.cgi found in the chap16 folder of the <chd2> CD-ROM, which you can upload to your server and use with your forms. It requires a UNIX-based server with Perl (version 5 or better) installed and the sendmail program (or one of the many sendmail equivalents). It will simply email the information from the form to an address that you provide. If you want to do something more specific, we recommend picking up a copy of any of the many excellent books on CGI programming or hiring a qualified programmer.

Using mailform.cgi

In order to use Bill's CGI program, you will need to edit the Perl source to set your email address, the default subject line for the messages, and the location of the sendmail program on your server. Then you must get the program onto your server, make sure it's executable, and make sure it follows whatever conventions your server uses for running CGI. Finally, you will have to get the correct URL into the ACTION attribute of your FORM tag.

This is not a trivial process, and it requires that you understand something about how your server works. You will have to talk to your system administrator to get this information. If we tell you how this works on our server, it will do you no good. It almost certainly works differently on your server. If you are not technically inclined, we strongly recommend that you hire a professional to help you.

After you have the program configured and running on your server, you will need to fill in the METHOD and ACTION attributes on the FORM tag. Here's what we used for our server:

```
<FORM METHOD=POST ACTION=" /cgi-bin/
mailform.cgi">
```

The METHOD attribute is either GET or POST. The GET method sends the data to the server as part of the URL, and the POST method sends it as a separate message to the server, which is not visible to the user. We like to use the POST method unless there is a reason to bookmark the data itself, so we used POST here.

The ACTION attribute is the URL for the CGI program that will handle the data. Don't just copy this value, it may well be very different on your server.

After the program is installed, and you press the Send button, it will send you an email message with the results. The message will look similar to this one:

```
Date: Tue, 30 Sep 1997 01:37:54 -0500
From: billw@sirius
X-Mailer: mailform.cgi 1.0 (by Bill
Weinman <wew@bearnet.com>)
To: billw@sirius
Subject: Ducks In A Row Feedback Form

Ducks In A Row Feedback Form:

Email : wew@bearnet.com
Name : Bill Weinman
Enthusiast : on
HendrixFan : on
Other : Web Programmer
Retail : Consumer
message : I would like to know more
about your stamps!
submit.x : 45
submit.y : 20


---
  Sent by mailform.cgi 1.0 (by Bill
Weinman <wew@bearnet.com>)
```

This includes all the information on your form. In fact, this same program will work with any form, and will work with both the POST and GET methods. On the other hand, you may need something better formatted, in which case you are welcome to modify the program or hire someone else to do that for you.

▶ chapter sixteen summary

Forms

Using HTML forms is an excellent tool for gathering all sorts of data from your customers. There are many, many programs available on the web for all sorts of different purposes, from online ordering, to banner exchange programs, to surveys, and even games.

These are a couple of our favorite locations for free CGI programs are:

Matt's Script Archives:
http://www.worldwidemart.com/scripts/

Selena Sol's Digital Soul:
http://www.selenasol.com/selena/

Both of these sites use scripts that allow the designer to rework the HTML, using the techniques you have learned here, to make your pages look as good as they work.

"It's kind of fun to do the impossible."
—*Walt Disney*

Animation & Sound

hype vs. truth

▶ **contents**

animation process

animation production

aesthetics of animation

animation technologies

sound technologies

sound production

If you're considering adding animation and/or sound to your website design, there are lots of choices and possibilities. Even experienced digital animators and musicians who want to publish to the web will discover new rules, standards, terminology, and tools. This chapter focuses on helping you sort out the various decisions—from how to make the content, to what tools to use, to what delivery methods and file formats to choose from.

In addition to our focus on how to create animation and sound, we also share our opinions about aesthetic considerations. The hype of the web is that the more bells and whistles you add to your site, the more it will attract visitors. In many cases, nothing could be further from the truth.

Animation & Sound

Animation Process

Animation is one of the biggest digital design challenges, because it requires knowledge of a variety of design and technical areas. This is the animation decision-making process in order of importance:

Concept: You must start with a strong concept. The concept can be formed from a number of considerations, such as what you are trying to communicate, the strengths and limitations of the animation tool you are using, and the overall aesthetic of your site.

Storyboard: A storyboard can be simple or complex. It can be scribbled on a napkin or beautifully rendered in Photoshop, depending on what you are trying to accomplish. If you are using your storyboard to work out the "idea" of your animation, scribbled napkins are fine. If you are using your storyboard to convince a client to buy your animation idea, then you might need to go with a slicker presentation method.

Preparation: Preparing your artwork is the key to the success of an animation. You will need to prepare artwork differently for different animation tools. We will show the preparation process for some of the animations we created for the Ducks In A Row site later in this chapter.

Execution: Use the animation tool to realize your idea.

Coding: Put the finished results into a web page, and watch it work!

Ducks In A Row Animation Case Study

Phase 1: Concept

We've already covered some brainstorming methods in the "Metaphors" section of Chapter 11, *"Planning."* We used these methods to come up with concepts for the animations on the DIAR site. We decided to produce simple animations that mimic stamping with rubber stamps. Our idea was to create banner graphics that start with a simple image, and to "stamp" out the rest of the graphic elements over time. Our concepts were built around the artwork style of the rubber stamps. There's no reason to make 3D rubber stamps rotating in a starfield being zapped by laser beams. Sometimes the clichés in computer animation don't fit the subject matter at hand.

Phase 2: Storyboard

It's always helpful to create a storyboard for animations, even if it's just a scribbled note to yourself. This example walks you through a sample animation that Lynda created for the DIAR site.

Lynda's "crude" storyboard, which served as a simple map of her animation idea.

She planned to start with the words Ducks In A Row, and the tag line Fine Art Rubber Stamps. Each duck would then fade up in a row. When the last duck had faded in, the words Ducks In A Row would glow for a moment.

Phase 3: Production

Production techniques for producing animation vary dramatically depending on the animation concept and delivery. Making artwork for an animated feature film, for example, would be quite different than making artwork for the web. We've already covered many of the distinctive characteristics of web graphics (low resolution, browser-safe colors, optimizing graphics, etc.), so there's no need to repeat them all here. Instead, we'll look at a case study of an animation, which offers an example of production methodology in the context of a real animation project:

This scan is called duckscan.pct, and is found in the chap17 folder of the <chd2> CD-ROM.

▶ e x e r c i s e

Creating Artwork for an Animation in Photoshop 6.0

Photoshop is a great program for creating artwork for an animation, but it does not have the capability to program the animation. I used Photoshop 6.0 to color the black-and-white scan of my artwork. I could have used ImageReady or Photoshop for this task.

I started with a black-and-white scan of the logo, and reduced it to web size and resolution in Photoshop. I changed its dimensions to fit well within a 640×480 browser winow, and set the resolution to 72 dpi, which is always the proper resolution for web images.

I wanted to paint the black-and-white logo with browser-safe colors. First, I converted the image to RGB mode by selecting **Image:Mode:RGB Color**.

Next, I used the **Magic Eraser** tool and changed the settings on the Options Bar to uncheck Contiguous. The Magic Eraser tool erases a color to transparency. If Contiguous is not checked, it will erase every instance of whatever color is clicked on. In this case, I clicked on white, and all the white in the document dissappeared to transparency.

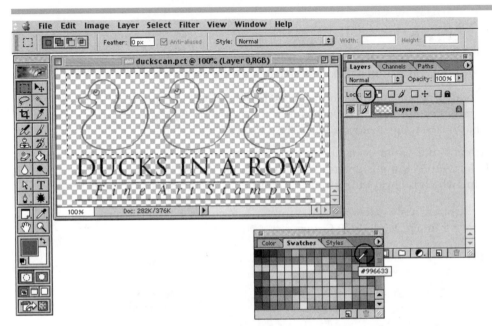

Next, I chose to **Lock Transparent Pixels** (shown circled above in the Layers palette).With this setting, it ensures that you areas that have pixels, not areas that contain transparency, are filled with a new color. I selected the duck images with the Marquee tool, selected a color, and then chose **Edit:Fill**. This filled the areas with non-transparent pixels with the new color. I then selected the words below and filled them with a different color using the same technique.

It's important to name your layers so to keep track of them, so I **Option-double-clicked** (Mac) or **Alt-double-clicked** (Windows) to rename the layer ducks. I clicked on the New Layer icon at the bottom of the Layers palette to create a new layer. I **Option-double-clicked** (Mac) or **Alt-double-clicked** (Windows) to name it background color. I filled it with a light cream color.

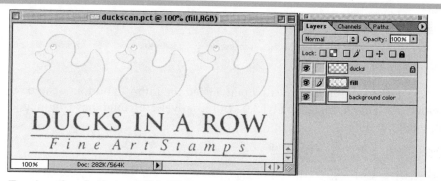

To give the ducks a solid fill, I created a third new layer and moved it in between the other two layers. I painted this layer with a paintbrush, and kept within the lines of the stroke of the duck shapes.

When I finished, I saved the artwork as duckscolors.psd. You can open the file from the chap17 folder of the CD-ROM to check the results of my coloring efforts.

▶ e x e r c i s e

Animating Artwork in ImageReady 3.0

With the duckscolors.psd file I'd made in Photoshop still open, I used the Jump To button located on the toolbar (circled below) to launch ImageReady 3.0. (Alternatively, I could have launched ImageReady and then opened the file.)

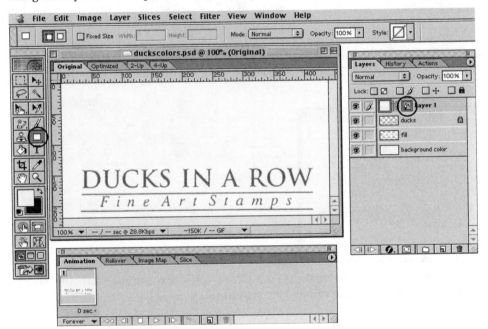

I used the Eyedropper tool to pick up the same color as the background to the image. Using the **Rectangle** tool, I drew a rectangle over the ducks. A new layer was automatically created by ImageReady, as shown above.

With the Animation palette open (**Window:Show Animation**), I clicked on the **New Frame** icon. Using the **Move** tool, I moved the artwork I just created for **Layer 1** to reveal a single duck from the layer underneath. This recorded the change to **Frame 2**.

I clicked on the New Frame icon again to create **Frame 3**. I moved **Layer 1** to the right again to reveal the second duck.

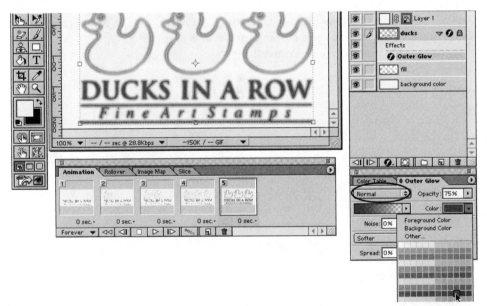

I created another frame of animation by clicking on the New Frame icon and moved **Layer 1** over more to reveal all three ducks.

I created another frame of animation by clicking on the New Frame icon and selected the layer called **ducks** in my Layers palette. I clicked on the Layer Effects icon (*f*) at the bottom of the Layers palette and selected **Outer Glow**. I changed the Outer Glow settings to **Normal** mode and selected a dark color from the Color pop-up.

I created one last frame of animation and changed the Outer Glow setting to have a **0%** Opacity.

With all the frames now made, I just needed to set their timings and create an in-between. I wanted **Frame 1** to hold for **1 second**, so I changed its pop-up menu to reflect that setting.

I wanted frames **2 – 4** to hold for a **half second**. Using the **Shift** key, I selected each frame and then changed its setting to **.5** second.

I selected **Frames 5** and **6** by holding down the **Shift** key. I clicked on the **in-between** button to create a five-frame animation. The Tween dialog box opened, and I clicked **OK**. This created five new frames of animation of the Outer Glow fading out.

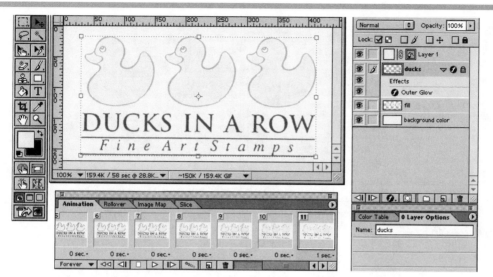

I clicked on the last frame in the animation (**Frame 11**) and changed it to last for **1 second**.

I clicked on the Animation palette to set the looping to **Once**. This means the animation will only play one time. I clicked the **Preview in Browser** button on my toolbar to see the animation play in a browser on my system. If you'd like to see my finished file, open duckscolor_final.psd in ImageReady from your chap17 folder on the <chd2> CD-ROM.

In order to save this as an animated GIF, it's necessary to optimize it properly. Make sure the settings are set to **GIF**, and that the fewest number of colors are chosen to reduce file size. Once I got the file as small as I could with it still looking acceptable, I chose **File:Save Optimized As**. I renamed the file ducksanim.gif. This file is also located inside the chap17 folder, if you want to see the finished result.

Phase 5: Coding

The next step was to insert the animated GIF I had saved from ImageReady. I chose to also include a background tile similar to the original catalog sample. The file measures 100×100 pixels at 72 dpi and is named tile.GIF in the chap17 folder of the <chd2> CD-ROM.

Here's the HTML:

```
<HTML>
<HEAD><TITLE>Animation in Action!</TITLE>
</HEAD>
<BODY LINK="#663333" BACKGROUND="tile.GIF">
<P><CENTER>
<A HREF="http://ducks.htmlbook.com">
<IMG SRC="duckanim.gif" WIDTH=419
  HEIGHT=219 ALIGN=bottom></A>
</CENTER>
</BODY>
</HTML>
```

Here's the final result! Open the duckanim.html **file from the** chap17 **folder of the** <chd2> **CD-ROM inside your browser to watch the animated GIF move.**

LOWSRC Animation Trick

In addition to the many different web animation file formats, there are also several HTML tricks for achieving limited animation effects. The LOWSRC attribute to the IMG tag enables a single image separate from the final image to load first, creating a two-frame animation.

To see this effect in action, open lowsrc1.html from the chap17 folder of the <chd2> CD-ROM. Here's the HTML deconstructed:

```
    <HTML>
    <HEAD><TITLE>LOW SRC TEST!</TITLE>
</HEAD>
    <BODY BGCOLOR=" #FFFFFF'">
1.  <IMG SRC=" catalog2.gif"
    LOWSRC=" lowcat.gif">
    </BODY>
    </HTML>
```

1. The LOWSRC image loads first in the browser, but is listed second in the tag.

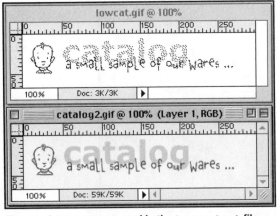

The two image sources used in the lowsrc.html **file.**

This effect is typically used with a small black-and-white graphic for the LOWSRC image, but it's possible to build variations of this effect.

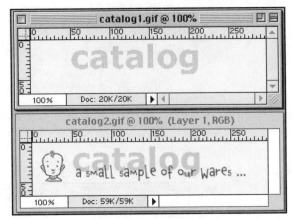

By choosing two color images with different versions of the same artwork, you can create two-frame animation effects that cause the graphics to look like they're "building" on screen. This example, lowsrc2.html, is also inside the chap17 folder of the <chd2> CD-ROM.

Client Pull for Slideshows

Client pull relies on the client (your web browser) to request (pull) the next page after a specified delay. This creates a slideshow effect. Because it's client-sided, client pull can be viewed locally from a hard drive or from within an intranet, without the need to post the source images or HTML to a live server. If you post the client pull HTML files to your server, it can also be viewed from the web.

Client pull involves the META tag, which can be programmed to display a series of HTML pages. The META tag includes a REFRESH attribute, which can be set using the CONTENT element with delays. A delay of 1 would theoretically program a one-second delay for loading the next page, although time measures vary depending on server speed and file sizes.

The pull1.html through pull3.html files are located inside the chap17 folder of the <chd2> CD-ROM. The META tag always goes inside the HEAD tag. Besides the TITLE tag, this is the only other tag that belongs inside the HEAD in HTML standards.

Here's the code for pull1.html:

```
<HTML>
<HEAD><TITLE>Client Pull Test</TITLE>
<META HTTP-EQUIV=Refresh
CONTENT="5; URL=pull2.html">
</HEAD>
<BODY BGCOLOR="#FFFFFF">
<IMG SRC="lowcat.gif">
</BODY>
</HTML>
```

Here's the code for pull2.html:

```
<HTML>
<HEAD><TITLE>Client Pull Test 2</TITLE>
<META HTTP-EQUIV=Refresh
CONTENT="5; URL=pull2.html">
</HEAD>
<BODY BGCOLOR="#FFFFFF">
<IMG SRC="catalog.gif">
</BODY>
</HTML>
```

Here's the code for pull3.html:

```
<HTML>
<HEAD><TITLE>Client Pull Test 3</TITLE>
</HEAD>
<BODY BGCOLOR="#FFFFFF">
<IMG SRC="catalog2.gif">
</BODY>
</HTML>
```

The CONTENT attribute is what instructs the browser to display and wait before loading the next HTML page. In our example, the CONTENT attribute is set for five seconds (this is dependent on many factors, so it's somewhat inaccurate). You can insert any value inside the CONTENT attribute.

Because client pull has to load each file as a separate page, this effect is much more like a slideshow than fluid animation. This technique is great to use with JPEGs and PNGs, which cannot animate like GIFs.

▶ **warning**

Client Pull Disadvantages

If you implement client pull on your web site, keep in mind that your viewers might get annoyed that they've lost control of their browsers. Each page your client pull requested is stacked up in your end viewer's cache, meaning that if they want to click backwards to the page they started from, they might have a long, cumbersome path of clicking backward arrows in their way.

The Aesthetics of Animation

We'd like to stop a moment and consider the broader issue—the aesthetics of animation. With the exception of multimedia, the web is the first medium to combine animation and body text on a single page. For this reason, it's totally understandable that many people struggle to use animation effectively.

Here are some general, personal guidelines we would like to share:

- In most instances, animation that cycles or loops endlessly will eventually become annoying.

- If you use more than one animation on a single page, the effect may be overwhelming to the end viewer instead of impressive.

- Animation calls attention to itself much more than static images on a page

- Make sure that the content of your animation is, in fact, the thing that you want to receive the most attention on your page. If it isn't, the animation will effectively detract from what you're trying to communicate.

- Using animation for a button is a great idea because the animation will invite the end user to click it more than a static button will.

- Make sure your animation loads quickly. If you make your audience wait too long for the animation or plug-in to load, they'll move on before ever seeing it.

Web Animation Technology Overview

In many instances, it's necessary to pick an animation technology before you create the animation. While there are many translation programs that convert one animation file format to another, it's good to have an overview of the technologies before you commit to an animation delivery method. A brief synopsis of different animation delivery choices follows.

Animated GIFs

Animated GIFs, or for the more technically-inclined, multi-part GIF89a's, have been in existence since the late 1980s. The great news is that all the major web browsers currently support the animated GIF spec, making it possible to include these files on web pages without worrying about excluding any potential end viewers.

The GIF89a file format allows for multiple images to be stored inside a single GIF document. When displayed within browser software that recognizes the multiple images, the artwork streams in to the web page in a predetermined sequence, creating a slide-show style animation. Animated GIFs support looping (the capability to repeat multiple images indefinitely) and timing delays between frames of artwork. Animated GIFs also support limited masking, meaning that animations can use the same type of transparency supported by static GIF images.

Animated GIFs do not require plug-ins or programming, and don't even require a live web connection, making them perfect for intranets and testing locally on your machine. Animated GIFs are simple to make, easy to include in HTML, and effortless for your web-viewing audience to see. They are one of the most elegant solutions to web animation and lack only in that they cannot include interactivity or sound. For an animated logo or button, however, animated GIFs are a pretty smart option.

To include animated GIFs in web pages, you'll use the standard IMG tag. A simple example of the code looks like this:

```
<IMG SRC="my_animation.gif">
```

Many enhanced animation options are possible through plug-ins, such as Shockwave, Flash, QuickTime, and more obscure formats. Plug-ins need to be installed by the end viewer, which can be a cumbersome process. A viewer must first download the plug-in, install it in the browser plug-in folder, and restart the browser. Plug-ins do not exactly support effortless web surfing, and the truth is that many people will choose to click off a page that requires a plug-in rather than endure the bothersome interruption or time-consuming installation process.

If you do decide to choose an animation format that requires a plug-in, you should keep in mind that your choice to do so probably excludes a portion of your potential audience. You might consider including a link so that your visitors can download the plug-in before viewing the screen that requires it. Notifying your audience that you're using a plug-in is a courtesy, and creating alternate pages for those who won't bother with the plug-in installation process is a recommended practice. An exercise that walks you through some of these processes, titled "Plugging-In," follows later in this chapter.

If your end user doesn't have the plug-in installed, they'll get a broken plug-in icon. Typically, whenever you include content that requires a plug-in, you should consider providing alternate content for your users who don't have the plug-in. In the past, Internet Explorer required the OBJECT tag, and Netscape the EMBED tag when specifying plug-in content.

If you are using the OBJECT tag, you can put your alternate inside the OBJECT container. For example:

```
<OBJECT CODETYPE="application/
x-coolanimation"
   CLASSID="my_suave_animation.foo"
   WIDTH=100 HEIGHT=100>

      <IMG SRC="other_animation.gif"
   WIDTH=100 HEIGHT=100
         ALT="Your browser doesn't
         support CoolAnim!">

</OBJECT>
```

If you are using the EMBED tag, you use the NOEMBED element inside the EMBED container:

```
<EMBED SRC="myanimation.xxx"
WIDTH=400 HEIGHT=200>
   <NOEMBED>
      Your browser doesn't support the
      Really Cool plug-in!
   </NOEMBED>
</EMBED>
```

The OBJECT tag is part of the HTML 4.0 standard and is the preferred way to implement all plug-ins today, but it may not be understood by all browsers. Older Netscape browsers—before Navigator 3.0—use the EMBED tag for plug-ins, and do not understand the OBJECT tag at all. It's up to you to decide which one to use. We tend to lean toward using OBJECT when we can. Just make sure you test your code on all the browsers you wish to support.

> ▶ **note**
>
> ### HEIGHT and WIDTH
>
> Whenever you use an EMBED or OBJECT tag in your HTML, you must always use the HEIGHT and WIDTH attributes to define the size for any plug-in-based content.

Animated GIFs in Detail

In our opinion, the animated GIF is one of the most sensible choices of web animation formats. Animated GIFs include the following features:

- The capability to set looping, or number of repeats

- The capability to set delays between individual frames

- The capability to optimize the graphics by using different disposal methods

- Palettes

- Transparency

- Interlacing

Looping: As stated earlier, be careful of unlimited looping animations as they can be annoying to your audience.

Frame delays: Frame delays can be used to alter the timing of animations. In ImageReady, you can set frame delays inside the Animation Palette. Other programs that create animated GIFs might use different unit measurements, but most of them allow you to set frame delays.

Download speeds: The initial download time of the animated GIF will depend on your end user's connection speed, but after the animation has fully downloaded, it will depend on the processor speed of his computer. This can make for wildly different frame delay timings on different systems, regardless of what frame delays you program. Almost all GIF animation software packages support frame delays.

Optimization: Animated GIFs can be optimized, just like regular GIFs. The same rules that applied to file size savings for regular web files apply here. Like other GIFs, you want to make sure that you use as few colors as needed and try to avoid dithering or noise in your image.

Transparency and disposal methods: Disposal methods are a scary sounding term for how the animation is displayed in terms of its transparency. With a single image, this is a nonissue. A transparent image shows through to its background, and that's the end of the story.

With a multiple-frame GIF, however, this presents a bigger issue. Let's say you've animated a ball that's bouncing. If you make the ball transparent, and the image before it has already loaded, the transparency might show part or all of the preceding frame. Instead of the illusion of motion, the result would be the nonillusion of each frame of the ball animation visible at once.

The disposal method is what instructs the GIF animation how to display preceding frames of the animation. Disposal methods are set within whatever GIF animation software package you're using. These are the terms used by some programs to describe disposal methods. The names for these disposal methods will vary depending on which GIF animation tool you're using.

Palettes: Most GIF animation software allows you to create bit-depth settings. Lower bit-depth settings will result in smaller, faster animated GIFs. One problem that animated GIFs suffer from is that often the software or browser defaults to accepting a different palette for each frame, which will cause palette flashing (a psychedelic feast for the eyes, to be sure)—most likely not the effect you were wishing to see.

The best way to avoid GIF animation palette problems is to map each frame of your animation to a common palette. Some programs (ImageReady and Fireworks for example) do this automatically.

Interlacing: Adding the interlace feature to a single or multiple GIF image will cause it to look blocky until it comes into focus. We personally dislike the effect, and especially dislike the effect in the context of animation. It sort of breaks the illusion of motion to see each individual frame come into full focus, don't you think?

Sound on the Web

Sound options on the web are as diverse as animation options. It's possible to program your site to provide background ambient noise, animations with sound, real-time audio on-demand, or sound that can be downloaded and played on external sound players. The following sections examine these options and other issues related to sound.

Shockwave Case Study

We created a sample synchronized sound and animation file using Macromedia Director 6.0 and saving the results as a Shockwave file. This enabled us to combine the GIF animation exercise shown earlier with synchronized and unsynchronized sound.

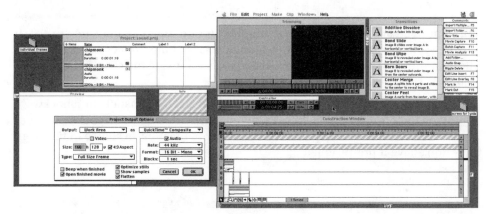

We mixed the sound in Adobe Premiere. It included a recording of Lynda's daughter, Jamie, and some generic quack sounds, which were both stored in the AIFF file format. We figured out the timing for the quacks based on appearance of each duck in the GIF animation.

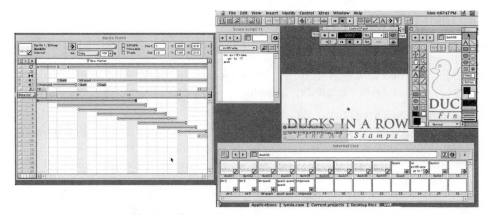

We imported each frame of the GIF animation into Macromedia Director 6.0. It enables you to combine images and sound. We saved the project as a Shockwave file with the .dcr file extension. You'll find ducks.dcr inside the chap17 folder in the <chd2> CD-ROM.

In order to view this file, your end user would need to install the Shockwave plug-in in their browser. It's helpful to include instructions on a page that includes a plug-in, and a link to help guide your end user to the plug-in source in the event they don't have it pre-installed.

```
<HTML>
<HEAD><TITLE>Ducks Shockwave</TITLE></HEAD>
<BODY>
<EMBED SRC="ducks.dcr" WIDTH="419" HEIGHT="219">
</BODY>
</HTML>
```

Shockwave is much more robust than standard HTML; it enables you to include synchronized sound, rollovers with different artwork for mouse over, mouse down and mouse click, and animations that are triggered by events (needed for creating web-based games). The learning curve is high, although the results are worth it to many. One problem with Shockwave, besides the plug-in barrier, is file size. The GIF animation was only 24k. The Shockwave file was 165k. Is the sound worth it? For some purposes yes, and others no. You'll have to be the judge on your own projects!

Sound Aesthetics

Just because you can add sound to your site doesn't mean you should. Keep in mind that people have very strong musical tastes, and while you might love Balinese gamelan music as much as I do, your end viewer might prefer Martin Denny.

Our suggestion is that you are careful about looping sounds, in the event that your end viewer can't stand your choice of music or sound effect and you are effectively driving them away.

Our point is, sound can be a wonderful thing to one person, and an annoyance to another. Embedding ambient sound on a web page is discussed later in this chapter, along with techniques to enable your end user to access audio controls to turn sound on and off for your site. You might think you are adding an enhancement to your site by including automatic sound, but it's our job to tell you that others might not agree.

Getting Sound Files into Your Computer

Just like images have to be scanned or created directly in the computer, sounds have to be scanned or digitized or created from scratch as well. This is a complex or easy undertaking, depending on whether you're attempting to achieve professional-level sound, or are willing to accept a few snaps, crackles, and pops. Here are some ideas for obtaining sound file sources:

Capture Sound from CDs

Most sound-capture software enables you to capture sound from audio CDs. Tips for capturing from CD sources are listed later in this chapter.

Be careful about copyrights and other rights—it is not legal to take sound from your favorite band and stick it on your web site or otherwise use it. For more information about copyright laws and music, check out:

http://home.earthlink.net/~ivanlove/music.html

Purchase Royalty-Free Sound Libraries

There are zillions of web sites and CD-ROMs that include royalty-free music and sound effects. Check with your favorite search engine to find sources that you like.

Use the microphone that ships with many Macs and PCs to record your voice for narration, greetings, or sound effects.

Macs and PCs often ship with microphones and simple sound editing software. This is a great way to add a personal greeting to your site. Lynda has wonderful sound bytes of her daughter singing songs and saying silly things as she was growing up that were all captured this way. Be aware, however, that professional sound designers would cringe at this recommendation! If you are planning to do professional-quality sound, use a professional! They have all kinds of equipment you won't begin to understand that do things like normalize, equalize, remove noise, mixing, dithering, resampling, and more...

Use Sound Editing Software

You can use sound editing software to produce computer generated sounds. There are dedicated sound editing packages, just like there are dedicated image editing software packages. Sound editing software can cut together disparate clips of sound, create transitions like fades and dissolves, and process the sound with effects like echo, reverb, and playing in reverse.

You might try reading the computer and sound trades to find hardware and software that fits your needs and budget. Or visit your favorite search engines to locate some online.

▶ definition

Digital Audio Terminology

Sample rates: Sample rates are measured in kilohertz (KHz). Sound editing software is where the initial sample rate settings are established. Standard sample rates range from 11.025 KHz, 22.050 KHz, 44.10 KHz, to 48 KHz. The higher the sample rate, the better the quality. The sample rate affects the "range" of digitized sound, which describes its highs and lows.

Bit-depth or sampling resolution: Sampling resolution affects quality, just like dpi resolution affects the quality of images. Standard sampling resolutions are 8-bit mono, 8-bit stereo, 16-bit mono, and 16-bit stereo. The most common setting is 44.1 KHz at 16 bits. That is the setting used for music on CDs.

To Stream or Not to Stream?

Streaming is the process whereby sound is downloading as it is playing. This enables your end user to hear the sound as it's downloading. Streaming is a good thing, but not always appropriate. There are times when you'll prefer to set up music archives on a site for downloading. This is especially true if you want to distribute high-quality sound that is too large in file size for smooth streaming. Streaming is appropriate for some things, and not for others. While streaming is much more convenient than downloading, your sound and music will take a quality hit in the process. Since both streaming and non-streaming audio standards still exist, this chapter covers both topics.

If you are going to prepare audio files for downloading off your site, you'll need to know a few new tricks. We'll look at the HTML tags required to do this, how to make your movies and sounds small, and decide which types of helper applications you and your audience will need

▶ **note**

Streaming as a Form of Copy Protection

Some people choose to stream audio or video because they think it prevents copying. Unfortunately, streaming does not prevent copying—it only makes it a bit more difficult.

Any time you put any information on the web, it will be copied. In fact a digital copy must be made just for the user to legitimately view or listen to your content on their computer. There are currently several applications freely available on the web that allow users to store copies of streamed content.

New paradigms will have to be created to deal with protection of intellectual property on the Internet. The current definitions don't work, nor do the current technologies offer any protection. In the mean time, we will all have to consider carefully what we make available and what we don't.

Making Small Audio Files

Audio on the web has most of the same limitations as images—many files are too large to hear as inline components of a page. In this event, your audience will be required to download audio files in order to listen to them, and it's your job to choose a file format and compression rate. You will base these decisions on what platform you're authoring sounds from, and how to make the files as small as possible while still sounding as good as possible.

Here's a look at the various audio standards and ways to reduce the size of audio files.

Rates and Bits

There are two components of an audio file that make it sound good (and take up space): the sampling rate and the bit depth, which is referred to as the sample resolution.

Sample rates are measured in kilohertz. The sample rate affects the range of a digitized sound, which defines its highs and lows. Higher sample rates result in larger file sizes. The sampling rate is set when the sound is digitized (captured) into the computer. Sound editing software is where the initial sample rate settings are established, and it should be set according to the type of sound being sampled. Some types of sounds can deal with lower sampling rates better. Narration, for example, doesn't depend on high and low ranges to sound good. Here are some typical sampling rates:

8 KHz

11 KHz

22.05 KHz

44.1 KHz

48 KHz

Sampling resolution dictates how much range the sound has in highs and lows. Higher kilohertz settings result in a bigger file size. The sampling resolution is also set when the sound is digitized (captured) into the computer. Sound editing software allows users to dictate which sample resolution the sound is captured at. Because noise is introduced at lower sample rates, it's necessary to evaluate individual sound elements to see how far down the sampling resolution can be set without introducing unacceptable noise. You can create digital sound at the following resolutions:

8-bit mono

8-bit stereo

16-bit mono

16-bit stereo

Generally, when you first digitally record or "sample" a sound, you want to record it at 16-bit resolution at the 44.1 KHz sampling rate. Later, after processing the sound to your satisfaction with digital audio editing applications, you would resample the final file down to 8-bit, 22.05 KHz.

Audio File Formats

Many types of audio files are used and found on the web. Choosing which one to use is often determined by what kind of computer system and software you're authoring sounds from. Here's a breakdown of the various formats:

μ-law

μ-law used to be the only file format you'd find on the web, as it is generated by UNIX platforms. Now that Macs and Windows are the predominant platforms, μ-law files are not seen as much. The sound quality is generally considered much lower than the other sound formats described here. It is used much less often now, as a result. If you are going to author μ-law files, they should be saved with an .au extension.

AIFF

AIFF was developed by Apple and is used on Macintoshes and SGIs. It stands for Audio Interchange File Format. It can store digital audio at all the sample rates and resolutions possible. You'll also hear about MACE (Macintosh Audio Compression/Expansion), which is the built-in compression standard for AIFF files. Just like in video, the compression method you use is invisible to the end listener. It does dictate the size and quality of your end result, however. If you are going to author AIFF files, they should be saved with an .aif extension.

WAV

WAV was developed by Microsoft and IBM and is the native sound file format to Windows platforms. Like AIFF, it can store digital audio at all the sample rates and resolutions possible. Basically, WAV and AIFF files are considered equals in terms of quality and compression, and are easier to use depending on which platform you are authoring from. If you are going to author WAV files, they should be saved with a .wav extension.

MPEG

MPEG (level 3, or .mp3) is quickly becoming the most popular audio format on the web. The compression scheme is virtually the same as that used for JPEG graphic files. It offers excellent audio quality with relatively small file size. There is a growing number of encoders and players available on the web. Here are some that we feel are worth checking out:

Audio Catalyst
http://www.xingtech. com

MP3 software resource
http://www.mp3.com/software/

MP3 Mac Endoder:
http://www.soundjam.com

MP3 Windows Encoder:
http://www.musicmatch.com/
http://www.xingtech.com/mp3/encoder/
http://www.audioactive.com/

RealAudio

RealAudio was the first example of streaming audio on the web. Streamed audio files come over the phone lines in small chunks, so the entire file doesn't have to be downloaded before it can be heard. The file can be up to one hour long because the data is coming in as you're hearing it—not downloading fully first to your hard drive. The sound quality is often compared to that of an AM radio station. Because of quality limits, it's best used for narration and not for music or other sounds. You must have the RealAudio player installed on your system to hear sounds play as soon as you click on a link that supplies real audio source material. You can author RealAudio content by using the RealAudio encoder, which can be obtained at http://www.real.com/. You won't be able to offer RealAudio files from your web site unless your provider has installed the Real server. Recently, **Progressive Networks**, the owners of RealAudio, have started distributing its servers for free. Contact their site for more information.

Tips for Making Web-Based Sound Files

Several free or shareware applications can convert from or to μ-law, AIFF, WAV, and MPEG files, so chances are your audience will be able to access your sounds regardless of which file format you choose to support. Typically, Mac authors will choose AIFF, PC authors will choose WAV or MPEG, and UNIX authors will pick μ-law because those are the file formats supported natively by their systems.

To properly prepare the files, however, you might want to use a sound editing program that offers features like peak level limiting, normalizing, down sampling, and dithering from 16-bit to 8-bit. Premiere is a great entry level video and sound editor, though professional videographers and sound engineers will typically own higher-end dedicated editing programs.

Here are some tips for making web-based sound files:

- Digitize at the standard audio CD sample rate and resolution (44 KHz and 16-bit). Down sample the file to the preferred sample size of 22 KHz or 11 KHz. Typically, the lower the sample rate, the less high end or duller the sound will be. For dialogue or sounds where high end doesn't matter, lowering the sample rate creates smaller files that will be of acceptable quality.

- Halving the sample rate will half the file size. Additionally, changing the file from stereo to mono cuts the file size in half. Use the Mix feature of most audio software packages to create a mono version of a stereo file.

- If the 16-bit file is still too large, you can use dithering algorithms on audio (just like on images) to take the files down to 8-bit. Dithering will add noise in the form of hiss (and in the worse case, electronic buzzing and chattering). Dithering will be most noticeable in files with silences between sounds.

- Because of the electronic noise, dithering should be avoided on dialogue. Dithering works great for rich, full music files such as hard rock and industrial. Another alternative is to re-digitize the 16-bit audio file at 8-bit by playing back and recording a prerecorded 16-bit, 44.1 KHz sound into your digitizer. Often, this creates cleaner 8-bit samples with more "punch."

- When naming audio files, as with all files being prepped for Internet distribution, they must be named with no spaces. Unlike inline images, these files are going to be downloaded by your audience. Therefore, names should be under eight characters long with room for a three-letter file extension, or Windows platform users won't get to hear them!

- Make sure you've done all your sound editing (such as mixing from stereo to mono, filtering, peak level limiting, normalizing, or down sampling) before you convert to 8-bit. If you edit an 8-bit sound and then resave it, you will add electronic noise to your file. Always start with higher bit depth, and do your editing in that file before you save or dither it to 8-bit.

HTML for Downloading Sound Files

A sound file gets the <A HREF></A> tag, just like its video and image-based counterparts. Unlike video, where there might be an associated thumbnail image, sounds are usually indicated by a sound icon, or hypertext. Here are a few variations, with the code you would use.

Here's the code to link your audience to a sound and let them know what file size and format it is:

```
<A HREF=" snd1.aif">
<FONT SIZE=5>Click here to download
this sound!</A></FONT>
<p>
Excerpt from CD:<BR>
WebaWorld<P>
Cut: Spider<P>
AIFF Sound<BR>
:30<BR>
567k
```

or, if you want to add an icon, too:

```
<A HREF=" snd1.aif">
<FONT SIZE=5><IMG SRC=" ear.gif">Click
here to download this sound!</A></FONT>
<P>
Excerpt from CD:<BR>
WebaWorld<P>
Cut: Spider<P>
AIFF Sound<BR>
:30<BR>
567k
```

MSIE Audio Tags

The BGSOUND element is an MS Internet Explorer 2.0 enhancement. SRC specifies the URL of the audio file to be played. To view Microsoft's tutorial page on these tags and attributes, check out:

http://support.microsoft.com/support/kb/articles/q156/1/54.asp

> ### ▶ note
>
> ### Cross-Browser Compatibility
>
> Now that you've reviewed the tags for each of the browsers, suppose you want to make a site that works for both?
>
> Try this:
>
> ```
> <EMBED SRC=" sound.wav"
> autostart=TRUE hidden=TRUE>
> <NOEMBED><BGSOUND=" sound.wav">
> </NOEMBED>
> </EMBED>
> ```

Other Sound Options

Sound is a huge subject worthy of entire books! There are many other sound options available to you for web delivery. Here is a brief synopsis of a few noteworthy ones:

QuickTime

QuickTime movies can be hidden from view, or can include control consoles. This makes their MIDI-compatible file format ideal for streaming audio. Check out the specs for QuickTime sound options at:

http://www.quicktime.apple.com

Macromedia Director/Streaming Audio

Director is one of the oldest authoring tools around for multimedia. Shockwave, a plug-in for web browsers, enables Director content to be viewed on web pages. Streaming audio is now a feature supported by the Shockwave plug-in. To develop streaming audio content, you need to learn to use Director and program interactivity with a proprietary language called Lingo. For more about Director, Shockwave, and Lingo, visit Macromedia's site:

http://www.macromedia.com/support/shockwave/

RealAudio

RealAudio is the oldest streaming and most well-known audio technology on the web. It has three components:

- The RealAudio Player plays files encoded in the RealAudio format

- The RealAudio Encoder encodes files into the RealAudio format

- The RealAudio Server delivers RealAudio over the Internet or your company network

In order to hear RealAudio files, you must have the plug-in. In order to author RealAudio files, you need to convert your sound files so they work in the RealAudio format. To download the encoder:

http://www.real.com/products/producer/

The RealAudio Server is the only piece of the puzzle that costs money. It enables you to distribute real audio content from your site. (Late breaking news: Progressive Networks, the owners of RealAudio, are now offering a 60-stream server for free.)

http://www.real.com

Flash

Flash is an authoring tool from Macromedia that creates animation, interactivity, and sound. You can import AIFF or WAV files and export them in the SWF format. This format supports MP3 sound, so you can bring larger audio files in and export them as highly compressed MP3 files. Flash content, like Director content, requires a plug-in that can be downloaded from the Macromedia site. You can learn more about visiting the Flash site:

http://www.macromedia.com/software/flash/

▶ chapter seventeen summary

Animation & Sound

The web promises to be a place of change, with animation and sound options getting better and easier as the medium matures. Whichever animation or sound technology path you choose to travel, always keep your site's goals and audience in mind. Although animation can add a lot to your site's appeal, it can also create exclusionary walls that only the elite few with fast speed, loads of RAM, and high-end computers can break through. Make sure your medium fits your message, and use animation wisely and sparingly to help make the web a more inviting place.

"If you build it, they will come."
—Field of Dreams, "The Voice"

Get Listed
increasing visibility

▶ **contents**

search engines
directories
site listing
meta tags
ad banners

As you've probably noticed by now, building web sites is a lot of work. The amount of time you personally devote to making your web site may shock you by the time you finish. What would be an even worse shock, however, would be if no one could find your site (or your client's site) once your efforts were complete.

We waited until the end of the book to discuss techniques for getting listed because listing methods involve writing HTML. Now that you have studied HTML for the past 17 chapters, our recommendation to learn some new code shouldn't be too surprising or intimidating.

This chapter covers the steps required to list your site with search engines, how to ensure that "keywords" exist on your site so that it can be easily found by search engines, and how advertising banners can play a role in leading your audience to your web site.

Get Listed

Using Search Engines and Directories

Using a search engine or directory is a great way to find things you need to know about web design (or anything else in the universe, for that matter). If you're looking for advice, tutorials, reviews, or new software or hardware, look to the web first! It's the greatest encyclopedia ever created.

Before discussing the use of search engines and directories, it's important to learn the distinction between the two.

A **search engine** is actually a software robot (sometimes called a spider or a crawler) that constantly visits web sites, following their links and maintaining a database of where the search engine has recently visited. Because it is constantly surfing the web, a search engine is likely to have many more sites than a directory.

A **directory** is really just a large catalog built and maintained by humans. People submit their web sites to the directory, and the staff places the listings in the appropriate categories. Because all the listings in a directory are placed there intentionally, the listings in a directory are often more reliable than those found by a search engine. Knowing which type of search engine to use can help yield better search results. For example, if I wanted to help my daughter get information about barn swallows for her bird report, I would choose a spider-based search engine. It would show me all the instances of the words "barn swallow" on the web. Some subjects are too big for a global search. For example, if I wanted to find out about the GIF file format, I might choose to use a directory. This would better enable me to hone in on the category file format instead of searching for the word GIF, which is so ubiquitous on the web, I doubt most search engines could even count the number of responses!

> ▶ **note**
>
> ### The Trusting Web?
>
> Because the web is such an easy and inexpensive place to publish, many searches will reveal large numbers of sites. Keep in mind that the content of some of those sites will not be as accurate as, say, the Encyclopedia Britannica. Consider the source: Does the site appear well-researched? Are there references to where the data came from? It's anarchy out there folks! Don't believe everything you read on the web!

Search Engines

One of the newest entries in the search engine field, Google is based on technology specifically designed for the web, and as such it tends to return more accurate and relevant search results. Google is also unique in today's world because it is only a search engine. Most of the other search engines today are also trying to be "portals" and offer a lot of other services.

Google

Google just wants to be the best and the fastest search engine, and they succeed well at that.

http://www.google.com

AltaVista

Originally started by Digital Equipment Corporation (now part of Compaq) as a demonstration of its minicomputer technology, Alta Vista is a large fast search engine that combines directory and portal services.

http://www.altavista.com

Wired's HotBot

HotBot, one of the newer search engines, is closely tied to its parent, *Wired* magazine. This search engine is built on a distributed-computing model that holds promise of scaling well as the web grows. This means that it is likely to keep up with the explosive growth that the web is experiencing.

http://www.hotbot.com

Excite

Excite is not the oldest and not the fastest search engine, but it may be approaching the rank of largest. Excite recently purchased two other major search engines, and if it finds a way to combine them, it may find itself with the largest engine on the Net. Excite also licenses its search engine to smaller web sites for local searches.

http://www.excite.com

Lycos

Lycos, the oldest search engine on the Net, is still very effective. Many people use this one exclusively just because it works and they haven't bothered to try the newer engines.

http://www.lycos.com

Search Engine Tips

http://www.searchenginewatch.com/facts/index.html

http://www.webreference.com/content/search/

Search Engine Tutorials

http://www.searchenginewatch.com/tutorials.htm

Directories

Yahoo!
The de facto directory on the Net. It's the oldest and the largest, and its reputation as the best is well-deserved. Yahoo! is a directory, and as such it does not go out and search for new sites on its own. In order to get listed on Yahoo! a site must be submitted to and approved by the staff.

http://www.yahoo.com

Search Engine Watch Site
Here is an excellent comparison of search engines and directories. As well as knowing which to use, it's very important to know how to use a search engine. Most have help-based tutorials that can make all the difference. The goal of a search is to come up with the exact matches you want. Most engines fail to find the correct response or correct number of responses because the search is too broad.

http://www.searchenginewatch.com

List Your Site with Search Engines

Most search engines have easy procedures for accepting web site listings. This is usually a free but time-consuming process. Most search engines require that you summarize your site in 20 words or less. It can help to assemble a list of "keywords" before you visit these sites so that you can easily fill out their submittal forms. Here are some URLs to contact:

- http://www.yahoo.com
- http://altavista.com
- http://www.excite.com
- http://www.lycos.com
- http://go.com
- http://www.magellan.excite.com
- http://www.webcrawler.com
- http://www.hotbot.com
- http://www.nln.com
- http://shareware.cnet.com

If you don't want to do the work of contacting multiple search engines yourself, there are several online services that will submit your site listing to many different search engines. The charge for this service varies, so it's best to contact the listing agencies yourself. We're sure there are more, but here are some listing services we're aware of:

- http://www.submit-it.com/
- http://www.position-it.com/
- http://www.webpromote.com

META Tag for Search Engines

Many search engines use automatic processes called "robots" or "spiders" that constantly troll the web looking for sites to list. The processes scan your HTML to determine the content of your site, and use what they've learned to automatically determine which categories to list the site under. (See "Using Search Engines and Directories" in Chapter 2, *"First Page."*)

Using the META tag, you can create special headers for your web pages that will help the automated services list your site more accurately. Use the NAME and CONTENT attributes to form the correct headers, like this:

1. `<HEAD><TITLE>`Sample Meta Page`</TITLE>`
   `<META NAME="`description`" CONTENT="`Ducks In A Row is a wholesaler to retail stores of custom rubber stamps designed by renowned illustrator Joan Farber."`>`
2. `<META NAME="`keywords`"`
   `CONTENT="`rubber stamps, greeting cards, illustration, hobby, design, crafts, birth announcements, wedding announcements, creativity"`>`
3. `</HEAD>`

1. The "description" header is where you enter a one or two sentence description of your site. You can write a longer description, but most search engines limit their scans to 20 or so words.

2. The "keywords" header is for the keywords that best describe your site. You can include more keywords, but most search engines limit their scans to 20 or so words.

3. The META tag must always go inside the HEAD element.

If you'd like to see this HTML in full, open the meta.html file from the chap18 folder of the <chd2> CD-ROM.

If you'd like to visit a free online service that will automatically create META tags for search engine purposes, visit http://vancouver-webpages.com/VWbot/mk-metas.html.

Here's a thorough index of all the different headers you can set with META: http://vancouver-webpages.com/META/.

Ad Banners: From Heaven or Hell?

Ad banners are really nothing more than buttons that link to other sites. Making an ad banner is not the hard part—understanding the dynamics of creating a successful ad banner campaign is. Just like TV commercials, ad banners can be either incredibly annoying or incredibly entertaining.

The purpose of an ad banner is to direct the end user to click on it. The success of an ad banner is usually judged by its number of "click-through hits" (how many people clicked on it). Ad banners are a form of commercialism, and commercialism is usually annoying unless it fulfills another function besides selling. If an ad banner provides entertainment or education, it is normally more accepted than if its sole purpose is to sell.

There are no standard specs for ad banners. You might be asked to design a variety of sizes for a variety of purposes. The site on which your ad banner is placed will dictate the size standard. Most ad banners are accepted in GIF or JPEG format. Animated GIFs (see Chapter 17, *"Animation & Sound"*) are a great file format for ad banners.

There are numerous markets for ad banners. If you are a professional web designer, you may have clients request that you design ads for them. Strangely enough, many web design firms make more money creating ad banners than entire web sites! If you are responsible for your own site's promotion, you may want to place your ad banners on other sites. There are no set advertising rates.

Many traditional advertising agencies set up web-based ad programs for their clients, and the methods for where to place these ads are as diverse as the web itself. If you want to place an ad banner on someone's site, the best method is to contact the webmaster to get information about their rates, formats, and size requirements.

To educate yourself on how much it costs to place ad banners, and what some of the major issues are, pay a visit to http://www.doubleclick.net, a web advertising placement service.

Click Here

Click Here, written by Raymond Pirouz and developed with Lynda Weinman, is the best resource available for understanding how to increase your site's appeal and increase your click-throughs and hits. This book has so much great advice that it's a must-read for anyone interested in marketing their site effectively. Raymond is responsible for some of the coolest ad banners on the web, and knows what it takes to create effective web banner campaigns.

It includes advice on how to:

- Make sure that banner advertisements do not cause your audience to leave your site

- Evaluate your audience effectively

- Create imaginative copy

- Integrate animation

- Make small and fast-loading ad banners

Click Here
Author: Raymond Pirouz
Publisher: New Riders Publishing
ISBN: 1562057928

▶ **note**

Exchanging Links for Links

There are several banner-exchange programs on the Net that provide free banner advertising for your site. In exchange for your banner appearing in the program, you agree to run the program's banners on your site. Typically, the more times the program banner is viewed on your site, the more times your banner will appear on other sites.

You can find an exhaustive list of banner exchange programs by entering "**banner exchange**" in the search form at Yahoo!: http://www.yahoo.com. Visit the **Link Exchange Digest** (http://digest.bcentral.com/) for a moderated discussion list with the goal to provide helpful information to those engaged in building traffic to their web sites. Discussions center on the topic of web site promotion on the Internet and World Wide Web, which includes banner advertising.

▶ chapter eighteen summary

Get Listed

Sadly, it isn't enough to master HTML and web design. Unless you understand some of the methods available to promote your site, you run the risk of creating something wonderful that no one will see.

This chapter covered the use of the META tag and its description and keywords headers. We touched on the advantages and pitfalls of ad banners, and made suggestions that should get you going on the path to better visibility. Be sure to visit the links listed in this chapter to learn more about this important aspect of web publishing.

*"You can't fake quality
any more than you can fake a good meal."*
—*William Burroughs (1914–1997)*

Good HTML
making it work right

▶ contents

why write good html?
html terminology
what you see
what you get
common html gotchas

The purpose of a web page is the message. The message of the page is sometimes in the words, sometimes in the images, and sometimes in other elements of the page, but the message is rarely in the code itself. So why bother writing good HTML?

The way the message is delivered can have impact on how it is received. HTML is one link in the chain of media that carries your web-based message. Ask a painter why they choose one type of canvas over another, or ask a musician why they choose a type of string or reed or bow for their instrument. You may not be able to discern what type of strings are on a guitar by listening to a recording (although Bill says he can), but it does affect the overall quality of the experience.

Good HTML

Why Write Good HTML?

There are both subjective and objective reasons for writing good HTML. Subjectively, it may or may not be important to you that you do as good a job as possible on every level of every project that you take on. We feel that doing something well is its own reward, but we recognize that it's not always practical.

On the other hand, there are some very pragmatic reasons to at least make sure that your HTML is correct, in spite of the fact that it may already work. As a practical illustration, here's a page that works fine in browsers that are based on the original NCSA Mosaic (including Microsoft Internet Explorer and older Netscape browsers), but does not work in the current Netscape:

```
<HTML>
<HEAD>
<TITLE> Bad Table </TITLE>
</HEAD>
<BODY BGCOLOR=WHITE>

<TABLE>
<TR><TD>

<H1>This entire page is in a table.
</H1>

</BODY>
</HTML>
```

Notice that there is no end tag for the TABLE element (/TABLE). This works just fine in Microsoft Internet Explorer.

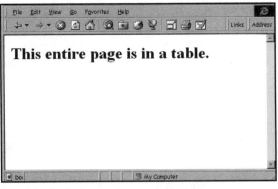

bad-table.html **in Microsoft Internet Explorer 4.**

The end tag is required for the TABLE element—according to both the table specification and the HTML 4 specification. Netscape Navigator (beginning with version 3) won't display a table without an end tag.

bad-table.html **in Netscape Navigator 3.**

In the case of the missing table end tags, there were a number of web sites that virtually "disappeared" when Netscape 3 was released. A similar problem happened with body backgrounds with the release of Netscape 4 (see the example later in this chapter).

HTML Terminology

Probably the single most important thing you can learn about HTML is the distinction between tags, attributes, containers, and elements. Once you understand these terms, it will be much easier for you to tell when your code is correct. Here's what they mean:

- **Tag:** A tag is an HTML instruction enclosed in angle-brackets (e.g., <P>). Some tags may also have end tags that begin with a slash (e.g., </P>). The tag without the slash is sometimes called a begin tag or a start tag.

- **Attribute:** An attribute is a property that works with a tag. Attributes go after the name of the tag, and before the right angle-bracket. For example, if you want a horizontal rule without the shading effect, you can use the NOSHADE attribute (e.g., <HR NOSHADE>). Some attributes have values like the ALIGN attribute (e.g., <P ALIGN=CENTER>), or the HREF attribute for the destination of a link (e.g., <A HREF="http://www.htmlbook. com">). The part to the right of the equal sign is called the value of the attribute.

- **Container:** A container is a tag that has both a beginning and an end, and generally has content that is placed in between. The beginning of a container is marked by a begin tag, and the end is marked by an end tag. For example, TITLE is a container because it has a distinct beginning and end. The content of a TITLE is in between the tags, (e.g., <TITLE> content </TITLE>). In contrast, BR is not a container because it has no end tag; everything it needs is between the brackets of the BR tag.

  Some containers, like P for instance, do not require end tags if the end can be accurately determined by context. But they are still containers because they have content and a limited scope of operation. In the absence of an end tag, the effects of a P tag end when the next P, or some other tag that is not valid content for P, is encountered. This is true of many containers with optional end tags.

- **Element:** Element is a general term for a chunk of HTML that can be treated as a distinct unit in some context. A container, along with all its content, can be considered an element (e.g., <STRONG> This is a STRONG element </STRONG>). A stand-alone tag, like IMG, can also be considered an element (e.g., <IMG SRC= "element.gif">). This term is used as a convenience of nomenclature whenever we need to discuss some distinct part of a document or code.

What You See AIN'T What You Get

WYSIWYG editors are a wonderful invention, and we encourage you to use them for proto-typing your web sites. The use of a WYSIWYG editor can greatly reduce the amount of time it takes you to layout, view, and re-layout your site while you are in the process of designing it.

But for production work, we implore you to be careful. An excellent example is the "disappearing background" problem that happened with the release of Netscape 4.

The HTML specification allows for one BODY element per page. Both the begin and end tags are optional (that is, the body of the document can be implied if the default properties are acceptable), but you are not allowed to have more than one BODY element in a single document.

However, there are evidently some WYSIWYG editors that don't follow this rule. We have seen a number of sites with two or more BODY tags, and this has created problems with some browsers.

The early release versions of Netscape Navigator 4 would ignore the additional BODY tags and only use the attributes of the first one.

For example, consider this HTML:

```
<HTML>
<HEAD>
<TITLE> Bad Body </TITLE>
</HEAD>
<BODY>
<BODY background=white.gif>

<H1>This document has two BODY tags.
</H1>

</BODY>
</HTML>
```

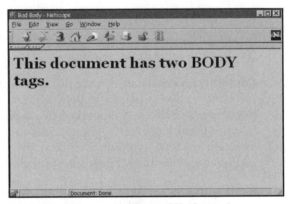

bad-body.html in an early release of Navigator 4.

Later releases of Navigator 4 (beginning with 4.03) accumulate attributes from BODY tags. But you really can't count on a browser guessing what your HTML means when it's not correct. For instance, Mosaic 3.0 (the last version) also shows a gray background for this error.

The best defense is good HTML.

Cleaning Up After a WYSIWYG Editor

As an example of the sorts of things you need to watch out for with your WYSIWYG editors, I have created a little page using Alaire's Home Site. Here's a screenshot of the page in the editor:

homesite-1.html in Home Site's viewer.

Now here is what it looks like in Netscape Navigator:

homesite-1.html in Netscape Navigator.

Notice anything different?

Let's look at the code and see if we can fix it up.

```
<!-- This document was created with
HomeSite 2.5 -->
<!DOCTYPE HTML PUBLIC "-//W3C//DTD
HTML 3.2 Final//EN">

<HTML>
<HEAD>
   <TITLE>Test Page</TITLE>
</HEAD>

<BODY BACKGROUND="/usr/BILL/htmlbook/
working/ch19/lgreentile.gif"
TEXT="Navy" LINK="Olive"
VLINK="#999933" ALINK="Silver">

<TABLE BORDER=0 CELLSPACING=8 CELL-
PADDING=5 VALIGN="TOP"
BGCOLOR="#CCFF99" WIDTH=350>
<TR>
   <TD>Something here</TD>
   <TD>Something Else</TD>
</TR>
<TR>
   <TD>Something New</TD>
   <TD>Something Blue</TD>
</TR>
<TR>
   <TD>Other things</TD>
   <TD>Things X, Y, and Z</TD>
</TR>
<TR>
   <TD>The Cat in the Hat</TD>
   <TD>Dr Seuss' Toothbrush</TD>
</TR>
</TABLE>

<P> Here's a paragraph created
in Home Site. It has
<B>bold and
<I>italic text in it.</I></B></P>

</BODY>
</HTML>
```

The most glaring problem in the HTML on the previous page is that the background image didn't show up in the browser (even though it was fine in the editor's preview screen). Notice that the URL for the BACKGROUND attribute is not a proper relative URL. This is easy to fix, but it shows a flaw in the editor.

The point here is for you to expect flaws in the code that the editor puts out. Always expect to have to fix the code that an automated tool generates. Some people say that the tools will get better, and that's probably true. But the fact remains that after 20 years of trying, there are still no automated tools for any programming language that do as good a job as a careful human. The promise of artificial intelligence that can better a human's creative efforts is yet to be realized. We don't expect that overall situation to change any time soon.

We also noticed that the tool doesn't break its lines to fit an 80-column screen (this is important for those of us who use multiple platforms to work on the same files), and the use of tabs for indenting is also not portable. Again, these are easy problems to fix, but they require effort. Always prepare for more complicated pages to have more complicated problems.

As a rule, we feel that the WYSIWYG editors are excellent tools for prototyping, but not for production use. If you must create and maintain a large and complex web site with constantly up-dated information (like a large news or periodical site), we recommend that you either create custom tools for that particular site (as most of the large major sites do) or retain the services of a programmer to do that for you. For large one-time sites that won't change much over time, you can prototype with your WYSIWYG editor and then modify or rewrite the code by hand to make it correct.

Common HTML Gotchas

There are many common HTML "gotchas" that we see a lot on the web. Of course, each of us has our own peculiar predilection for error, and as such, our problems will not always fit nicely into a preordained list. But we've compiled a short list that you may want to watch out for anyway. These are some of the most frequent HTML problems we see on public web pages.

What's in a Quote?

Quotation marks (either double " or single ') are used in HTML to contain the values of some attributes. When do you need to use quotes? If all the characters in the value are either letters (a-z), numbers (0-9), periods (.), or hyphens (-), you don't need to use quotes. If you have any characters besides those mentioned, you need to use quotes. When in doubt, use the quotes. They can't hurt.

The most common type of value that requires quotes, and often doesn't have them, is the URL (e.g., `<A HREF=http://www.htmlbook.com/>Creative HTML Book Site</A>` is not legal HTML because it is missing the quotes around `"http://www.htmlbook.com/"`). Most URLs have slashes, colons, and other characters that must be quoted to be correct. We are not looking forward to the day Netscape starts requiring quotes around attributes that really need them. A lot of the web will need to be fixed!

Hanging Quotes

On the other hand, you have to use your quotes in matching pairs! For example, this doesn't work well:

```
<HTML>
<HEAD>
<TITLE> Bad Quotes </TITLE>
</HEAD>
<BODY BGCOLOR=white>

<P>This is a <a
href=" link.html>link</a> with a
missing quote.

<P>You won't see any of this
text until
<a href=" link.html">after</a>
this other link.

</BODY>
</HTML>
```

Notice the missing quote in the first link. You don't see it? Look here then:

bad-quote.html in the View:Source of Netscape Navigator.

The folks at Netscape gave us this handy-dandy missing quote finder in their **View:Source** menu, starting with version 3. When you view the source of a document with a missing quote, all the text that's affected will be highlighted and blinking. Try this for yourself: find the bad-quote.html file in the chap19 folder of the <chd2> CD-ROM and look at it in Netscape Navigator. Be sure to select **View:Source**. See it blink? Tell a friend.

Straddling Containers

Considering the fact that a container—along with all of its content—is a single distinct element, it is reasonable that one container can have other containers as part of its content. That's why you can write something like this:

```
<P> This paragraph has <EM> emphasized
and <STRONG> strong </STRONG> text </EM>
inside it. </P>
```

In this perfectly legal example, the P element contains the EM element, which in turn contains the STRONG element.

Now consider this example:

```
<P> This paragraph has <EM> emphasized
and <STRONG> strong </EM> text </STRONG>
inside it. </P>
```

Here we decided to end the EM element before the end of the STRONG element. What's wrong with this picture? Notice that EM no longer contains STRONG (nor does STRONG contain EM). The elements are straddling each other.

It is perfectly legal to have one element contain another element, as long as the inner element is valid content for the outer element. But it is not legal to have two elements straddle each other. As with many common HTML errors, this may work in some browsers today, and it may not work in later versions of those same browsers.

Line Endings

Unless you are actually trying to make your HTML unreadable (some people actually want to make it a little tougher to "steal" their code), you should keep your lines to under 80 characters wide (75 is a good rule of thumb). That makes it easier to view your source code in the browser and to work on it on the widest possible variety of platforms.

You should also set your editor to use UNIX line-endings, especially if your server runs under UNIX.

There are three different types of line endings:

- **Carriage Return**—used by Macs

- **Carriage Return + Line Feed**—used by Windows

- **Line Feed only**—used by UNIX

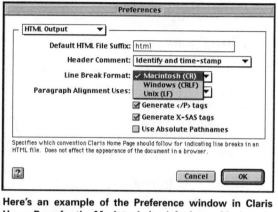

Here's an example of the Preference window in Claris Home Page for the Macintosh. Its default was Macintosh, but you can and should change it to UNIX.

The line endings are invisible to you, but visible to your web server and many HTML editors. You will probably find the setting for UNIX line endings in the Preferences menu of your HTML editor or word processor.

A Brief History of Line Endings

Now that your lines are less than 80 charac-ters wide, you may be surprised to find that users of different operating systems may still see your code as one long line of text. The reason for this? The operating system has to know where the end of the line is, and different operating systems tend to represent the end of a line of text differently.

Internally, text—like everything else on a computer—is represented as a string of bytes. In order to display distinct lines of text on a screen or a printer, the computer must know where one line ends and the next one begins. It does this with a special character called a line ending, which tells the computer, "this line is over now," kind of like the Return key on your keyboard.

Originally, before video displays existed, computers used mechanical printers that looked like massive typewriters to display text. The printer used a rubberized platen (also called a carriage) to position the paper on the printer. A special character called **c**arriage-**r**eturn (CR) would move the paper to the left margin, and another special character called **l**ine-**f**eed (LF) would advance the paper to the next line. Because of this, lines of text were traditionally ended with a CR-LF sequence.

By the time UNIX became popular, video displays were more prevalent, and UNIX systems began using LF alone to represent line endings (like many features of UNIX, this was designed to save space).

In contrast, the designers of the Macintosh OS opted to use CR alone to represent line-endings. Windows, because its operating system is based on DOS, which was based on CP/M, which was based on older DEC operating systems that go back to the days of line-printers, use the full CR-LF sequence.

System	Line Ending
UNIX	LF-only
MacOS	CR-only
DOS/Windows	CR-LF sequence

The bottom line is simple. If you want your code to be truly portable, use UNIX line endings wherever possible.

Entities vs. Numbers vs. Embedded Characters

HTML uses something called "entities" for characters outside of the normal English alpha-numeric character set (there's a nice list of them here: http://luna.bearnet.com/iso8859-1.html). Named entities (e.g, © for the © symbol) are preferable to the numbered entities (e.g, © also for the © symbol), because the names will work on multiple platforms. The numbered entities will not work on all platforms, nor will characters embedded from your word processor. (Some WYSIWYG editors use numbered entities by default.)

- **Color Names Not Browser Safe:** Remember that the named colors (e.g, "teal") are not all browser safe. Most of them will dither in 256-color systems. Use the hexadecimal colors instead (e.g, "#669999"). (Some WYSIWYG editors use color names by default.) In-depth information about browser-safe colors is in Chapter 4, *"Web Color."*

- **Empty ALT Attributes:** The ALT attribute for the IMG tag is an important tool for making your pages work on non-graphical systems, but an empty ALT attribute (e.g, ALT="") can be annoying. In non-graphical systems, it will take up space without saying anything; and in many graphical systems, it will show an empty little tool-help (usually a little yellow square) when the mouse is passed over the graphic. If you don't have content for your ALT attributes, don't include them at all. (Some WYSIWYG editors insert these by default.)

- **Case-Sensitive File Names:** Most web servers run under UNIX, which uses case-sensitive file names. Most web authors use Mac or Windows platforms, which do not use case-sensitive file names. That means that if you have a file named Image.gif and you refer to it as IMAGE.GIF, it may work on your system at home, but not on the web. We recommend that you use all lowercase file names, just to avoid problems. They're easier to type anyway.

- **Relative vs. Absolute Links:** Always use relative links when possible. (See Chapter 12, *"Organization."*) Absolute links will become a major headache for you when you eventually have to move your site to another machine, or even just another folder on the same machine. (Some WYSIWYG editors use absolute links by default.)

▶ chapter nineteen summary

Good HTML

Writing good HTML is not required. No one is going to force you to do it, and most people won't even notice if you don't. But it's a discipline that will serve you well in the long run. It will make life easier on you when new tools and browsers are released and whenever you need to make substantial changes to your site (which will likely be more often than you plan for).

In this chapter, you have seen some of the common problems with incorrect HTML, and how to correct them when they are encountered.

We encourage you to use the HTML Reference in the back of this book as an authoritative source.

HTML 4.01 Reference

▶ **contents**

introduction
categorized
alphabetical
supplemental

The purpose of this reference is to document the HTML 4.01 language, as thoroughly and accurately as possible. By providing this reference, we hope to give you a place to turn when you need to know the details of a particular tag or attribute.

This reference grew out of our own personal need to have all the elements of HTML documented in one place, clearly and concisely. The HTML DTDs distributed by the W3C (**W**orld **W**ide **W**eb **C**onsortium) are neither convenient nor concise. The DTDs document the exact syntax of the language—if you can figure out how to read them—but their descriptions of the purposes of the various elements and attributes are either lacking in detail, or missing entirely. This reference is designed to fill that need by clearly and succinctly stating the purpose and usage of every HTML element and attribute.

HTML Reference

▶ table of contents

HTML 4.0 Reference

Section 1. *Introduction*

What Version of HTML Is This?	429
Are They Tags or Elements?	430
The Concept of Content	431
General Content Models	432
Reference Layout	433
Global Attribute Groups	435
Core Attributes	435
Internationalization Attributes	436
Event-Related Attributes	437

Section 2. *Categorized Reference*

Document Structure Elements	438
Font Markup	441
Phrase Markup	442
List Elements	443
Block Elements	444
Special Text-Level Elements	446
Forms Elements	451
Table Elements	456
Frames Elements	459
Miscellaneous Elements	461

Section 3. *Alphabetical Reference*

All Tags	463
All Attributes	470

Section 4. *Supplemental Reference*

Character Entities	486

Section 1: *Introduction*

What Version of HTML Is This?

The information in this reference is based on the "Transitional" version of the HTML 4.01 DTD (**D**ocument **T**ype **D**efinition), as of the W3C's finalized recommendation of 24 December 1999. Keep in mind that internet-related specifications and standards are rarely final in the rapidly changing world of the Web (even when they are officially called "final"), nor are the browser vendors likely to implement any particular HTML specification completely or accurately (even though they all claim to).

We chose not to use the "strict" version of the DTD because it omits many elements that are in common use today, such as FONT and CENTER, and many more attributes commonly used for formatting and decoration, such as BACKGROUND and BGCOLOR. We don't think the W3C (**W**orld **W**ide **W**eb **C**onsortium) intended for people to stop using these features— on the contrary, we believe that they are trying to encourage the software makers to implement full support for the more powerful and flexible formatting capabilities of HTML style sheets. Until that happens—and perhaps even after—designers and programmers will continue to use the features that work for their applications, so we have documented the full set of HTML elements here.

Are They Tags or Elements?

There is some measure of controversy regarding the proper terminology for referring to the parts of an HTML document. Some HTML purists actually take offense when the term "Tag" is applied more broadly than they feel is correct. The current HTML specification includes this comment:

- **Elements are not tags!** Some people refer incorrectly to elements as tags (e.g., "the P tag"). Remember that the element is one thing, and the tag (be it start or end tag) is another. For instance, the HEAD element is always present, even though both start and end HEAD tags may be missing in the markup.

If you can understand what they mean by that, then more power to you! We find it confusing. We have chosen to use the word "Tag" more loosely than some would like, for several reasons:

- The word "**Tag**" is small and neat, and fits nicely in the headings of our tables.

- The word "**Element**" can be ambiguous. Logically, the P element includes all the content of the container, whereas the P tag does not.

Our goal is to have our readers understand how to write good HTML. We feel this can be better accomplished by using familiar terminology. With that in mind, here's our definitions:

- **Tag:** Everything between the "<" and ">" characters. For example, <P> is a P tag; <IMG SRC=" foo.gif"> is an IMG tag; </P> is an end tag for the P element.

- **Element:** A unit of markup. For example, this is a P element: <P> Here's a small paragraph. </P>

We recognize that this seems persnickety, but when you get as much email as we do, you do what you can to answer it in advance.

The Concept of Content

When you are deciding what tags to use, and where to use them, it is useful to understand what it means to put content into an HTML element. In order to understand that, let's take a look at the concept of content.

The content of an HTML element is all the stuff between the start tag and the end tag. Some HTML elements are simply start tags. They don't have an end tag, and so they cannot have any content. The tag itself, along with its attributes, is the element. For example, this IMG tag *is* the whole element:

```
<IMG SRC=" foo.gif">
```

Other elements have content. These elements are called **containers**. The content is what goes inside the container, that is, between the start and end tags. For example, consider this P container:

```
<P> This is the content of a paragraph element. </P>
```

The content of the P container is the sentence of text. There are some things that are allowed inside a P container, and some other things that are not.

If everything inside the container is allowed, then the browser will generally do what you expect. On the other hand, if you try to put something inside that is not allowed, the element will automatically end just before the disallowed content. That can cause confusion!

For example, consider this code:

```
<P> Text here <H1> Heading </H1> Other text here. </P>
```

In this example, the paragraph ends just after "Text here," because the H1 element is not allowed inside a paragraph. The "Other text here" part is not in a paragraph at all, and the </P> end tag is superfluous (and ignored).

With an element like P, that doesn't require an end tag, the browser automatically ends the element when it encounters disallowed content. So it's common, and perfectly legal, to write our previous example like this:

```
<P> Text here
<H1> Heading </H1>
<P> Other text here.
```

The first paragraph ends where the heading begins, and the next paragraph starts right after the following P tag.

General Content Models

What is, and what is not, allowed inside a given element is called the **Content model** for that element. Some elements allow just a few certain elements as content, while others are far more generalized.

There are two general content models which are shared by a large number of elements. Because so many elements use these same models, we use a shorthand notation to refer to them.

The **Inline** content model includes written text, and all the elements that can be included in a paragraph. These are the tags that are part of the Inline content model:

Inline Content Model

```
A/ABBR/ACRONYM/APPLET/B/BASEFONT/BDO/BIG/BR/BUTTON/CITE/CODE/
DFN/EM/FONT/I/IFRAME/IMG/INPUT/KBD/LABEL/MAP/OBJECT/Q/S/SAMP/
SCRIPT/SELECT/SMALL/SPAN/STRIKE/STRONG/SUB/SUP/TEXTAREA/TT/
U/VAR
```

The **Block** content model includes mostly tags that are not rendered inline, or are used to enclose other Text content. It does not include written text. The Block content model includes all the following tags:

Block Content Model

```
ADDRESS/BLOCKQUOTE/CENTER/DIR/DIV/DL/FIELDSET/FORM/H1/H2/H3/
H4/H5/H6/HR/ISINDEX/MENU/NOFRAMES/NOSCRIPT/OL/P/PRE/TABLE/UL
```

For example, consider the P element. According to the specification, the allowable content for a P element is Text. So, anything in the Text content model is allowed in a P element, and other stuff is not. So if we try to put, say, an H1 element inside a P element, the P element will simply end, and the H1 element will begin:

```
<P> Text here
<H1> Heading </H1>
<P> Other text here.
```

In this example, the H1 tag will create an automatic end to the P element because H1 is not part of the *Text* content model. The text "Other text here" is in a separate paragraph.

Reference Layout

The HTML reference itself is organized in tables of **Tags** and **Attributes**. The tables are designed to quickly tell you what you need to know, in order to use the elements described.

The **Tag** tables have the following structure:

Tag	End Tag	Content	Attributes	Description / Notes
TAG	*Req or Opt*	Content-model	ATTRIBUTE ATTRIBUTE ATTRIBUTE	A description of what the tag is for, with special notes where necessary.

Tag: The name of the tag. The name of the tag is always the part immediately following the left angle-bracket (<TAG>).

End tag: *Req* if the end tag is required, *Opt* if the end tag is optional. Optional end tags can be omitted if the end of the element is otherwise obvious. Usually, that means that the element will end at the first occurrence of any content that is not allowed within the element.

Content: What content (if any) is allowed within this element. This may be the name of one or more of the general content models (*Inline* or *Block*), or it could be a list of tags. Sometimes it will be a combination of content models and tags.

Attributes: A list of the attributes that can be used with this tag.

Description/Notes: A description of the tag and its usage, sometimes with additional notes about the tag.

The **Attribute** tables have the following structure:

Attribute	Required	Value(s)	Parent Tag	Description / Notes
ATTRIBUTE	*Req or Opt*	Value	TAG TAG TAG	A description of what the attribute is for, and how to use it.

Attribute: The name of the attribute. Attributes always go after the name of the tag, but still between the angle-brackets: For example, in `<P ALIGN=RIGHT>`, the name of the tag is `P`, the name of the attribute is `ALIGN`, and `RIGHT` is the value of the `ALIGN` attribute. Tags can have more than one attribute, e.g., `<IMG SRC="foo.gif" ALIGN=RIGHT BORDER=0>`.

Required: *Req* if the attribute is required, *Opt* if the attribute is optional.

Value(s): The allowed value(s), if any, for this attribute.

Parent Tag: The tag(s) that this attribute may be used with. One attribute name may be listed more than once, if it is used differently for different parent tags. For example, the `SIZE` attribute is used for `HR` (the thickness of the rule), `FONT` (the size of the font), and `INPUT` (the number of characters wide to render the text box). Each of those uses are listed separately because the attributes have different meanings (even though they are spelled the same!).

Description/Notes: A description of the attribute, its values, and how to use them.

In the **Categorized Reference** section, tags are listed in a logical order, with the most significant tags at the top of the table. Sometimes those are the most commonly used tags; other times they are the tags which contain other tags in that category.

Attributes in the Categorized Reference section are organized alphabetically by *Attribute*, and then by *Parent Tag* within *Attribute*. Hopefully this will allow you to quickly find related tags and attributes.

In the **Alphabetical Reference** section, all 86 tags are listed alphabetically, followed by an alphabetical listing of all 178 associated attributes.

GLOBAL ATTRIBUTE GROUPS

There are 86 different tags, and 178 different attributes (including different attributes that are spelled the same) in the HTML 4.01 specification. Some of the attributes can be used by nearly all of the tags, so it made sense to group them here, rather than redundantly list them in every category. We call these the *Global Attribute Groups*.

The global attributes are further broken down into three groups, as they are generally applicable in these groups. The groups are *Core*, *Internationalization*, and *Event*.

Core Attributes

The core attributes are those that apply to style sheets and advisory titles. These are the most globally applicable attributes. In the reference tables, we refer to this group as *Core*.

For example, to apply a style class to a paragraph, you would use the CLASS attribute like this:

```
<P CLASS="classname"> This paragraph has class. </P>
```

The *Core* attributes are CLASS, ID, STYLE, and TITLE:

Attribute	Required	Value(s)	Parent Tag	Description / Notes
CLASS	*Opt*	List of class names	*All elements except:* BASE•BASEFONT HEAD•HTML•META PARAM•SCRIPT STYLE•TITLE	Specifies a class (or a space-separated list of classes) for applying style-sheet properties to the element.
ID	*Opt*	#Unique-ID	*All elements except:* BASE•BASEFONT HEAD•HTML•META PARAM•SCRIPT STYLE•TITLE	Unique ID for an individual instance of an element. The "#" character must be used before the value.
STYLE	*Opt*	Style	*All elements except:* BASE•BASEFONT HEAD•HTML•META PARAM•SCRIPT STYLE•TITLE	Style information to associate with the element.
TITLE	*Opt*	Text	*All elements except:* BASE•BASEFONT HEAD•HTML•META PARAM•SCRIPT STYLE•TITLE	An advisory title. May display as a *tool-tip* or be spoken or rendered some other way for non-visual browsers.

Internationalization Attributes

The internationalization attributes are used to apply language-specific formatting to elements of text. In the reference tables, we refer to this group as *Int'l*.

For example, if you want a paragraph to read right-to-left, you can use the DIR attribute:

```
<P> Paul McCartney's voice: <Q DIR=RTL> I'm dead! </Q>
```

Which would look like this, in a browser that supports the DIR attribute:

      Paul McCartney's voice: "!daed m'I"

The *Internationalization* attributes are DIR and LANG:

Attribute	Required	Value(s)	Parent Tag	Description / Notes
DIR	*Opt*	LTR or RTL	*All tags except:* APPLET • BASE BASEFONT • BDO BR • FRAME FRAMESET IFRAME • PARAM SCRIPT	Direction of text. LTR = Left to Right RTL = Right to Left
LANG	*Opt*	Lang-ID	*All tags except:* APPLET • BASE BASEFONT • BDO BR • FRAME FRAMESET IFRAME • PARAM SCRIPT	Language identifier, as specified in RFC1766.

Event-Related Attributes

The event-related attributes are for linking various visual elements with events, for use with scripting languages such as JavaScript (ECMA-Script). In the reference tables, we refer to this group as *Event*.

For example, if you want a JavaScript routine to run whenever the mouse passes over a link, you can use the ONMOUSEOVER attribute like this:

```
<A HREF="intheroad.html" ONMOUSEOVER="doit(intheroad)">
```

The *Event* attributes are ONCLICK, ONDBLCLICK, ONKEYDOWN, ONKEYPRESS, ONKEYUP, ONMOUSEDOWN, ONMOUSEMOVE, ONMOUSEOUT, ONMOUSEOVER, and ONMOUSEUP:

Attribute	Required	Value(s)	Parent Tag	Description / Notes
ONCLICK	*Opt*	Script	*All tags except:* APPLET•BASE BASEFONT•BDO BR•FONT•FRAME FRAMESET•HEAD HTML•IFRAME ISINDEX•META PARAM•SCRIPT STYLE•TITLE	When the mouse button is clicked on the element.
ONDBLCLICK	*Opt*	Script	"	When the mouse button is double-clicked on the element.
ONKEYDOWN	*Opt*	Script	"	When a key is pressed down within the element.
ONKEYPRESS	*Opt*	Script	"	When a key is pressed *and* released within the element.
ONKEYUP	*Opt*	Script	"	When a key is released in the element.
ONMOUSEDOWN	*Opt*	Script	"	When a mouse button is pressed over the element.
ONMOUSEMOVE	*Opt*	Script	"	When the mouse cursor is moved over the element.
ONMOUSEOUT	*Opt*	Script	"	When the mouse cursor moves out of the element's display space.
ONMOUSEOVER	*Opt*	Script	"	When the mouse cursor moves into the element's display space.
ONMOUSEUP	*Opt*	Script	"	When a mouse button is released over the element.

Section 2: *Categorized Reference*

Document Structure Elements

These elements are used to set up the structure of an HTML document.

Tag	End Tag	Content	Attributes	Description / Notes
HTML	*Opt*	HEAD•BODY PLAINTEXT	*Int'l* VERSION	Outer container for an HTML document.
HEAD	*Opt*	TITLE•ISINDEX BASE•META LINK•SCRIPT STYLE	*Int'l* PROFILE	Container for document header.
TITLE	*Req*	Document Title	*Int'l*	Provides a title for the document.
BODY	*Opt*	All	*Core• Int'l• Event* BACKGROUND BGCOLOR•TEXT LINK•VLINK ALINK•ONLOAD UNLOAD	Base URL for dereferencing relative URLs. Valid only within HEAD.
BASE	*None*	None	HREF•TARGET	Container for document body.
LINK	*None*	None	*Core• Int'l• Event* CHARSET•HREF HREFLANG•REL REV•TYPE MEDIA•TARGET	Defines relationships with other documents.
META	*None*	None	*Int'l* HTTP-EQUIV NAME•CONTENT SCHEME	Meta-information describing properties of the document. Generates HTTP header when used with HTTP-EQUIV. Valid only within HEAD.
STYLE	*Req*	Style Sheet	*Int'l* TYPE	Container for style-sheet definitions.

Attributes (Document Structure Elements)

Attribute	Required	Value(s)	Parent Tag	Description / Notes
ALINK	Opt	Color	BODY	Color of active links (e.g. while the mouse button is pressed on the link). (depreciated)
BACKGROUND	Opt	URL	BODY	URL for the background graphic.(depreciated)
BGCOLOR	Opt	Color	BODY	Background color of the document page. (depreciated)
CHARSET	Opt	Character Set Identifier	A•LINK•SCRIPT	Character encoding of the destination link.
CONTENT	Req	Text	META	Content of meta-information.
HREF	Opt	URL	A•AREA•LINK	The destination of the hypertext link.
HREF	Opt	URL	BASE	URL for the document base.
HTTP-EQUIV	Opt	Text	META	Name for HTTP header.
LINK	Opt	Color	BODY	Color of unvisited links. (depreciated)
MEDIA	Opt	Media	STYLE•LINK	Destination media for style. Defaults to ALL.
NAME	Opt	Text	META	Name of meta-information.
ONLOAD	Opt	Script	BODY	When the document is finished loading.
PROFILE	Opt	URL	HEAD	A meta-data profile.
REL	Opt	Link Types	A•LINK	The forward relationship for the linked resource.
REV	Opt	Link Types	A•LINK	The reverse relationship for the linked resource.

Attributes (Document Structure Elements) *continued ...*

Attribute	Required	Value(s)	Parent Tag	Description / Notes
SCHEME	*Opt*	Text	META	The scheme to be used in interpreting the content. Depends on context.
TARGET	*Opt*	Target	A•AREA•BASE FORM•LINK	The target window or frame for a hyperlink or form results. The following magic target names are also supported: _blank — a new blank window _self — the same window as the link _parent — the parent frameset _top — the full body of the window
TEXT	*Opt*	Color	BODY	Color of the document text. (depreciated)
TYPE	*Opt*	MIME	A•LINK	MIME-type for the TITLE content.
TYPE	*Req*	MIME	STYLE	MIME-type for the external style sheet.
VERSION	*Opt*	Text	HTML	Link to the DTD for this document. Redundant with use of DOCTYPE. (depreciated)
VLINK	*Opt*	Color	BODY	Color of visited links. (depreciated)

Font Markup Elements

The font markup elements are used to change the appearance of the characters on the screen, for parts of text. All of these elements may use the *Core*, *Int'l*, and *Event* attributes.

Tag	End Tag	Content	Attributes	Description / Notes
B	*Req*	Text	*Core• Int'l• Event*	Bold text.
BIG	*Req*	Text	*Core• Int'l• Event*	Larger text style.
I	*Req*	Text	*Core• Int'l• Event*	Italic.
S	*Req*	Text	*Core• Int'l• Event*	Strike-through (synonym for STRIKE). (depreciated)
SMALL	*Req*	Text	*Core• Int'l• Event*	Smaller size text.
STRIKE	*Req*	Text	*Core• Int'l• Event*	Strike-through (synonym for S).(depreciated)
TT	*Req*	Text	*Core• Int'l• Event*	Teletype (fixed width).
U	*Req*	Text	*Core• Int'l• Event*	Underline. (depreciated)

Phrase Markup

The phrase markup elements are used to indicate certain common parts of speech. All of these elements may use the *Core, Int'l,* and *Event* attributes. These elements may render a certain way on visual browsers, but may also have an effect with non-visual applications, such as Braille browsers or speech synthesizers.

Use these instead of the font markup elements, where possible, to make your site more accessible to the visually impaired.

Tag	End Tag	Content	Attributes	Description / Notes
ABBR	*Req*	Text	*Core• Int'l• Event*	Abbreviation (e.g. HTML, M., Inc., et al., etc)
ACRONYM	*Req*	Text	*Core• Int'l• Event*	Acronym (e.g., WAC, RADAR, etc.).
CITE	*Req*	Text	*Core• Int'l• Event*	Citation.
CODE	*Req*	Text	*Core• Int'l• Event*	Code fragment (usually presented in fixed-width text).
DFN	*Req*	Text	*Core• Int'l• Event*	Defining instance of a term.
EM	*Req*	Text	*Core• Int'l• Event*	Emphasis (usually *italic*).
KBD	*Req*	Text	*Core• Int'l• Event*	Keyboard—text to be typed by a user.
Q	*Req*	Text	*Core• Int'l• Event*	Inline Quotation (may be rendered with quotation marks).
SAMP	*Req*	Text	*Core• Int'l• Event*	Sample output from a program.
STRONG	*Req*	Text	*Core• Int'l• Event*	Strong emphasis (usually **bold**).
VAR	*Req*	Text	*Core• Int'l• Event*	Variable or argument in a program.

Attributes (Phrase Markup)

Tag	End Tag	Content	Attributes	Description / Notes
CITE	*Opt*	URL	BLOCKQUOTE• Q	Source document or message with information about the quotation.

List Elements

These are the elements for making lists. **Ordered** lists are automatically rendered with numbers (ordinal or roman); **unordered** lists are generally rendered with bullets; and **definition** lists are for lists of terms with associated definitions. **Menu** and **directory** lists are depreciated and should not be used.

Tag	End Tag	Content	Attributes	Description / Notes
OL	*Req*	LI	*Core• Int'l• Event* TYPE•START COMPACT	Ordered list.
UL	*Req*	LI	*Core• Int'l• Event* TYPE•COMPACT	Unordered List.
LI	*Opt*	Text Block	*Core• Int'l• Event* TYPE•VALUE	List item.
DL	*Req*	DT•DD	*Core• Int'l• Event* COMPACT	Definition list.
DD	*Opt*	Text Block	*Core• Int'l• Event*	The definition of a term.
DT	*Opt*	Text	*Core Int'l• Event*	A term being defined.
DIR	*Req*	LI –Block	*Core Int'l• Event* COMPACT	Directory list. (depreciated)
MENU	*Req*	LI –Block	*Core• Int'l• Event* COMPACT	Menu list. (depreciated)

Attributes (List Elements)

Attribute	Required	Value(s)	Parent Tag	Description / Notes
COMPACT	*Opt*	None	DIR•DL•MENU OL•UL	Render the list more compactly. (depreciated)
START	*Opt*	Number	LI	Starting sequence number. (depreciated)
TYPE	*Opt*	List style	LI•OL•UL	Style of bullet or numbering style. (depreciated) **For OL lists:** **For UL lists:** 1 1, 2, 3, 4, ... disc ● a a, b, c, d, ... square ■ A A, B, C, D, ... circle ○ i i, ii, iii, iv, ... I I, II, III, IV, ...
VALUE	*Opt*	Number	OL	Reset number sequence to the value given. (depreciated)

Block Elements

Block elements are generally containers for text. They are used for applying formatting or designating purpose to a block of text at a time.

Tag	End Tag	Content	Attributes	Description / Notes
ADDRESS	*Req*	Text + P	*Core• Int'l• Event* CITE	Information on author.
BLOCKQUOTE	*Req*	Block	*Core• Int'l• Event* CITE	For quoted passages. (usually depreciated)
CENTER	*Req*	Block	*Core• Int'l• Event*	For centering (alias for <DIV ALIGN=CENTER). (depreciated)
DIV	*Req*	Block	*Core• Int'l• Event* ALIGN	Null container for applying style and common attributes to block-level content.
H1 H2 H3 H4 H5 H6	*Req*	Text	*Core• Int'l• Event* ALIGN	Six different levels of headings.
HR	*None*	None	*Core• Int'l• Event* ALIGN•NOSHADE SIZE•WIDTH	Horizontal rule (line).
P	*Opt*	Text	*Core• Int'l• Event* ALIGN	Paragraph.
PRE	*Req*	Text - APPLET BASEFONT•BIG FONT•IMG OBJECT·SMALL SUB·SUP	*Core• Int'l• Event* CITE	Information on author.

Attributes (Block Elements)

Attribute	Required	Value(s)	Parent Tag	Description / Notes
ALIGN	*Opt*	LEFT•CENTER RIGHT•JUSTIFY	DIV•H1•H2•H3 H4•H5•H6•P	Alignment of the block of text. Defaults to LEFT. (depreciated)
ALIGN	*Opt*	RIGHT•LEFT• CENTER	HR	Alignment of horizontal rule. (depreciated)
CITE	*Opt*	URL	BLOCKQUOTE•Q	Source document or message with information about the quotation.
NOSHADE	*Opt*	None	HR	Render the horizontal rule without shading. (depreciated)
SIZE	*Opt*	Pixels	HR	The size (height in pixels) of the horizontal rule. (depreciated)
WIDTH	*Opt*	Pixels or Percentage	HR	Width of the horizontal rule. (depreciated)
WIDTH	*Opt*	Number	PRE	Number of characters wide for the display of fixed-width data. (depreciated)

Special Text-Level Elements

These are miscellaneous elements that are valid content as part of a block of text, but are not actually rendered as text.

Tag	End Tag	Content	Attributes	Description / Notes
A	*Req*	Text −A	*Core•Int'l•Event* ACCESSKEY CHARSET•COORDS HREF•HREFLANG NAME•ONFOCUS ONBLUR•REL•REV SHAPE•TABINDEX TARGET•TITLE	Anchor for a hypertext link or a named target for hypertext links.
APPLET	*Req*	Text +PARAM	*Core•Int'l•Events* SHAPE•COORDS HREF•NOHREF ALT•TARGET TABINDEX ACCESSKEY	Java applet. (depreciated)
AREA	*None*	None	*Core•Int'l•Events* SHAPE•COORDS HREF•NOHREF ALT•TARGET TABINDEX ACCESSKEY	Client-side image map area (hotzones) definition.
BASEFONT	*None*	None	ID•SIZE COLOR•FACE	Sets the default size of text. (depreciated)
BDO	*Req*	Text	*Core* LANG•DIR	Override direction of text.
BR	*None*	None	*Core•Int'l•Event* CLEAR	Force a line break. Moves point of text to the beginning of the next available line.
FONT	*Req*	Text	*Core•Int'l•Event* SIZE•COLOR•FACE	Sets the appearance of text. (depreciated)
IMG	*None*	None	*Core•Int'l•Event* SRC•ALT LONGDESC•ALIGN HEIGHT•WIDTH BORDER•HSPACE VSPACE•USEMAP ISMAP	An embedded image.
MAP	*Req*	AREA	*Core•Int'l•Event* NAME	Client-side image map.

Special Text-Level Elements *continued ...*

Tag	End Tag	Content	Attributes	Description / Notes
OBJECT	*Req*	Text Block PARAM	*Core•Int'l•Event* DECLARE•CLASSID CODEBASE•DATA TYPE•CODETYPE ARCHIVE•STANDBY ALIGN•HEIGHT WIDTH•BORDER HSPACE•VSPACE USEMAP•SHAPES NAME•TABINDEX	Generic mechanism for including objects.
PARAM	*None*	None	ID•NAME•VALUE VALUETYPE•TYPE	Named parameters (e.g. that can be read with Java's getParameter( ) method).
SPAN	*Req*	Text	*Core•Int'l•Event*	Null-container for applying styles to inline text-level content.
SUB	*Req*	Text	*Core•Int'l•Event*	Subscript.
SUP	*Req*	Text	*Core•Int'l•Event*	Superscript.

Attributes (Special Text-Level Elements)

Attribute	Required	Value(s)	Parent Tag	Description / Notes
ACCESSKEY	*Opt*	Text (single character)	A•AREA•BUTTON INPUT•LABEL LEGEND TEXTAREA	Assigns an access (shortcut) key to the associated element. Pressing this key will assign the focus to the associated element.
ALIGN	*Opt*	TOP MIDDLE BOTTOM LEFT RIGHT	APPLET•IFRAME IMG•INPUT OBJECT	Alignment of the element relative to surrounding text. (depreciated)
ALT	*Opt*	Text	APPLET	Alternate text for display in circumstances where the applet cannot be rendered. (depreciated)
ALT	*Req*	Text	AREA•IMAGE	Text associated with the image or area for use by text-only browsers and non-visual user agents that cannot display images.
ARCHIVE	*Opt*	Text	OBJECT	Preload resources for OBJECT. Note: List is space-separated for OBJECT.

Attributes (Special Text-Level Elements) *continued ...*

Attribute	Required	Value(s)	Parent Tag	Description / Notes
BORDER	*Opt*	Pixels	IMG•OBJECT	The size of the border when the IMG or OBJECT is used in a hyper-text link (A element). Set this to zero to suppress the border.
CHARSET	*Opt*	Character Set Identifier	A•LINK•SCRIPT	Character encoding of the destination link.
CLASSID	*Opt*	URL	OBJECT	URL for specific implementation.
CLEAR	*None*	LEFT•RIGHT ALL•NONE	BR	Move down past floating images. LEFT clears to the left margin; RIGHT clears to the right margin; ALL clears to both margins. (depreciated)
CODEBASE	*Opt*	URL	OBJECT	Base URL for resolving relative URLs for this object. Specifically used for the CLASSID URL.
CODETYPE	*Opt*	MIME	OBJECT	MIME-type for the object specified by CLASSID. Defaults to the value of TYPE attribute.
COLOR	*Opt*	Color	BASEFONT•FONT	Sets the color of text. (depreciated)
COORDS	*Opt*	Coordinates	A•AREA	List of coordinates, in pixel units, according to the given shape, e.g.: shape = default shape = rect coords = "*left-x, top-y, right-x, bottom-y*" shape = rect coords = "*left-x, top-y, right-x, bottom-y*"
DATA	*Opt*	URL	OBJECT	Location for the object's data.
DECLARE	*Opt*	None	OBJECT	Declare OBJECT only.
DIR	*Req*	LTR or RTL	BDO	Direction for overridden text.
FACE	*Opt*	List	BASEFONT•FONT	Comma-separated list of font names.
HEIGHT	*Opt*	Pixels or Percentage	IMG•OBJECT	The height of the image. Some browsers use this to reserve space for an image so that the page can be laid out before images are downloaded. Can also be used to override the height of the actual image or object.
HREF	*Opt*	URL	A•AREA•LINK	The destination of the hypertext link.

Attributes (Special Text-Level Elements) *continued ...*

Attribute	Required	Value(s)	Parent Tag	Description / Notes
HSPACE	*Opt*	Pixels or Pecercentage	APPLET•IMG OBJECT	The size of the horizontal gutter space around the image. Set this to zero to suppress the horizontal gutter. (depreciated)
ISMAP	*Opt*	None	IMG•INPUT	Indicates that this image is a server-side image map. Only valid for IMG when within an A (anchor) element with an HREF attribute.
LONGDESC	*Opt*	URL	IMG	Link to a long description. (complements ALT)
NAME	*Opt*	Text	A	The name of an anchor for use with a fragment identifier (#) in a hyperlink.
NAME	*Opt*	Text	INPUT•OBJECT	The name used to identify the form element (including use of an OBJECT as a form element) for use with a scripting language.
NAME	*Req*	Text	MAP	The name used to reference the map with USEMAP.
NAME	*Req*	Text	PARAM	Name of parameter.
NOHREF	*Opt*	None	AREA	Declares the area of a client-side imagemap to be a dead zone.
ONBLUR	*Opt*	Script	A•AREA•BUTTON INPUT•LABEL SELECT TEXTAREA	When the focus is removed from the element.
ONFOCUS	*Opt*	Script	A•AREA•BUTTON INPUT•LABEL SELECT TEXTAREA	When the element receives the focus.
REL	*Opt*	Link Types	A•LINK	The forward relationship for the linked resource.
REV	*Opt*	Link Types	A•LINK	The reverse relationship for the linked resource.
SHAPE	*Opt*	RECT•CIRCLE POLY•DEFAULT	A•AREA	Declares the shape of the area. DEFAULT indicates the entire image (use DEFAULT first to overlay the other shapes on top of it). May be used with the A element only within OBJECT.

Attributes (Special Text-Level Elements) *continued ...*

Attribute	Required	Value(s)	Parent Tag	Description / Notes
SIZE	*Opt*	Number	FONT	A number in the range 1–7 that specifies the size of displayed text. As an attribute to the FONT element, SIZE may be a relative number in the form +*n* or -*n*, where the resulting size will be relative to the default size or BASEFONT size. (depreciated)
SRC	*Req*	URL	IMG	Location of the image.
STANDBY	*Opt*	Text	OBJECT	Message to display while loading the object.
TABINDEX	*Opt*	Number	A • AREA • BUTTON INPUT • OBJECT SELECT TEXTAREA	Tabbing sequence for keyboard use.
TARGET	*Opt*	Target	A • AREA • BASE FROM • LINK	The target window or frame for a hyperlink or form results. The following magic target names are supported: _blank: a new blank window _self: the same window as the link _parent: the parent frameset _top: the full body of the window MIME type
TYPE	*Opt*	MIME	OBJECT • PARAM	MIME type.
USEMAP	*Opt*	URL	IMG • INPUT OBJECT	URL fragment identifier that points to a MAP element for a client-side image map.
VALUE	*Opt*	Text	PARAM	Value of the parameter.
VALUETYPE	*Opt*	DATA • REF OBJECT	PARAM	How to interpret VALUE. Defaults to DATA.
VSPACE	*Opt*	Pixels	APPLET • IMG OBJECT	The size of the vertical gutter space around the image. Set this to zero to suppress the vertical gutter. (depreciated)
WIDTH	*Opt*	Pixels or Percentage	IMG • OBJECT	The width of the image or object display space. Some browsers use this to reserve space for an image so that the page can be laid out before images are downloaded.

Forms Elements

The elements for creating forms and widgets.

Tag	End Tag	Content	Attributes	Description / Notes
BUTTON	*Req*	Text + Block – Forms – A	*Core• Int'l• Event* NAME•VALUE TYPE•DISABLED TABINDEX ACCESSKEY ONFOCUS•ONBLUR	A button for use with forms. Richer presentation possibilities than INPUT type buttons, but not supported by all browsers.
FIELDSET	*Req*	Text Block LEGEND	*Core• Int'l• Event*	Grouping form controls.
FORM	*Req*	All	*Core• Int'l• Event* ACTION•METHOD ENCTYPE ONSUBMIT ONRESET•TARGET ACCEPT-CHARSET	Outer container for all form fields.
INPUT	*None*	None	*Core• Int'l• Event* TYPE•NAME VALUE•CHECKED DISABLED READONLY•SIZE MAXLENGTH•SRC ALT•USEMAP ALIGN•TABINDEX ACCESSKEY ONFOCUS•ONBLUR ONSELECT ONCHANGE ACCEPT	Generalized tag for all non-container input fields.
LABEL	*Req*	Text - LABEL	*Core• Int'l• Event* FOR•DISABLED ACCESSKEY ONFOCUS•ONBLUR	For attaching labels to form control elements.
LEGEND	*Req*	Text	*Core• Int'l• Event* ALIGN ACCESSKEY	Assigns a caption (legend) to a FIELDSET.

Forms Elements *continued* ...

Tag	End Tag	Content	Attributes	Description / Notes
OPTGROUP	*Req*	OPTION	*Core• Int'l• Event* DISABLED LABEL	For grouping options with a SELECT container.
OPTION	*Opt*	Alphanumeric content	*Core• Int'l• Event* SELECTED DISABLED•VALUE	Container for individual options within a SELECT container.
SELECT	*Req*	OPTION OPTGROUP	*Core• Int'l• Event* NAME•SIZE MULTIPLE DISABLED TABINDEX ONFOCUS•ONBLUR ONCHANGE	Container for OPTION list.
TEXTAREA	*Req*	Alphanumeric content	*Core• Int'l• Event* NAME•ROWS COLS•DISABLED READONLY TABINDEX ONFOCUS•ONBLUR ONSELECT ONCHANGE	Container for multi-line text input field.

Attributes (Forms Elements)

Attribute	Required	Value(s)	Parent Tag	Description / Notes
ACCEPT	*Opt*	MIME	INPUT	List of MIME-types allowed by the server for upload. Used for FILE type INPUT elements.
ACCEPT-CHARSET	*Opt*	List	FORM	List of acceptable character encodings for the server processing this form.
ACCESSKEY	*Opt*	Text (single character)	A•AREA•BUTTON INPUT•LABEL LEGEND TEXTAREA	Assigns an access (shortcut) key to the associated element. Pressing this key will assign the focus to the associated element.
ACTION	*Req*	URL	FORM	Location of CGI program for handling form input.
ALIGN	*Opt*	TOP•MIDDLE BOTTOM•LEFT RIGHT	APPLET•IFRAME IMG•INPUT OBJECT	Alignment of the element relative to surrounding text. (depreciated)
ALIGN	*Opt*	TOP•BOTTOM LEFT•RIGHT	LEGEND	Alignment of the legend relative to the group of form controls. (depreciated)
ALT	*Opt*	Value	INPUT	Alternate text for display in circumstances where the graphic control cannot be rendered. (Valid only for TYPE=image controls.)
CHECKED	*Opt*	None	INPUT	Valid only for RADIO and CHECKBOX widgets. If specified, the default state will be true.
COLS	*Req*	Number	TEXTAREA	The number of visible columns in the text area.
DISABLED	*Opt*	None	BUTTON•INPUT OPTGROUP OPTION•SELECT TEXTAREA	Make the control unavailable. May be "grayed out" in some browsers.
ENCTYPE	*Opt*	MIME	FORM	MIME-type for METHOD=POST form submissions. Defaults to "application/x-www-form-urlencoded".
FOR	*Opt*	ID-value	LABEL	Explicitly associate a label with a control.
LABEL	*Req*	Text	OPTGROUP	Group name for hierarchical SELECT menus.

Attributes (Forms Elements) *continued ...*

Attribute	Required	Value(s)	Parent Tag	Description / Notes
MAXLENGTH	*Opt*	Number	INPUT	The maximum number of characters that can be typed into a TEXT or PASSWORD input field.
METHOD	*Req*	POST•GET	FORM	Method of submitting data to HTTP server. Defaults to GET.
MULTIPLE	*Opt*	None	SELECT	Indicates that multiple items may be selected at a time.
NAME	*Opt*	Text	BUTTON TEXTAREA	The name used to identify the control for use with a scripting language.
NAME	*Opt*	Text	INPUT•OBJECT	The name used to identify the form element (including use of an OBJECT as a form element) for use with a scripting language.
NAME	*Opt*	Text	SELECT	The name of the field for use with scripting.
ONBLUR	*Opt*	Script	A•AREA•BUTTON INPUT•LABEL SELECT TEXTAREA	When focus is removed from the element.
ONCHANGE	*Opt*	Script	INPUT•SELECT TEXTAREA	When the value of the element changes.
ONFOCUS	*Opt*	Script	A•AREA•BUTTON INPUT•LABEL SELECT TEXTAREA	When the element receives the focus.
ONRESET	*Opt*	Script	FORM	When the form is reset.
ONSELECT	*Opt*	Script	INPUT TEXTAREA	When text is selected within the widget.
ONSUBMIT	*Opt*	Script	FORM	When the form is submitted.
READONLY	*Opt*	None	INPUT	Data can be selected, but not modified. (Only valid for TEXT and PASSWORD input types.)
READONLY	*Opt*	None	TEXTAREA	Data can be selected by not modified.
ROWS	*Req*	Number	TEXTAREA	The number of rows of horizontal space to be rendered for the widget.

Attributes (Forms Elements) *continued ...*

Attribute	Required	Value(s)	Parent Tag	Description / Notes
SELECTED	*Opt*	None	OPTION	Indicates that this option is selected by default.
SIZE	*Opt*	Text	INPUT	The amount of space assigned for this input field. Valid only for types TEXT and PASSWORD.
SIZE	*Opt*	Number	SELECT	Number of visible rows to display for the SELECT widget.
SRC	*Opt*	URL	INPUT	The location of the image for an IMAGE type widget.
TABINDEX	*Opt*	Number	A • AREA • BUTTON INPUT • OBJECT SELECT TEXTAREA	Tabbing sequence for keyboard use.
TARGET	*Opt*	Target	A • AREA • BASE FORM • LINK	The target window or frame for a hyperlink or form results. The following magic target names are also supported: _blank: a new blank window _self: the same window as the link _parent: the parent frameset _top: the full body of the window.
TYPE	*Opt*	BUTTON • SUBMIT RESET	BUTTON	The type of button to use. Defaults to SUBMIT.
TYPE	*Text*	Input Type	INPUT	Type of widget to use for form element. Defaults to TEXT.
USEMAP	*Opt*	URL	IMG • INPUT OBJECT	URL fragment identifier that points to a MAP element for a client-side image map.
VALUE	*Opt*	Text	BUTTON	The value that is sent to the server when this button is pressed. Usually this value is also displayed on the button itself.
VALUE	*Opt*	Text	INPUT	The default value for text-oriented widgets.
VALUE	*Opt*	Text	OPTION	The value of the option when selected. Defaults to the content of the OPTION container.

Table Elements

These are the elements for creating tables. Tables can be used for displaying tabular information, or for relative positioning of visual content.

Tag	End Tag	Content	Attributes	Description / Notes
CAPTION	*Req*	Text	*Core• Int'l• Event* ALIGN	Captions and figures within tables.
COL	*None*	None	*Core• Int'l• Event* SPAN•WIDTH ALIGN•CHAR CHAROFF•VALIGN	For sharing attributes among table columns.
COLGROUP	*Opt*	COL	*Core Int'l Event* SPAN•WIDTH ALIGN•CHAR CHAROFF•VALIGN	Groups of table columns, for sharing attributes.
TABLE	*Req*	CAPTION•COL COLGROUP•THEAD TFOOT•TBODY	*Core• Int'l• Event* ALIGN•BGCOLOR BORDER• CELLSPACING CELLPADDING COLS•FRAME RULES•SUMMARY WIDTH	Outer container for table.
TBODY	*Opt*	TR	*Core• Int'l• Event* ALIGN•CHAR CHAROFF•VALIGN	For grouping table content. May allow browsers to independently scroll the body of a table.
TD	*Opt*	Block (including nested tables)	*Core• Int'l• Event* ABBR•AXIS•AXES NOWRAP•BGCOLOR ROWSPAN•SCOPE COLSPAN•WIDTH HEADERS•HEIGHT ALIGN•CHAR CHAROFF•VALIGN	Table data cell.

Table Elements *continued ...*

Tag	End Tag	Content	Attributes	Description / Notes
TFOOT	*Opt*	TR	*Core• Int'l• Event* ALIGN•CHAR CHAROFF•VALIGN	For grouping table content. May allow browsers to independently scroll the body of a table.
TH	*Opt*	Block (including nested tables)	*Core• Int'l• Event* ABBR•AXIS•AXES NOWRAP•BGCOLOR HEADERS ROWSPAN•SCOPE COLSPAN•WIDTH HEIGHT•ALIGN CHAR•CHAROFF VALIGN	Table heading cell.
THEAD	*Opt*	TR	*Core• Int'l• Event* ALIGN•CHAR CHAROFF•VALIGN	For grouping table content. May allow browsers to independently scroll the body of a table.
TR	*Opt*	TD TH	*Core• Int'l• Event* BGCOLOR•ALIGN-CHAR•CHAROFF VALIGN	Defines rows. At least one TR is required for each table.

Attributes (Table Elements)

Attribute	Required	Value(s)	Parent Tag	Description / Notes
ABBR	*Opt*	Text	TD•TH	Abbreviation for header cell.
ALIGN	*Opt*	TOP•BOTTOM	CAPTION	Positions the caption at the top or bottom of the table. More than one CAPTION tag per table is an error. (depreciated)
ALIGN	*Opt*	LEFT•CENTER RIGHT•JUSTIFY CHAR	COL•COLGROUP TBODY•TD TFOOT•TH THEAD•TR	Alignment of content within the cell(s). Defaults to LEFT.
ALIGN	*Opt*	LEFT•CENTER RIGHT	TABLE	Sets the position of the table on the page. (depreciated)
AXIS	*Opt*	Text	TD•TH	Relates a group of header cells for hierarchical table structures. (Comma-separated list.)
BGCOLOR	*Opt*	Color	TABLE	Sets the background color for a table. (depreciated)

Attributes (Table Elements) *continued ...*

Attribute	Required	Value(s)	Parent Tag	Description / Notes
BGCOLOR	*Opt*	Color	TD•TH	Sets the background color for a table cell. (depreciated)
BGCOLOR	*Opt*	Color	TR	Sets the background color for a table row. (depreciated)
BORDER	*Opt*	Pixels	TABLE	Number of pixels for the size of the table's border. Defaults to no border if the attribute is used without a value.
CELLPADDING	*Opt*	Number	TABLE	Sets the space between the border and the content of cells.
CELLSPACING	*Opt*	Number	TABLE	Sets the spacing between cells in the table (and consequently, the thickness of the borders between cells).
CHAR	*Opt*	Character	COL•COLGROUP TBODY•TD TFOOT•TH THEAD•TR	Alignment character for use with ALIGN=CHAR. Defaults to decimal point character for current language.
CHAROFF	*Opt*	Number	COL•COLGROUP TBODY•TD TFOOT•TH THEAD•TR	Offset for alignment character.
COLSPAN	*Opt*	Number	TD•TH	Causes the cell to span a number of columns.
FRAME	*Opt*	VOID•ABOVE BELOW•HSIDES LHS•RHS•VSIDES BOX•BORDER	TABLE	Which parts of the table frame to include.
HEADERS	*Opt*	ID-values(s)	TD•TH	Space-separated list of ID attributes for table cells that are to be treated as headers for this cell.
HEIGHT	*Opt*	Pixels or Percentage	TD•TH	Sets the height of the cell in pixels. (depreciated)
NOWRAP	*Opt*	None	TD•TH	Prevents word-wrapping within the cell. (depreciated)
ROWSPAN	*Opt*	Number	TD•TH	Causes the cell to span a number of rows (defaults to 1).
RULES	*Opt*	NONE•GROUPS ROWS•COLS•ALL	TABLE	Specifies which rules to display between table cells . Defaults to NONE. (depreciated)

Attributes (Table Elements) *continued ...*

Attribute	Required	Value(s)	Parent Tag	Description / Notes
SCOPE	*Opt*	ROW•COLUMN ROWGROUP COLGROUP	TD•TH	Specifies the set of data cells for which the current header cell provides information.
SPAN	*Opt*	Number	COL	Number of columns spanned by group. Defaults to 1.
SPAN	*Opt*	Number	COLGROUP	Default number of columns in group. Defaults to 1.
SUMMARY	*Opt*	Text	TABLE	Summary statement for non-visual browsers.
VALIGN	*Opt*	TOP•MIDDLE BOTTOM BASELINE	COL•COLGROUP TBODY•TD TFOOT•TH THEAD•TR	Sets the vertical alignment of content within the cells of the table row. Defaults to MIDDLE.
WIDTH	*Opt*	Pixels or Percentage	COL•COLGROUP	Width of the column or default width of the COLGROUP.
WIDTH	*Opt*	Pixels or Percentage	TABLE	Sets the overall width of the table, in pixels or a percentage of the width of the page (as *n*%).
WIDTH	*Opt*	Pixels or Percentage	TD•TH	Sets the width of the cell in pixels. (depreciated)

Frames Elements

Frames are distinct sub-windows within a visual browser. Each sub-window is effectively a separate browser environment.

Tag	End Tag	Content	Attributes	Description / Notes
FRAME	*None*	None	TITLE•SRC•NAME MARGINWIDTH MARGINHEIGHT SCROLLING NORESIZE FRAMEBORDER	Tag describing an individual frame.
FRAMESET	*Req*	FRAME•FRAME-SET NOFRAMES	TITLE•ROWS COLS•ONLOAD ONUNLOAD	Outer container for the frames.

Frames Elements *continued ...*

Tag	End Tag	Content	Attributes	Description / Notes
IFRAME	*Req*	Block	TITLE•NAME•SRC FRAMEBORDER MARGINWIDTH MARGINHEIGHT SCROLLING ALIGN•HEIGHT WIDTH	Inline frame (sub-window).
NOFRAME	*Req*	Non-frames document	*Core•Int'l•Event*	Container for a document that will be seen by non-frames-aware browsers.

Attributes (Frames Elements)

Attribute	Required	Value(s)	Parent Tag	Description / Notes
ALIGN	*Opt*	TOP•MIDDLE BOTTOM•LEFT RIGHT	APPLET•IFRAME IMG•INPUT OBJECT	Alignment of the element relative to surrounding text. (depreciated)
COLS	*Opt*	List of widths	FRAMESET	Comma-separated list of widths for the columns of frames. The number of columns in this list will be used to determine the number of frames in the document. Defaults to "100%." (depreciated)
FRAMEBORDER	*Opt*	1 or 0 or Yes or No	FRAME•IFRAME	Whether or not the borders for a particular frame are displayed. Defaults to Yes.
HEIGHT	*Opt*	Pixels or Percentage	IFRAME	The height of the frame's display space on the screen.
MARGINHEIGHT	*Opt*	Pixels	FRAME•IFRAME	Height of the top and bottom margins for the frame.
MARGINWIDTH	*Opt*	Pixels	FRAME•IFRAME	Width of the left and right margins for the frame.
NAME	*Opt*	Text	FRAME•IFRAME	Name of the frame (for use with the TARGET attribute).
NORESIZE	*Opt*	None	FRAME	If present, do not allow resizing of the frame.

Attributes (Frames Elements) *continued...*

Attribute	Required	Value(s)	Parent Tag	Description / Notes
ONLOAD	*Opt*	Script	FRAMESET	When all the frames are finished loading.
ONUNLOAD	*Opt*	Script	FRAMESET	When all the frames have been unloaded.
ROWS	*Opt*	Pixels or Percentage	FRAMESET	Comma-separated list of heights for the rows of frames. The number of rows in this list will be used to determine the number of elements in the document. (Defaults to 1 row of 100%.)
SCROLLING	*Opt*	YES • NO • AUTO	FRAME • IFRAME	Controls the display of scrollbars. YES: Always display scrollbars; NO: Never display scrollbars; AUTO: Display scrollbars if warranted. Defaults to AUTO.
SRC	*Opt*	URL	FRAME • IFRAME	The URL of the document to be displayed in this frame.
WIDTH	*Opt*	Pixels or Percentage	IFRAME	The width of the frame's display space on the screen.

Miscellaneous Elements

Elements that don't fit nicely in any of the other categories.

Tag	End Tag	Content	Attributes	Description / Notes
DEL	*Req*	Text	*Core • Int'l • Event* CITE • DATETIME	Deleted text.
INS	*Req*	Text	*Core • Int'l • Event* CITE • DATETIME	Inserted text.
ISINDEX	*None*	None	*Core • Int'l* PROMPT	Single line prompt. (depreciated)
NOSCRIPT	*Req*	Block	*Core • Int'l • Event*	Alternative content for browsers which don't understand SCRIPT.
SCRIPT	*Req*	Script	CHARSET • DEFER LANGUAGE • SRC TYPE	Container for in-line scripts. (Also used to specify external scripts.)

Attributes (Miscellaneous Elements)

Attribute	Required	Value(s)	Parent Tag	Description / Notes
CHARSET	*Opt*	Character Set Identifier	A • LINK • SCRIPT	Character encoding of the destination link.
CITE	*Opt*	URL	DEL • INS	Source document or message with information about the change.
DATETIME	*Opt*	ISO-Date	DEL • INS	When the change was made. ISO date format is: YYYY-MM-DDThh:mm:ssTZD YYYY = four-digit year MM = two-digit month DD = two-digit day of month T = Literal character "T" hh = two-digit hour (00–24) mm = two-digit minute ss = two-digit second TZD = time zone (Z or offset) Z = UTC (**U**niversal **C**oordinated **T**ime); offset is + or – from UTC *Examples* (both are equivalent to 1 January 1998, 9:49pm, US Eastern Standard Time): 1998-01-01T21:49:00-05:00 1998-01-02T02:49:00Z
LANGUAGE	*Opt*	Text	SCRIPT	Language the script is written in. (depreciated)
PROMPT	*Opt*	Text	ISINDEX	An optional prompt for ISINDEX. (depreciated)
SRC	*Opt*	URL	SCRIPT	Specifies the location of an external script.
TYPE	*Req*	MIME	SCRIPT	MIME type for the script URL.

Section 3: *Alphabetical Reference*

Alphabetical List of All HTML 4.0 Tags

Tag	End Tag	Content	Attributes	Description / Notes
A	*Req*	Text - A	*Core• Int'l• Events* ACCESSKEY CHARSET•COORDS HREF•HREFLANG NAME•ONFOCUS ONBLUR•REL•REV SHAPE•TABINDEX TARGET•TITLE	Anchor for a hypertext link or a name target for hypertext links.
ABBR	*Req*	Text	*Core• Int'l• Event*	Abbreviation (e.g. HTML, M., Inc., et al., etc.).
ACRONYM	*Req*	Text	*Core• Int'l• Event*	Acronym (WAC, radar, etc.).
ADDRESS	*Req*	Text + P	*Core• Int'l• Event* CITE	Information on author.
APPLET	*Req*	Text + PARAM	*Core• Int'l• Event* SHAPE•COORDS HREF•NOHREF ALT•TARGET TABINDEX ACCESSKEY	Java applet. (depreciated)
AREA	*None*	None	*Core• Int'l• Event* SHAPE•COORDS HREF•NOHREF ALT•TARGET TABINDEX ACCESSKEY	Client-side image map area (hotzones) definition.
B	*Req*	Text	*Core• Int'l• Event*	Bold text.
BASE	*None*	None	HREF•TARGET	Base URL for dereferencing realtive URLs. Valid only within HEAD.
BASEFONT	*None*	None	ID•SIZE COLOR•FACE	Sets the default size of text. (depreciated)
BDO	*Req*	Text	*Core* LANG•DIR	Override direction of text.
BIG	*Req*	Text	*Core• Int'l• Event*	Large text style.

Alphabetical List of All HTML 4.0 Tags *continued ...*

Tag	End Tag	Content	Attributes	Description / Notes
BLOCKQUOTE	*Req*	Block	*Core• Int'l• Event* CITE	For quoted passages (usually indented).
BODY	*Opt*	All	*Core• Int'l• Event* BACKGROUND BGCOLOR•TEXT LINK•VLINK ALINK•ONLOAD UNLOAD	Container for document body.
BR	*None*	None	*Core• Int'l• Event* CLEAR	Force a line break. Moves point of text to the beginning of the next available line.
BUTTON	*Req*	Text + Block - Forms - A	*Core• Int'l• Event* NAME•VALUE TYPE•DISABLED TABINDEX ACCESSKEY ONFOCUS•ONBLUR	A button for use with forms. Richer presentation possibilities than INPUT type buttons, but not supported by all browers.
CAPTION	*Req*	Text	*Core• Int'l• Event* ALIGN	Captions and figures within tables.
CENTER	*Req*	Block	*Core• Int'l• Event*	For centering (alias for <DIV ALIGN=CENTER>). (depreciated)
CITE	*Req*	Text	*Core• Int'l• Event*	Citation.
CODE	*Req*	Text	*Core• Int'l• Event*	Code fragment. (Usually presented in fixed-width for text.)
COL	*None*	None	*Core• Int'l• Event* SPAN•WIDTH ALIGN•CHAR CHAROFF•VALIGN	For sharing attributes among table columns.
COLGROUP	*Opt*	COL	*Core• Int'l• Event* SPAN•WIDTH ALIGN•CHAR CHAROFF•VALIGN	Groups of table columns, for sharing attributes.
DD	*Opt*	Text	*Core• Int'l• Event*	The definition of a term.
DEL	*Req*	Text	*Core• Int'l• Event* CITE•DATETIME	Deleted text.
DFN	*Req*	Text	*Core• Int'l• Event*	Defining instance of a term.
DIR	*Req*	LI - Block	*Core• Int'l• Event* COMPACT	Directory list. (depreciated)

Alphabetical List of All HTML 4.0 Tags *continued …*

Tag	End Tag	Content	Attributes	Description / Notes
DIV	*Req*	Block	*Core• Int'l• Event* ALIGN	Null container for applying style and common attributes to block-level content.
DL	*Req*	DT DD	*Core• Int'l• Event* COMPACT	Definition list.
DT	*Opt*	Text	*Core• Int'l• Event*	A term being defined.
EM	*Req*	Text	*Core• Int'l• Event*	Emphasis (usually italic).
FIELDSET	*Req*	Text Block LEGEND	*Core• Int'l• Event*	Grouping form controls.
FONT	*Req*	Text	*Core• Int'l• Event* SIZE•COLOR FACE	Sets the appearance of text. (depreciated)
FORM	*Req*	All	*Core• Int'l• Event* ACTION•METHOD ENCTYPE ONSUBMIT ONRESET•TARGET ACCEPTCHARSET	Outer container for all form fields.
FRAME	*None*	None	TITLE•SRC•NAME MARGINWIDTH MARGINHEIGHT SCROLLING NORESIZE FRAMEBORDER	Tag describing individual frame.
FRAMESET	*Req*	FRAME•FRAMESET NOFRAMES	TITLE•ROWS COLS•ONLOAD ONUNLOAD	Outer container for the frames.
H1 H2 H3 H4 H5 H6	*Req*	Text	*Core• Int'l• Event* ALIGN	Six different levels of headings.
HEAD	*Opt*	TITLE•ISINDEX BASE•META LINK•SCRIPT STYLE	*Int'l* PROFILE	Container for document header.
HR	*None*	None	*Core• Int'l• Event* ALIGN•NOSHADE SIZE•WIDTH	Horiztonal rule (line).
HTML	*Opt*	HEAD•BODY PLAINTEXT	*Int'l* VERSION	Outer container for an HTML document.

Alphabetical List of All HTML 4.0 Tags *continued ...*

Tag	End Tag	Content	Attributes	Description / Note
I	*Req*	Text	*Core• Int'l• Event*	Italic.
IFRAME	*Req*	Block	TITLE•NAME SRC FRAMEBORDER MARGINWIDTH MARGINHEIGHT SCROLLING ALIGN•HEIGHT WIDTH	Inline frame (subwindow).
IMG	*None*	None	*Core• Int'l• Event* SRC•ALT LONGDESC•ALIGN HEIGHT•WIDTH BORDER•HSPACE VSPACE•USEMAP ISMAP	An embedded image.
INPUT	*None*	None	*Core• Int'l• Event* TYPE•NAME VALUE•CHECKED DISABLED READONLY•SIZE MAXLENGTH•SRC ALT•USEMAP ALIGN•TABINDEX ACCESSKEY ONFOCUS•ONBLUR ONSELECT ONCHANGE•ACCEPT	Generalized tag for all non-container input fields.
INS	*Req*	Text	*Core• Int'l• Event* CITE•DATETIME	Inserted text.
ISINDEX	*None*	None	*Core• Int'l* PROMPT	Single line prompt. (depreciated)
KBD	*Req*	Text	*Core• Int'l• Event*	Keyboard—text to be typed by a user.
LABEL	*Req*	Text –(LABEL)	*Core• Int'l• Event* FOR•DISABLED ACCESSKEY ONFOCUS•ONBLUR	For attaching labels to form control elements.
LEGEND	*Req*	Text	*Core• Int'l• Event* ALIGN•ACCESSKEY	Assigns a caption (legend) to a FIELDSET.
LI	*Opt*	Text Block	*Core• Int'l• Event* TYPE•VALUE	List item.

Alphabetical List of All HTML 4.0 Tags *continued ...*

Tag	End Tag	Content	Attributes	Description / Notes
LINK	*None*	None	*Core• Int'l• Event* CHARSET•HREF HREFLANG•REL REV•REV•TYPE MEDIA•TARGET	Defines relationships with other documents.
MAP	*Req*	AREA	*Core• Int'l• Event* NAME	Client-side image map.
MENU	*Req*	LI – Block	*Core• Int'l• Event* COMPACT	Menu list. (depreciated)
META	*None*	None	*Int'l* HTTP-EQUIV NAME•CONTENT SCHEME	Meta-information describing properties of the document. Generates HTTP header when used with HTTP-EQUIV. Valid only within HEAD.
NOFRAMES	*Req*	Non-frames document	*Core• Int'l• Event*	Container for a document that will be seen by non-frames-aware browsers.
NOSCRIPT	*Req*	Block	*Core• Int'l• Event*	Alternative content for browsers which don't understand SCRIPT.
OBJECT	*Req*	Text Block PARAM	*Core• Int'l• Event* DECLARE•CLASSID CODEBASE•DATA TYPE•CODETYPE ARCHIVE•STANDBY ALIGN•HEIGHT WIDTH•BORDER HSPACE•VSPACE USEMAP•SHAPES NAME•TABINDEX	Generic mechanism for including objects.
OL	*Req*	LI	*Core• Int'l• Event* TYPE•START COMPACT	Ordered list.
OPTGROUP	*Req*	OPTION	*Core• Int'l• Event* DISABLED•LABEL	For grouping options within a SELECT container.
OPTION	*Opt*	Alphanumeric content	*Core• Int'l• Event* SELECTED DISABLED•VALUE	Container for individual options within a SELECT container.
P	*Opt*	Text	*Core Int'l Event* ALIGN	Paragraph.
PARAM	*None*	None	ID•NAME•VALUE VALUETYPE•TYPE	Named parameters (e.g. that can be read with Java's getParameter () method).

Alphabetical List of All HTML 4.0 Tags *continued ...*

Tag	End Tag	Content	Attributes	Description / Notes
PRE	*Req*	Text – APPLET BASEFONT BIG•FONT•IMG OBJECT•SMALL SUB•SUP	*Core• Int'l• Event* WIDTH	Preformatted text.
Q	*Req*	Text	*Core• Int'l• Event* CITE	Inline quotation (may be rendered with quotation marks).
S	*Req*	Text	*Core• Int'l• Event*	Strike-through (synonym for STRIKE). (depreciated)
SAMP	*Req*	Text	*Core• Int'l• Event*	Sample output from a program.
SCRIPT	*Req*	Script	CHARSET•DEFER LANGUAGE•SRC TYPE	Container for in-line scripts. (Also used to specify external scripts.)
SELECT	*Req*	OPTION OPTGROUP	*Core• Int'l• Event* NAME•SIZE MULTIPLE DISABLED TABINDEX ONFOCUS•ONBLUR ONCHANGE	Container for OPTION list.
SMALL	*Req*	Text	*Core• Int'l• Event*	Smaller size text.
SPAN	*Req*	Text	*Core• Int'l• Event*	Null-container for applying styles to inline text-level content.
STRIKE	*Req*	Text	*Core• Int'l• Event*	Strike-through (synonym for S). (depreciated)
STRONG	*Req*	Text	*Core• Int'l• Event*	Strong emphasis (usually **bold**).
STYLE	*Req*	Style-sheet	*Int'l•* TYPE MEDIA•TITLE	Container for style-sheet definitions.
SUB	*Req*	Text	*Core• Int'l• Event*	Subscript.
SUP	*Req*	Text	*Core• Int'l• Event*	Superscript.

Alphabetical List of All HTML 4.0 Tags *continued ...*

Tag	End Tag	Content	Attributes	Description / Notes
TABLE	*Req*	CAPTION•COL COLGROUP•THEAD TFOOT•TBODY	*Core• Int'l• Event* ALIGN•BGCOLOR BORDER CELLSPACING CELLPADDING COLS•FRAME RULES•SUMMARY WIDTH	Outer container for table.
TBODY	*Opt*	TR	*Core• Int'l• Event* ALIGN•CHAR CHAROFF•VALIGN	For grouping table content. May allow browsers to independently scroll the body of a table.
TD	*Opt*	Block (including nested tables)	*Core• Int'l• Event* ABBR•AXIS•AXES NOWRAP•BGCOLOR ROWSPAN•SCOPE COLSPAN WIDTH•HEADERS HEIGHT•ALIGN CHAR•CHAROFF VALIGN	Table Data cell.
TEXTAREA	*Req*	Alphanumeric content	*Core• Int'l• Event* NAME•ROWS COLS•DISABLED READONLY TABINDEX ONFOCUS•ONBLUR ONSELECT ONCHANGE	Container for multi-line text input field.
TFOOT	*Opt*	TR	*Core Int'l Event* ALIGN•CHAR CHAROFF•VALIGN	For grouping table content. May allow browsers to independently scroll the body of a table.
TH	*Opt*	Block (including nested tables)	*Core• Int'l• Event* ABBR•AXIS•AXES NOWRAP•BGCOLOR HEADERS ROWSPAN•SCOPE COLSPAN•WIDTH HEIGHT•ALIGN CHAR•CHAROFF VALIGN	Table heading cell.
THEAD	*Opt*	TR	*Core• Int'l• Event* ALIGN•CHAR CHAROFF•VALIGN	For grouping table content. May allow browsers to independently scroll the body of a table.

Alphabetical List of All HTML 4.0 Tags *continued ...*

Tag	End Tag	Content	Attributes	Description / Notes
TITLE	*Req*	Document title	*Int'l*	Provides a title for the document.
TR	*Opt*	TD•TH	*Core• Int'l• Event* BGCOLOR•ALIGN CHAR•CHAROFF VALIGN	Defines rows. At least one TR is required for each table.
TT	*Req*	Text	*Core• Int'l• Event*	Teletype (fixed width).
U	*Req*	Text	*Core• Int'l• Event*	Underline. (depreciated)
UL	*Req*	LI	*Core• Int'l• Event* TYPE•COMPACT	Unordered List.
VAR	*Req*	Text	*Core• Int'l• Event*	Variable or argument in a program.

Alphabetical List of All HTML 4.0 Attributes

Attribute	Required	Value(s)	Parent Tag	Description / Notes
ABBR	*Opt*	Text	TD•TH	Abbreviation for header cell.
ACCEPT	*Opt*	MIME	INPUT	List of MIME-types allowed by the server for file upload. Used for FILE type INPUT elements.
ACCEPT-CHARSET	*Opt*	List	FORM	List of acceptable character encodings for the server processing this form.
ACCESSKEY	*Opt*	Text (single character)	A•AREA BUTTON•INPUT LABEL•LEGEND TEXTAREA	Assigns an access (shortcut) key to the associated element. Pressing this key will assign focus to the associated element.
ACTION	*Opt*	FORM	FORM	Location of CGI program for handling form input.
ALIGN	*Opt*	TOP•MIDDLE BOTTOM•LEFT RIGHT	APPLET•IFRAME IMG•INPUT OBJECT	Alignment of the element relative to surrounding text. (depreciated)
ALIGN	*Opt*	TOP•BOTTOM	CAPTION	Positions the caption at the top or bottom of the table. More than one CAPTION tag per table is an error. (depreciated)

Alphabetical List of All HTML 4.0 Attributes *continued ...*

Attribute	Required	Value(s)	Parent Tag	Description / Notes
ALIGN	Opt	LEFT•CENTER RIGHT•JUSTIFY CHAR	COL•COLGROUP TBODY•TD TFOOT•TH THEAD•TR	Alignment of content within the cell(s). Defaults to LEFT.
ALIGN	Opt	LEFT•CENTER RIGHT•JUSTIFY	DIV•H1•H2•H3 H4•H5•H6•P	Alignment of the block of text. Defaults to LEFT. (depreciated)
ALIGN	Opt	RIGHT•LEFT CENTER	HR	Alignment of the horizontal rule. (depreciated)
ALIGN	Opt	TOP•BOTTOM LEFT•RIGHT	LEGEND	Alignment of the legend relative to the group of form controls. (depreciated)
ALIGN	Opt	LEFT•CENTER RIGHT	TABLE	Sets the position of the table on the page. (depreciated)
ALINK	Opt	Color	BODY	Color of active links (e.g. while the mouse button is pressed on the link). (depreciated)
ALT	Opt	Text	APPLET	Alternate text for display in circumstances where the applet or graphic control cannot be rendered. (depreciated)
ALT	Req	Text	AREA•IMAGE	Text associated with the image or area for use by text-only browsers and non-visual user agents that cannot display images.
ALT	Opt	Text	INPUT	Alternate text for display in circumstances whre the graphic control cannot be rendered. (Valid only for TYPE=image controls.)
ARCHIVE	Opt	Text	APPLET	Preload resources for APPLET. Note: List is comma-separated for APPLET. (depreciated)
ARCHIVE	Opt	Text	OBJECT	Preload resources for OBJECT Note: List is space-separated for OBJECT.
AXIS	Opt	Text	TD•TH	Relates a group of header cells for hierarchical table structures . (Comma-separated list.)
BACKGROUND	Opt	URL	BODY	URL for the background graphic. (depreciated)

Alphabetical List of All HTML 4.0 Attributes *continued* ...

Attribute	Required	Value(s)	Parent Tag	Description / Notes
BGCOLOR	*Opt*	Color	BODY	Background color of the document page. (depreciated)
BGCOLOR	*Opt*	Color	TABLE	Sets the background color for a table. (depreciated)
BGCOLOR	*Opt*	Color	TD•TH	Sets the background color for a table cell. (depreciated)
BGCOLOR	*Opt*	Color	TR	Sets the background color for a table row. (depreciated)
BORDER	*Opt*	Pixels	IMG•OBJECT	The size of the border when the IMG or OBJECT is used in a hypertext link (A element). Set this to zero to suppress the border.
BORDER	*Opt*	Pixels	TABLE	Number of pixels for the size of the table's border. Defaults to no border if the attribute is not used, or one pixel if the attribute is used without a value.
CELLPADDING	*Opt*	Number	TABLE	Sets the space between the border and the content of cells.
CELLSPACING	*Opt*	Number	TABLE	Sets the spacing between cells in the table (and consequently, the thickness of the borders between cells).
CHAR	*Opt*	Character	COL•COLGROUP TBODY•TD TFOOT•TH THEAD•TR	Alignment character for use with ALIGN=CHAR. Defaults to decimal point character for current language.
CHAROFF	*Opt*	Number	COL•COLGROUP TBODY•TD TFOOT•TH THEAD•TR	Offset for alignment character.
CHARSET	*Opt*	Character Set Identifier	A•LINK•SCRIPT	Character encoding of the destination link.
CHECKED	*Opt*	None	INPUT	Valid only for RADIO and CHECKBOX widgets. If specified, the default state will be true.
CITE	*Opt*	URL	BLOCKQUOTE•Q	Source document or message with information about the quotation.

Alphabetical List of All HTML 4.0 Attributes *continued ...*

Attribute	Required	Value(s)	Parent Tag	Description / Notes
CITE	*Opt*	URL	DEL•INS	Source document or message with information about the change.
CLASS	*Opt*	List of Class names	*All elements except:* BASE•BASEFONT FRAME•FRAMESET HEAD•HTML META•PARAM SCRIPT•STYLE TITLE	Specifies a class (or a space-separated list of classes) for applying style-sheet properties to the element.
CLASSID	*Opt*	URL	OBJECT	URL for specific implementation.
CLEAR	*None*	LEFT•RIGHT ALL•NONE	BR	Move down past floating images. LEFT clears to the left margin; RIGHT clears to the right margin; ALL clears to both margins. (depreciated)
CODE	*Opt*	Applet File	APPLET	The name of the file that contains the applet's compiled subclass. This file is relative to the CODEBASE location, if specified (otherwise it is relative to the URL of the document). It cannot be an absolute URL. (depreciated)
CODEBASE	*Opt*	URL	APPLET	Base URL for resolving relative URLs for this applet. Specifically used for resolving the CODE URL.
CODEBASE	*Opt*	URL	APPLET	Base URL for resolving relative URLs for this object. Specifically used for the CLASSID URL. (depreciated)
CODETYPE	*Opt*	MIME	OBJECT	MIME-type for the object specified by CLASSID. Defaults to the value of the TYPE attribute.
COLOR	*Opt*	Color	BASEFONT•FONT	Sets the color of text. (depreciated)
COLS	*Opt*	List of widths	FRAMESET	Comma-separated list of widths for the columns of frames. The number of columns in this list will be used to determine the number of frames in the document. Defaults to "100%." (depreciated)
COLS	*Req*	Number	TEXTAREA	The number of visible columns in the text area.

Alphabetical List of All HTML 4.0 Attributes *continued ...*

Attribute	Required	Value(s)	Parent Tag	Description / Notes
COLSPAN	*Opt*	Number	TD•TH	Causes the cell to span a number of columns.
COMPACT	*Opt*	None	DIR•DL•MENU OL•UL	Render the list more compactly. (depreciated)
CONTENT	*Req*	Text	META	Content of meta-information.

COORDS	*Opt*	Coordinates	A•AREA	List of coordinates, in pixel units, according to the given shape, e.g.:
				
				 shape = default
				 shape = rect coords =
				     "left-x, top-y, right-x, bottom-y"
				 shape = circle coords =
				     "center-x, center-y, radius"
				 shape = poly coords =
				     "x1,y1, x2, y2,x3,y3, ..."

DATA	*Opt*	URL	OBJECT	Location for the object's data.

DATETIME	*Opt*	ISO-date	DEL•INS	When the change was made. ISO date format is: YYYY-MM-DDThh:mm:ssTZD
				 YYYY = four-digit year
				 MM = two-digit month
				 DD = two-digit day of month
				 T = Literal character "T"
				 hh = two-digit hour (00–24)
				 mm = two-digit minute
				 ss = two-digit second
				 TZD = time zone (Z or offset)
				 Z = UTC (**U**niversal **C**oordinated **Time**); offset is + or – from UTC
				 Examples (both are equivalent to 1 January 1998, 9:49pm, US Eastern Standard Time):
				 `1998-01-01T21:49:00-05:00`
				 `1998-01-02T02:49:00Z`

DECLARE	*Opt*	None	OBJECT	Declare OBJECT only.

Alphabetical List of All HTML 4.0 Attributes *continued* ...

Attribute	Required	Value(s)	Parent Tag	Description / Notes
DIR	*Opt*	LTR *or* RTL	*All tags except* APPLET•BASE BASEFONT•BDO BR•FRAME FRAMESET IFRAME•PARAM SCRIPT	Direction of text.
DIR	*Req*	LTR *or* RTL	BDO	Direction for overridden text.
DISABLED	*Opt*	None	BUTTON•INPUT OPTGROUP OPTION•SELECT TEXTAREA	Make the control unavailable. May be "grayed out" in some browsers.
ENCTYPE	*Opt*	MIME	FORM	MIME-type for METHOD=POST form submissions. Defaults to "application/x-www-form-urlencoded".
FACE	*Opt*	List	BASEFONT•FONT	Comma-separated list of font names.
FOR	*Opt*	ID-value	LABEL	Explicitly associate a label with a control.
FRAME	*Opt*	VOID•ABOVE BELOW•HSIDES LHS•RHS•VSIDES BOX•BORDER	TABLE	Which parts of the table frame to include.
FRAMEBORDER	*Opt*	1 or 0 or YES or NO	FRAME•IFRAME	Whether or not the borders for a particular frame are displayed. Defaults to Yes.
HEADERS	*Opt*	ID-value(s)	TD•TH	Space-separated list of ID attributes for table cells that are to be treated as headers for this cell.
HEIGHT	*Req*	Pixels or Percentage	APPLET	The height of the applet's display space on the screen. Used to reserve space for the applet on the page so that the page can be laid out before applet is executed. (depreciated)
HEIGHT	*Opt*	Pixels or Percentage	IFRAME	The height of the frame's display space on the screen.
HEIGHT	*Opt*	Pixels or Percentage	IMG•OBJECT	The height of the image. Some browsers use this to reserve space for an image so that the page can be laid out before images are downloaded. Can also be used to override the height of the actual image or object.

Alphabetical List of All HTML 4.0 Attributes *continued ...*

Attribute	Required	Value(s)	Parent Tag	Description / Notes
HEIGHT	*Opt*	Pixels or Percentage	TD•TH	Sets the height of the cell in pixels. (depreciated)
HREF	*Opt*	URL	A•AREA•LINK	The destination of the hypertext link.
HREF	*Opt*	URL	BASE	URL for the document base.
HSPACE	*Opt*	Pixels	APPLET•IMAGE OBJECT	The size of the horizontal gutter space around the image. Set this to zero to suppress the horiztonal gutter. (depreciated)
HTTP-EQUIV	*Opt*	Text	META	Name for HTTP header.
ID	*Opt*	ID	*All elements except* BASE•HEAD META•SCRIPT STYLE•TITLE	Unique ID for an individual instance of an element.
ISMAP	*Opt*	None	IMG•INPUT	Indicates that this image is a server-side image map. Only valid for IMG when within an A (anchor) element with an HREF attribute.
LABEL	*Req*	Text	OPTGROUP	Group name for hierarchical SELECT menus.
LABEL	*Opt*	Text	OPTION	Item name for hierarchical SELECT menus.
LANG	*Opt*	Lang-ID	*All elements except* APPLET•BASE BASEFONT•BR FRAME•FRAMESET IFRAME•PARAM SCRIPT	Language identifier, as specified in RFC-1766.
LANGUAGE	*Opt*	Text	SCRIPT	Language the script is written in. (depreciated)
LINK	*Opt*	Color	BODY	Color of unvisited links. (depreciated)
LONGDESC	*Opt*	URL	FRAME•IFRAME	Link to a long description (complements TITLE).
LONGDESC	*Opt*	URL	IMG	Link to a long description (complements ALT).

Alphabetical List of All HTML 4.0 Attributes *continued ...*

Attribute	Required	Value(s)	Parent Tag	Description / Note
MARGINHEIGHT	*Opt*	Pixels	FRAME•IFRAME	Height of the top and bottom margins for the frame.
MARGINWIDTH	*Opt*	Pixels	FRAME•IFRAME	Width of the left and right margins for the frame.
MAXLENGTH	*Opt*	Number	INPUT	The maximum number of characters that can be type into a TEXT or PASSWORD input field.
MEDIA	*Opt*	Media	STYLE•LINK	Destination media for style. Defaults to ALL.
METHOD	*Req*	POST•GET	FORM	Method of submitting data to HTTP server. Defaults to GET.
MULTIPLE	*Opt*	None	SELECT	Indicates that multiple items may be selected at a time.
NAME	*Opt*	Text	A	The name of an anchor for use with a fragment identifier (#) in a hyperlink.
NAME	*Opt*	Text	APPLET	A name for the applet instance. This allows multiple applets on the same page to communicate with each other. (depreciated)
NAME	*Opt*	Text	BUTTON•TEXTAREA	The name used to identify the control for use with a scripting language.
NAME	*Opt*	Text	FORM	The name used to identify the entire form for use with a scripting language.
NAME	*Opt*	Text	FRAME•IFRAME	Name of the frame (for use with the TARGET attribute).
NAME	*Opt*	Text	IMG	The name used to identify the image for use with a scripting language.
NAME	*Opt*	Text	INPUT•OBJECT	The name used to identify the form element (including use of an OBJECT as a form element) for use with a scripting language.
NAME	*Req*	Text	MAP	The name used to reference the map with USEMAP.
NAME	*Opt*	Text	META	Name for meta-information.

Alphabetical List of All HTML 4.0 Attributes *continued ...*

Attribute	Required	Value(s)	Parent Tag	Description / Notes
NAME	*Req*	Text	PARAM	Name of paramter.
NAME	*Opt*	Text	SELECT	The name of the field for use with scripting.
NOHREF	*Opt*	None	AREA	Declares the area of a client-side imagemap to be a dead zone.
NORESIZE	*Opt*	None	FRAME	If present, do not allow resizing of the frame.
NOSHADE	*Opt*	None	HR	Render the horizontal rule without shading. (depreciated)
NOWRAP	*Opt*	None	TD•TH	Prevents word-wrapping within the cell. (depreciated)
OBJECT	*Opt*	Text	APPLET	Serialized data for the applet. (depreciated)
ONBLUR	*Opt*	Script	A•AREA•BUTTON INPUT•LABEL SELECT TEXTAREA	When focus is removed from the element.
ONCHANGE	*Opt*	Script	INPUT•SELECT TEXTAREA	When the value of the element changes.
ONCLICK	*Opt*	Script	*All elements except:* APPLET•BASE BASEFONT•BDO BR•FONT•FRAME FRAMESET•HEAD HTML•IFRAME ISINDEX•META PARAM•SCRIPT STYLE•TITLE	When the mouse is clicked on the element.
ONDBLCLICK	*Opt*	Script	*All elements except:* APPLET•BASE BASEFONT•BDO BR•FONT•FRAME FRAMESET•HEAD HTML•IFRAME ISINDEX•META PARAM•SCRIPT STYLE•TITLE	When the mouse is double-clicked on the element.

Alphabetical List of All HTML 4.0 Attributes *continued ...*

Attribute	Required	Value(s)	Parent Tag	Description / Notes
ONFOCUS	*Opt*	Script	A•AREA•BUTTON INPUT•LABEL SELECT TEXTAREA	When the element receives the focus.
ONKEYDOWN	*Opt*	Script	*All elements except:* APPLET•BASE BASEFONT•BDO BR•FONT•FRAME FRAMESET•HEAD HTML•IFRAME ISINDEX•META PARAM•SCRIPT STYLE•TITLE	When a key is pressed down within the element.
ONKEYPRESS	*Opt*	Script	*All elements except:* APPLET•BASE BASEFONT•BDO BR•FONT•FRAME FRAMESET•HEAD HTML•IFRAME ISINDEX•META PARAM•SCRIPT STYLE•TITLE	When a key is pressed and released within the element.
ONKEYUP	*Opt*	Script	*All elements except:* APPLET•BASE BASEFONT•BDO BR•FONT•FRAME FRAMESET•HEAD HTML•IFRAME ISINDEX•META PARAM•SCRIPT STYLE•TITLE	When a key is released in the element.
ONLOAD	*Opt*	Script	BODY	When the document is finished loading.
ONLOAD	*Opt*	Script	FRAMESET	When all the frames are finished loading.
ONMOUSEDOWN	*Opt*	Script	*All elements except:* APPLET•BASE BASEFONT•BDO BR•FONT•FRAME FRAMESET•HEAD HTML•IFRAME ISINDEX•META PARAM•SCRIPT STYLE•TITLE	When a mouse button is depressed on the element.

Alphabetical List of All HTML 4.0 Attributes *continued ...*

Attribute	Required	Value(s)	Parent Tag	Description / Notes
ONMOUSEMOVE	*Opt*	Script	*All elements except:* APPLET•BASE BASEFONT•BDO BR•FONT•FRAME FRAMESET•HEAD HTML•IFRAME ISINDEX•META PARAM•SCRIPT STYLE•TITLE	When the mouse cursor is moved within the element.
ONMOUSEOUT	*Opt*	Script	*All elements except:* APPLET•BASE BASEFONT•BDO BR•FONT•FRAME FRAMESET•HEAD HTML•IFRAME ISINDEX•META PARAM•SCRIPT STYLE•TITLE	When the mouse cursor moves out of the element's display space.
ONMOUSEOVER	*Opt*	Script	*All elements except:* APPLET•BASE BASEFONT•BDO BR•FONT•FRAME FRAMESET•HEAD HTML•IFRAME ISINDEX•META PARAM•SCRIPT STYLE•TITLE	When the mouse cursor is moved over the element's display space.
ONMOUSEUP	*Opt*	Script	*All elements except:* APPLET•BASE BASEFONT•BDO BR•FONT•FRAME FRAMESET•HEAD HTML•IFRAME ISINDEX•META PARAM•SCRIPT STYLE•TITLE	When a mouse button is released over the element.
ONRESET	*Opt*	Script	FORM	When the form is reset.
ONSELECT	*Opt*	Script	INPUT•TEXTAREA	When text is selected within the widget.
ONSUBMIT	*Opt*	Script	FORM	When the form is submitted.
ONUNLOAD	*Opt*	Script	BODY	When the document is unloaded (e.g., another document has been called for).
ONUNLOAD	*Opt*	Script	FRAMESET	When all the frames have been unloaded.

Alphabetical List of All HTML 4.0 Attributes *continued ...*

Attribute	Required	Value(s)	Parent Tag	Description / Note
PROFILE	*Opt*	URL	HEAD	A meta-data profile.
PROMPT	*Opt*	Text	ISINDEX	An optional prompt for ISINDEX. (depreciated)
READONLY	*Opt*	None	INPUT	Data can be selected, but not modified. (Only valid for TEXT and PASSWORD input types.)
READONLY	*Opt*	None	TEXTAREA	Data can be selected but not modified.
REL	*Opt*	Link type(s)	A•LINK	The forward relationship for the linked resource.
REV	*Opt*	Link type(s)	A•LINK	The reverse relationship for the linked resource.
ROWS	*Opt*	Pixels or Percentage	FRAMESET	Comma-separated list of heights for the rows of frames. The number of rows in this list will be used to determine the number of frames in the document (defaults to 1 row of 100%).
ROWS	*Req*	Number	TEXTAREA	The number of rows of horizontal space to be rendered for the widget.
ROWSPAN	*Opt*	Number	TD•TH	Causes the cell to span a number of rows (defaults to 1).
RULES	*Opt*	NONE•GROUPS ROWS•COLS•ALL	TABLE	Specifies which rules to display between table cells (defaults to NONE). (depreciated)
SCHEME	*Opt*	Text	META	The scheme to be used in interpreting the content. Depends on content.
SCOPE	*Opt*	ROW•COL ROWGROUP COLGROUP	TD•TH	Specifies the set of data cells for which the current header cell provides information.
SCROLLING	*Opt*	YES•NO•AUTO	FRAME•IFRAME	Controls the display of scrollbars. YES: Always display scrollbars; NO: Never display scrollbars; AUTO: Display scrollbars if warranted. Defaults to AUTO.

Alphabetical List of All HTML 4.0 Attributes *continued ...*

Attribute	Required	Value(s)	Parent Tag	Description / Notes
SELECTED	*Opt*	None	OPTION	Indicates that this option is selected by default.
SHAPE	*Opt*	RECT•CIRCLE POLY•DEFAULT	A•AREA	Declares the shape of the area. DEFAULT indicates the entire image (use DEFAULT first to overlay the other shapes on top of it). May be used with the A element only within OBJECT.
SIZE	*Req*	Number	BASEFONT•FONT	A number in the range 1-7 that specifies the size of displayed text. As an attribute to the FONT element, SIZE may be a relative number in the form +n or -n, where the result-ing size will be relative to the default size or BASEFONT size. (depreciated)
SIZE	*Opt*	Pixels	HR	The size (height in pixels) of the horizontal rule. (depreciated)
SIZE	*Opt*	Number	INPUT	The amount of space assigned for this input field. Valid only for types TEXT and PASSWORD.
SIZE	*Opt*	Number	SELECT	Number of visible rows to display for the SELECT widget.
SPAN	*Opt*	Number	COL	Number of columns spanned by group. Defaults to 1.
SPAN	*Opt*	Number	COLGROUP	Default number of columns in group. Defaults to 1.
SRC	*Opt*	URL	FRAME•IFRAME	The URL of the document to be displayed in this frame.
SRC	*Req*	URL	IMG	Location of the image.
SRC	*Opt*	URL	INPUT	The location of the image for an IMAGE type widget.
SRC	*Opt*	URL	SCRIPT	Specifies the location of an external script.
STANDBY	*Opt*	Text	OBJECT	Message to display while loading the object.
START	*Opt*	Number	OL	Starting sequence number. (depreciated)

Alphabetical List of All HTML 4.0 Attributes *continued ...*

Attribute	Required	Value(s)	Parent Tag	Description / Notes
STYLE	*Opt*	Stylesheet	*All elements except:* BASE•BASEFONT HEAD•HTML•META PARAM•SCRIPT STYLE•TITLE	Style information to associate with the element.
SUMMARY	*Opt*	Text	TABLE	Summary statement for non-visual browsers.
TABINDEX	*Opt*	Number	A•AREA•BUTTON INPUT•OBJECT SELECT TEXTAREA	Tabbing sequence for keyboard use.
TARGET	*Opt*	Target	A•AREA•BASE FORM•LINK	The target window or frame for hyperlinks. The following magic target names are also supported: _blank a new blank window _self the same window as the link _parent the parent frameset _top the full body of the window
TEXT	*Opt*	Color	BODY	Color of the document text. (depreciated)
TITLE	*Opt*	Text	*All elements except:* BASE•BASEFONT HEAD•HTML•META PARAM•SCRIPT STYLE•TITLE	An advisory title. May display as a tool-tip or be spoken or rendered some other way for non-visual browsers.
TYPE	*Opt*	MIME	A•LINK	MIME-type for the TITLE content.
TYPE	*Opt*	BUTTON•SUBMIT RESET	BUTTON	The type of button to use. Defaults to SUBMIT.
TYPE	*TEXT*	Input Type	INPUT	Type of widget to use for form element. Defaults to TEXT.
TYPE	*Opt*	List Style	LI•OL•UL	Style of bullet or numbering style. (depreciated) For OL lists: 1 1, 2, 3, 4, … a a, b, c, d, … A A, B, C, D, … i i, ii, iii, iv, … I I, II, III, IV, … For UL lists: disc ● square ■ circle ○
TYPE	*Opt*	MIME	OBJECT•PARAM	MIME type.
TYPE	*Req*	MIME	SCRIPT	MIME type for the script URL.
TYPE	*Req*	MIME	STYLE	MIME type for the external style sheet.

Alphabetical List of All HTML 4.0 Attributes *continued ...*

Attribute	Required	Value(s)	Parent Tag	Description / Notes
USEMAP	*Opt*	URL	IMG•INPUT OBJECT	URL fragment identifer that points to a MAP element for a client-side imagemap.
VALIGN	*Opt*	TOP•MIDDLE BOTTOM BASELINE	COL•COLGROUP TBODY•TD•TFOOT TH•THEAD•TR	Sets the vertical alignment of content within the cells of the table row. Defaults to MIDDLE.
VALUE	*Opt*	Text	BUTTON	The value that is sent to the server when this button is pressed. Usually this value is also displayed on the button itself.
VALUE	*Opt*	Text	INPUT	The default value for text-oriented widgets.
VALUE	*Opt*	Number	LI	Reset number sequence to the value given. (depreciated)
VALUE	*Opt*	Text	OPTION	The value of the option when selected. Defaults to the content of the OPTION container.
VALUE	*Opt*	Text	PARAM	Value of the parameter.
VALUETYPE	*Opt*	DATA•REF OBJECT	PARAM	How to interpret VALUE. Defaults to DATA.
VERSION	*Opt*	Text	HTML	Link to the DTD for this document. Redundant with use of DOCTYPE. (depreciated)
VLINK	*Opt*	Color	BODY	Color of visited links. (depreciated)
VSPACE	*Opt*	Pixels	APPLET•IMAGE OBJECT	The size of the vertical gutter space around the image. Set this to zero to suppress the vertical gutter. (depreciated)

Attribute	Required	Value(s)	Parent Tag	Description / Notes
WIDTH	*Req*	Pixels or Percentage	APPLET	The width of the applet's display space on the screen. Used to reserve space for the applet on the page so that the page can be laid out before applet is executed. (depreciated)
WIDTH	*Opt*	Pixels or Percentage	COL•COLGROUP	Width of the column or default width of the COLGROUP.
WIDTH	*Opt*	Pixels or Percentage	HR	Width of the horizontal rule. (depreciated)
WIDTH	*Opt*	Pixels or Percentage	IFRAME	The width of the frame's display space on the screen.
WIDTH	*Opt*	Pixels or Percentage	IMG•OBJECT	The width of the image or object display space. Some browsers use this to reserve space for an image so that the page can be laid out before images are downloaded.
WIDTH	*Opt*	Number	PRE	Number of characters wide for the display of fixed-width data. (depreciated)
WIDTH	*Opt*	Pixels or Percentage	TABLE	Sets the overall width of the table, in pixels or a percentage of the width of the page (as n%).
WIDTH	*Opt*	Pixels	TD•TH	Sets the width of the cell in pixels. (depreciated)

Section 4: *Supplemental Reference*

Character Entities (ISO 8859-1)

The 98 characters here are the character entities supported by HTML 4.0. There are other characters which may be supported in the future, including Greek, Math, and other international character sets. These entities are all supported by the current versions of the major browsers but are not likely to be supported by older versions.

Name	Number	Symbol	Description
&quot;	&#34;	"	quotation mark
&amp;	&#38;	&	ampersand
&lt;	&#60;	<	less-than sign
&gt;	&#62;	>	greater-than sign
			no-break space
&iexcl;	&#161;	¡	inverted exclamation mark
&cent;	&#162;	¢	cent sign
&pound;	&#163;	£	pound sterling sign
&curren;	&#164;	¤	general currency sign
&yen;	&#165;	¥	yen sign
&brvbar;	&#166;	¦	broken (vertical) bar
&sect;	&#167;	§	section sign
&uml;	&#168;	¨	umlaut (dieresis)
&copy;	&#169;	©	copyright sign
&ordf;	&#170;	ª	ordinal indicator, feminine
&laquo;	&#171;	«	angle quotation mark, left
&not;	&#172;	¬	not sign
&shy;	&#173;		soft hyphen
&reg;	&#174;	®	registered sign
&macr;	&#175;	¯	macron
&deg;	&#176;	°	degree sign
&plusmn;	&#177;	±	plus-or-minus sign

Character Entities (ISO 8859-1) *continued ...*

Name	Number	Symbol	Description
²	²	^{2}	superscript two
³	³	^{3}	superscript three
´	´	´	acute accent
µ	µ	µ	micro sign
¶	¶	¶	pilcrow (paragraph sign)
·	·	·	middle dot
¸	¸	¸	cedilla
¹	¹	^{1}	superscript one
º	º	º	ordinal indicator, masculine
»	»	»	angle quotation mark, right
¼	¼	¼	fraction one-quarter
½	½	½	fraction one-half
¾	¾	¾	fraction three-quarters
¿	¿	¿	inverted question mark
À	À	À	capital A, grave accent
Á	Á	Á	capital A, acute accent
Â	Â	Â	capital A, circumflex accent
Ã	Ã	Ã	capital A, tilde
Ä	Ä	Ä	capital A, dieresis or umlaut mark
Å	Å	Å	capital A, ring
Æ	Æ	Æ	capital AE diphthong (ligature)
Ç	Ç	Ç	capital C, cedilla
È	È	È	capital E, grave accent
É	É	É	capital E, acute accent
Ê	Ê	Ê	capital E, circumflex accent
Ë	Ë	Ë	capital E, dieresis or umlaut mark

Character Entities (ISO 8859-1) *continued ...*

Name	Number	Symbol	Description
Ì	Ì	Ì	capital I, grave accent
Í	Í	Í	capital I, acute accent
Î	Î	Î	capital I, circumflex accent
Ï	Ï	Ï	capital I, dieresis or umlaut mark
Ð	Ð	Ð	capital Eth, Icelandic
Ñ	Ñ	Ñ	capital N, tilde
Ò	Ò	Ò	capital O, grave accent
Ó	Ó	Ó	capital O, acute accent
Ô	Ô	Ô	capital O, circumflex accent
Õ	Õ	Õ	capital O, tilde
Ö	Ö	Ö	capital O, dieresis or umlaut mark
×	×	×	multiply sign
Ø	Ø	Ø	capital O, slash
Ù	Ù	Ù	capital U, grave accent
Ú	Ú	Ú	capital U, acute accent
Û	Û	Û	capital U, circumflex accent
Ü	Ü	Ü	capital U, dieresis or umlaut mark
Ý	Ý	Ý	capital Y, acute accent
Þ	Þ	Þ	capital THORN, Icelandic
ß	ß	ß	small sharp s, German (sz ligature)
à	à	à	small a, grave accent
á	á	á	small a, acute accent
â	â	â	small a, circumflex accent
ã	ã	ã	small a, tilde
ä	ä	ä	small a, dieresis or umlaut mark
å	å	å	small a, ring

Character Entities (ISO 8859-1) *continued ...*

Name	Number	Symbol	Description
æ	æ	æ	small æ dipthong (ligature)
ç	ç	ç	small c, cedilla
è	è	è	small e, grave accent
é	é	é	small e, acute accent
ê	ê	ê	small e, circumflex accent
ë	ë	ë	small e, dieresis or umlaut mark
ì	ì	ì	small i, grave accent
í	í	í	small i, acute accent
î	î	î	small i, circumflex accent
ï	ï	ï	small i, dieresis or umlaut mark
ð	ð	ð	small eth, Icelandic
ñ	ñ	ñ	small n, tilde
ò	ò	ò	small o, grave accent
ó	ó	ó	small o, acute accent
ô	ô	ô	small o, circumflex accent
õ	õ	õ	small o, tilde
ö	ö	ö	small o, dieresis or umlaut mark
÷	÷	÷	divide sign
ø	ø	ø	small o, slash
ù	ù	ù	small u, grave accent
ú	ú	ú	small u, acute accent
û	û	û	small u, circumflex accent
ü	ü	ü	small u, dieresis or umlaut mark
ý	ý	ý	small y, acute accent
þ	þ	þ	small thorn, Icelandic
ÿ	ÿ	ÿ	small y, dieresis or umlaut mark

▶ reference additions

A place for your terms…

"What is the meaning of this...."
—End User

Glossary
creative html design.2

#

8-bit graphics: A color or grayscale graphic or movie that has 256 colors or less.

8-bit sound: 8-bit sound has a dynamic range of about 48 dB (decibels).

16-bit graphics: A color image or movie that has 65,536 colors.

16-bit sound: Standard CD-quality sound quality. 16-bit sound has a dynamic range of about 96 dB.

24-bit graphics: A color image or movie that has 16.7 million colors.

32-bit graphics: A color image or movie that has 16.7 million colors plus an 8-bit masking channel.

µ-law: µ-law is a sound file format used by Unix platforms. These files have the .au file extension.

a

active navigation: Point-and-click navigation, where the end user guides the information flow.

adaptive dithering: A form of dithering in which the program looks to the image to determine the best set of colors when creating an 8-bit or smaller palette. See *dithering*.

additive color: The use of projected light to mix color. This is the type of color we see on video monitors.

AIFC: A sound file format. AIFC is a new spec for the older Audio Interchange File Format (AIFF). Both AIFF and AIFF-C files can be read by this format. This format is commonly used by Apple and Silicon Graphics computers.

aliasing: In bitmapped graphics, the jagged boundary along the edges of different-colored shapes within an image. See *anti-aliasing*.

animated GIF: A single GIF file with multiple images and information for displaying them sequentially.

anti-aliasing: A technique for reducing the jagged appearance of aliased bit-mapped images, usually by interpolating the color and value of pixels at the boundaries of adjacent colors.

artifacts: Image imperfections, usually caused by compression.

attribute: A modifier to an HTML tag (for example, `<TAG ATTRIBUTE>`).

authoring tools: Creation tools for interactive media.

AVI: Audio-Video Interleaved. Microsoft's file format for desktop video movies.

b

bit depth: The number of bits used to repre-sent the color of each pixel in a digital image. Specifically: bit depth of 1 = 2 colors (usually black and white); bit depth of 2 = 4 colors; bit depth of 4 = 16 colors; bit depth of 8 = 256 colors; bit depth of 16 = 65,536 colors; bit depth of 24 = 16,777,216 colors. (See *Chapter 2.*)

bitmapped graphics: Also called raster graphics. Bitmapped graphics are images that have a specific number of pixels. As such, they are fixed into a particular grid of so many vertical and horizontal lines of pixels. This grid is called a "raster," and images that are fixed to such a grid are said to be "rasterized." The GIF and JPEG images that you commonly use on the web are bitmapped. See *vector graphics*.

browser: Also called user agent. An application that enables you to access World Wide Web pages. Most browsers provide the capability to view web pages, copy and print material from web pages, download files from the web, and navigate throughout the web.

browser-safe colors: The 216 colors that do not shift between platforms, operating systems, or most web browsers.

c

cache: A storage area that keeps frequently accessed data or program instructions readily available so that you do not have to retrieve them repeatedly.

CERN: The European Laboratory for Particle Physics (formerly **C**onseil **E**uropèenne pour la **R**echerche **N**uclèaire). A joint project of the European Economic Community, where the World Wide Web was first conceived.

CGI: **C**ommon **G**ateway **I**nterface. The programmatic interface between a web server and other programs running on that server. Commonly used for extending the interactivity of a site.

Cinepak: Cinepak is a form of very high compression for movies. The compression type is called "lossy" because it causes a visible loss in quality.

client: A computer that requests information from a network server. See *server*.

client pull: Client pull creates a slideshow effect with HTML text or inline images. It is programmed within the <META> tag.

client side: Client side means that the web element or effect can run locally off a computer and does not require the presence of a server.

client-side imagemap: A client-side imagemap is programmed in HTML and does not require a separate map definition file or a live web server to operate.

CLUT: **C**olor **L**ook**U**p **T**able. An 8-bit or lower image file uses a CLUT to define its palette.

color mapping: A color map refers to the color palette of an image. Color mapping means assigning colors to an image.

color names: Some browsers support using the name of a color instead of the color's hexadecimal value.

container: An element that encloses other objects, for example, <STRONG> </STRONG>.

compression: Reduction of the amount of data required to re-create an original file, graphic, or movie. Compression is used to reduce the transmission time of media and application files across the Internet.

contrast: The degrees of separation between values.

d

data rate: The data rate is the amount of data used or captured per second of real-time media. It is commonly used for both sound and movies.

data streaming: The ability to deliver media in real-time, much like a VCR, rather than having to download all the information before it can be played.

decibel (dB): The measure of relative intensity between two signals, usually used in measuring sound. Decibels are a logarithmic measurement, where twice the power is equal to 3 dB.

dithering: The positioning of different-colored pixels within an image to approximate colors that are not in the available palette. A dithered image often looks noisy, or composed of scattered pixels. See *adaptive dithering*.

document: Any individual object (text, image, media) on the web.

dpi: **D**ots **P**er **I**nch. A common measurement related to the resolution of an image. See *screen resolution*.

dynamic range: The measure of the listenable range of sound—that is, above the level of background noise and below the level of distortion. The larger the number the better the quality of the sound.

e

element: An object in an HTML file.

entity: Special characters (such as ©, ®, or @) that are defined by ASCII character combinations (such as ©, ®, or @).

extension: Abbreviated code at the end of a file usually used to identify the type of file. For example, a JPEG file may have the .jpg extension.

f

fps: **F**rames **P**er **S**econd. A movie contains a certain number of frames per second, and the fewer frames, the more jerky the motion and the smaller the file size.

frames: Frames offer the ability to divide a web page into multiple regions, with each region acting as a nested web page.

FTP: **F**ile **T**ransfer **P**rotocol. An Internet protcol that enables users to remotely access files on other computers. An ftp site houses files that can be downloaded to your computer.

g

gamma: Gamma measures the contrast that affects the midtones of an image. Adjusting the gamma lets you change the brightness values of the middle range of gray tones without dramatically altering the shadows and highlights.

gamut: A viewable or printable color range.

GIF: A bitmapped, color graphics file format. GIF is commonly used on the web because it employs an efficient compression method. See *JPEG*.

GIF89a: The most current GIF specification.

guestbook: A type of form that enables end users to enter comments on a web page.

h

hexadecimal: The base-16 number system. Often used in scripts and code. Hexadecimal code is required by HTML to describe RGB values of color for the web.

HTML: **H**yper**T**ext **M**arkup **L**anguage. The common language for interchange of hypertext between the World Wide Web client and server. Web pages are written using HTML. See *hypertext*.

HTTP: **H**yper**T**ext **T**ransfer **P**rotocol is the protocol that the browser and the web server use to communicate with each other.

hue: Defines a linear spectrum of the color wheel.

hyperlink: Linked text, images, or media.

hypertext: Text that is linked to documents on the web.

i

imagemaps: Portions of images that are hypertext links. Using a mouse-based web client such as Netscape or Mosaic, the user clicks on different parts of a mapped image to activate different hypertext links. See *hypertext*.

inline graphic: A graphic that sits inside an HTML document instead of the alternative, which would require that the image be downloaded and then viewed by using an outside system.

interlaced GIFs: The GIF file format allows for "interlacing," which causes the GIF to load quickly at low or chunky resolution and gradually come into full or crisp resolution.

ISP: Internet Service Provider.

j

Java: A programming language developed by Sun Microsystems that is cross-platform compatible and supported by some web browsers.

JavaScript: A scripting language that enables you to extend the capabilities of HTML. Developed by Netscape. No relation to Java (except the name).

JPEG: Joint Photographic Experts Group; also the graphic format developed by them. JPEG graphics use a lossy compression technique that can reduce the size of the graphics file by as much as 96 percent. See *GIF*.

l

links: Words or graphics in a hypertext document that act as pointers to other web objects. Links are generally underlined and may appear in a different color. When you click on a link, you can be transported to a different web site that contains information about the work or phrase used as the link. See *hypertext*.

lossless compression: A data compression technique that reduces the size of a file without sacrificing any of the original data. In lossless compression, the expanded or restored file is an exact replica of the original file before it was compressed. See *compression*.

lossy compression: A data compression technique in which some data is deliberately discarded in order to achieve massive reductions in the size of the compressed file. See *compression*.

m - n

mask: The process of blocking out areas in a computer graphic.

MIME: Multipurpose Internet Mail Extensions. An Internet standard for transferring nontext-based data such as sounds, movies, and images.

MPEG: Moving Pictures Experts Group. Also the name of a high-quality media format for both audio and video.

NCSA: National Center for Supercomputing Applications. A project of the University of Illinois.

o

object: Any distinct component of HTML, such as a tag, attribute, image, text file, etc.

p

passive navigation: Animation, slideshows, streaming movies, and audio. Basically, anything that plays without the end user initiating the content.

plug-in: Plug-ins are supported by some browsers and extend the capability of standard HTML.

PNG: (pronounced, "ping") **P**ortable **N**etwork **G**raphics. PNG is a lossless file format that supports interlacing, 8-bit transparency, and gamma information.

PostScript: A page description language used for printing text and graphics on laser printers and other high-resolution printing devices.

PP: (also **IPP**) Acronym for (Internet) **P**resence **P**rovider. Usually a web-hosting service.

progressive JPEG: A type of JPEG that produces an interlaced effect as it loads, much like interlaced GIFs.

provider: Provides Internet access. See *ISP*.

q

QuickTime: System software developed by Apple Computer for presentation of desktop video.

r

raster graphics: See *bitmapped graphics*.

rollover: A type of navigation button that changes when the end user's mouse rolls over it.

s

sample rate: Sample rates are measured in kilohertz (KHz). Sound-editing software is where the initial sample rate settings are established. Standard sample rates range from 11.025 KHz, 22.050 KHz, 44.10 KHz, to 48 KHz.

The higher the sample rate, the better the quality. The sample describes its highs and lows. See *data rate*.

sampling resolution: Sampling resolution affects media quality, just like dpi resolution affects the quality of images.

saturation: Defines the intensity of color.

screen resolution: Screen resolution, measured in dots per inch, (dpi), generally refers to the resolution of common computer monitors. 72 dpi is an agreed upon average, although you will also hear of 96 dpi being the resolution of larger displays.

search engine: A type of application, commonly found on the web, that enables you to search by keywords for information or URLs.

server: A computer that provides services for users of its network. The server receives requests for services and manages the requests so that they are answered in an orderly manner. See *client*.

server push: Server push is the method of requesting images or data from the server and automating their playback. It involves CGI and the presence of a live web server.

server side: Server side means any type of web page element that depends on being loaded to a server. It also implies the use of a CGI script.

server-side imagemap: A server-side imagemap requires that the information about the image-map be saved within a "map definition file" that needs to be stored on a server and accessed by a CGI script.

splash screen: A main menu screen or opening graphic to a web page.

sprite: An individual component of an animation, such as a character or graphic that moves independently.

t

tables: Tables create rows and columns, as in a spreadsheet, and can be used to align data and images.

tag: An HTML directive, enclosed in "<" and ">".

texture map: 2D artwork that is applied to the surface of a 3D shape.

transparent GIFs: A subset of the original GIF file format that adds header information to the GIF file, which signifies that a defined color will be masked out.

true color: The quality of color provided by 24-bit color depth. 24-bit color depth results in 16.7 million colors, which is usually more than adequate for the human eye.

u

user agent: See *browser*.

URL: **U**niform **R**esource **L**ocator. The address for a web site.

v

value: The range from light to dark in an image.

vector graphics: Images that are stored as lines and curves, instead of pixels. Vector graphics can be rendered in various sizes, resolutions, and media, without losing information. See *bitmapped graphics*.

Video for Windows: A multimedia architecture and application suite that provides an outbound architecture that lets applications developers access audio, video, and animation from many different sources through one interface. As an application, Video for Windows primarily handles video capture and compression, and video and audio editing. See *AVI*.

w

WYSIWYG: Pronounced, "wizzy-wig". Acronym for **W**hat **Y**ou **S**ee **I**s **W**hat **Y**ou **G**et. A design philosophy in which formatting commands directly affect the text displayed onscreen so that the screen shows the appearance of printed text.

▶ glossary additions

A place for your terms...

Index
creative html design.2

symbols

(hash marks), hexadecimal numbers, 28
.. (two dots), in relative URLs, 270
µ-law audio file format, 401
24-bit color, 69
24-bit PNG images, large file size, 63
216-color palette. *See* browser-safe colors

a

<A> tag (anchor text), 26, 446, 463
  bullets as hyperlinks, 173
  creating hot images, 105
  hyperlinks in bulleted lists, 166
  sound files, 404
ABBR attribute, 457, 470
<ABBR> tag, 442, 463
absolute links, writing good HTML code, 425
absolute positioning of images, 295-296
absolute URLs
  converting relative URLs to, 271
  versus relative URLs, 268
ACCEPT attribute, 453, 470
ACCEPTCHARSET attribute, 453, 470
ACCESSKEY attribute, 447, 453, 470

accuracy of web site sources, evaluating, 408
<ACRONYM> tag, 442, 463
ACTION attribute, 371, 453, 470
ad banners, 412-413
adaptive palettes, 94
<ADDRESS> tag, 444, 463
addresses, URLs (Uniform Resource
  Locators), 266
    absolute versus relative URLs, 268
    fragments, 326-327
    parts of, 267
    relative URLs
        converting to absolute URLs, 271
        examples, 270-271
        as links, 272-273
        paths in, 269
    web sites for information, 273
Adobe online graphics services, 91
AIFF audio file format, 401
aliased images, color editing in Photoshop 6.0,
  157-159
aliased type, versus anti-aliased type, 246
aliasing
    in Photoshop, 46-49
    versus anti-aliasing, 44-45
ALIGN attribute, 470-471
    <CAPTION> tag, 457
    <DIV> tag, 205, 445
    forms elements, 453
    frames elements, 460
    <H#> tag, 445
    <HR> tag, 163, 445
    <IMG> tag, 208-209
    <LEGEND> tag, 453
    <P> tag, 203-204, 445
    special text-level elements, 447
    table elements, 457
    <TABLE> tag, 457
alignment, 201
    graphic alignment, 207

 tag (line breaks), 210-211
        floating images, 209
        image gutters, 212-213
        <IMG> tag, 208
    offset, 186
    tables, 214-216
        borders in Netscape, 219
        bulleted lists, creating, 232
        cell colors, 217
        cell spacing, 218-219
        centering images, 232

odd numbers of cells, 223-224
slicing images, 225, 229-230
spacing text and graphics, 220-222
versus single-pixel GIFs, 231
vertical rules, creating, 233
    text alignment, 202
        <CENTER> tag, 206
        <DIV> tag, 205
        <P> tag, 203-204
ALINK attribute, 29, 439, 471
alpha-channel transparency (PNG), 62
alphabetical lists, 168
ALT attribute, 471
    <APPLET> tag, 447
    <AREA> tag, 447
    <INPUT> tag, 453
    <IMG> tag, 107, 121-123, 425, 447
AltaVista search engine, 409
anchor text. See <A> tag (anchor text)
animated GIFs, 391-394
animation
    aesthetics, 390
    animated GIFs, 391-394
    animating artwork in ImageReady 3.0,
      380-386
    client pull, 389
    creating artwork in Photoshop 6.0, 377-379
    Ducks In A Row case study, 375-387
    LOWSRC attribute (<IMG> tag), 388
    plug-ins, 391-392
    process overview, 374
    storyboards, 375
anti-aliased images, color editing
    in ImageReady 3.0, 153-156
    in Photoshop 6.0, 148-152
anti-aliased type, versus aliased type, 246
anti-aliasing
    transparent GIFs, 187-189
    versus aliasing, 44-45
<APPLET> tag, 446, 463
ARCHIVE attribute, 447, 471
<AREA> tag, 446, 463
Arial font, compared to Verdana screen-based
  font, 244
artwork, planning web sites, 260-261
attributes (HTML)
    ABBR, 457, 470
    ACCEPT, 453, 470
    ACCEPTCHARSET, 453, 470
    ACCESSKEY, 447, 453, 470
    ACTION, 371, 453, 470

ALIGN, 470-471
    <CAPTION> tag, 457
    <DIV> tag, 205, 445
    forms elements, 453
    frames elements, 460
    <H#> tag, 445
    <HR> tag, 163, 445
    <IMG> tag, 208-209
    <LEGEND> tag, 453
    <P> tag, 203-204, 445
    special text-level elements, 447
    table elements, 457
    <TABLE> tag, 457
ALINK, 29, 439, 471
alphabetical list, 470-485
ALT, 471
    <APPLET> tag, 447
    <AREA> tag, 447
    <IMG> tag, 107, 121-123, 425, 447
    <INPUT> tag, 453
ARCHIVE, 447, 471
AXIS, 457, 471
BACKGROUND, 30, 180, 439, 471
BGCOLOR, 472
    <BODY> tag, 29, 178-179, 439
    table cells, 217
    tables, 100, 457-458
block elements, 445
BORDER, 472
    <FRAMESET> tag, 311
    <IMG> tag, 106, 448
    <OBJECT> tag, 448
    tables, 215, 219, 458
CELLPADDING, 218, 458, 472
CELLSPACING, 218, 458, 472
CHAR, 458, 472
CHAROFF, 458, 472
CHARSET, 439, 448, 462, 472
CHECKED, 453, 472
CITE, 442, 445, 462, 472-473
CLASS, 293, 473
CLASSID, 448, 473
CLEAR, 210-211, 448, 473
CODE, 473
CODEBASE, 448, 473
CODETYPE, 448, 473
COLOR, 240, 448, 473
COLS, 473
    <FRAMESET> tag, 307, 310, 460
    <TEXTAREA> tag, 453
COLSPAN, 223-224, 458, 474

COMPACT, 443, 474
CONTENT, 389, 411, 439, 474
COORDS, 448, 474
Core attributes, 435
DATA, 448, 474
DATETIME, 462, 474
DECLARE, 448, 474
defined, 14, 417
DIR, 448, 475
DISABLED, 453, 475
document-structure elements, 439-440
ENCTYPE, 453, 475
Event attributes, 437
FACE, 448, 475
FOR, 453, 475
forms elements, 453-455
FRAME, 458, 475
FRAMEBORDER, 460, 475
frames elements, 460-461
HEADERS, 458, 475
HEIGHT, 475-476
      <IFRAME> tag, 460
      <IMG> tag, 108-109, 213, 448
      <OBJECT> tag, 448
      plug-ins, 392
      tables, 220-222, 458
HREF, 439, 448, 476
HSPACE, 212, 449, 476
HTML reference layout, 434
HTTP-EQUIV, 439, 476
ID, 476
Internationalization attributes, 436
ISMAP, 449, 476
LABEL, 453, 476
LANG, 476
LANGUAGE, 462, 476
LINK, 29, 106, 439, 476
list elements, 443
LONGDESC, 449, 476
LOWSRC, 388
MARGINHEIGHT, 315, 460, 477
MARGINWIDTH, 315, 460, 477
MAXLENGTH, 454, 477
MEDIA, 439, 477
METHOD, 371, 454, 477
miscellaneous elements, 462
MULTIPLE, 454, 477
NAME, 477-478
      <A tag>, 325, 449
      <BUTTON> tag, 454
      <FRAME> tag, 312, 460

<IFRAME> tag, 460
<INPUT> tag, 449, 454
<MAP> tag, 449
<META> tag, 411, 439
<OBJECT> tag, 449, 454
<PARAM> tag, 449
<SELECT> tag, 454
<TEXTAREA> tag, 454
NOHREF, 449, 478
NORESIZE, 460, 478
NOSHADE, 163, 445, 478
NOWRAP, 458, 478
OBJECT, 478
ONBLUR, 449, 454, 478
ONCHANGE, 454, 478
ONCLICK, 478
ONDBLCLICK, 478
ONFOCUS, 449, 454, 479
ONKEYDOWN, 479
ONKEYPRESS, 479
ONKEYUP, 479
ONLOAD, 479
      <BODY> tag, 439
      <FRAMESET> tag, 461
ONMOUSEDOWN, 479
ONMOUSEMOVE, 480
ONMOUSEOUT, 480
ONMOUSEOVER, 480
ONMOUSEUP, 480
ONRESET, 454, 480
ONSELECT, 454, 480
ONSUBMIT, 454, 480
ONUNLOAD, 461, 480
phrase markup elements, 442
PROFILE, 439, 481
PROMPT, 462, 481
quotation marks around, 421
READONLY, 454, 481
REL, 439, 449, 481
REV, 439, 449, 481
ROWS, 481
      <FRAMESET> tag, 307, 310, 461
      <TEXTAREA> tag, 454
ROWSPAN, 223-224, 458, 481
RULES, 458, 481
SCHEME, 440, 481
SCOPE, 459, 481
SCROLLING, 314, 461, 481
SELECTED, 455, 482
SHAPE, 449, 482

SIZE, 482
      <FONT> tag, 240, 450
      <HR> tag, 163, 445
      <INPUT> tag, 455
      <SELECT> tag, 455
spaces in, 21
SPAN, 459, 482
special text-level elements, 447-450
SRC, 482
      <FRAME> tag, 461
      <IFRAME> tag, 461
      <IMG> tag, 18, 450
      <INPUT> tag, 455
      <SCRIPT> tag, 462
STANDBY, 450, 482
START, 443, 482
STYLE, 483
SUMMARY, 459, 483
TABINDEX, 450, 455, 483
table elements, 457-459
TARGET, 440, 450, 455, 483
TEXT, 29, 440, 483
TITLE, 483
TYPE, 483
      <A> tag, 440
      <BUTTON> tag, 455
      <INPUT> tag, 362-363, 455
      <LI> tag, 167-168, 443
      <LINK> tag, 440
      <OBJECT> tag, 450
      <OL> tag, 443
      <PARAM> tag, 450
      <SCRIPT> tag, 462
      <STYLE> tag, 288, 440
      <UL> tag, 443
USEMAP, 119, 450, 455, 484
VALIGN, 215, 459, 484
VALUE, 484
      <BUTTON> tag, 455
      <INPUT> tag, 455
      <OL> tag, 443
      <OPTION> tag, 455
      <PARAM> tag, 450
VALUETYPE, 450, 484
VERSION, 440, 484
VLINK, 29, 440, 484
VSPACE, 450, 484
WIDTH, 485
      <COL> tag, 459
      <COLGROUP> tag, 459
      <HR> tag, 163, 445

<IFRAME> tag, 461
<IMG> tag, 108-109, 213, 450
<OBJECT> tag, 450
plug-ins, 392
<PRE> tag, 445
tables, 220-222, 459
audio. *See* sound
auto-slices (Photoshop 6.0), 228
AXIS attribute, 457, 471

b

<B> tag (bold text), 238, 441, 463
BACKGROUND attribute, 30, 180, 439, 471
background color
matching for transparency, 176
with hex values, 178-179
in ImageReady 3.0, 181-184
with tiled images, 180
transparent GIFs, 188-189
background tiles, 30-31, 125
advantages of, 126
color editing
aliased images in Photoshop 6.0,
157-159
anti-aliased images in ImageReady 3.0,
153-156
anti-aliased images in Photoshop 6.0,
148-152
color matching, 180
file formats, 130
full-screen backgrounds
advantages of, 128
disadvantages of, 129
JPEG or GIF, 177
pattern size, determining, 127
seamless, 131
in ImageReady 3.0, 132-137
in Photoshop 6.0, 138-144
seams, 130-131
special effects, 145
text readability, 146-147
in web pages, 30-31
bandwidth, selecting Internet providers, 4
banner ads, 412-413
<BASE> tag, 438, 463
base URLs, building relative URLs, 269
<BASEFONT> tag, 446, 463
<BDO> tag, 446, 463

BGCOLOR attribute, 472
<BODY> tag, 29, 178-179, 439
table cells, 217
tables, 100, 457-458
<BGSOUND> tag, 404
<BIG> tag, 441, 463
bit-depth
animated GIFs, 394
sound, 398, 400
blank images in rollovers, warning about, 356
<BLINK> tag, 239
blinking text, 239
Block content model, 432
block elements, 444-445
<BLOCKQUOTE> tag, 444, 464
<BODY> tag, 438, 464
background images, 30
color in web pages, 28-29
extras inserted by WYSIWYG editors, 418
HTML color, 101
body type, versus headline type, 237
bold text (<B> tag), 238, 441, 463
BORDER attribute, 472
<FRAMESET> tag, 311
<IMG> tag, 106, 448
<OBJECT> tag, 448
tables, 215, 219, 458
borderless frames, 311
borders
background tiles, 131
hot images
resizing, 106
identifying, 104
tables in Netscape, 219

 tag (line breaks), 170, 446, 464
graphic alignment, 210-211
browser-safe colors, 425
color names chart, 97
color pickers, 86
hex color choices example, 82-85
for HTML color, 75-85
illustration-based artwork, 87-90
converting to browser-safe colors,
warning about, 92
JPEG file format, 93
loading into Photoshop 6.0, 76-77
mathematical organization of, 67
online graphics services for, 91
previsualizing in Photoshop 6.0, 78-81
photographic-based artwork, 94-95
reasons for using, 66, 68
when to use, 74

browsers
color preferences, 177
older browsers, frames on, 308
operational overview, 15
bulleted lists
creating with tables, 232
defined, 443
bullets, 165
changing shape of, 167
clip art for, 169
custom-made, 170-172
HTML code for, 166
as hyperlinks, 173
hyperlinks in, 166
text crowding, troubleshooting, 170
<BUTTON> tag, 451, 464
buttons. *See* bullets
Buzan, Tony (Mind Maps), 256

c

caching images, 110
<CAPTION> tag, 216, 456, 464
carriage returns in HTML, 19
Carter, Matthew (screen-based font
development), 242-244
Cascading Style Sheets. *See* CSS
case sensitivity
filenames, 20, 425
tags (HTML), 19
case studies
Ducks In A Row case study (animation),
375-387
Shockwave case study (sound), 395-396
Caslon, William (history of typography), 242
CDs, capturing sound from, 397
CELLPADDING attribute, 218, 458, 472
cells (tables)
color, 217
odd numbers of, 223-224
spacing, 218-219
CELLSPACING attribute, 218, 458, 472
<CENTER> tag, 206, 239, 444, 464
centering
images with tables, 232
text, 202. *See also* <CENTER> tag
centimeters, 290
CGI (Common Gateway Interface) programs, 370
retrieving data from forms, 370-371
web sites for, 372

CHAR attribute, 458, 472
character entities, list of, 486-489
Character Shape Player (CSP), 245
Character Shape Recorder (CSR), 245
CHAROFF attribute, 458, 472
CHARSET attribute, 439, 448, 462, 472
checkboxes in forms, 365
CHECKED attribute, 453, 472
CITE attribute, 442, 445, 462, 472-473
<CITE> tag, 442, 464
CLASS attribute, 293, 435, 473
class selectors (CSS), 293
    versus ID selectors, 296
CLASSID attribute, 448, 473
CLEAR attribute, 210-211, 448, 473
Click Here (Raymond Pirouz), 413
clickable images. *See* hot images
client-side imagemaps
    compared to server-side imagemaps, 113
    creating in ImageReady 3.0, 114-117
    HTML code for, 118-119
client-pull animation, 389
clip art
    for bullets, 169
    web sites for, 165
CMYK color, converting RGB color to, 86
code (HTML). *See* attributes (HTML); elements
  (HTML); good HTML code; tags (HTML)
CODE attribute, 473
<CODE> tag, 442, 464
CODEBASE attribute, 448, 473
CODETYPE attribute, 448, 473
<COL> tag, 456, 464
cold type, 251
<COLGROUP> tag, 456, 464
color
    background color
        matching for transparency, 176-184
        text readability, 146-147
        transparent GIFs, 188-189
    borders on hot images, changing, 106
    browser-safe colors, 425
        color names chart, 97
        color pickers, 86
        hex color choices example, 82-85
        for HTML color, 75-85
        illustration-based artwork, 87-90
        JPEG file format, 93
        loading into Photoshop 6.0, 76-77
        mathematical organization of, 67

online graphics services for, 91
photographic-based artwork, 94-95
previsualizing in Photoshop 6.0, 78-81
reasons for using, 66, 68
warning about converting images to, 92
when to use, 74
editing background tiles
    aliased images in Photoshop 6.0,
      157-159
    anti-aliased images in ImageReady 3.0,
      153-156
    anti-aliased images in Photoshop 6.0,
      148-152
HTML color
    hyperlinks, 99
    lines of text, 98
    names, using instead of hexadecimal
      color, 96-97
    in tables, 100
    tags for, 101
reducing in GIF images with Photoshop,
  38-43
RGB color, 69
    converting to CMYK color, 86
    hexadecimal values, 71-73
    web hex converters, 73
screen-based color versus print-based
  color, 65
table cells, 217
of text, printing web pages, 147
in web pages, 28-29
COLOR attribute, 240, 448, 473
color pickers (browser-safe colors), 86
color preferences, in browsers, 177
COLS attribute, 473
    <FRAMESET> tag, 307, 310, 460
    <TEXTAREA> tag, 453
COLSPAN attribute, 223-224, 458, 474
columns (tables), cells spanning multiple, 223-224
combination rollovers, 358
comments
    HTML
        nesting frames, 309
        SSI in, 279
        style sheets, 286-287
    JavaScript, 340
Common Gateway Interface. *See* CGI programs
COMPACT attribute, 443, 474
compression. *See* file compression
computer screen-based color. *See*
  screen-based color

containers (HTML)
    defined, 14, 18, 417, 431
    straddling containers, problems with, 422
content, defined, 431
CONTENT attribute, 389, 411, 439, 474
content models, 432
controls. *See* widgets (forms)
COORDS attribute, 448, 474
copy protection (streaming audio), 399
copyright information web site, 397
Core attributes (HTML), 435
crawlers. *See* search engines
CSP (Character Shape Player), 245
CSR (Character Shape Recorder), 245
CSS (Cascading Style Sheets), 283
    absolute positioning, 295-296
    class selectors, 293
    defined, 284
    internal style sheets, 285
    measurement units, 290-291
    parts of, 288-289
    <SPAN> tag, 294
    text-related properties, 292
cursor, identifying hot images, 104
custom swatches (Photoshop 6.0), creating, 76
custom-made bullets, 170
    changing size in Photoshop 6.0, 171-172

d

DATA attribute, 448, 474
DATETIME attribute, 462, 474
<DD> tag (definition lists), 167, 443, 464
decimal system
    RGB color, 69
    versus hexadecimal system, 70
DECLARE attribute, 448, 474
dedicated HTML editors, 10
default HTML fonts, 236
definition lists, 167, 443
<DEL> tag, 461, 464
design medium, HTML as, 8
<DFN> tag, 442, 464
DHTML (Dynamic HTML), 358-359
digital audio. *See* sound
DIR attribute, 436, 448, 475
<DIR> tag, 443, 464
Director, streaming audio, 405
directories (of web sites), 408-410

directory information (FTP), 25
directory structure, organization of HTML files, 274
DISABLED attribute, 453, 475
display size, navigation of web sites, 318-319
disposal methods (animated GIFs), 394
dithering
  avoiding with browser-safe colors, 87-90
  correcting, 88-90
  with Photoshop, 52
  sound files, 403
  versus non-dithering, 50-51
<DIV> tag, 444, 465
  absolute positioning, 295-296
  text alignment, 205
<DL> tag (definition lists), 167, 443, 465
Document Type Definition (DTD), 429
document-structure elements, 438-440
documents, 14
dots (..), in relative URLs, 270
download speeds, animated GIFs, 393
Dreamweaver, web site for, 359
drop shadows (transparent GIFs), 188-189
<DT> tag (definition lists), 443, 465
DTD (Document Type Definition), 429
Ducks In A Row case study (animation), 375-387
Dynamic HTML (DHTML), 358-359

e

editors (HTML)
  dedicated HTML editors, 10
  text-based editors, 9
  WYSIWYG editors, 11
    extra <BODY> tags, 418
    problems writing good HTML code, 419-420
electronic typesetting, 251
elements (HTML). See also tags (HTML)
  block elements, 444-445
  content, 431
  content models, 432
  defined, 14, 417, 430
  document-structure elements, 438-440
  font markup elements, 441
  forms elements, 451-455
  frames elements, 459-461
  list elements, 443

miscellaneous elements, 461-462
phrase markup elements, 442
special text-level elements, 446-450
table elements, 456-459
versus tags, 430
em, defined, 290
<EM> tag, 238, 442, 465
<EMBED> tag, 392
embedded characters, 425
embedding fonts, 245
en, defined, 290
ENCTYPE attribute, 453, 475
entities (HTML), numbered entities versus named entities, 425
Event attributes (HTML), 437
Excite search engine, 409
exercises
  animation
    animating artwork in ImageReady 3.0, 380-386
    creating artwork in Photoshop 6.0, 377-379
  background color matching
    with hex values, 178-179
    in ImageReady 3.0, 181-184
  background tiles, color editing
    aliased images in Photoshop 6.0, 157-159
    anti-aliased images in ImageReady 3.0, 153-156
    anti-aliased images in Photoshop 6.0, 148-152
  browser-safe colors
    correcting dithering, 88-90
    hex color choices, 82-85
    loading into Photoshop 6.0, 76-77
    previsualizing in Photoshop 6.0, 78-81
  bullets, changing size in Photoshop 6.0, 171-172
  client-side imagemaps, creating in ImageReady 3.0, 114-117
  GIF images
    aliasing in Photoshop, 46-49
    reducing colors with Photoshop, 38-43
  highlighting rollovers, 357-358
  hot image options, 111
  images, slicing in Photoshop 6.0, 226-229
  JPEG images, compression in Photoshop, 55-59
  pointing rollovers, 343

rollovers, creating in ImageReady 3.0, 331-335
seamless background tiles
  in ImageReady 3.0, 132-137
  in Photoshop 6.0, 138-144
slideshow rollovers, 349-350
transparent GIFs, creating
  in ImageReady 3.0, 191-194
  in Photoshop 6.0, 195-198
web pages
  background patterns, 31
  color in, 29
  hyperlinks on, 26
  image hyperlinks, 27
  uploading, 22-25
  writing, 16-17
extensions, filenames, 20
external style sheets, 284

f

FACE attribute, 448, 475
feedback forms, HTML code for, 364-365
FETCH program, 24
<FIELDSET> tag, 451, 465
file compression
  GIF
    aliasing in Photoshop, 46-49
    aliasing versus anti-aliasing, 44-45
    compression overview, 37
    compression tables, 51
    dithering versus non-dithering, 50
    dithering with Photoshop, 52
    reducing colors with Photoshop, 38-43
    reducing image size, 38
    versus JPEG, 60
  JPEG
    compression overview, 54
    image compression in Photoshop, 55-59
    progressive JPEGs, warning about, 59
    versus GIF, 60
  PNG
    compression overview, 61
    large file size for 24-bit images, 63
    in Photoshop, 63
file formats
  background tiles, 130
  sound, 401-402

file names
    case sensitivity, 425
    extensions, 20
    highlighting rollovers, 352
    SSI, 277
file sizes, determining, 34
File Transfer Protocol. *See* FTP
files (HTML). *See* web pages
Flash authoring tool, 405
floating images, graphic alignment, 209-211
flowcharts, planning web sites, 263
folder names (SSI), 277
folders, organization of HTML files, 266
font markup elements, 441
<FONT> tag, 240-241, 446, 465
    coloring lines of text, 98
    HTML color, 101
font-family property (CSS), 288, 292
fonts
    anti-aliased versus aliased type, 246
    changing sizes, 239
    default HTML fonts, 236
    embedding, 245
    in forms, using tables with, 366-368
    native fonts on Windows and Macs, 241
    screen-based fonts
        Verdana and Georgia, 243-244
        versus print-based fonts, 242
    web sites for repositories, 253
<FONTSIZE> tag, 239
FOR attribute, 453, 475
<FORM> tag, 362, 451, 465
forms, 361
    CGI programs, web sites for, 372
    feedback forms, HTML code for, 364-365
    images as submit buttons, 369
    retrieving data from, 370-371
    tables, using with, 366-368
    widgets, 362-363
forms elements, 451-455
fragments (HTML), 325-327
FRAME attribute, 458, 475
frame delays (animation), 393
<FRAME> tag, 307, 459, 465
FRAMEBORDER attribute, 460, 475
frames, 306
    aesthetics of, 316
    borderless frames, 311
    framesets, 307
    margins in, 315
    nesting, 309

    on older browsers, 308
    resizing, 310
    screen size considerations, 320-323
    scrollbars in, 314
    targeted links in, 312-313
    web sites for information, 325
frames elements, 459-461
<FRAMESET> tag, 307, 459, 465
framesets, 307
fringe (transparent GIFs), avoiding, 188
FTP (File Transfer Protocol)
    host and directory information, 25
    instructions
        Macintoshes, 24
        Windows, 22-23
full-screen backgrounds
    advantages of, 128
    disadvantages of, 129

g

gamma correction (PNG), 61
Garamond, Claude (history of typography), 242
Georgia screen-based font, 243-244
GET method (sending server messages), 371
GIF images
    adaptive palettes, 94
    aliasing
        in Photoshop, 46-49
        versus anti-aliasing, 44-45
    animated GIFs, 391-394
    background color matching, 177
    background tiles, 130
    compression overview, 37
    compression tables, 51
    dithering
        with Photoshop, 52
        versus non-dithering, 50
    interlaced GIFs, 110
    patent controversy, 53
    pronunciation of, 36
    reducing
        colors with Photoshop, 38-43
        image size, 38
    single-pixel GIFs
        image gutters, 213
        indented type, 252
        leading tricks, 249
        versus tables for alignment, 231

    transparent GIFs, 185
        anti-aliasing, 187
        creating in ImageReady 3.0, 191-194
        creating in Photoshop 6.0, 195-198
        glows, drop shadows, soft edges, 188-189
        HTML code for, 190
        in rollovers, warning about, 356
        when to use, 186
        versus JPEG, 60
GIF89a file format. *See* animated GIFs
gigabytes, 34
Gill, Eric (history of typography), 242
glows (transparent GIFs), 188-189
goals, determining (planning web sites), 259
good HTML code
    ALT attribute (<IMG> tag), 425
    browser-safe colors, 425
    case-sensitive file names, 425
    line endings, 423-424
    missing quotation marks, 422
    numbered versus named entities, 425
    quotation marks around attribute values, 421
    reasons for writing, 416
    relative versus absolute links, 425
    straddling containers, 422
    WYSIWYG editors
        extra <BODY> tags, 418
        problems with, 419-420
Google search engine, 409
Gould Stewart, Margaret (storyboarding process), 263
graphics-based typography, 248
    leading tricks, 250
graphics. *See* images
Gutenberg, Johannes (history of typography), 242
gutters (graphic alignment), 212-213

h

<H#> tag (headings), 18, 238, 444, 465
halos (transparent GIFs), avoiding, 188
hash marks (#), hexadecimal numbers, 28
<HEAD> tag, 18, 438, 465
HEADERS attribute, 458, 475
headings
    <H#> tag, 18, 238, 444, 465
    tables, 216
headline type, versus body type, 237

HEIGHT attribute, 475-476
    <IFRAME> tag, 460
    <IMG> tag, 108-109, 213, 448
    <OBJECT> tag, 448
    plug-ins, 392
    tables, 220-222, 458
hexadecimal calculators, 73
hexadecimal system
    background color matching, 178-179
    browser-safe colors, hex color choices
    example, 82-85
    color in web pages, 28
    HTML color, using names instead of
    hexadecimal color, 96-97
    RGB color values, 71-72
        converting with hex calculators, 73
        web hex converters, 73
    versus decimal system, 70
hiding borders on hot images, 106
highlighting rollovers
    defined, 336
    JavaScript for, 351-358
    naming conventions, 352
history of line endings, 424
horizontal rules (<HR> tag), 162, 444, 465
    images as, 164
    options for, 163
hosting companies. See IPPs
hosts
    FTP, 25
    URLs, 267
hot images, 103. See also imagemaps
    borders, resizing, 106
    exercise, 111
    identifying, 104
    <IMG> and <A> tags, 105
    versus imagemaps, 120
hot type, defined, 251
HotBot search engine, 409
HotWired, study on scrolling in web pages, 317
<HR> tag (horizontal rules), 162-163, 444, 465
HREF attribute, 439, 448, 476
HSPACE attribute, 212, 449, 476
HTML (HyperText Markup Language), 7
    advantages of learning, 8
    attributes. See attributes (HTML)
    dedicated HTML editors, 10
    as design medium, 8
    editors. See editors (HTML)
    elements. See elements (HTML)
    good HTML code. See good HTML code
    online tutorials, 9

    purpose of, 7
    tags. See tags (HTML)
    text-based editors, 9
    WYSIWYG editors, 11
HTML color
    browser-safe colors
        selecting, 75-85
        when to use, 74
    hyperlinks, 99
    lines of text, 98
    names, using instead of hexadecimal color,
    96-97
    in tables, 100
    tags for, 101
<HTML> tag, 18, 438, 465
HTML-based typography, 238-241
    indents, 252
    leading tricks, 249-250
    unreliability of leading tricks, 251
HTTP (HyperText Transport Protocol), 370
HTTP-EQUIV attribute, 439, 476
hyperlinks
    back to top of page, 327
    in bulleted lists, 166
    bullets as, 173
    defined, 14
    hot images, 103
        exercise, 111
        identifying, 104
        <IMG> and <A> tags, 105
        resizing borders, 106
    HTML color, 99
    image hyperlinks on web pages, 27
    imagemaps, 112
        ALT text with, 121-123
        client-side imagemaps, 113-119
        server-side imagemaps, 113, 120
        versus multiple images, 120
    link exchanges (publicizing web sites), 413
    on web pages, exercise, 26
    operational overview, 15
    relative URLs as, 272-273
    relative versus absolute links, writing good
    HTML code, 425
    targeted links in frames, 312-313
hypertext, 14
HyperText Markup Language. See HTML
HyperText Transport Protocol (HTTP), 370

i

<I> tag (italic text), 238, 441, 466
icons of images, saving in Photoshop, 35
ID attribute, 435, 476
ID selectors (CSS), 295
    versus class selectors, 296
<IFRAME> tag, 460, 466
illustration-based artwork (browser-safe colors),
87-90
    JPEG file format, 93
    warning about converting to, 92
    when to use, 74
image hyperlinks on web pages, 27
imagemaps, 112
    ALT text with, 121-123
    client-side imagemaps, 113
        creating in ImageReady 3.0, 114-117
        HTML code for, 118-119
    server-side imagemaps, 113, 120
    versus multiple images, 120
ImageReady 3.0
    anti-aliased images, color editing, 153-156
    artwork, animating, 380-386
    background color matching, 181-184
    browser-safe colors, color pickers, 86
    client-side imagemaps, creating, 114-117
    dithering, correcting, 88-90
    rollovers, creating, 331-335
    seamless background tiles, 132-137
    slicing images, 332
    transparent GIFs, creating, 191-194
images
    absolute positioning, 295-296
    alignment, 207

 tag (line breaks), 210-211
        floating images, 209
        gutters, 212-213
        <IMG> tag, 208
        with tables, 220-222
    ALT text, 107
    animation. See animation
    background tiles. See background tiles
    centering with tables, 232
    converting to browser-safe colors, warning
    about, 92
    dithering
        avoiding with browser-safe colors,
        87-90
        correcting, 88-90

file size, determining, 34
GIF. *See* GIF images
as horizontal rules, 164
hot images, 103
    exercise, 111
    identifying, 104
    <IMG> and <A> tags, 105
    resizing borders, 106
imagemaps, 112
    ALT text with, 121-123
    client-side imagemaps, 113-119
    server-side imagemaps, 113, 120
    versus multiple images, 120
interlaced GIFs, 110
JPEG. *See* JPEG images
layering with text, 297-303
online graphics services, 91
photographs, browser-safe colors, 94-95
PNG
    alpha-channel transparency, 62
    compression in Photoshop, 63
    compression overview, 61
    gamma correction, 61
    large file size for 24-bit images, 63
preloading, 110
rollovers. *See* rollovers
saving icons in Photoshop, 35
slicing
    in ImageReady 3.0, 332
    in Photoshop 6.0, 226-229
    for table alignment, 225, 229-230
as submit buttons, 369
thumbnail graphics, 324
WIDTH and HEIGHT attributes 108-109
<IMG> tag, 18, 446, 466
    creating hot images, 105
    custom-made bullets, 170
    exercise, 111
    graphic alignment, 208-209
    graphics-based typography, 248
    transparent GIFs, 190
inches, 290
include keyword (SSI), 279
indents (typography), 252
Inline content model, 432
inline graphics, 207
inline quotations (<Q> tag), 442, 468
<INPUT> tag, 362-363, 451, 466
<INS> tag, 461, 466
interactive buttons. *See* hot images
interlaced GIFs, 110, 394
internal style sheets, 285

Internationalization attributes (HTML), 436
Internet, relationship to World Wide Web, 14
Internet Explorer, <BGSOUND> tag, 404
Internet Presence Providers. *See* IPPs
Internet providers, selecting, 2-3
    See also IPPs; ISPs
    bandwidth, 4
    other services, 5
    overhead, 4
Internet Service Providers. *See* ISPs
IPPs (Internet Presence Providers), 2
    authors' use of, 6
    compared with ISPs, 2-3
<ISINDEX> tag, 461, 466
ISMAP attribute, 449, 476
ISPs (Internet Service Providers), 2
    compared with IPPs, 2-3
    web site for comparison study, 6
italic text (<I> tag), 238, 441, 466

j

JavaScript
    comments in, 340
    highlighting rollovers, 351-358
    pointing rollovers, 337-343
    slideshow rollovers, 344-350
    types of rollovers, 336
    writing your own versus software-generated
        code, 330
JPEG images
    background color matching, 177
    background tiles, 130
    browser-safe colors, 93
    color palettes, 94
    compression overview, 54
    compression in Photoshop, 55-59
    progressive JPEGs, warning about, 59
    versus GIF, 60
justified text, 202

k

<KBD> tag, 442, 466
keywords, <META> tag, 411
kilobytes, 34
Kuniavsky, Mike (study on scrolling in
    web pages), 317

l

LABEL attribute, 453, 476
<LABEL> tag, 451, 466
LANG attribute, 436, 476
LANGUAGE attribute, 462, 476
Layer Effects feature (ImageReady 3.0), 335
Layer Opacity feature (ImageReady 3.0), 335
Layer Visibility feature (ImageReady 3.0), 335
layering text and images, 297-303
leading (typography)
    defined, 251
    line-height property (CSS), 292
    tricks (HTML-based typography), 249-251
left property (CSS), 295
left-justified text, 202
<LEGEND> tag, 451, 466
<LI> tag (list items), 166, 443, 466
line breaks (
 tag), 170, 210-211, 446, 464
line endings
    good HTML code, 423
    history of, 424
line-height property (CSS), 292
lines of text, HTML color, 98
LINK attribute, 29, 106, 439, 476
<LINK> tag, 438, 467
links. *See* hyperlinks
list elements, 443
lists
    bullets, 165
        changing shape of, 167
        clip art for, 169
        creating with tables, 232
        custom-made, 170-172
        HTML code for, 166
        as hyperlinks, 173
        hyperlinks in, 166
    definition lists, 167
    ordered lists, 167-168
LONGDESC attribute, 449, 476
lossless compression, 61
lossy compression, 41
lowercase type, 251
LOWSRC attribute (<IMG> tag), 388
Lycos search engine, 409
LZW (Lempel Ziv Welch) file compression, 37

m

Macs
line endings, 423-424
native fonts, 241
mailform.cgi (retrieving data from forms), 370-371
<MAP> tag, 446, 467
MARGINHEIGHT attribute, 315, 460, 477
margins
in frames, 315
in Netscape, 204
variable width in browsers, 220
MARGINWIDTH attribute, 315, 460, 477
masking. *See* transparency
mathematics of browser-safe colors, 67
matte lines (transparent GIFs), avoiding, 188
MAXLENGTH attribute, 454, 477
measurement units, typography, 290-291
MEDIA attribute, 439, 477
megabytes, 34
<MENU> tag, 443, 467
<META> tag, 389, 411, 438, 467
metaphors, planning web sites, 262
METHOD attribute, 371, 454, 477
microphone recordings, 397-398
Microsoft
OpenType font format, 247
TrueType Embedding font format, 245
web fonts package, 241
millimeters, 290
mind maps, planning web sites, 257
miscellaneous elements, 461-462
missing quotation marks, 422
monospaced fonts, 236
MP3 audio file format, 402
MPEG audio file format, 402
MS Sans font, compared to Verdana
screen-based font, 243
multimedia. *See* animation; sound
MULTIPLE attribute, 454, 477

n

NAME attribute, 477-478
<A tag>, 325, 449
<BUTTON> tag, 454
<FRAME> tag, 312, 460

<IFRAME> tag, 460
<INPUT> tag, 449, 454
<MAP> tag, 449
<META> tag, 411, 439
<OBJECT> tag, 449, 454
<PARAM> tag, 449
<SELECT> tag, 454
<TEXTAREA> tag, 454
named entities, versus numbered entities, 425
names of colors
browser-safe colors, 97
using instead of hexadecimal color, 96-97
naming conventions, highlighting rollovers, 352
native fonts on Windows and Macs, 241
navbars, screen size considerations, 320-323
navigation of web sites, 305
DHTML, 358-359
display size, 318-319
flowcharts, planning web sites, 263
fragments, 325-327
frames, 306
aesthetics of, 316
borderless frames, 311
framesets, 307
margins in, 315
nesting, 309
on older browsers, 308
resizing, 310
scrollbars in, 314
size considerations, 320-323
targeted links in, 312-313
web sites for information, 325
links back to top of page, 327
rollovers, 329
blank images in, warning about, 356
combination rollovers, 358
creating in ImageReady 3.0, 331-335
highlighting rollovers, 351-358
JavaScript, writing your own versus
software-generated code, 330
pointing rollovers, 337-343
slideshow rollovers, 344-350
types of, 336
scrolling in web pages, study on, 317
nested bulleted lists, 166
nested frames, 309
Netscape
margins in, 204
table borders, 219
TrueDoc font files, 245
<NOEMBED> tag (plug-ins), 392

<NOFRAMES> tag, 308, 460, 467
NOHREF attribute, 449, 478
NORESIZE attribute, 460, 478
<NOSCRIPT> tag, 461, 467
NOSHADE attribute, 163, 445, 478
NOWRAP attribute, 458, 478
numbered entities, versus named entities, 425
numbered lists, 167, 443

o

OBJECT attribute, 478
<OBJECT> tag, 447, 467
plug-ins, 392
objects (HTML), defined, 14
offset (alignment), 186
<OL> tag (ordered lists), 167, 443, 467
older browsers, frames on, 308
ONBLUR attribute, 449, 454, 478
ONCHANGE attribute, 454, 478
ONCLICK attribute, 437, 478
ONDBLCLICK attribute, 437, 478
ONFOCUS attribute, 449, 454, 479
ONKEYDOWN attribute, 437, 479
ONKEYPRESS attribute, 437, 479
ONKEYUP attribute, 437, 479
online graphics services, 91
online tutorials (HTML), 9
ONLOAD attribute, 479
<BODY> tag, 439
<FRAMESET> tag, 461
ONMOUSEDOWN attribute, 437, 479
ONMOUSEMOVE attribute, 437, 480
ONMOUSEOUT attribute, 437, 480
ONMOUSEOVER attribute, 437, 480
ONMOUSEUP attributes, 437, 480
ONRESET attribute, 454, 480
ONSELECT attribute, 454, 480
ONSUBMIT attribute, 454, 480
ONUNLOAD attribute, 461, 480
OpenType font format, 245, 247
<OPTGROUP> tag, 452, 467
optimization, animated GIFs, 393
<OPTION> tag, 363, 452, 467
ordered lists
alphabetic and Roman numerals, 168
defined, 443
<OL> tag, 167, 443, 467

organization of HTML files, 265
- directory structure, 274
- folders, importance of, 266
- planning web sites, 256
- relative URLs. *See* relative URLs
- repeating elements, 275
- SSI. *See* SSI
overhead, selecting Internet providers, 4

p

<P> tag (paragraphs), 18, 444, 467
- invalid content in, 431
- leading tricks, 249
- text alignment, 203-204
pairs of tags. *See* containers (HTML)
palettes, animated GIFs, 394. *See also* color
paragraphs
- indenting with style sheets, 293
- <P> tag, 18, 444, 467
  - invalid content in, 431
  - leading tricks, 249
  - text alignment, 203-204
<PARAM> tag, 447, 467
patent controversy, GIF images, 53
paths (URLs)
- defined, 267
- in relative URLs, 269
patterns (background) in web pages, 30
- determining size of, 127
- exercise, 31
PCs
- line endings, 423-424
- native fonts, 241
PFR (Portable Font Resource) file, 245
photographic-based artwork, browser-safe colors, 74, 94-95
Photoshop 5 and earlier swatches, warning about, 77
Photoshop 6.0
- aliased images, 46-49
  - color editing, 157-159
- animation artwork, creating, 377-379
- anti-aliased images, color editing, 148-152
- browser-safe colors
  - color pickers, 86
  - loading, 76-77
  - previsualizing, 78-81
- bullets, changing size, 171-172

dithering images, 52
- correcting, 88-90
GIF images, reducing colors in, 38-43
icons of images, saving, 35
JPEG image compression, 55-59
PNG image compression, 63
seamless background tiles, 138-144
slicing images, 226-229
transparent GIFs, creating, 195-198
phrase markup elements, 442
picas, 290
Pirouz, Raymond (*Click Here*), 413
pixels, 290
planning web sites, 255
- artwork, 260-261
- flowcharts, 263
- goal determination, 259
- metaphors, 262
- mind maps, 257
- organization, 256
- resources for information, 258
plug-ins, animation, 391-392
PNG (Portable Network Graphics), 61
- alpha-channel transparency, 62
- compression in Photoshop, 63
- compression overview, 61
- gamma correction, 61
- large file size for 24-bit images, 63
- transparency, 199
pointing rollovers
- defined, 336
- JavaScript for, 337-343
pointing-hand cursor, identifying hot images, 104
points, 290
Portable Font Resource (PRF) file, 245
Portable Network Graphics. *See* PNG
position property (CSS), 295
POST method (sending server messages), 371
PostScript, 247
<PRE> tag, 239, 250, 444, 468
preloading images, 110
preparation. *See* planning web sites
print-based color, versus screen-based color, 65
print-based fonts, versus screen-based fonts, 242
printing web pages, color issues, 147
PROFILE attribute, 439, 481
PROMPT attribute,, 462 481
pronunciation of GIF, 36
properties (CSS)
- defined, 288
- text-related properties, 292

proportional-spaced fonts, 236
publicizing web sites, 407
- ad banners, 412-413
- *Click Here* (Raymond Pirouz), 413
- directories, 408, 410
- link exchanges, 413
- listing with search engines, 410
- <META> tag, 411
- search engines, 408-409

q

<Q> tag (inline quotations), 442, 468
QBullets, 169
QuickTime audio format, 405
quotation marks
- around attribute values, 421
- missing, 422
quotations (<Q> tag), 442, 468

r

radio buttons in forms, 365
readability of text over background tiles, 146-147
READONLY attribute, 481
- <INPUT> tag, 454
- <TEXTAREA> tag, 454
RealAudio audio file format, 402, 405
REL attribute, 439, 449, 481
relative URLs
- converting to absolute URLs, 271
- examples, 270-271
- as links, 272-273
- paths in, 269
- versus absolute URLs, 268
- writing good HTML code, 425
repeating elements, organization of HTML files, 275
repeating tiles. *See* background tiles
resizing
- borders on hot images, 106
- images, 109
REV attribute, 439, 449, 481
RGB color, 69
- converting to CMYK color, warning about, 86
- hexadecimal values, 71-72
  - converting with hex calculators, 73
  - web hex converters, 73

RGBA (Red, Green, Blue, Alpha) palettes, 62
right-justified text, 202
rims (transparent GIFs), avoiding, 188
RLE (Run-Length Encoding) file compression, 37
robots. *See* search engines
rollovers, 329
    blank images in, warning about, 356
    combination rollovers, 358
    creating in ImageReady 3.0, 331-335
    JavaScript, 336
        highlighting rollovers, 351-358
        pointing rollovers, 337-343
        slideshow rollovers, 344-350
        writing your own versus
           software-generated code, 330
Roman numeral lists, 168
rows (tables), cells spanning multiple, 223-224
ROWS attribute, 481
    <FRAMESET> tag, 307, 310, 461
    <TEXTAREA> tag, 454
ROWSPAN attribute, 223-224, 458, 481
royalty-free sound libraries, 397
rules, origin of term, 162. *See also* horizontal
 rules; vertical rules
RULES attribute, 458, 481
Run-Length Encoding (RLE) file compression, 37

S

<S> tag (strikethrough text), 441, 468
<SAMP> tag, 442, 468
sample rates (sound), 398, 400
sampling resolution (sound), 398, 400
sans serif fonts, 236
SCHEME attribute, 440, 481
schemes (URLs), 267
SCOPE attribute, 459, 481
screen size, navigation of web sites, 318-319
screen-based color, versus print-based color, 65
screen-based fonts
    Verdana and Georgia, 243-244
    versus print-based fonts, 242
<SCRIPT> tag, 340, 461, 468
scrollbars in frames, 314
SCROLLING attribute, 314, 461, 481
scrolling in web pages, study on, 317
seamless background tiles, 131
    in ImageReady 3.0, 132-137
    in Photoshop 6.0, 138-144

seams in background tiles, 130-131
Search Engine Watch web site, 410
search engines
    defined, 408
    list of, 409
    listing web sites with, 410
    <META> tag, 411
<SELECT> tag, 363, 452, 468
SELECTED attribute, 455, 482
selecting Internet providers, 2-3
    bandwidth, 4
    other services, 5
    overhead, 4
selectors (CSS)
    class selectors, 293
    defined, 288
    ID selectors, 295-296
serif fonts, 236
server-side imagemaps, 113, 120
Server-Side Includes. *See* SSI
SHAPE attribute, 449, 482
Shockwave
    case study (sound), 395-396
    streaming audio, 405
simplicity, organization of HTML files, 266
single-pixel GIFs
    image gutters, 213
    indented type, 252
    leading tricks, 249
    versus tables for alignment, 231
SIZE attribute, 482
    <FONT> tag, 240, 450
    <HR> tag, 163, 445
    <INPUT> tag, 455
    <SELECT> tag, 455
size considerations
    frames and navbars, 320-323
    screen size, 318-319
size of pattern (background tiles),
 determining, 127
slicing images
    in ImageReady 3.0, 332
    in Photoshop 6.0, 226-229
    for table alignment, 225, 229-230
slideshow rollovers
    defined, 336
    JavaScript for, 344-350
slideshows, client pull, 389
small caps, HTML tagging, 239
<SMALL> tag, 441, 468
soft edges (transparent GIFs), 188-189

sound
    aesthetics, 397
    capturing from audio CDs, 397
    Director, 405
    editing software, 398
    file formats, 401-402
    Flash authoring tool, 405
    HTML code for downloading, 404
    microphone recordings, 397-398
    QuickTime, 405
    RealAudio file format, 405
    royalty-free sound libraries, 397
    sample rates, 398, 400
    sampling resolution, 398, 400
    Shockwave case study, 395-396
    streaming audio, 399
    tips for file preparation, 403
spaces
    in filenames, 20
    in tags and attributes, 21
spacing
    table cells, 218-219
    in tables, single-pixel GIFs versus table
     alignment, 231
    text and graphics with tables, 220-222
SPAN attribute, 459, 482
<SPAN> tag, 294, 447, 468
special effects, background tiles, 145
special text-level elements, 446-450
spiders. *See* search engines
SRC attribute, 482
    <FRAME> tag, 461
    <IFRAME> tag, 461
    <IMG> tag, 18, 450
    <INPUT> tag, 455
    <SCRIPT> tag, 462
SSI (Server-Side Includes), 276
    file and folder names, 277
    HTML code for, 278-281
    potential problems with, 276
    web sites for information, 276
STANDBY attribute, 450, 482
START attribute, 443, 482
storyboarding
    Ducks In A Row case study (animation), 375
    planning web sites, 263
straddling containers, problems with, 422
streaming audio
    advantages and disadvantages, 399
    Director, 405
    QuickTime, 405
    RealAudio file format, 402, 405

<STRIKE> tag, 441, 468
strikethrough text
        <S> tag, 441, 468
        <STRIKE> tag, 441
<STRONG> tag, 238, 442, 468
STYLE attribute, 435, 483
style sheets
        CSS (Cascading Style Sheets), 283
                absolute positioning, 295-296
                class selectors, 293
                defined, 284
                internal style sheets, 285
                measurement units, 290-291
                parts of, 288-289
                <SPAN> tag, 294
                text-related properties, 292
        defined, 283
        external style sheets, 284
        layering text and images, 297-303
        <STYLE> tag, 286-287, 438, 468
        web sites for information, 303
<STYLE> tag, 286-287, 438, 468
        parts of, 288
<SUB> tag (subscript text), 447, 468
submit buttons on forms, images as, 369
SUMMARY attribute, 459, 483
<SUP> tag (superscript text), 447, 468
swatches
        Photoshop 5 and earlier, warning about, 77
        Photoshop 6.0, loading browser-safe colors,
        76-77

t

TABINDEX attribute, 450, 455, 483
table elements, 456-459
<TABLE> tag, 214-216, 416, 456, 469
tables, 214-216
        borders in Netscape, 219
        bulleted lists, creating, 232
        cells
                color, 217
                odd numbers of, 223-224
                spacing, 218-219
        forms, using with, 366-368
        graphic alignment, slicing images, 225,
        229-230
        HTML color in, 100-101
        images, centering, 232

indented type, 252
spacing text and graphics, 220-222
versus single-pixel GIFs for alignment, 231
vertical rules, creating, 233
tags (HTML). See also elements (HTML)
        <A> (anchor text), 26, 446, 463
                bullets as hyperlinks, 173
                creating hot images, 105
                hyperlinks in bulleted lists, 166
                sound files, 404
        <ABBR>, 442, 463
        <ACRONYM>, 442, 463
        <ADDRESS>, 444, 463
        alphabetical list, 463-470
        <APPLET>, 446, 463
        <AREA>, 446, 463
        attributes. See attributes (HTML)
        <B> (bold text), 238, 441, 463
        <BASE>, 438, 463
        <BASEFONT>, 446, 463
        <BDO>, 446, 463
        <BGSOUND>, 404
        <BIG>, 441, 463
        <BLINK>, 239
        <BLOCKQUOTE>, 444, 464
        <BODY>, 438, 464
                background images, 30
                color in web pages, 28-29
                extras inserted by WYSIWYG
                editors, 418
                HTML color, 101

 (line breaks), 170, 210-211, 446, 464
        <BUTTON>, 451, 464
        <CAPTION>, 216, 456, 464
        case sensitivity, 19
        <CENTER>, 206, 239, 444, 464
        <CITE>, 442, 464
        client-side imagemaps, 118-119
        <CODE>, 442, 464
        <COL>, 456, 464
        <COLGROUP>, 456, 464
        for color, 101
        comments
                nesting frames, 309
                SSI in, 279
                style sheets, 286-287
        <DD> (definition lists), 167, 443, 464
        defined, 14, 18, 417, 430
        <DEL>, 461, 464
        <DFN>, 442, 464
        <DIR>, 443, 464

<DIV>, 444, 465
        absolute positioning, 295-296
        text alignment, 205
<DL> (definition lists), 167, 443, 465
<DT> (definition lists), 443, 465
<EM>, 238, 442, 465
<EMBED>, 392
<FIELDSET>, 451, 465
<FONT>, 240-241, 446, 465
        coloring lines of text, 98
        HTML color, 101
<FONTSIZE>, 239
<FORM>, 362, 451, 465
<FRAME>, 307, 459, 465
<FRAMESET>, 307, 459, 465
<H#> (headings), 18, 238, 444, 465
<HEAD>, 18, 438, 465
<HR> (horizontal rules), 162-163, 444, 465
<HTML>, 18, 438, 465
HTML reference layout, 433
<I> (italic text), 238, 441, 466
<IFRAME>, 460, 466
<IMG>, 18, 446, 466
        creating hot images, 105
        custom-made bullets, 170
        exercise, 111
        graphic alignment, 208-209
        graphics based typography, 248
        transparent GIFs, 190
<INPUT>, 362-363, 451, 466
<INS>, 461, 466
<ISINDEX>, 461, 466
<KBD>, 442, 466
<LABEL>, 451, 466
<LEGEND>, 451, 466
<LI>, 166, 443, 466
<LINK>, 438, 467
<MAP>, 446, 467
<MENU>, 443, 467
<META>, 389, 411, 438, 467
<NOEMBED> (plug-ins), 392
<NOFRAMES>, 308, 460, 467
<NOSCRIPT>, 461, 467
<OBJECT>, 392, 447, 467
<OL> (ordered lists), 167, 443, 467
<OPTGROUP>, 452, 467
<OPTION>, 363, 452, 467
<P> (paragraphs), 18, 444, 467
        invalid content in, 431
        leading tricks, 249
        text alignment, 203-204

<PARAM>, 447, 467
<PRE> (preformatted text), 239, 250, 444, 468
<Q> (inline quotations), 442, 468
repeating elements, organization of HTML
  files, 275
<S> (strikethrough text), 441, 468
<SAMP>, 442, 468
<SCRIPT>, 340, 461, 468
<SELECT>, 363, 452, 468
<SMALL>, 441, 468
spaces in, 21
<SPAN>, 294, 447, 468
<STRIKE>, 441, 468
<STRONG>, 238, 442, 468
<STYLE>, 286-288, 438, 468
<SUB> (subscript text), 447, 468
<SUP> (superscript text), 447, 468
<TABLE>, 214-216, 416, 456, 469
<TBODY>, 456, 469
<TD>, 214-215, 456, 469
<TEXTAREA>, 363, 452, 469
<TFOOT>, 457, 469
<TH>, 216, 457, 469
<THEAD>, 457, 469
<TITLE>, 18, 438, 470
<TR>, 214-215, 457, 470
<TT> (teletype), 441, 470
<U> (underlined text), 441, 470
<UL> (unordered lists), 166, 443, 470
<VAR>, 442, 470
versus elements, 430
TARGET attribute 440, 450, 455, 483
targeted links in frames, 312-313
<TBODY> tag, 456, 469
<TD> tag, 214-215, 456, 469
teletype text (<TT> tag), 441, 470
templates for web pages, 21
text
    alignment, 202
        <CENTER> tag, 206
        <DIV> tag, 205
        <P> tag, 203-204
        with tables, 220-222
    crowding into bullets, troubleshooting, 170
    HTML color, 98
    layering with images, 297-303
    readability over background tiles, 146-147
TEXT attribute, 29, 440, 483
text color, printing web pages, 147
text elements, special text-level elements, 446-450
text-based HTML editors, 9

text-indent property (CSS), 293
text-related properties (CSS), 292
<TEXTAREA> tag, 363, 452, 469
<TFOOT> tag, 457, 469
<TH> tag, 216, 457, 469
<THEAD> tag, 457, 469
thumbnail graphics, 324
tiled backgrounds. See background tiles
Times font, compared to Georgia screen-based
  font, 244
Times New Roman font, compared to Georgia
  screen-based font, 243
TITLE attribute, 435, 483
<TITLE> tag, 18, 438, 470
top of page, links back to, 327
top property (CSS), 295
<TR> tag, 214-215, 457, 470
transparency, 175. See also transparent GIFs
    animated GIFs, 394
    background color matching, 176
        with hex values, 178-179
        in ImageReady 3.0, 181-184
        with tiled images, 180
    PNG file format, 199
transparent GIFs, 185
    anti-aliasing, 187
    creating
        in ImageReady 3.0, 191-194
        in Photoshop 6.0, 195-198
    glows, drop shadows, soft edges, 188-189
    HTML code for, 190
    in rollovers, warning about, 356
    when to use, 186
troubleshooting HTML code. See
  good HTML code
TrueDoc font format
    anti-aliased type, 246
    defined, 247
    font files, 245
TrueType embedding font format, 245
TrueType font format, 247
Tschichold, Jan (history of typography), 242
<TT> tag (teletype), 441, 470
two dots (..), in relative URLs, 270
TYPE attribute, 483
    <A> tag, 440
    <BUTTON> tag, 455
    <INPUT> tag, 362-363, 455
    <LI> tag, 167-168, 443
    <LINK> tag, 440
    <OBJECT> tag, 450

<OL> tag, 443
<PARAM> tag, 450
<SCRIPT> tag, 462
<STYLE> tag, 288, 440
<UL> tag, 443
Type1 font format, 247
typography, 235
    definitions, 251
    graphics-based typography, 248
        leading tricks, 250
    HTML-based typography, 238-241
        anti-aliased versus aliased type, 246
        body type versus headline type, 237
        default HTML fonts, 236
        embedding fonts, 245
        indents, 252
        leading tricks, 249-250
        problems with web typography, 242
        screen-based fonts, Verdana and
          Georgia, 243-244
        unreliability of leading tricks, 251
    measurement units, 290-291
    resources for, 247
    web sites for information and font
      repositories, 253

u

<U> tag (underlined text), 441, 470
<UL> tag (unordered lists), 166, 443, 470
underlined text (<U> tag), 441, 470
Uniform Resource Locators. See URLs
Unisys (GIF patent controversy), 53
units of measurement, typography, 290-291
UNIX line endings, 423-424
unordered lists (<UL> tag), 166, 443, 470
uploading web pages, 22-25
uppercase type, 251
URLs (Uniform Resource Locators), 266
    absolute versus relative URLs, 268
    defined, 15
    fragments, 326-327
    parts of, 267
    relative URLs
        converting to absolute URLs, 271
        examples, 270-271
        as links, 272-273
        paths in, 269
    web sites for information, 273

USEMAP attribute, 119, 450, 455, 484
user interaction. *See* forms
user-based slices (Photoshop 6.0), 228

V

VALIGN attribute, 215, 459, 484
VALUE attribute, 484
    \<BUTTON\> tag, 455
    \<INPUT\> tag, 455
    \<OL\> tag, 443
    \<OPTION\> tag, 455
    \<PARAM\> tag, 450
VALUETYPE attribute, 450, 484
\<VAR\> tag, 442, 470
variable margins in browsers, 220
Verdana screen-based font, 243-244
VERSION attribute, 440, 484
versions of HTML in reference section, 429
vertical rules, 164, 233
virtual keyword (SSI), 279
VLINK attribute, 29, 440, 484
VSPACE attribute, 450, 484

W

W3C (World Wide Web Consortium), 61, 284
WAV audio file format, 401
web, defined, 14
web browsers. *See* browsers
web hex converters, 73
web hosting companies. *See* IPPs
web pages
    background patterns, 30-31
    color, 28-29
    file size, determining, 34
    hyperlinks on, exercise, 26
    image hyperlinks, exercise, 27
    links back to top of page, 327
    printing, color issues, 147
    scrolling in, study on, 317
    templates for, 21
    uploading, exercise, 22-25
    viewing locally, 16
    writing, exercise, 16-17

web sites
    accuracy of sources, evaluating, 408
    CGI programs, 372
    clip art collections, 165
    copyright information, 397
    dedicated HTML editors, 10
    directories of, 410
    Dreamweaver, 359
    external style sheet information, 284
    font repositories, 253
    frames information, 325
    HTML online tutorials, 9
    imagemap resources, 119
    ISP comparison study, 6
    link exchange information, 413
    Microsoft web fonts package, 241
    MP3 information, 402
    navigation. *See* navigation of web sites
    online graphics services, 91
    organization. *See* organization of HTML files
    planning, 255
        artwork, 260-261
        flowcharts, 263
        goal determination, 259
        metaphors, 262
        mind maps, 257
        organization, 256
        resources for information, 258
    PNG information, 61, 199
    publicizing. *See* publicizing web sites
    RGB hex converters, 73
    search engine listings, 409-410
    SSI information, 276
    style sheet information, 303
    typography information, 253
    URL information, 273
whitespace in HTML, 19
widgets (forms), 362-363
WIDTH attribute, 485
    \<COL\> tag, 459
    \<COLGROUP\> tag, 459
    \<HR\> tag, 163, 445
    \<IFRAME\> tag, 461
    \<IMG\> tag, 108-109, 213, 450
    \<OBJECT\> tag, 450
    plug-ins, 392
    \<PRE\> tag, 445
    tables, 220-222, 459
World Wide Web, relationship to Internet, 14

World Wide Web Consortium (W3C), 61, 284
WS_FTPprogram, 22-23
WYSIWYG editors, 11
    extra \<BODY\> tags, 418
    problems writing good HTML code, 419-420

X-Z

x-height, 290

Yahoo! web site, 410

z-index property (CSS), 295

Solutions from experts you know and trust.

www.informit.com

OPERATING SYSTEMS

WEB DEVELOPMENT

PROGRAMMING

NETWORKING

CERTIFICATION

AND MORE...

Expert Access.
Free Content.

New Riders has partnered with **InformIT.com** to bring technical information to your desktop. Drawing on New Riders authors and reviewers to provide additional information on topics you're interested in, **InformIT.com** has free, in-depth information you won't find anywhere else.

- **Master the skills you need, when you need them**

- **Call on resources from some of the best minds in the industry**

- **Get answers when you need them, using InformIT's comprehensive library or live experts online**

- **Go above and beyond what you find in New Riders books, extending your knowledge**

As an **InformIT** partner, **New Riders** has shared the wisdom and knowledge of our authors with you online. Visit **InformIT.com** to see what you're missing.

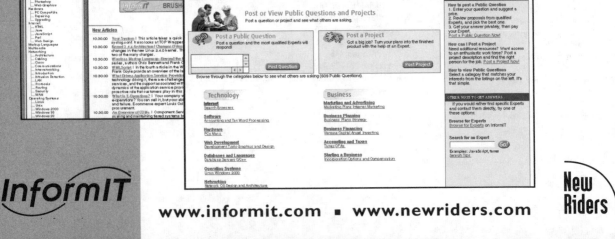